Service-Oriented Architecture

A Field Guide to Integrating XML and Web Services

About Prentice Hall Professional Technical Reference

With origins reaching back to the industry's first computer science publishing program in the 1960s, and formally launched as its own imprint in 1986, Prentice Hall Professional Technical Reference (PH PTR) has developed into the leading provider of technical books in the world today. Our editors now publish over 200 books annually, authored by leaders in the fields of computing, engineering, and business.

Our roots are firmly planted in the soil that gave rise to the technical revolution. Our bookshelf contains many of the industry's computing and engineering classics: Kernighan and Ritchie's *C Programming Language*, Nemeth's *UNIX System Adminstration Handbook*, Horstmann's *Core Java*, and Johnson's *High-Speed Digital Design*.

PH PTR acknowledges its auspicious beginnings while it looks to the future for inspiration. We continue to evolve and break new ground in publishing by providing today's professionals with tomorrow's solutions.

Service-Oriented Architecture

A Field Guide to Integrating XML and Web Services

Thomas Erl

PRENTICE HALL

PROFESSIONAL TECHNICAL REFERENCE

UPPER SADDLE RIVER, NJ 07458

WWW.PHPTR.COM

A CIP catalog record for this book can be obtained from the Library of Congress

Editorial/production supervision: *Techne Group*
Cover design director: *Jerry Votta*
Cover design: *Anthony Gemmellaro*
Art director: *Gail Cocker-Bogusz*
Manufacturing manager: *Alexis R. Heydt-Long*
Manufacturing buyer: *Maura Zaldivar*
Editor-in-Chief: *Mark Taub*
Editorial assistant: *Noreen Regina*
Marketing manager: *Chanda Leary-Coutu*
Full-service production manager: *Anne R. Garcia*

Prentice Hall PTR offers excellent discounts on this book when ordered in quantity for bulk purchases or special sales. For more information, please contact: U.S. Corporate and Government Sales, 1-800-382-3419, corpsales@pearsontechgroup.com. For sales outside of the U.S., please contact: International Sales, 1-317-581-3793, international@pearsontechgroup.com.

Printed in the United States of America

Third Printing

ISBN 0-13-142898-5

Pearson Education Ltd.
Pearson Education Australia Pty., Limited
Pearson Education South Asia Pte. Ltd.
Pearson Education Asia Ltd.
Pearson Education Canada, Ltd.
Pearson Educación de Mexico, S.A. de C.V.
Pearson Education-Japan
Pearson Malaysia S.D.N. B.H.D.

Contents

Part I

The technical landscape

Chapter 2

Introduction to XML technologies

Chapter 3

Introduction to Web services technologies

Chapter 4

Introduction to second-generation (WS-*) Web services technologies

Part II

Integrating technology

Chapter 5

Integrating XML into applications

Chapter 6

Integrating Web services into applications   187

Chapter 7

Integrating XML and databases

Chapter 10

Service-oriented architectures for enterprise integration

Part IV
Integrating the enterprise

Chapter 12
Thirty best practices for integrating XML

Chapter 13
Thirty best practices for integrating Web services   449

Chapter 14

Building the service-oriented enterprise (SOE) 475

Preface

My father runs a placer mine, far North in a remote part of the Yukon wilderness. For almost half a century, he's made his living plowing through mountains with his bulldozers, looking for gold. Due to the climate, he gets only a limited amount of time during which he can actually mine. His priority, therefore, is to keep his business fully operational throughout this period. Any disruption results in lost revenue. Despite his best efforts, though, he is constantly faced with obstacles.

He's had to contend with volatile, sometimes even violent environmental conditions. He's had to confront bears that roamed into his camp, looking for food. He's even chased thieves off his land in the middle of the night. Once, the hydraulic pump on his front-end loader collapsed, crushing his hand. Instead of "wasting" two days to get to the nearest hospital, he simply wrapped a diesel soaked rag around his broken fingers and kept on going.

The worst kind of problem he's ever had to face, though, is mechanical failure. If a key piece of equipment breaks, if an engine slows or stops, or if any other part of his infrastructure seizes, his business comes to a (literally) grinding halt. It can take weeks to get new equipment or spare parts — a delay that can be devastating to his bottom line.

When faced with these challenges in the past, he's had only himself to rely on. I asked him once how he deals with these situations. He told me that there are very few problems in life that can't be solved with a blowtorch and a welding rod.

I think about that "life philosophy" sometimes, when staring at the cursor, blinking hypnotically amidst some problem displayed on my computer screen. I've always been involved with new technology. It has the mystery of the unknown and the attraction of potential. It's also put me in more "impossible" situations than I care to remember.

Although I have respect for the expertise required to produce product documentation and tutorials, I generally classify this information as "option A." It is surprising how often option A does not work in integrated environments. But, that's what option B is for. Option B is when I roll up my sleeves and light my own blowtorch.

This attitude is important when working on integration projects. Some integration tasks are easy. Making two compatible pieces of software talk to each other can be straightforward, involving a predictable development and deployment effort. Others, though, can be a nightmare. Sometimes two pieces of software aren't just "not compatible," they seem violently opposed to each other's very existence.

The goal of this guide is to help you define your own options for whatever integration challenges you might be facing. I am fortunate to be writing a book about integration strategy at a time when the IT community has at its disposal a platform that fosters integration and interoperability like never before.

I hope that you will find this guide not only useful, but that it will lead you to view XML, Web services, and service-oriented principles as problem-solving tools. So that no matter what obstacles cross your path, you will be able to use your own blowtorch to carve out that perfect solution.

Acknowledgments

My thanks to the friends and family who encouraged me throughout the creation of this guide. I must also acknowledge the many technical reviewers who selflessly gave their time to ensure the quality of this book, as well as the staff at Pearson/Prentice Hall PTR that made it all happen.

Finally, a special thanks to Charles F. Goldfarb who supported this project from its inception.

Introduction

1.1　Why this guide is important

"Hype," by definition, is an exaggeration of fact. Both XML and Web services have had their share. When looking back at the rise of these technologies and the excitement that surrounded them, many who bought into the hype are beginning to feel disappointed. Organizations are realizing that their technical environments are not magically transformed simply by adding XML or Web services to the mix.

I actually believe that much of this publicity has been warranted. This platform's potential is real, and its importance cannot be understated. When properly applied, it not only improves the technology of an organization, but also the manner in which business automation is delivered. *When properly applied.*

What's been exaggerated isn't as much the potential, but its perceived simplicity. A well-designed, service-oriented environment can simplify and streamline many aspects of information technology, but achieving this state is no simple matter. The technology set introduced by XML and Web services is diversely complex. In order to truly leverage its benefits, you first need to appreciate the implications of this complexity. Then, you need to strategize.

1.1.1　The hammer and XML

It all starts with XML. Like a hammer, XML is a tool. If you pay attention to how you use it, you'll hit the nail every time; if you don't, chances are your thumb will take a beating. On its own, it does not solve or create problems—the results of using XML are directly related to how intelligently it is applied.

For years, industry analysts have theorized and speculated about the benefits XML will introduce to the age of online data sharing. Because this technology platform provides a potential ideal for a universal data format, it will lead the world into a new era of information unity and parity.

The potential is real, but the manner in which XML is being applied in the real world is anything but ideal. XML is a specification, a revolutionary innovation that exists in a document that describes a simple idea, with huge implications. The fact that XML has been adopted into the IT mainstream is good. It establishes a common technology used for a common purpose. Simply using XML, however, in no way guarantees that you will realize any of its true benefits. You will be staying current, complying with a worldwide platform shift, and you will not feel left out when reading about how others are riding the XML wave, but… you will not see anything revolutionary happening in your world.

1.1.2 XML and Web services

If XML is a hammer, then Web services are… what? The nail? The hand that holds it? Whatever it is you're building, Web services are the building blocks you can use after you've first pounded out a solid foundation with XML. That doesn't mean you can't start using Web services without first properly integrating XML, but then there's nothing stopping you from building that dream house in the swamplands either.

This guide, in fact, is mostly about integration with Web services technologies and service-oriented design principles. This makes it no less of a book about XML, since the Web services platform is a natural continuation of the XML movement.

1.1.3 Web services and Service-Oriented Architecture

As you read through this book, you will notice that the path to building service-oriented architecture is riddled with pitfalls and risks. Too often, organizations investing in Web services discover the errors of their ways once entire solutions have been built and deployed. This is not necessarily a bad or neglectful occurrence. It's simply a tribute to the vastness of this platform.

With its complex and comprehensive feature set, though, comes a load of power. Use this technology the right way, and you truly can build a better enterprise. That statement goes beyond IT, because service-oriented concepts can reach out and change the way you model your business. Grasping the potential is an important first step. Equally as important, though, is understanding what's involved with realizing this potential. That takes us back to integration strategy.

1.1.4 Service-Oriented Architecture and the hammer

Unfortunately, the majority of corporate IT departments do not employ any form of integration or migration strategy. Without a planned integration, standards cannot be positioned, and the resulting ad hoc usage of these technologies only ends up contributing to existing disparity. It's the equivalent of construction workers building a home without direction and without a blueprint. With the absence of a planned and coordinated effort, a group of hammering workers will not only *not* create a quality foundation, they won't be building anything resembling a foundation at all.

1.1.5   The hammer and you

Strategizing with a foreknowledge of how to best incorporate XML, Web services, and service-oriented design principles into the various domains that make up your automated enterprise, however, will put you on a path at the end of which lies a sophisticated and adaptive automation environment. It will allow you to transition toward an integrated enterprise with superior data sharing and unprecedented control of your corporate business models.

This guide is your map. The strategies, recommendations, and best practices provided here collectively form a framework that offers direction and guidance through the twists and turns along the road to building service-oriented architecture and, ultimately, a service-oriented enterprise. So, grab your hammer and enjoy the ride!

1.2   The XML & Web Services Integration Framework (XWIF)

As an independent consultant, I've worked for many companies. More often than not, I've been part of projects that involved highly complex environments, unique problems, and difficult integration issues. Solutions frequently required an element of creativity that ventured beyond traditional mindset boundaries. Many of the ideas expressed in this guide, therefore, may be new to you, and hopefully will provide you with alternative perspectives to common integration problems.

The contents of this book are part of an integration framework that I've been developing for a number of years through my company, XMLTC Consulting Inc. The XML & Web Services Integration Framework (XWIF) consists of an enterprise standardization strategy, supported by a series of best practices, integration strategies, and processes for planning and delivering service-oriented integration projects.

Each piece of this collective intelligence is designed with the common goal of transitioning an organization toward a service-oriented enterprise.

Table 1.1   An Overview of XWIF

XML & Web Services Integration Framework		
Best practices	Standards	Processes
Strategies	Service Models	Roles

Much of what XWIF preaches is a common-sense approach to resolving typical integration issues with XML and Web services. Some of the guidelines provided are in use elsewhere in the industry, whereas others are unique to XWIF. Many best practices and strategies, and all processes in this guide were developed exclusively as part of this framework.[1]

> **NOTE**
> This book isn't about XWIF, nor does it discuss this framework in any detail. Much of the information provided here was borrowed from XWIF and assembled into this generic field guide. To learn more about XWIF, visit www.xwif.com.

1.3 How this guide is organized

The Field Guide is different from most IT books; it doesn't prescribe to the traditional tutorial or process-oriented formats. This guide provides a collection of strategies and best practices that have one common theme: the integration of XML, Web services, and service-oriented architecture.

As I put this book together, it became evident that I had to include background information on the many technologies it discussed. Therefore, the three chapters in Part I contain a series of lightweight tutorials for the primary technologies that form contemporary XML and Web services architectures.

Since the guide is intended for a range of IT professionals that no doubt will be using it under different circumstances, there was no perfect way of organizing its many topics. After a number of iterations, I decided to categorize the XWIF strategies and best practices into Parts II, III, and IV, as illustrated in Figure 1.1.

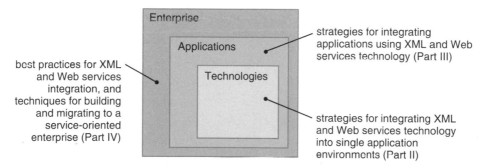

Figure 1.1
Three categories representing Parts II, III, and IV of this guide.

---

1.   Even though the framework is occasionally referenced throughout this book, I've avoided prefixing every single strategy, process, and best practice with "XWIF."

Here is a quick reference overview of what is covered in each part and chapter.

1.3.1   Part I: The technical landscape

Nearly 30 XML and Web services specifications are discussed throughout this part of the book, with a focus on the 17 core standards listed in Table 1.2.

Table 1.2   Reference Matrix of Technology Tutorials

XML technologies (Chapter 2)	Web services technologies (Chapter 3)	Second-generation Web services technologies (Chapter 4)
XML	WSDL	WS-Coordination
DTD	SOAP	WS-Transaction
XSD	UDDI	BPEL4WS
XSLT		WS-Security
XQuery		WS-ReliableMessaging
XPath		WS-Policy
		WS-Attachments
		WS-Addressing

Note that Chapter 3 also covers numerous concepts relating to the Web services framework, including:

- requestor and provider roles
- intermediaries
- initial sender and ultimate receiver roles
- message paths
- message exchange patterns
- correlation
- choreography
- activities

Also note that Chapter 3 introduces service-oriented architecture (SOA) concepts. Later, Chapter 14 continues this discussion with a detailed tutorial on SOA design principles.

1.3.2 Part II: Integrating technology

As shown in Figure 1.2, Part II confines the scope of topics to single application environments in order to focus on strategies for integrating technology within application tiers.

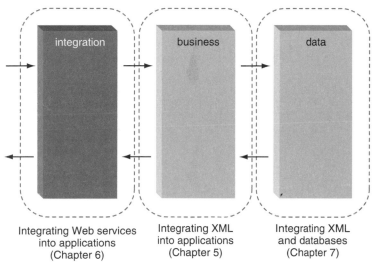

Integrating Web services
into applications
(Chapter 6)

Integrating XML
into applications
(Chapter 5)

Integrating XML
and databases
(Chapter 7)

Figure 1.2
The three chapters in Part II roughly correspond to the three backend tiers
of a distributed application architecture.

Within Part II we clearly separate integration issues relating to XML and Web services. This allows XML strategies to be used independently of service-oriented environments, if required.

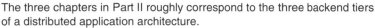

Integrating XML into applications (Chapter 5)
The scope of this chapter is the integration of core XML technologies with the purpose of establishing a fundamental data management architecture. Numerous strategies for addressing common integration issues are provided, organized according to the functional areas most likely to be affected by the integration, as follows:

- XML data representation strategies for conceptually and technically incorporating XML as a data representation format and delivery mechanism
- XML data validation strategies that explore the utilization of schema definitions, with an emphasis on XSD
- an XML schema administration process that highlights the importance of centralizing ownership of XML schema definitions

- XML transformation strategies that cover the integration of XSLT for structural and aesthetic transformation of XML documents

- XML data querying strategies that position XQuery as a technology to centralize and abstract data access logic

These sections assume you have a base knowledge of the discussed technologies. If you don't, you should study the tutorials in Chapter 2 first.

Integrating Web services into applications (Chapter 6)

Here we focus on fundamental design concepts that allow you to establish a foundation for a service-oriented architecture, and prepare an application for future interoperability. The scope of this chapter, therefore, is limited to the integration of Web services technology within application environments.

The following XWIF service models are established:

- utility services

- business services

- controller services

XWIF also supplies us with these two modeling processes:

- modeling service-oriented component classes

- modeling Web service interfaces

A collection of integration and optimization strategies are provided next, addressing the use of service assemblies, Web services performance, and interface design.

Integrating XML and databases (Chapter 7)

XML opens up a whole new world of data modeling that contrasts traditional approaches to structuring and defining schemas. This chapter is dedicated to exploring techniques for integrating the hierarchical structure of XML documents with traditional relational repositories. Since this is a common area for which knowledge and resources typically are limited, we explore issues with more syntactical detail than in other chapters.

First, we compare XML and relational databases in order to establish their fundamental differences and to contrast how each platform relates to and manages data. Next, the basics of data mapping are covered, as well as issues relating to performance and platform disparity. We then get into the details of mapping the hierarchical XML data model to relational databases.

Finally, we take a look at the common ways in which current database products support XML through the use of proprietary extensions. The implications of using these extensions, along with some techniques on how to mitigate their impact, also are provided. This chapter concludes with an overview of native XML databases.

1.3.3   Part III: Integrating applications

We now carry the discussion forward into the realm of application integration. The chapters in Part III are almost entirely centered around the use of Web services, as numerous traditional and service-oriented integration scenarios are explored and contrasted. Figure 1.3 illustrates the scope of Part III chapters, as they relate to application tiers.

The mechanics of application integration (Chapter 8)
Fundamental integration concepts are introduced, and the differences between traditional and contemporary application integration architectures are discussed. This chapter is more of a primer for cross-application integration, as it also provides a guide to middleware products, and explores common paths for evolving an enterprise integration environment.

If integration architecture is new to you, I recommend you read through this chapter prior to proceeding with Chapters 9 and 10.

Service-oriented architectures for legacy integration (Chapter 9)
Here we dive into the multi-varied world of legacy integration architectures. We begin by describing the following set of XWIF services models:

- proxy services
- wrapper services
- coordination services (for atomic transactions)

We then explain the roles of common integration components, including:

- legacy adapters
- intermediary services
- service interceptors

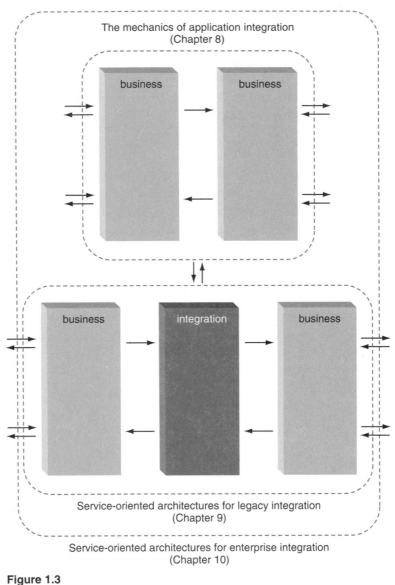

Figure 1.3
The architectural scopes of Part III chapters.

Many legacy integration architectures are then explored. Each of the following sections separately illustrates an integration architecture in a traditional and service-oriented state:

- one-way integration architecture: batch export and import
- one-way integration architecture: direct data access

- point-to-point architecture: tightly-coupled integration between homogenous legacy applications
- point-to-point architecture: tightly-coupled integration between heterogeneous applications
- point-to-point architecture: integration between homogenous component-based applications
- point-to-point architecture: integration between heterogeneous component-based applications
- centralized database architecture

These sections are supplemented further with architectural comparison matrices that contrast key architectural aspects within traditional and service-oriented contexts. The chapter concludes with an analysis process for assessing the feasibility of introducing service-oriented design principles within legacy architectures.

Service-oriented architectures for enterprise integration (Chapter 10)
The scope now broadens to encompass enterprise integration architectures. The roles of broker and orchestration components are demonstrated, along with the introduction of the following XWIF service models:

- process services
- coordination services (for business activities)

Both traditional and contemporary EAI architectures are then explored, including:

- hub and spoke
- messaging bus (publish and subscribe)
- enterprise service bus (ESB)

How Web services can be integrated within these environments is illustrated, and supplemented with numerous design considerations.

Service-oriented integration strategies (Chapter 11)
To supplement and expand on the topics covered in Chapters 9 and 10, the following collection of integration strategies are provided:

- strategies for streamlining integration endpoint interfaces
- strategies for optimizing integration endpoint services

- strategies for integrating legacy architectures
- strategies for enterprise solution integration
- strategies for integrating Web services security

1.3.4   Part IV: Integrating the enterprise

This part of the book provides a clear roadmap to a standardized service-oriented enterprise, and consists of a collection of best practices and processes for planning and implementing an enterprise-wide integration strategy.

Here's a brief overview of the chapters:

Thirty best practices for integrating XML (Chapter 12)
Chapter 12 describes a wide variety of best practices and recommendations for various aspects of XML integration, including:

- planning XML migration projects
- knowledge management within XML projects
- standardizing XML applications
- designing XML applications

Thirty best practices for integrating Web services (Chapter 13)
Chapter 13 details a set of best practices that provide guidance and insight for managing and integrating Web services. The following areas are covered:

- planning service-oriented projects
- standardizing Web services
- designing service-oriented environments
- managing service-oriented development projects
- implementing Web services

Building the service-oriented enterprise (SOE) (Chapter 14)
Our last chapter contains perhaps the most important information within this guide. First, it delves into the details of service-oriented modeling concepts and design principles. A detailed tutorial breaks down the components of a service-oriented architecture into activities, services, and processes.

It then applies these concepts to a service-oriented enterprise by establishing a series of business modeling and technology building blocks for the design of service-oriented environments. Examples are provided, establishing problems that are then solved using these service-oriented design principles.

Finally, the XWIF Layered Scope Model (LSM) is introduced, establishing a comprehensive migration strategy for the controlled integration of XML and Web services technologies through a series of phases that gradually transition an organization toward the service-oriented enterprise. This last section draws upon information provided throughout the Field Guide, by listing the XWIF service models, processes, and strategies most appropriate for each LSM phase.

1.3.5   The extended enterprise

Service-oriented concepts and architecture allow an enterprise to be extended beyond its organizational boundaries. The enterprise standardization process in Chapter 14 identifies a migration path into the extended enterprise; however, the XWIF business-to-business interchange model is not an area of integration we cover in this guide.

1.4   www.serviceoriented.ws

Updates, samples, a glossary of terms, and various other supporting resources can be found at `www.serviceoriented.ws`. I am interested in your feedback. Any experiences you'd like to share, or suggestions you may have as to how I can continue to improve this book would be much appreciated.

1.5   Contact the author

To contact me directly, visit my bio site at `www.thomaserl.com`.

PART

I

The technical landscape

I can remember, just a few years ago, listening to colleagues complain about having to learn the difference between HTML and these new "extensible documents." Now, here I am, writing a book about contemporary integration strategies, and I need to spend the next 3 chapters providing you with introductions to 16 different technologies before I even get to use the word "strategy" in a section title (and that covers only the core platform).

It's not just a testament to "how far we've come," but more so a validation that there is an ever-growing confidence in these platforms — that XML and Web services are truly establishing a new foundation for the new enterprise.

Even though I occasionally refer to the individual sections in these chapters as tutorials, they really are just simple introductions. Each gives you a high-level description of the purpose and concepts behind a particular technology, with an emphasis on its role in common integration scenarios.

These introductions were included to accommodate readers with varying degrees of exposure to the range of integration-related specifications referenced throughout this book. Hopefully they will help you better understand and appreciate the numerous strategies and guidelines we discuss later.

NOTE

To actually become proficient with any of these technologies, you will need to supplement this guide with specialized tutorials. I maintain a list of recommended reading materials and online resources at www.service-oriented.ws.

Introduction to XML technologies

A sking someone if they "know XML" is about as concise as asking whether they know how to program. Though you can isolate the XML language as a technology, it rarely ventures out into the real world unaccompanied. A closer look at any serious XML architecture will reveal a variety of supplemental technologies occupying key positions wherein they perform specialized processing of XML formatted data.

As the core family of XML specifications grows, so too does the complexity of the technology that implements it. You would not think to deploy XML documents without a supporting schema technology, nor would you design an integration channel between applications expecting different data formats, without first considering the use of XSLT.

Supplemental specifications add consistent functional dimensions to an architecture. This deepens an application's control over XML data, but also increases the potential dependencies on the technologies that realize these functions.

As a result, many of these technologies embed themselves deeply within your applications. They become permanent residents of your technical environments, until the day they are uprooted by the next data technology revolution. It is because of these (often intrinsic) dependencies that an understanding of the various roles assumed by XML technologies is important. The following collection of "lightweight" tutorials is intended to provide a starting point toward achieving that understanding.

NOTE

This chapter's focus is on XML specifications relevant to integration architectures (as illustrated in Figure 2.1). The technical landscape portrayed here, therefore, is not representative of a standard XML technology framework. For instance, although introductions for seven key XML specifications are provided, some (such as XSL-FO) have been omitted intentionally. This by no means lessens the importance of these specifications — they are just not key factors in typical integration environments.

2.1 Extensible Markup Language (XML)

To appreciate the meaning of XML, let's take a quick look back at what motivated its creation. In the mid-1970s, Charles F. Goldfarb introduced the world to the Standard

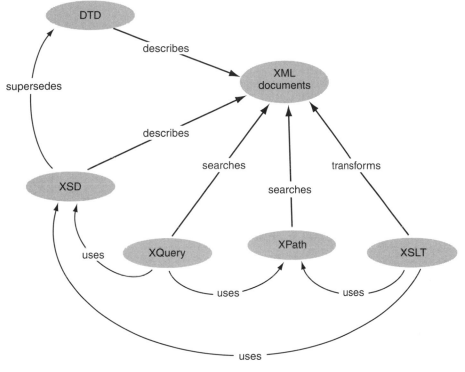

Figure 2.1
Relationship between XML specifications.

Generalized Markup Language (SGML). This hugely successful meta language established an international standard for data representation. SGML empowered organizations to take control of corporate intelligence, and evolved into a universal format for information exchange.

Over a decade later, Tim Berners-Lee conceived the World Wide Web, and soon thereafter, he founded the World Wide Web Consortium (W3C). One of the first initiatives of this organization was to create a formal specification for the Hypertext Markup Language (HTML), a language based on SGML.

HTML provides a syntax used to describe the formatting and layout of document text. Its compact size and overall simplicity allowed it to become the standard document format for Web publishing, and perhaps the most widely used technical language in the world.

In the mid-to-late 1990s it became evident that the Internet would be used for more than just document publishing. The advent of e-business identified a compelling need for a standard, business-centric data representation format. The W3C responded by once again turning to SGML. The result was the Extensible Markup Language. A meta language intended to supplement HTML's presentation features with the ability to describe the nature of the information being presented.

Without XML, information passed over the Internet has little meaning or context beyond its presentation value. XML adds a layer of intelligence to information, proportional to the intelligence with which it is applied. This layer can be extended throughout an organization, and beyond.

2.1.1 Concepts

A good point of reference for learning about XML is the HTML language. HTML allows us to describe how information should be rendered by a Web browser. Therefore, an HTML document cannot tell us anything about the nature of the data being displayed. A financial report may be clearly formatted and displayed by an HTML document, but the data being presented has no underlying meaning — it is, in effect, nothing more than a picture.

Why is this a problem? Let's say company A and company B want to do business over the Internet. If company A sends company B the results of its financial report as an HTML document, someone at company B would need to read and interpret the document ("look at the picture") in order to further use this information. This lack of "information quality" limits its usefulness and severely inhibits the potential of the Internet as a mechanism for information sharing. This is where XML comes in.

XML solves this problem by allowing us to supplement content with "meta information," self-descriptive labels for each piece of text that go wherever the document goes. This turns each Web document into a self-contained, mini-repository.

If company A sends company B its financial report using XML, company B can:

- programmatically manipulate the report's data
- import the report data into a database
- store the report within its corporate document set
- create different views of the report by sorting and filtering the data

… and so on.

Elements, Documents, and Vocabularies

As with HTML, XML is implemented using a set of *elements*. Unlike HTML, however, XML elements are not predefined. They can be customized to represent data in unique contexts. A set of related XML elements can be classified as a *vocabulary*. Elements are demonstrated and further discussed in the upcoming examples.

Vocabularies can be created to describe specific types of business documents, such as invoices or purchase orders. An instance of a vocabulary, therefore, is called an *XML document*. An XML document is the most fundamental building block of an XML architecture. Figure 2.2 establishes the symbol used in diagrams throughout this book to represent XML documents.

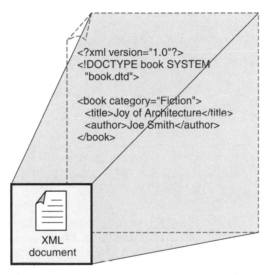

Figure 2.2
The standard symbol used by this book to represent
an XML document.

Organizations that need to exchange information can agree on a standard set of vocabularies. Alternatively, they can enlist a transformation technology to translate vocabulary formats dynamically (transformation is discussed in the XSLT tutorial, later in this chapter).

2.1.2   Schemas

Vocabularies can be defined formally using a *schema definition language*. The same way database schemas establish a structural model for the data they represent, XML schemas define the structure of XML documents. As shown in Figure 2.3, they protect the integrity of XML document data by providing structure, validation rules, type constraints, and inter-element relationships. In other words, XML schemas dictate what can and cannot be done with XML data.

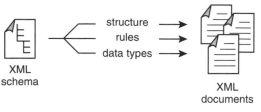

Figure 2.3
How XML schemas relate to XML documents.

Numerous XML schema languages exist. The two most common are explained in the "Document Type Definitions (DTD)" and "XML Schema Definition Language (XSD)" tutorials, following this section.

2.1.3   Programming models

XML documents can be manipulated using *tree-based*, *event-based,* or *class-based* interfaces. The W3C provides a standard tree-based API called the Document Object Model (DOM). The most popular event-based API is the Simple API for XML (SAX), and most development platforms offer proprietary data binding APIs that supply a class-based interface into XML documents.

Vendor-specific implementations of DOM and SAX APIs can vary in their compliance to the DOM and SAX standards. Some that do comply further increase standard functionality by adding proprietary extensions. Using a compatible programming language, you can interact with the parser's API to manipulate XML documents in many different ways.

The Document Object Model expresses an XML document using a hierarchical tree view. Each branch of the tree represents an element in the hierarchy. The DOM classifies these elements as *nodes,* and the API provided by the DOM is also referred to as the *node interface.* Other XML specifications that reference or utilize the node interface also refer to elements as nodes.

Though the use of DOM-compliant APIs is very common, they can introduce some performance challenges. The API loads the entire XML tree view into memory, which can consume a significant amount of resources when processing larger sized documents.

The event-based API provided by SAX establishes a linear processing model that notifies the application logic of certain events prior to delivering the data. This approach is very efficient, and addresses many of the performance concerns of DOM. The SAX and

DOM APIs complement each other and collectively provide a flexible programming model for XML.

Data binding APIs are a departure from the structure-oriented nature of DOM and SAX. They allow for a data-centric programming approach, where business classes are provided as the interface into XML document data. Many variations of data binding APIs exist, each with a unique feature set. (XML APIs are further discussed and compared in Chapter 6.)

2.1.4   Syntax

Let's take a brief look inside a simple XML document. The first line of markup you will encounter is the *XML declaration*. It establishes the version of the XML specification being used.

```
<?xml version="1.0"?>
```

Example 2.1   The XML declaration

The part of a document within which data is represented is considered the *document instance*. It consists of a series of elements that tag data values with meta information.

An XML document instance orders its information into a hierarchical structure, defined by parent-child relationships between elements. Typically, the parent element establishes a context that is inherited by the child element.

In the example below, for instance, the book element has two child elements, `title` and `author`.

```
<book>
    <title>Joy of Integration</title>
    <author>Joe Smith</author>
</book>
```

Example 2.2   A simple parent-child relationship between elements

Individual elements also can have properties, known as *attributes*. Whereas a parent element can have multiple layers of nested child elements, it can have only a one-to-one relationship with an attribute.

In our example, we've added the `category` attribute to the book element.

```
<book category="Fiction">
   ...
</book>
```

Example 2.3   An element with an attribute

To associate a document with a schema, a separate declaration statement typically is required. Here we link a Document Type Definition to our XML document.

```
<!DOCTYPE book SYSTEM "book.dtd">
```

Example 2.4   A document type declaration

Finally, here's a look at the entire document we just built.

```
<?xml version="1.0"?>
<!DOCTYPE book SYSTEM "book.dtd">
<book category="Fiction">
   <title>Joy of Architecture</title>
   <author>Joe Smith</author>
</book>
```

Example 2.5   A complete XML document

The syntactical conventions introduced here form the basis for all specifications that exist as specialized implementations (or applications) of XML. This includes most of the subsequent specifications covered in this chapter, as well as all Web services markup languages discussed in Chapters 3 and 4.

NOTE

We linked our sample document to a DTD as a way of transitioning this section into the next tutorial about Document Type Definitions. XML documents used by the other technologies covered in Part I of this book most likely require the use of XSD definitions, which are discussed later in this chapter.

SUMMARY OF KEY POINTS

- XML adds a layer of intelligence, establishing business-centric data representation.

- Elements can be combined into vocabularies that represent logical business data entities.

- Vocabularies can be defined formally using XML schemas.

For more information regarding XML standards, visit www.specifications.ws.

2.2 Document Type Definitions (DTD)

Through the use of Document Type Definitions you can define simple schemas for XML documents.

DTDs have been in use for a long time and, as a result, have established themselves as a core part of both the SGML and HTML landscapes. When designing schemas to represent XML data in enterprise application environments, the features offered by the DTD language may be insufficient. The need for more complex document structures and validation rules, and a larger selection of data types, often require more sophisticated schema definition languages, such as the XML Schema Definition Language (XSD).

There are, however, situations where DTDs are appropriate. An entire section in Chapter 5 is dedicated to discussing the applicability of DTDs compared to XML schema definitions. Additionally, since DTDs are so established, you are bound to run into them when delving into the world of legacy integration. It is therefore worth your while to familiarize yourself with the basics of the DTD language.

2.2.1   Concepts

Within a DTD you can declare element types and attributes, establish parent-child relationships between element types, and assign simple data types and validation rules. There are also techniques for utilizing predefined DTD attributes to simulate inter-element relationship constraints. (This topic is explored further in Chapter 7.)

HTML, for instance, uses a standard DTD that declares each of its element types, parent-child relationships between element types, nesting rules, attributes, and rules that ensure that element and attribute data are valid.

In the XML world, DTDs are used in the same way, defining the XML document structure (element types and parent-child relationships) and all of the rules that govern document content. Unlike HTML, however, which supplies a predefined DTD with a fixed set of element types, XML documents and their corresponding DTD can be completely customized. The symbol used to represent DTDs in this book is shown in Figure 2.4.

2.2.2   Syntax

Even though DTD information can be embedded within an XML document, typically it is kept in a separate file to which XML documents link using a header statement as follows:

```
<!DOCTYPE book SYSTEM "book.dtd">
```

Example 2.6   A declaration of a document type definition

Inside a DTD, the document structure is created through a series of element type declarations, which establish a hierarchy of elements.

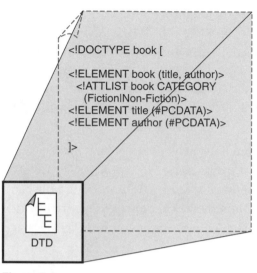

Figure 2.4
The standard symbol used by this book to represent
an XML schema, in this case a DTD.

The DTD begins with a document type declaration that represents the root element. This declaration corresponds to the header statement added to the XML document.

```
<!DOCTYPE book [
```
Example 2.7   A DOCTYPE definition

Characteristics of each element, such as data types and parent-child relationships, are also established, as follows:

```
<!ELEMENT book (title, author)>
<!ELEMENT title (#PCDATA)>
<!ELEMENT author (#PCDATA)>
```
Example 2.8   Three elements are declared — one as the parent, the other two as its children

Additional element characteristics, such as attributes and validation rules, can also be defined:

```
<!ATTLIST book CATEGORY (Fiction|Non-Fiction)>
```
Example 2.9   The category attribute is provided with a list of allowable values

Here, the `book` element was assigned an attribute called `category`, which has a validation rule limiting its possible value assignments to `Fiction` or `Non-Fiction`.

Finally, a closing statement for the DOCTYPE definition is added to complete the document.

```
]>
```

Example 2.10   The closing DOCTYPE statement

The entire contents of this simple DTD file are displayed below:

```
<!DOCTYPE book [
<!ELEMENT book (title, author)>
    <!ATTLIST book CATEGORY (Fiction|Non-Fiction)>
<!ELEMENT title (#PCDATA)>
<!ELEMENT author (#PCDATA)>
]>
```

Example 2.11   A complete document type definition

A physical instance (in the form of an XML document) of the document type in the above DTD would appear as follows:

```
<?xml version="1.0"?>
<!DOCTYPE book SYSTEM "book.dtd">
<book category="Fiction">
    <title>Joy of Integration</title>
    <author>Joe Smith</author>
</book>
```

Example 2.12   Look familiar? This document is the same one we built in the previous XML tutorial.

The preceding example demonstrates only a basic application of a DTD. The Document Type Definition syntax provides several features for the creation of more complex content models, including the use of entity references, and a series of keywords that provide processing instructions.

SUMMARY OF KEY POINTS

- DTDs supply a basic schema definition language for XML.

- DTD documents consist of a series of element type and attribute declarations.

- DTD functionality is limited. A number of more powerful schema languages exist, however, XSD is considered its primary successor.

Additional resources for DTDs are located at www.specifications.ws.

2.3 XML Schema Definition Language (XSD)

XSD is a comprehensive data modeling language for XML documents, and the one XML schema specification that has received the broadest industry support across contemporary XML and Web services technologies.

> **NOTE**
>
> The XML Schema Definition Language is sometimes also represented with the abbreviation XSDL.

2.3.1   Concepts

Unlike DTDs, the XML Schema Definition Language is an actual implementation of the XML language; schemas are themselves XML documents. XSD provides the structural and validation-related features offered by the DTD language within an extended feature set consisting of many more variations and options in how to model and establish validation criteria for XML document data.

One of the most important features introduced by the XML Schema specification is the wide range of support for data types. This greatly refines the quality of XML data representation, and further underscores its role as an enterprise data transport standard. XSD schemas also provide support for *namespaces*. This enables the schema author to establish logical domains to which some or all parts of a schema can be applied. Figure 2.5 provides the symbol used to represent XSD schemas in diagrams throughout this book.

The XML Schema document format is very flexible and highly extensible. Each schema definition is capable of containing multiple schema documents. This allows for the creation of modular schemas that can be combined or individually processed (see Figure 2.6).

Each schema can be dynamically extended with supplementary constructs. This allows schemas to adapt to different data representation requirements (see Figure 2.7).

Parts of a schema definition can be redefined (overridden) by other schema definitions. This allows you to create a series of schema classes (see Figure 2.8).

Strategies and further details regarding these features are covered in Chapter 5. Additionally, much of Chapter 7 is dedicated to exploring how XSD schemas can simulate relational database characteristics, such as inter-element constraints.

2.3.2   Syntax

In the following example we represent the DTD definition from the previous tutorial, within an XSD schema.

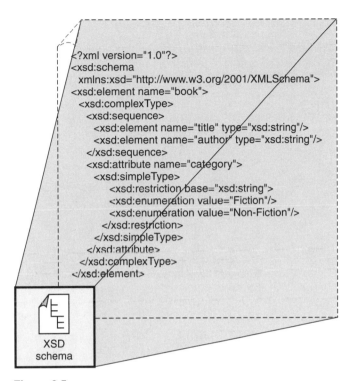

```
<?xml version="1.0"?>
<xsd:schema
  xmlns:xsd="http://www.w3.org/2001/XMLSchema">
<xsd:element name="book">
  <xsd:complexType>
    <xsd:sequence>
      <xsd:element name="title" type="xsd:string"/>
      <xsd:element name="author" type="xsd:string"/>
    </xsd:sequence>
    <xsd:attribute name="category">
      <xsd:simpleType>
        <xsd:restriction base="xsd:string">
        <xsd:enumeration value="Fiction"/>
        <xsd:enumeration value="Non-Fiction"/>
        </xsd:restriction>
      </xsd:simpleType>
    </xsd:attribute>
  </xsd:complexType>
</xsd:element>
```

XSD
schema

Figure 2.5
The standard symbol used by this book to represent an XML
schema, in this case an XSD schema.

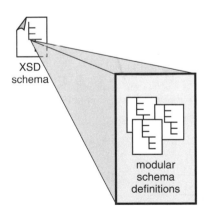

XSD
schema

modular
schema
definitions

Figure 2.6
A schema document hosting multiple
schema definitions.

extended
XSD schema

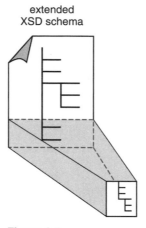

Figure 2.7
The schema data model being
extended by a supplementary
construct.

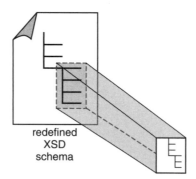

redefined
XSD
schema

Figure 2.8
Part of a schema definition being overridden
by a supplementary construct.

The XSD schema is defined using the following header statements:

```
<?xml version="1.0"?>
<xsd:schema xmlns:xsd="http://www.w3.org/2001/XMLSchema">
```

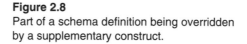

Example 2.13   The schema element used to establish the schema

Note the use of the xmlns:xsd attribute, which declares the namespace. This value is
carried forward throughout the schema by the use of the xsd: prefix. Schemas can be
fully customized, and developers can create and link schemas to their own
namespaces, by using custom prefixes.

```
<xsd:element name="book">
  <xsd:complexType>
    <xsd:sequence>
```

Example 2.14   These statements open the construct establishing the parent book element

XML schema elements have either *simple* or *complex* types, depending on whether or not they contain attributes or child elements. Since book is a parent element that will have child elements, it has a complex type. The sequence element acts as a compositor, setting up the sequence of the nested child elements.

```
    <xsd:element name="title" type="xsd:string"/>
    <xsd:element name="author" type="xsd:string"/>
  </xsd:sequence>
```

Example 2.15   The child title and author elements have simple types within the complexType construct

Since neither of the title or author elements have attributes or child elements, they have simple types, namely the built-in type xsd:string.

The book element, however, does have an attribute, which is declared separately within the complexType construct.

```
<xsd:attribute name="category">
  <xsd:simpleType>
    <xsd:restriction base="xsd:string">
      <xsd:enumeration value="Fiction"/>
      <xsd:enumeration value="Non-Fiction"/>
    </xsd:restriction>
  </xsd:simpleType>
</xsd:attribute>
```

Example 2.16   The category attribute receives its own simpleType construct wherein a list of allowable values is set

Note that the use of this attribute also introduces the schema's first validation rule. The category attribute is limited to one of two values, through the use of the restriction element. Also, notice the use of the simpleType element — since XML attributes cannot contain further attributes or child elements, they always have simple types.

The declaration of the book element (along with its nested child elements and its attribute) is completed by closing off the complexType and element constructs.

```
  </xsd:complexType>
</xsd:element>
```

Example 2.17   The book element declaration is completed

Finally, the schema construct itself is closed:

```
</xsd:schema>
```

Example 2.18   The schema ends with the closing element

The entire XSD schema definition appears as follows:

```
<?xml version="1.0"?>
<xsd:schema xmlns:xsd="http://www.w3.org/2001/XMLSchema">
<xsd:element name="book">
  <xsd:complexType>
    <xsd:sequence>
        <xsd:element name="title" type="xsd:string"/>
        <xsd:element name="author" type="xsd:string"/>
    </xsd:sequence>
    <xsd:attribute name="category">
        <xsd:simpleType>
           <xsd:restriction base="xsd:string">
               <xsd:enumeration value="Fiction"/>
               <xsd:enumeration value="Non-Fiction"/>
           </xsd:restriction>
        </xsd:simpleType>
    </xsd:attribute>
  </xsd:complexType>
</xsd:element>
</xsd:schema>
```

Example 2.19   A complete XSD schema definition

This schema can now be implemented using an XML document, such as our familiar example:

```
<?xml version="1.0"?>
<book xmlns="http://www.xmltc.com"
  xmlns:xsi="http://www.w3.org/2001/XMLSchema-instance"
  xsi:noNamespaceSchemaLocation="book.xsd"
  category="Fiction">
  <title>Joy of Integration</title>
  <author>Joe Smith</author>
</book>
```

Example 2.20   An XML document based on our schema definition

This introduction to XSD schemas has only scratched the surface of this technology's capabilities. The XML Schema Definition Language provides a number of advanced content modeling features, including:

- support for a wide variety of data types
- advanced validation syntax
- the ability to simulate relational schema models through the use of constraints and keys
- extensibility via the `any` element
- modularization using the `include` and `import` elements
- a form of validation inheritance using the `redefine` element

With its great many features comes a significant amount of complexity. This book explores numerous integration scenarios in which XSD schemas play a key role. To fully understand the extent to which this important technology can be utilized, you should read through a comprehensive tutorial. (See `www.serviceoriented.ws` for a list of recommended resources.)

SUMMARY OF KEY POINTS

- XSD is an advanced and complex language that supports the creation of sophisticated XML schemas.

- XSD schemas provide a number of features that go beyond establishing a data model and providing data validation.

- Many XML and Web services specifications natively incorporate XSD schema features.

To learn more about XSD and other XML schema languages, visit `www.specifications.ws`.

2.4 Extensible Stylesheet Language Transformations (XSLT)

Within just about any application design, there will be a requirement for the format of data to be altered between the time it is first retrieved to when it reaches its final destination. Because XML provides a clear separation of content, structure, and presentation, the output format of an XML document can be completely transformed.

Unlike with XML schemas, where you have a series of languages to choose from and combine, XML transformation relies on one core standard: XSLT. There aren't many alternatives, but there are some supplementary technologies that can be used to extend and optimize this part of an architecture. The diagram symbol used in this book to illustrate XSLT style sheets is established in Figure 2.9.

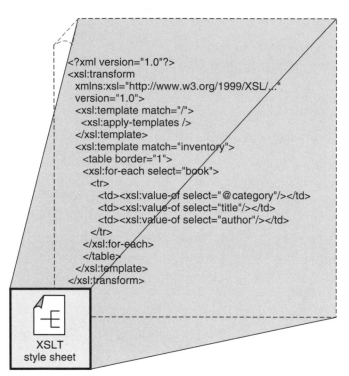

```
<?xml version="1.0"?>
<xsl:transform
  xmlns:xsl="http://www.w3.org/1999/XSL/..."
  version="1.0">
  <xsl:template match="/">
    <xsl:apply-templates />
  </xsl:template>
  <xsl:template match="inventory">
    <table border="1">
    <xsl:for-each select="book">
      <tr>
        <td><xsl:value-of select="@category"/></td>
        <td><xsl:value-of select="title"/></td>
        <td><xsl:value-of select="author"/></td>
      </tr>
    </xsl:for-each>
    </table>
  </xsl:template>
</xsl:transform>
```

XSLT
style sheet

Figure 2.9
The standard symbol used by this book to represent
XSLT style sheets.

2.4.1   Concepts

XSLT performs the following two primary transformation tasks:

Structural transformation
The conversion of one XML document type into another, as shown in Figure 2.10.

Aesthetic transformation
The formatting of an XML document into human-readable output, by conversion to a page-description vocabulary.

As demonstrated in Figure 2.11, for instance, an XSLT style sheet can be used to transform an XML document into an XSL-FO rendition that ultimately will make it suitable for published output, such as a PDF document. Alternatively, XSLT can be used to convert one XML document into another based on a different XML language, such as WML (Wireless Markup Language).

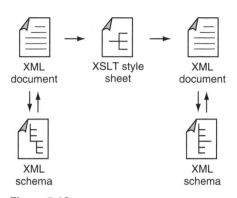

Figure 2.10
An XSLT style sheet is used to transform
XML document types.

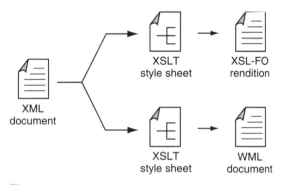

Figure 2.11
XSLT style sheets used to transform an XML document
into different presentation renditions.

Put simply, XSLT allows for the efficient conversion of XML documents into a number of different output formats. The XSLT feature set facilitates the manipulation, ordering, and filtering of XML document data to provide alternative views and renditions of information for any number of document transformation scenarios.

2.4.2   Syntax

To demonstrate the use of a simple XSLT template, we'll transform the following XML document into an HTML table. (To distinguish XSLT markup from HTML, HTML markup is bolded.)

```
<?xml version="1.0"?>
<inventory>
  <book category="Fiction">
    <title>Joy of Integration</title>
    <author>Joe Smith</author>
  </book>
  <book category="Non-Fiction">
    <title>Integration for Dummies</title>
    <author>John Doe</author>
  </book>
</inventory>
```

Example 2.21   An expanded version of the XML document we've been using in previous tutorials

To the preceding document we need to add a reference to the XSLT template we'll be building.

```
<?xml-stylesheet type="text/xsl" href="book.xsl" ?>
```

Example 2.22   A style sheet declaration

Note that XML documents do not need to have this statement embedded — the linking of an XML document and an XSLT template can be accomplished dynamically at runtime.

The XSLT template begins with the following header statements that simply identify it as an XML document conforming to the W3C XSLT specification.

```
<?xml version="1.0"?>
<xsl:transform
  xmlns:xsl="http://www.w3.org/1999/XSL/Transform"
  version="1.0">
```

Example 2.23   XSLT template header declarations

The following construct establishes the base node of the XML document, to which the template applies:

```
<xsl:template match="/">
  <xsl:apply-templates />
</xsl:template>
```

Example 2.24   A template construct that establishes the scope of the template

The `match="/"` fragment identifies the root node, which tells the XSLT processor that this template applies to the entire XML document (as opposed to a subset of the document tree).

The following construct uses XPath expressions to locate and loop through each instance of the book element. Every iteration through the loop results in the insertion of a table row consisting of category, title, and author column values.

```
<xsl:template match="inventory">
  <table border="1">
  <xsl:for-each select="book">
    <tr>
      <td><xsl:value-of select="@category"/></td>
      <td><xsl:value-of select="title"/></td>
      <td><xsl:value-of select="author"/></td>
    </tr>
  </xsl:for-each>
  </table>
</xsl:template>
```

Example 2.25 A loop construct that supplements filtered data with HTML tags

The XSLT syntax is interspersed with HTML tags responsible for building the table. Note the use of the @ symbol, which identifies a value as being an attribute, as opposed to an element.

The XSLT template is completed with the following closing element:

```
</xsl:transform>
```

Example 2.26 The final statement in the template

Here is the template in its entirety.

```
<?xml version="1.0"?>
<xsl:transform
  xmlns:xsl="http://www.w3.org/1999/XSL/Transform"
  version="1.0">

  <xsl:template match="/">
    <xsl:apply-templates />
  </xsl:template>

  <xsl:template match="inventory">
    <table border="1">
    <xsl:for-each select="book">
      <tr>
        <td><xsl:value-of select="@category"/></td>
        <td><xsl:value-of select="title"/></td>
        <td><xsl:value-of select="author"/></td>
      </tr>
    </xsl:for-each>
```

```
  </table>
 </xsl:template>

</xsl:transform>
```

Example 2.27   The complete template

Upon opening the XML document, the sample template will generate HTML formatted output that a browser should render as follows:

Fiction	Joy of Integration	Joe Smith
Non-Fiction	Integration for Dummies	John Doe

SUMMARY OF KEY POINTS

- XSLT allows for the structural and aesthetic conversion of XML document types.

- XSLT is a key integration technology, and is utilized by many EAI products.

- XSLT enables the formatting of XML data output by converting it to various formatting vocabularies, such as XSL-FO.

For a look at the XSLT specification and related standards, visit www.specifications.ws.

2.5 XML Query Language (XQuery)

The XQuery specification establishes a comprehensive data query language, designed specifically for XML documents.

XQuery is aligned (and overlaps considerably) with release 2.0 of the XPath specification. It uses the XPath language to define data source addressing, and even adds some new XPath extensions.

2.5.1 Concepts

XQuery statements can be isolated into independent *functions*. Functions can then be logically organized into *modules*, which are represented by the symbol provided in Figure 2.12.

A module can contain a collection of XQuery functions that can be imported into other modules, as shown in Figure 2.13.

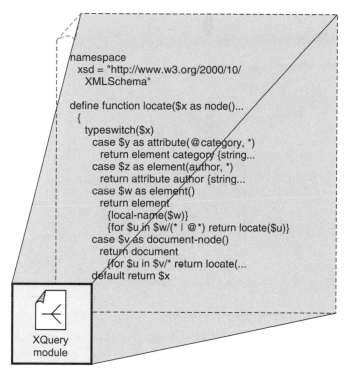

```
namespace
 xsd = "http://www.w3.org/2000/10/
    XMLSchema"

define function locate($x as node()...
  {
    typeswitch($x)
      case $y as attribute(@category, *)
        return element category {string...
      case $z as element(author, *)
        return attribute author {string...
      case $w as element()
        return element
          {local-name($w)}
          {for $u in $w/(* | @*) return locate($u)}
      case $v as document-node()
        return document
          {for $u in $v/* return locate(...
      default return $x
```

XQuery
module

Figure 2.12
The standard symbol used by this book to represent an XQuery module.

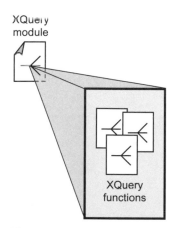

XQuery
module

XQuery
functions

Figure 2.13
An XQuery module hosting multiple
XQuery functions.

XQuery *expressions* can be embedded within an XML document (in which case they are enclosed within braces). Figure 2.14 provides a simple XQuery expression contained within an XML document.

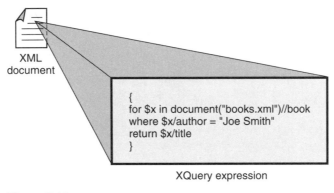

XQuery expression

Figure 2.14
An XQuery expression embedded within an XML document.

XQuery is often compared to the Structured Query Language (SQL). In fact, some XQuery features are even derived from traditional SQL statements. A significant characteristic of XQuery is that it enables you to perform a search across multiple XML repositories with a single query statement. As illustrated in Figure 2.15, this establishes a data source independence that broadens the application of XQuery beyond that of SQL.

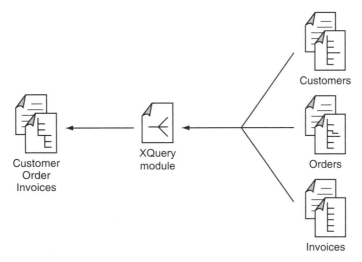

Figure 2.15
A single query against multiple data sources returns an XML document with a unique context.

Depending on the nature of the data you are searching and the type of query expression you need to build, you can choose from one of several available expression formats, including:

- FLWR (pronounced "flower"), which provides a series of keywords that are comparable to those used by SQL.
- Path expressions, which allow you to access elements and attributes of an input document.
- Element constructors that enable the dynamic creation of new XML elements and values.
- Conditional expressions that can add complex logic to query statements using the well-known `if-then-else` construct.
- Quantified expressions that allow for the inclusion of quantifying logic. Using keywords, such as `some` and `every`, submitted test expressions result in either false or true.

2.5.2   Syntax

For our example we'll be building a FLWR query expression using the `for`, `where`, and `return` keywords.

The following `for` clause provides a variable that is bound to the `book` element of the `books.xml` document. The values that will be output are defined by the subsequent XQuery clauses.

```
for $x in document("books.xml")//book
```

Example 2.28   A for clause starting off our query statement

The `where` fragment is very similar to the SQL WHERE clause, in that it defines the search criteria. In this case, we are searching for all books written by Joe Smith.

```
where $x/author = "Joe Smith"
```

Example 2.29   The where keyword used to define search criteria

To define what data from the queried XML tree we actually want returned, XQuery provides the `return` keyword (much like an SQL SELECT statement). In response to our query, we'd like to get the titles written by Joe Smith.

```
return $x/title
```

Example 2.30   The return keyword specifying the requested output values

When the following XQuery statement:

```
for $x in document("books.xml")//book
where $x/author = "Joe Smith"
return $x/title
```

Example 2.31   A complete XQuery statement

queries this document:

```
<inventory>
  <book category="Fiction">
    <title>Joy of Integration</title>
    <author>Joe Smith</author>
  </book>
  <book category="Non-Fiction">
    <title>Integration for Dummies</title>
    <author>John Doe</author>
  </book>
</inventory>
```

Example 2.32   The XML document acting as our data source

it returns the following result:

```
<title>Joy of Integration</title>
```

Example 2.33   The query result

With numerous types of expressions at its disposal, the XQuery specification can be used to create complex query logic. Key features to look out for include support for XSD data types, XPath functions, SQL aggregation functions, and many other SQL features, such as grouping, joins, and sorting.

SUMMARY OF KEY POINTS

- XQuery provides a full-featured language for creating complex queries across multiple XML data sources.

- XQuery modules can contain libraries of query functions. Numerous expression options exist for the creation of query statements.

- FLWR is a common XQuery expression format that provides a set of keywords comparable to those found in SQL.

The current XQuery specification and related resources can be found at www.specifications.ws.

2.6 XML Path Language (XPath)

By abstracting certain utility functions, a relatively modular set of XML specifications has emerged. Functional redundancy is avoided by allowing these supplementary features to be reused by other standards. XPath is an example of such a utility specification. It can be used independently within custom programming logic to interact directly with the XML Document Object Model, or it can be intrinsically incorporated within other specifications.

Essentially, XPath provides an expression syntax used to create location paths.

2.6.1 Concepts

Elements or element values within XML documents can be searched and filtered using a variety of XPath functions. Statements that identify location paths are called *expressions*. XPath expressions are mobile, in that they can be embedded within other types of XML documents (as shown in Figure 2.16).

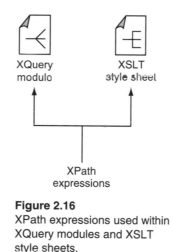

Figure 2.16
XPath expressions used within
XQuery modules and XSLT
style sheets.

XPath is one of the few remaining XML specifications that does not consist of an XML-compliant syntax itself. Its nature is purely functional, and its expression syntax has become highly integrated with the XQuery and XSLT specifications. Figure 2.17 shows how version 2.0 of the XPath specification shares the same data model as Query 1.0 and XSLT 2.0.

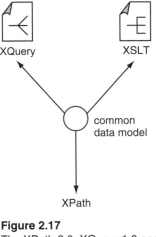

Figure 2.17
The XPath 2.0, XQuery 1.0 and
XSLT 2.0 specifications sharing
the same data model.

XPath approaches the addressing of an XML document tree similarly to how traditional file paths refer to directory structures, or how virtual paths refer to internal Web site structures. As a result, XPath addresses can also be relative or absolute.

> **NOTE**
>
> When discussing elements within the context of a document tree, the term *node* is frequently used instead.

Although it is important to have a basic understanding of how XPath works, in particular when supporting XSLT, it is not a technology that commonly acts as a key part of an integration architecture. XPath statements are typically found within XSLT templates and various programming routines that interact with the XML parser API.

2.6.2   Syntax

The following example starts a path with the forward slash symbol indicating that the statement applies to the root node:

```
/book
/book/author
```

Example 2.34   A statement identifying elements or nodes within a document

The first statement selects the root node `book`; the second selects all `author` elements that have the `book` element as a parent.

Starting the path statement with a double forward slash indicates that elements anywhere in the document that match the path are selected, as follows:

```
//title
```

Example 2.35   An expression restricting the criteria to the title element(s)

These are very basic applications of XPath. Much more complex path definitions can be created, for instance:

```
//author[normalize-space(@location)='Vancouver']
//*[count(category)=3]
```

Example 2.36   An example of a slightly more complex XPath expression

The first statement selects all `author` elements that have a location attribute with the value 'Vancouver'. The second selects all elements that have exactly three `category` child elements.

> ### SUMMARY OF KEY POINTS
>
> - XPath provides an expression syntax used to locate elements and element values within XML documents.
>
> - XPath expressions are often embedded within XSLT templates and XQuery modules.
>
> - XPath itself is not an XML-compliant language.

For resources and more information about XPath, visit `www.specifications.ws.`

Introduction to Web services technologies

efore we delve into the concepts and technology behind Web services, let's complete the timeline we began at the beginning of the previous chapter. In 2000, the W3C accepted a submission for the Simple Object Access Protocol (SOAP). This XML-based messaging format established a transmission framework for inter-application (or inter-service) communication via HTTP. As a vendor-neutral technology, SOAP provided an attractive alternative to traditional proprietary protocols, such as CORBA and DCOM.

During the following year, the W3C published the WSDL specification. Another implementation of XML, this standard supplied a language for describing the interface of Web services. Further supplemented by the Universal Description, Discovery, and Integration (UDDI) specification that provided a standard mechanism for the dynamic discovery of service descriptions, the first generation of the Web services platform had been established. Figure 3.1 illustrates, on a high level, the relationship between these standards.

Since then, Web services have been adopted by vendors and manufacturers at a remarkable pace. Industry-wide support furthered the popularity and importance of this platform and of service-oriented design principles. This led to the creation of a second generation of Web services specifications (discussed in Chapter 4).

3.1 Web services and the service-oriented architecture (SOA)

3.1.1 Understanding services

The concept of services within an application has been around for a while. Services, much like components, are intended to be independent building blocks that collectively represent an application environment. Unlike traditional components, though, services have a number of unique characteristics that allow them to participate as part of a service-oriented architecture.

One of these qualities is complete autonomy from other services. This means that each service is responsible for its own domain, which typically translates into limiting its scope to a specific business function (or a group of related functions).

This design approach results in the creation of isolated units of business functionality loosely bound together by a common compliance to a standard communications

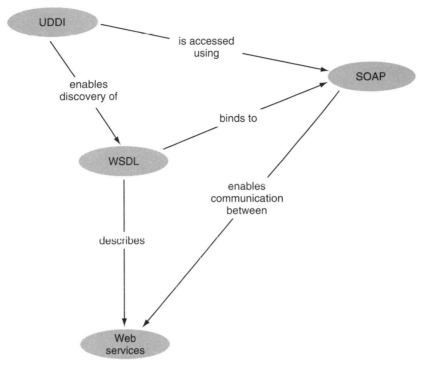

Figure 3.1
The relationship between first-generation specifications.

framework. Due to the independence that services enjoy within this framework, the programming logic they encapsulate does not need to comply to any one platform or technology set.

3.1.2   XML Web services

The most widely accepted and successful type of service is the *XML Web service* (from hereon referred to as *Web service* or, simply, *service*).

This type of service has two fundamental requirements:

- it communicates via Internet protocols (most commonly HTTP)
- it sends and receives data formatted as XML documents

That's pretty much it. You can write a simple ASP or JSP script that resides on a Web server sending and receiving XML formatted messages via HTTP, and you can go out and get yourself an "I'm Service-Oriented" T-shirt.

Broad acceptance of the Web service design model has resulted in the emergence of a set of supplementary technologies that have become de facto standards. An industry standard Web service, therefore, generally is expected to:

- provide a service description that, at minimum, consists of a WSDL document
- be capable of transporting XML documents using SOAP over HTTP

These technologies do not alter the core functionality of a Web service as much as they do its ability to represent itself and communicate in a standard way. Many of the architectural conventions expressed in this chapter assume that SOAP and WSDL are part of the described Web services framework.

Additionally, it is common for Web services to:

- be able to act as both the requestor and provider of a service
- be registered with a discovery agent through which they can be located

In a typical conversation with a Web service, the client initiating the request is a Web service as well. As shown in Figure 3.2, any interface exposed by this "client service" also qualifies it as a service from which other services can request information. Therefore, Web services do not fit into the classic client-server model. Instead, they tend to establish a peer-to-peer system, where each service can play the role of client or server.

NOTE
The tutorials in this part of the book cover technology only. SOA design principles, as they apply to business and architecture modeling, are covered in detail in Chapter 14. If you are interested in supplementing the technical knowledge provided here with service-oriented design theory, I highly recommend you read through the "SOA modeling basics" section.

3.1.3   Service-oriented architecture (SOA)

As previously mentioned, it is not too much trouble to append an application with a few Web services. This limited integration may be appropriate as a learning experience, or to supplement an existing application architecture with a service-based piece of functionality that meets a specific project requirement. It does not, however, establish a service-oriented architecture.

There is a distinct difference between:

- an application that uses Web services
- an application based on a service-oriented architecture

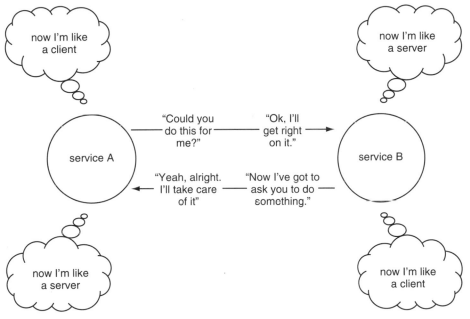

Figure 3.2
Web services swapping roles during a conversation.

An SOA is a design model with a deeply rooted concept of encapsulating application logic within services that interact via a common communications protocol. When Web services are used to establish this communications framework, they basically represent a Web-based implementation of an SOA.

The resulting architecture essentially establishes a design paradigm within which Web services are a key building block. This means that when migrating your application architecture to an SOA, you are committing yourself to Web services design principles and the accompanying technologies as core parts of your technical environment.

An SOA based on XML Web services builds upon established XML technology layers, with a focus on exposing existing application logic as loosely coupled services. In support of this model, an SOA promotes the use of a discovery mechanism for services via a service broker or discovery agent.

Figure 3.3 shows how an SOA alters the existing multi-tier architecture by introducing a logical layer that, through the use of standard programmatic interfaces (provided by Web services), establishes a common point of integration.

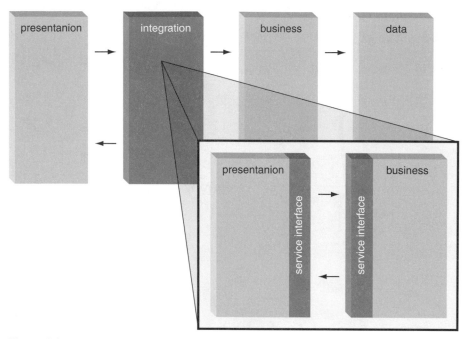

Figure 3.3
A logical representation of a service-oriented architecture (for a single multi-tier application).

This *service integration layer* forms the basis of a new model that can extend beyond the scope of a single application to unify disparate legacy platforms into an openly interoperable environment. When Web services are used for cross-application integration (as in Figure 3.4's logical service-oriented integration architecture), they establish themselves as part of the enterprise infrastructure.

It is important to understand the increased design complexities introduced by enterprise SOAs. Even more so than in n-tier environments, application designers need to appreciate fully how the introduction of services will affect existing data and business models, especially if current or future EAI initiatives need to comply to a service-oriented model.

As the utilization of services diversifies, the significance of security and scalability requirements are amplified. Well-designed service-oriented environments will attempt to address these challenges with adequate infrastructure, rather than custom, application-specific solutions.

For detailed information about service-oriented architecture design principles, and how SOAs can lead to the evolution of a service-oriented enterprise, see Chapter 14.

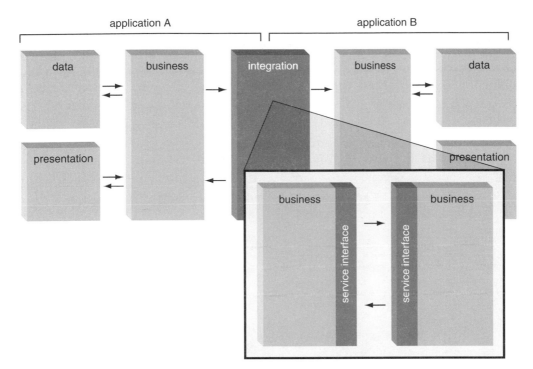

Figure 3.4
A logical representation of a service-oriented integration architecture.

SUMMARY OF KEY POINTS

- XML Web services are a Web-based implementation of service-oriented principles.

- The service-oriented architecture introduces a new logical layer within the distributed computing platform.

- The service integration layer establishes a common point of integration within application tiers and across application boundaries.

NOTE

The roles and scenarios illustrated in the next two sections are limited to the involvement of Web services only. The underlying SOAP messaging framework is explained separately, later in this chapter.

3.1.4   Web service roles

Services can assume different roles when involved in various interaction scenarios. Depending on the context with which it's viewed, as well as the state of the currently running task, the same Web service can change roles or be assigned multiple roles at the same time.

Service provider

When acting as a *service provider*, a Web service exposes a public interface through which it can be invoked by requestors of the service. A service provider promotes this interface by publishing a service description. In a client-server model, the service provider is comparable to the server (Figure 3.5).

> ### NOTE
> The term "service provider" can also be used to describe the organization or environment hosting (providing) the Web service.

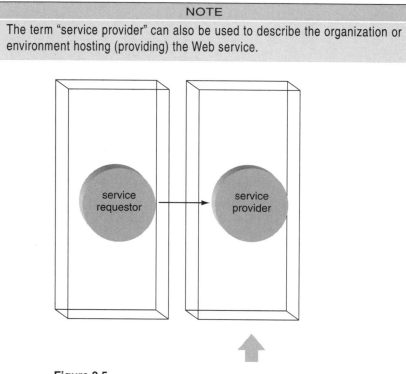

Figure 3.5
A service provider receiving a request from a service requestor.

A service provider can also act as a service requestor. For example, a Web service can play the role of service provider when a service requestor asks it to perform a function. It can then act as a service requestor when it later contacts the original service requestor (now acting as a service provider) to ask for status information.

Service requestor

A *service requestor* is the sender of a Web service message or the software program requesting a specific Web service. As shown in Figure 3.6, the service requestor is comparable to the client within the standard client-server model.

NOTE
Service requestors are sometimes referred to as *service consumers*.

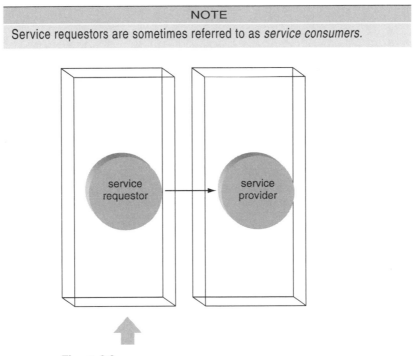

Figure 3.6
A service requestor initiating a request to a service provider.

A service requestor can also be a service provider. For instance, in a request and response pattern, the initiating Web service first acts as a service requestor when initially requesting information from the service provider. The same Web service then plays the role of a service provider when responding to the original request.

Intermediary

The role of *intermediary* is assumed by the Web service when it receives a message from a service requestor, and then forwards the message to a service provider. Figure 3.7 explains how, during the time that an intermediary processes a message, it too can act as a service provider (receiving the message) and as a service requestor (sending the message forward).

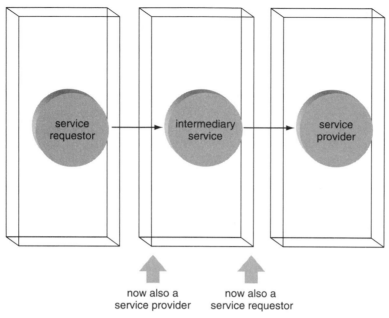

Figure 3.7
An intermediary service transitioning through two roles while relaying a message.

Intermediaries can exist in many different forms. Some are passive, and simply relay or route messages, whereas others actively process a message before passing it on. Typically, intermediaries are allowed only to process and modify the message header. To preserve the integrity of a message, its data should not be altered. (Intermediaries are discussed in more detail in Chapter 9.)

Initial sender
As the Web services responsible for initiating the transmission of a message, *initial senders* also can be considered service requestors (Figure 3.8). This term exists to help differentiate the first Web service to send a message, from intermediaries also classified as service requestors.

Ultimate receiver
The last Web service to receive a message is the *ultimate receiver*. As shown in Figure 3.9, these services represent the final destination of a message, and also can be considered service providers.

3.1.5   Web service interaction

When messages are passed between two or more Web services, a variety of interaction scenarios can be played out. Following are common terms used to identify and label these scenarios.

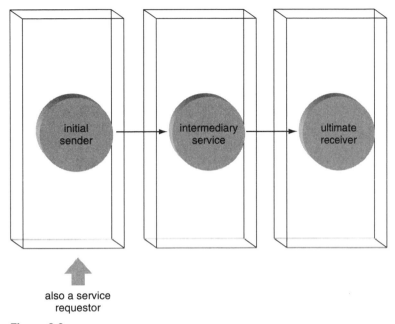

also a service
requestor

Figure 3.8
The first Web service is identified as the initial sender.

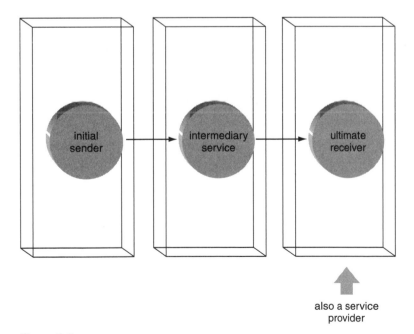

also a service
provider

Figure 3.9
A service acting as the ultimate receiver.

Message path

The route along which a message travels is the *message path*. It must consist of one initial sender, one ultimate receiver, and can contain zero or more intermediaries. Figure 3.10 illustrates a simple message path.

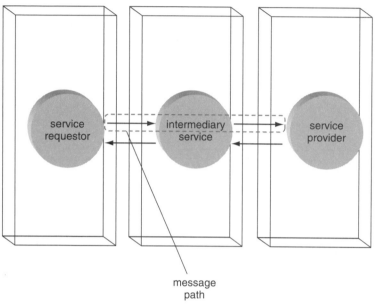

message
path

Figure 3.10
A message path consisting of three Web services.

The actual transmission path traveled by a message can be dynamically determined by routing intermediaries. Routing logic may be invoked in response to load balancing requirements, or it can be based on message characteristics and other variables read and processed by the intermediary at runtime. Figure 3.11 explains how a message is sent via one of two possible message paths, as determined by a routing intermediary.

Message exchange pattern

Services that interact within a service-oriented environment typically participate in one of a number of predefined *message exchange patterns*.

Typical patterns include:

- request and response (see Figure 3.12)
- publish and subscribe
- fire and forget (one-to-one)
- fire and forget (one-to-many or broadcast)

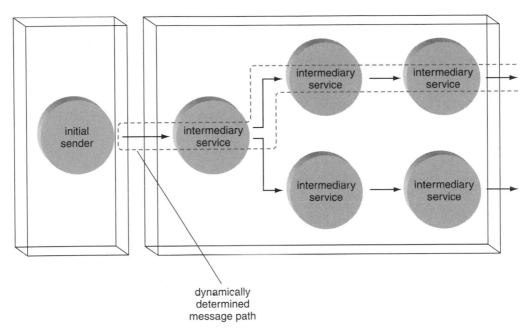

Figure 3.11
A message determined dynamically by a routing intermediary.

The request and response pattern is more common when simulating synchronous data exchange. The remaining patterns are used primarily to facilitate asynchronous data transfer.

Correlation

Correlation is a technique used to match messages sent along different message paths. As illustrated in Figure 3.13, it is commonly employed in a request and response message exchange pattern, where the response message needs to be associated to the original message initiating the request.

Embedding synchronized ID values within the related messages is a frequently used technique to achieve correlation.

Choreography

Rules that govern behavioral characteristics relating to how a group of Web services interact can be applied as a *choreography*. These rules include the sequence in which Web services can be invoked, conditions that apply to this sequence being carried out, and a usage pattern that further defines allowed interaction scenarios. The scope of a choreography is typically tied to that of an activity or task (see Figure 3.14 for an example).

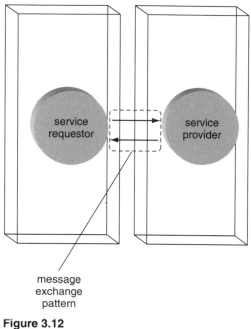

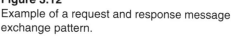

message
exchange
pattern

Figure 3.12
Example of a request and response message
exchange pattern.

Activity

Message exchange patterns form the basis for service *activities* (also known as *tasks*). An activity consists of a group of Web services that interact and collaborate to perform a function or a logical group of functions. Figure 3.15 shows a simple service activity.

The difference between a choreography and an activity is that the activity is generally associated with a specific application function, such as the execution of a business task.

3.1.6   Service models

Depending on the extent to which they are utilized, Web services can introduce a great deal of standardization on a number of levels, including:

* application architecture
* enterprise infrastructure
* global data exchange

Despite their contribution to establishing a consistent framework for information interchange, Web services themselves do not come in standard shapes or sizes. A

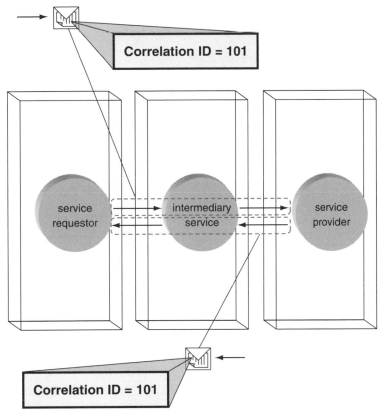

Figure 3.13
Correlation used in a request and response message exchange pattern.

NOTE
A choreography is similar in concept, but still different from orchestration. Orchestration is an implementation of a choreography within the context of a workflow or business process. To learn more about orchestration, read through Chapter 10.

service can be based on one of a number of design models, each with its own role and function.

This book documents a number of the common XWIF design models for Web services (listed in Table 3.1). Consider these a starting point, and feel free to customize them to whatever extent they assist in meeting your requirements. As the overall acceptance of service-oriented designs increases, and as Web services and their associated technology set become more integrated into the IT mainstream, this list is sure to evolve.

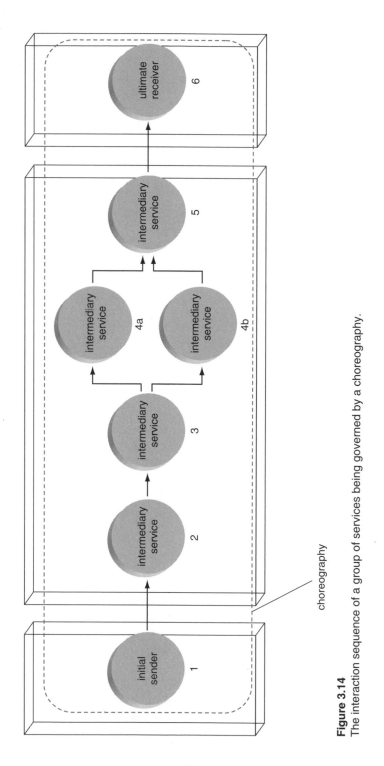

Figure 3.14
The interaction sequence of a group of services being governed by a choreography.

choreography

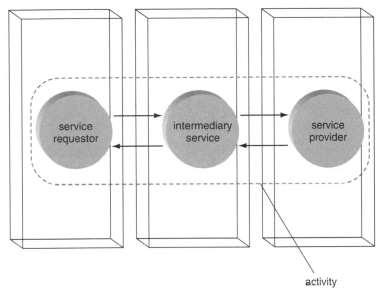

Figure 3.15
A service activity involving three services.

Table 3.1   Service models and the locations of their respective descriptions within this book

XWIF Service Model	Location
utility service	Chapter 6
business service	Chapter 6
controller service	Chapter 6
proxy service	Chapter 9
wrapper service	Chapter 9
coordination service (for atomic transactions)	Chapter 9
process service	Chapter 10
coordination service (for business activities)	Chapter 10

3.1.7   Web service description structure

An XML Web service is described through a stack of definition documents that constitute a service description. Figure 3.16 illustrates the relationship between these documents, each of which is described individually, thereafter.

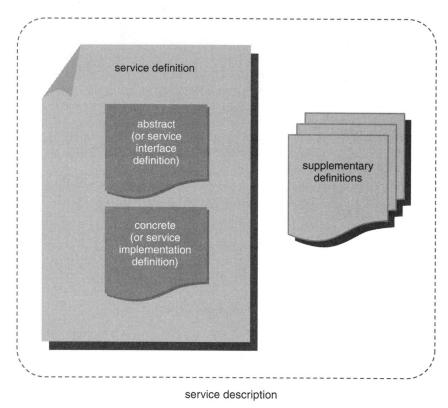

service description

Figure 3.16
Contents of a service description.

Definition documents acts as building blocks for a service description:

> *Abstract + Concrete = Service Definition*
>
> *Service Definition + Supplementary Definitions = Service Description*

Abstract

The description of a Web service interface, independent of implementation details, is referred to as the *abstract*. Within a WSDL document, this abstract interface definition is primarily made up of the `interface` and `message` constructs. It is further supported by the `types` construct, which is often classified separately. (Descriptions of these elements are provided later in this chapter, as part of the WSDL tutorial.) In a component-based architecture, the service interface is often compared to the Interface Definition Language (IDL) file used to describe a component interface.

> **NOTE**
>
> The term "abstract" superseded the term "service interface definition" as of the May 14, 2003 working draft release of the W3C Web services architecture specification.

Concrete

Specific location and implementation information about a Web service are the *concrete* parts of a WSDL document, as represented by the `binding`, `service`, and `endpoint` (or `port`) elements.

> **NOTE**
>
> The term "service implementation definition" was replaced with the term "concrete" in the May 14, 2003 working draft release of the W3C Web services architecture specification.

Service definition

Generally, the contents of a WSDL document constitute a *service definition*, which includes the interface (abstract) and implementation (concrete) definitions.

Service description

Often a *service description* consists of only a WSDL document providing a service definition; however, it can include a number of additional definition documents that can provide supplemental information (such as how this service relates to others)

3.1.8   Introduction to first-generation Web services

The W3C framework for Web services consists of a foundation built on top of three core XML specifications:

- Web Services Definition Language (WSDL)
- Simple Object Access Protocol (SOAP)
- Universal Description, Discovery, and Integration (UDDI)

These technology standards, coupled with service-oriented design principles, form a basic XML-driven SOA. This *first-generation Web services architecture* allows for the creation of independent Web services capable of encapsulating isolated units of business functionality. It also has a number of limitations, which have been addressed in a second generation of specifications. (Key second-generation Web services specifications are introduced through a series of tutorials in Chapter 4.)

The next three sections provide introductory tutorials to each of the first-generation Web services technologies.

3.2 Web Services Definition Language (WSDL)

Web services need to be defined in a consistent manner so that they can be discovered by and interfaced with other services and applications. The Web Services Definition Language is a W3C specification providing the foremost language for the description of Web service definitions.

The integration layer introduced by the Web services framework establishes a standard, universally recognized and supported programmatic interface. As shown in Figure 3.17, WSDL enables communication between these layers by providing standardized endpoint descriptions.

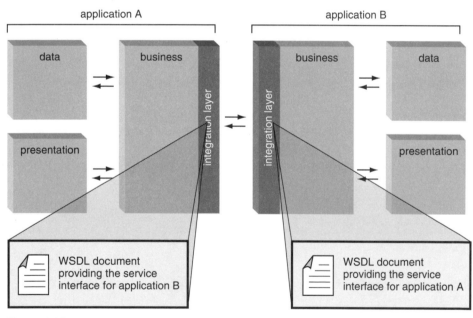

Figure 3.17
WSDL documents representing Web services to applications.

The best way to understand how a Web service is defined and expressed by a WSDL document is to step through each of the constructs that collectively represent this definition. Let's begin with the root `definitions` element, which acts as the container for the entire service definition.

```
<definitions>
  <interface name="Catalog">
    ...
  </interface>
  <message name="BookInfo">
    ...
  </message>
  <service>
    ...
  </service>
  <binding name="Binding1">
    ...
  </binding>
</definitions>
```

Example 3.1   A service definition, as expressed by the definitions construct

A WSDL definition can host collections of the following primary constructs:

- `interface` (previously known as `portType`)[1]
- `message`
- `service`
- `binding`

Figure 3.18 illustrates how the first two constructs represent the service interface definition, and the latter two provide the service implementation details.

3.2.1   Abstract interface definition

Individual Web service interfaces are represented by WSDL `interface` elements. These constructs contain a group of logically related operations. In a component-based architecture, a WSDL `interface` is comparable to a component interface. An operation is therefore the equivalent of a component method, as it represents a single action or function.

```
<definitions>
  <interface name="Catalog">
    <operation name="GetBook">
      ...
    </operation>
  </interface >
</definitions>
```

Example 3.2   A Web service interface represented by the interface element

---

1.   As of June 11, 2003, the WSDL specification changed the name of this element from `portType` to `interface`.

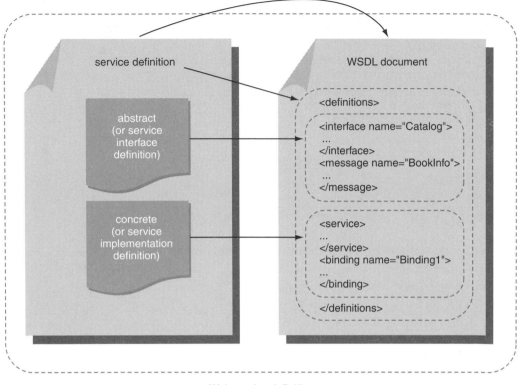

Web service definition

Figure 3.18
The contents of a WSDL document, as they relate to a service definition.

A typical `operation` element consists of a group of related input and output messages. The execution of an operation requires the transmission or exchange of these messages between the service requestor and the service provider.

Operation messages are represented by `message` constructs that are declared separately under the `definitions` element. The message names then are referenced in the operation's `input` or `output` child elements.

```
<definitions>
  <message name="BookInfo">
    ...
  </message>
  <interface name="Catalog">
    <operation name="GetBook">
      <input name="Msg1" message="BookInfo" />
    </operation>
```

```
  </interface>
</definitions>
```

Example 3.3   The input element within an operation construct referencing a message block

A `message` element can contain one or more input or output parameters that belong to an operation. Each `part` element defines one such parameter. It provides a name/value set, along with an associated data type. In a component-based architecture, a WSDL `part` is the equivalent of an input or output parameter (or a return value) of a component method.

```
<definitions>
  <message name="BookInfo">
    <part name="title" type="xs:string">
      Field Guide
    </part>
    <part name="author" type="xs:string">
      Mr. T
    </part>
  </message>
</definitions>
```

Example 3.4   A message block with part constructs representing operation parameters

Here's a brief summary of the fundamental constructs that can be assembled to establish an abstract interface definition:

- `interfaces` represent service interfaces, and can contain multiple `operations`
- `operations` represent a Web service function, and can reference multiple `messages`
- `messages` represent collections of input or output parameters, and can contain multiple `parts`
- `parts` represent either incoming or outgoing `operation` parameter data

3.2.2   Concrete (implementation) definition

On to the implementation details. Using the elements described in this section, a WSDL document can establish concrete binding details for protocols, such as SOAP and HTTP.

Within a WSDL document, the `service` element represents one or more endpoints at which the Web service can be accessed. These endpoints consist of location and protocol information, and are stored in a collection of `endpoint` (previously known as `port`)[2] elements.

---

2.   As of June 11, 2003, the WSDL specification changed the name of this element from `port` to `endpoint`.

```
<definitions>
  <service name="Service1">
    <endpoint name="Endpoint1" binding="Binding1">
      ...concrete implementation details...
    </endpoint>
  </service>
</definitions>
```

Example 3.5   The endpoint element

Now that we've described how a Web service can be accessed, we need to define the invocation requirements of each of its operations. The binding element associates protocol and message format information to operations. The operation construct that resides within the binding block resembles its counterpart in the interface section.

```
<definitions>
  <service>
    <binding name="Binding1">
      <operation>
        <input name="Msg1" message="book" />
      </operation>
    </binding>
  </service>
</definitions>
```

Example 3.6   The binding element representing an existing operation

The description of concrete information within a WSDL document can be summarized as follows:

- service elements host collections of endpoints represented individually by endpoint elements
- endpoint elements contain endpoint data, including physical address and protocol information
- binding elements associate themselves to operation constructs
- each endpoint can reference a binding element, and therefore relates the endpoint information to underlying operation

3.2.3   Supplementary constructs

An additional feature used to provide data type support for Web service definitions is the types element. Its construct allows XSD schemas to be embedded or imported into the definition document.

```
<definitions>
  <types>
    <xsd:schema
      targetNamespace="http://www.examples.ws/"
      xmlns="http://www.w3.org/2000/10/XMLSchema">
      ...
    </xsd:schema>
  </types>
</definitions>
```

Example 3.7   The types element establishing XSD data types

Finally, the optional `documentation` element allows supplementary annotations to be added.

```
<definitions>
  <documentation>
    I wrote this service definition some time ago,
    when I was younger and times were simpler for us all...
  </documentation>
</definitions>
```

Example 3.8   The documentation element allows you to supplement service definitions with annotations

---

SUMMARY OF KEY POINTS

- A service definition can be represented by the contents of a WSDL document, as defined within the `definitions` construct.

- The abstract interface definition is described by the `interface`, `message`, and `types` constructs. This part of the WSDL document provides a mobile, platform-independent description of the Web service interface.

- Concrete implementation information is contained within the `binding`, `service`, and `endpoint/port` elements. This part of the WSDL document is used to bind an abstract interface to specific protocols, such as SOAP and HTTP.

For more information regarding WSDL features and resources, visit `www.specifica-tions.ws`.

3.3 Simple Object Access Protocol (SOAP)

Although originally conceived as a technology to bridge the gap between disparate RPC-based communication platforms, SOAP has evolved into the most widely supported messaging format and protocol for use with XML Web services. Hence the

SOAP acronym is frequently referred to as the Service-Oriented Architecture (or Application) Protocol, instead of the Simple Object Access Protocol.

The SOAP specification establishes a standard message format that consists of an XML document capable of hosting RPC and document-centric data (see Figure 3.19). This facilitates synchronous (request and response) as well as asynchronous (process-driven) data exchange models. With WSDL establishing a standard endpoint description format for applications, the document-centric message format is much more common.

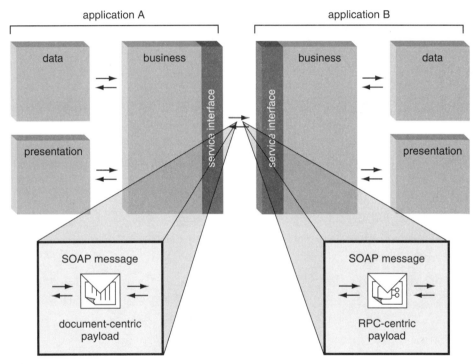

Figure 3.19
SOAP establishes two primary standard message formats.

The architectures we explore throughout this book make reference to both types of message formats using the standard diagram symbols provided in Figures 3.20 and 3.21.

Additionally, we discuss the use of SOAP message attachments, which are described in separate second-generation Web services specifications. (Specifically, the WS-Attachments and SOAP Messages with Attachments (SwA) standards, are covered in Chapter 4.) SOAP messages containing attachments are represented with the symbol shown in Figure 3.22.

SOAP
envelope
document-centric

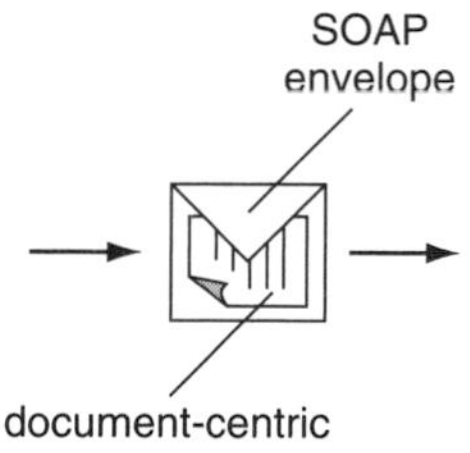

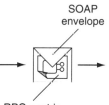

Figure 3.20
The symbol used to represent a SOAP message with a document-centric payload.

SOAP
envelope
RPC-centric

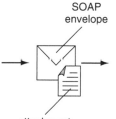

Figure 3.21
The symbol used to represent a SOAP message with an RPC-centric payload.

SOAP
envelope
attachment

Figure 3.22
The symbol used to represent a SOAP message delivering its data as an attachment.

3.3.1 SOAP messaging framework

SOAP institutes a method of communication based on a processing model that is in relative alignment with the overall Web services framework described at the beginning of this chapter. It differs only in that it introduces terms and concepts that relate specifically to the manner in which SOAP messages need to be handled (within a technical implementation of this framework).

Note that the diagram symbols used to identify SOAP nodes in the following sections are not displayed in other chapters. Their existence is implied in subsequent architectural diagrams that include Web services.

SOAP nodes

A *SOAP node* represents the processing logic responsible for transmitting, receiving, and performing a variety of processing tasks on SOAP messages. An implementation of a SOAP node is typically platform specific, and is commonly labeled as a *SOAP server* or a *SOAP listener*. Specialized variations also exist, such as *SOAP routers*. Conceptually, all are considered SOAP nodes. Figure 3.23 establishes the SOAP node as the underlying transport mechanism for a Web service.

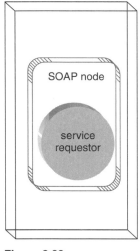

Figure 3.23
A SOAP node.

SOAP nodes are best viewed as the technical infrastructure that powers all of the communication scenarios explored in the earlier section, "Web service interaction." When discussing the involvement of SOAP nodes, however, a slight departure from the terms and concepts established by the Web services framework needs to be incorporated.

SOAP node types

Like Web services, SOAP nodes can exist as initial senders, intermediaries, and ultimate receivers. Whereas Web services are also classified as requestors and providers, SOAP nodes performing the equivalent tasks (sending, receiving) are referred to as *SOAP senders* and *SOAP receivers* (see Figure 3.24). The SOAP specification, however, does not classify these as roles. For the purpose of this book, we'll refer to them as "types" of SOAP nodes.

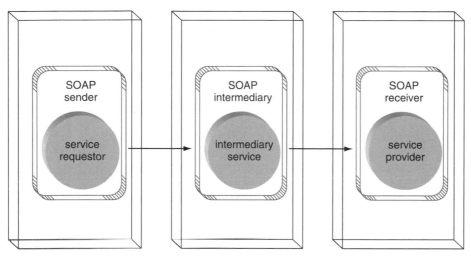

Figure 3.24
Fundamental SOAP node types along a message path.

As illustrated in Figure 3.25, a node type of SOAP initial sender is also a SOAP sender, and the SOAP ultimate receiver is also a SOAP receiver.

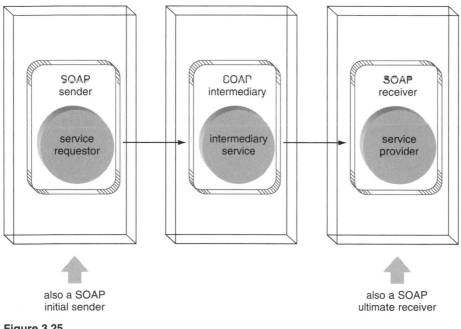

Figure 3.25
SOAP nodes with multiple types.

Figure 3.26 shows how a SOAP node, acting as an intermediary, transitions through both SOAP sender and receiver types during the processing of a SOAP message.

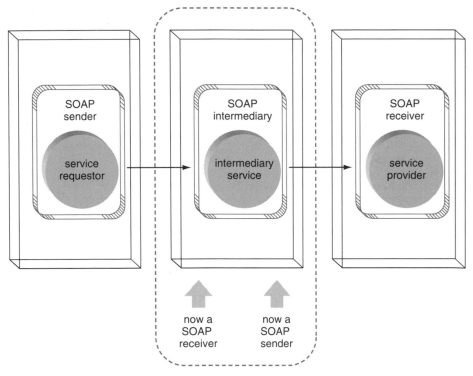

Figure 3.26
A SOAP node going through the transition of being a SOAP receiver and sender during the processing of a SOAP message.

As with Web service roles, the same SOAP node can act as different types depending on its position within the message path and the state of the current business activity. For instance, a SOAP node transmitting a message as the initial sender can later receive a response as the ultimate receiver.

NOTE
Roles for SOAP nodes also exist, but are described separately at the end of this section.

3.3.2   SOAP message structure

The container of SOAP message information is referred to as a *SOAP envelope*. Let's open it and take a brief look at the underlying structure of a typical SOAP message.

The root `Envelope` element that frames the message document consists of a mandatory body section and an optional header area.

```
<env:Envelope xmlns:env="http://www.w3.org/2003/05/soap-envelope">
  <env:Header>
    ...
  </env:Header>
  <env:Body>
    ...
  </env:Body>
</env:Envelope>
```

Example 3.9 A skeleton envelope construct

The SOAP header is expressed using the `Header` construct, which can contain one or more sections or blocks.

```
<env:Envelope xmlns:env="http://www.w3.org/2003/05/soap-envelope">
  <env:Header>
    <n:shipping >
      UPS
    </n:shipping>
  </env:Header>
  <env:Body>
    ...
  </env:Body>
</env:Envelope>
```

Example 3.10 The Header construct with a header block

Common uses of header blocks include:

- implementation of (predefined or application-specific) SOAP extensions, such as those introduced by second-generation specifications
- identification of target SOAP intermediaries
- providing supplementary meta information about the SOAP message

While a SOAP message progresses along a message path, intermediaries may add, remove, or process information in SOAP header blocks. Although an optional part of a SOAP message, the use of the header section to carry header blocks is commonplace when working with second-generation Web services specifications.

The one part of a SOAP message that is not optional is the body. As represented by the `Body` construct, this section acts as a container for the data being delivered by the

SOAP message. Data within the SOAP body is often referred to as the *payload* or *payload data*.

```
<env:Envelope xmlns:env="http://www.w3.org/2003/05/soap-envelope">
  <env:Header>
    ...
  </env:Header>
  <env:Body>
    <x:Book xmlns:x="http://www.examples.ws/">
      <x:Title>
        Service-Oriented Architecture
        A Field Guide to Integrating XML
        and Web services
      </x:Title>
    </x:Book>
  </env:Body>
</env:Envelope>
```

Example 3.11   The Body construct

The `Body` construct can also be used to host exception information within nested `Fault` elements. Although fault sections can reside alongside standard data payloads, this type of information is often sent separately in response messages that communicate error conditions.

The `Fault` construct consists of a series of system elements used to identify characteristics of the exception.

```
<env:Envelope xmlns:env="http://www.w3.org/2003/05/soap-envelope">
  <env:Body>
    <env:Fault>
      <env:Code>
        <env:Value>
          env:VersionMismatch
        </env:Value>
      </env:Code>
      <env:Reason>
        <env:Text xml:lang="en">
          versions do not match
        </env:Text>
      </env:Reason>
    </env:Fault>
  </env:Body>
</env:Envelope>
```

Example 3.12   A sample fault construct providing error information

SOAP node roles

Now that you've had a look at the internal structure and syntax of a SOAP message, let's finish by briefly introducing *SOAP node roles*. When discussing SOAP nodes, roles relate to an optional `env:role`[3] attribute that a SOAP message can use to identify header blocks intended for specific types of SOAP receivers. Therefore, SOAP roles are associated only to types of SOAP nodes that perform a receiving function. In other words, intermediaries and ultimate receivers (see Figure 3.27).

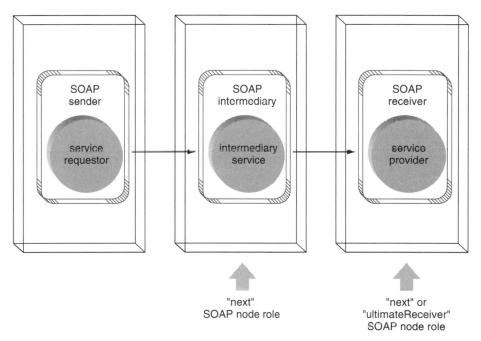

Figure 3.27
Roles that can be assumed by receiving SOAP nodes

The two most common `env:role` attribute values are `next` and `ultimateReceiver`. An intermediary node will process only header blocks identified with the `next` role, whereas a node acting as the ultimate receiver will process both.

To learn more about SOAP, header blocks, and how they relate to second-generation Web services, visit `www.specifications.ws`.

---

3.   The `env:role` attribute was introduced in version 1.2 of the SOAP specification. It was previously named `env:actor`.

> ### SUMMARY OF KEY POINTS
>
> - Implementations of the SOAP messaging framework can be collectively conceptualized as an end-to-end messaging engine that drives communication throughout contemporary service-oriented architectures.
>
> - A SOAP message consists of a simple XML document structure. The parent `envelope` construct houses an optional `header` and a required `body` construct. Exception information can be placed in a special `Fault` element that is nested within the message body.
>
> - The utilization of SOAP header blocks by second-generation Web services specifications is an important aspect of this framework that vastly increases its power and complexity.

3.4 Universal Description, Discovery, and Integration (UDDI)

One of the fundamental components of a service-oriented architecture is a mechanism for Web service descriptions to be discovered by potential requestors. To establish this part of a Web services framework, a central directory to host service descriptions is required. Such a directory can become an integral part of an organization or an Internet community, so much so, it is considered an extension to infrastructure.

This is why the Universal Description, Discovery, and Integration specification has become increasingly important. A key part of UDDI is the standardization of profile records stored within such a directory, also known as a *registry*. Depending on who the registry is intended for, different implementations can be created.

A *public business registry* is a global directory of international business service descriptions. Instances of this registry are hosted by large corporations (also referred to as *node operators*) on a series of dedicated UDDI servers. UDDI records are replicated automatically between repository instances. Some companies also act as UDDI registrars, allowing others to add and edit their Web service description profiles. The public business registry is complemented by a number of *service marketplaces* offering generic Web services for sale or lease.

Private registries are service description repositories hosted within an organization (see Figure 3.28). Those authorized to access this directory may include select external business partners. A registry restricted to internal users only can be referred to as an *internal registry*.

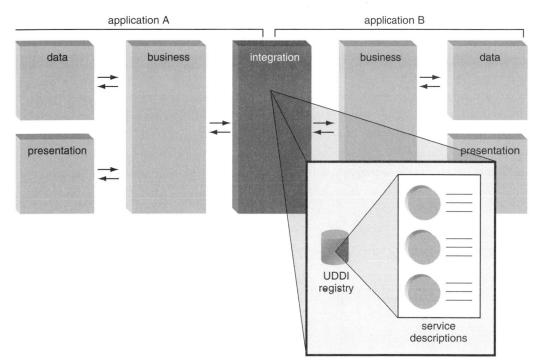

Figure 3.28
Service descriptions centralized in a private UDDI registry

The discovery process can occur in various situations depending on why service information is required. For instance:

- An organization seeking to establish new business relationships for online transactions can search for (and compare) suitable business partners using a public business registry.
- When building an inter-enterprise integration channel, the architect working for an organization's business partner will need to learn about the organization's external contact points. Service interfaces and the logic they express will form the basis for the Web services designed by the business partner. Access to the organization's private registry allows the architect to efficiently gather this information.
- An architect designing a new e-Business application may first want to research the availability of generic programming logic within an organization. By reading through existing service descriptions, opportunities for reuse may be discovered. Centralizing service descriptions in an internal registry provides a convenient resource repository for public endpoint descriptions within an enterprise.

- That same architect may also want to shop for a third-party Web service providing pre-built application logic that could be incorporated (locally or remotely) within the e-Business application. Service marketplaces offer venues to purchase or lease third-party Web services.

- A developer building new services will need to access interface definitions for existing services. The internal registry spares the developer from having to worry about whether the service interfaces being incorporated are current.

UDDI registries organize registry entries using six primary types of data:

- business entities
- business services
- specification pointers
- service types
- business relationships
- subscriptions

Business entity data, as represented by the businessEntity element, provides profile information about the registered business, including its name, a description, and a unique identifier.

Here is a sample XML document containing a businessEntity construct.

```
<businessEntity xmlns:xsd="http://www.w3.org/2001/XMLSchema"
  xmlns:xsi="http://www.w3.org/2001/XMLSchema-instance"
  businessKey="e9355d51-32ca-49cf-8eb4-1ce59afbf4a7"
  operator="Microsoft Corporation"
  authorizedName="Thomas Erl"
  xmlns="urn:uddi-org:api_v2">
  <discoveryURLs>
    <discoveryURL useType=
      "businessEntity">http://test.uddi.microsoft.com/discovery
      ?businesskey=e9355d51-32ca-49cf-8eb4-1ce59afbf4a7
    </discoveryURL>
  </discoveryURLs>
  <name xml:lang="en">
    XMLTC Consulting Inc.
  </name>
  <description xml:lang="en">
    XMLTC has been building end-to-end enterprise
```

```
      eBusiness solutions for corporations and
      government agencies since 1996. We offer a
      wide range of design, development and
      integration services.
    </description>
    <businessServices>
      <businessService
        serviceKey="1eeecfa1-6f99-460e-a392-8328d38b763a"
        businessKey="e9355d51-32ca-49cf-8eb4-1ce59afbf4a7">
        <name xml:lang="en-us">
          Corporate Home Page
        </name>
        <bindingTemplates>
          <bindingTemplate
            bindingKey="48b02d40-0312-4293-a7f5-4449ca190984"
            serviceKey="1ccccfa1-6f99-460c-a392-8328d38b763a">
            <description xml:lang="en">
              Entry point into the XMLTC Web site
              through which a number of resource
              sites can be accessed.
            </description>
            <accessPoint URLType="http">
              http://www.xmltc.com/
            </accessPoint>
            <tModelInstanceDetails />
          </bindingTemplate>
        </bindingTemplates>
        <categoryBag>
          <keyedReference
            tModelKey="uuid:c1acf26d-9672-4404-9d70-39b756e62ab4"
            keyName="Namespace" keyValue="namespace" />
        </categoryBag>
      </businessService>
    </businessServices>
  </businessEntity>
```

Example 3.13　An actual business entity document retrieved from a public service registry

NOTE
This document can be retrieved manually or programmatically using the URL `http://test.uddi.microsoft.com/discovery?businesskey` `=e9355d51-32ca-49cf-8eb4-1ce59afbf4a7`

Let's take this document apart to study the individual constructs.

```
<businessEntity xmlns:xsd="http://www.w3.org/2001/XMLSchema"
  xmlns:xsi="http://www.w3.org/2001/XMLSchema-instance"
  businessKey="e9355d51-32ca-49cf-8eb4-1ce59afbf4a7"
  operator="Microsoft Corporation"
  authorizedName="Thomas Erl"
  xmlns="urn:uddi-org:api_v2">
```

Example 3.14   The parent businessEntity element with a number of attributes

When I registered XMLTC Consulting Inc. it was given a unique identifier of
e9355d51-32ca-49cf-8eb4-1ce59afbf4a7, which was then assigned to the
businessKey attribute of the businessEntity parent element. Since Microsoft
acted as the node operator providing an instance of the UDDI registry, its name is displayed in the businessEntity element's operator attribute.

The discoveryURL element identifies the address used to locate this XML document.

```
<discoveryURLs>
  <discoveryURL useType="businessEntity">
    http://test.uddi.microsoft.com/discovery
    ?businesskey=e9355d51-32ca-49cf8eb4-1ce59afbf4a7
  </discoveryURL>
</discoveryURLs>
```

Example 3.15   The discoveryURLs construct containing the original URL

The name element simply contains the official business name.

```
<name xml:lang="en">
  XMLTC Consulting Inc.
</name>
```

Example 3.16   The name element providing the business name

Business service records representing the actual services offered by the registered business are nested within the businessEntity construct.

```
<businessServices>
  <businessService
    serviceKey="1eeecfa1-6f99-460e-a392-8328d38b763a"
    businessKey="e9355d51-32ca-49cf-8eb4-1ce59afbf4a7">
    <name xml:lang="en-us">
      Corporate Home Page
    </name>
    <bindingTemplates>
      <bindingTemplate
        bindingKey="48b02d40-0312-4293-a7f5-4449ca190984"
        serviceKey="1eeecfa1-6f99-460e-a392-8328d38b763a">
```

```
            <description xml:lang="en">
              Entry point into the XMLTC Web site
              through which a number of resource
              sites can be accessed.
            </description>
            <accessPoint URLType="http">
              http://www.xmltc.com/
            </accessPoint>
            <tModelInstanceDetails />
        </bindingTemplate>
    </bindingTemplates>
    <categoryBag>
      <keyedReference
        tModelKey="uuid:c1acf26d-9672-4404-9d70-39b756e62ab4"
        keyName="Namespace" keyValue="namespace" />
    </categoryBag>
  </businessService>
</businessServices>
```

Example 3.17   The businessServices construct

A business service is identified with a unique value assigned to the `serviceKey` attribute. Its parent `businessEntity` element is referenced by the `businessKey` attribute.

```
<businessService
  serviceKey="1eeecfa1-6f99-460e-a392-8328d38b763a"
  businessKey="e9355d51-32ca-49cf-8eb4-1ce59afbf4a7">
  ...
</businessService>
```

Example 3.18   The businessService element's serviceKey and businessKey attributes

The only business service associated with this business entity is the business's Web site home page, as identified by the `name` element.

```
<name xml:lang="en-us">
  Corporate Home Page
</name>
```

Example 3.19   The name element with the service name

Each business service provides *specification pointers*. Also known as *binding templates*, these records consist of addresses linking the business service to implementation information. Using service pointers, a developer can learn how and where to physically bind to a Web service.

```
<bindingTemplates>
  <bindingTemplate
    bindingKey="48b02d40-0312-4293-a7f5-4449ca190984"
    serviceKey="1eeecfa1-6f99-460e-a392-8328d38b763a">
    <description xml:lang="en">
      Entry point into the XMLTC Web site
      through which a number of resource
      sites can be accessed.
    </description>
    <accessPoint URLType="http">
      http://www.xmltc.com/
    </accessPoint>
    <tModelInstanceDetails />
  </bindingTemplate>
</bindingTemplates>
```

Example 3.20   The bindingTemplates construct housing concrete location information

The `bindingTemplate` construct displayed in the preceding example establishes the location and description of the service using the `accessPoint` and `description` elements.

Various categories can be assigned to business services. In our example, the URL we identified has been classified as a namespace using the `keyedReference` child element of the `categoryBag` construct.

```
<categoryBag>
  <keyedReference
    tModelKey="uuid:c1acf26d-9672-4404-9d70-39b756e62ab4"
    keyName="Namespace" keyValue="namespace" />
</categoryBag>
```

Example 3.21   The categoryBag element providing a categorization using the nested keyedReference element

There is no formal relationship between UDDI and WSDL. A UDDI registry provides a means of pointing to service interface definitions through the use of a *tModel*. Though it would most likely be a WSDL document, it does not have to be. The tModel represents the definition of the UDDI *service type*, and also can provide information relating to message formats, as well as message and security protocols.

Finally, business relationship and subscription data is represented by `publisher-Assertion` and `subscription` elements, respectively. `publisherAssertion` constructs provide a means of establishing the relationship of the current `businessEntity` with another. `Subscription` allows subscribers to be notified when business entity profile information is updated.

You can interface programmatically with a UDDI registry. The UDDI specification provides a number of APIs that can be grouped into two general categories: *inquiry* and *publishing*. For instance, you could issue a SOAP message to search for a company by name with the following payload:

```
<find_business xmlns="urn:uddi-org:api_v3">
  <findQualifiers>
    <findQualifier>
        uddi:uddi.org:findQualifier:exactMatch
    </findQualifier>
  </findQualifiers>
  <name>
    XMLTC Consulting Inc.
  </name>
</find_business>
```

Example 3.22   The find_business construct encasing a command for the UDDI inquiry API

Although this brief overview has discussed the fundamentals of UDDI (with a focus on the structure of business entities), it has not delved into the heart of a UDDI registry: the tModel. This important construct provides access to the technical details required for requestors to interface and interact with available Web services.

> ### SUMMARY OF KEY POINTS
>
> - UDDI directories can be implemented as public business registries, private registries, and internal registries.
>
> - Registry entries consist of the following profile information: business entities, business services, specification pointers, service types, business relationships, and subscriptions.
>
> - UDDI provides inquiry and publishing APIs, allowing applications to interface programmatically with a registry.

To learn more about the tModel and UDDI in general, visit `www.specifications.ws`.

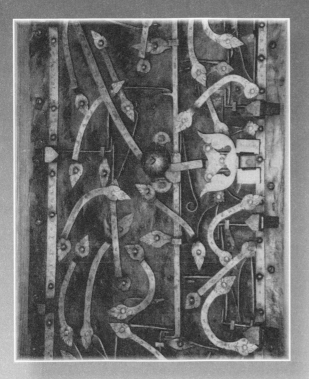

Introduction to second-generation (WS-*) Web services technologies

4.1 Second-generation Web services and the service-oriented enterprise (SOE)

The driving motivation behind extending the capabilities of the first-generation Web services framework is to empower service-oriented architectures to represent and even improve upon the range of business functions required for contemporary enterprises.

The army of second-generation Web service specifications that have emerged position SOAs as a viable successor to prior distributed platforms. Their feature sets continue to broaden, as do vendor-sponsored variations of the specifications themselves. The continuing maturity of these standards and their implementations sets the stage for the viable evolution of a *service-oriented enterprise*.

The diagram in Figure 4.1 illustrates how various Web services specifications relate to the technology layers of the SOE model. (The service-oriented enterprise model is explained in Chapter 14.)

This chapter provides high-level introductions to the following key specifications:

- WS-Coordination
- WS-Transaction
- Business Process Execution Language for Web Services (BPEL4WS)
- WS-ReliableMessaging
- WS-Addressing
- WS-Policy
- WS-PolicyAssertions
- WS-PolicyAttachments
- WS-Attachments
- SOAP with Attachments (SwA)

Additionally, the following security specifications are discussed:

- WS-Security Framework
- Extensible Access Control Markup Language (XACML)

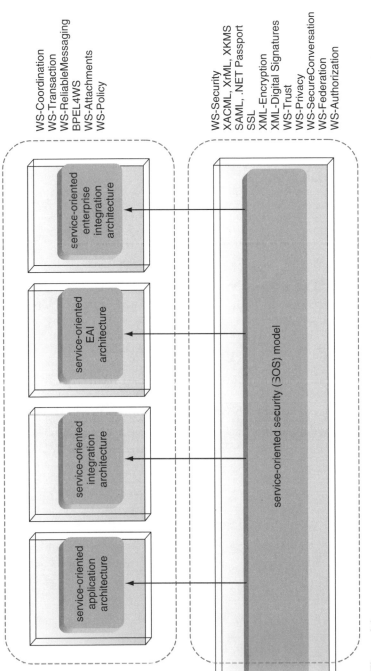

WS-Coordination
WS-Transaction
WS-ReliableMessaging
BPEL4WS
WS-Attachments
WS-Policy

WS-Security
XACML, XrML, XKMS
SAML, .NET Passport
SSL
XML-Encryption
XML-Digital Signatures
WS-Trust
WS-Privacy
WS-SecureConversation
WS-Federation
WS-Authorization

service-oriented
enterprise
integration
architecture

service-oriented
EAI
architecture

service-oriented
integration
architecture

service-oriented
application
architecture

service-oriented security (SOS) model

Figure 4.1
Second-generation specifications and the SOE.

91

- Extensible Rights Markup Language (XrML)
- XML Key Management (XKMS)
- Security Assertion Markup Language (SAML)
- .NET Passport
- XML-Encryption
- Secure Sockets Layer (SSL)
- XML-Digital Signatures
- WS-Trust
- WS-Privacy
- WS-SecureConversation
- WS-Federation
- WS-Authorization

4.1.1   Problems solved by second-generation specifications

In order to understand why these specifications were created, we need to take a look at some of the fundamental business automation requirements that have not been met by first-generation Web services.

Context and transaction management

The initial set of Web services technologies lacked the ability to support the structured maintenance of context throughout a service activity. Without an active, stateful context, Web services act independently and cannot support distributed transactions. The WS-Coordination standard provides a context management system, which is applied to support atomic and long-running transactions, using protocols described in the WS-Transaction specification.

For more information, see section 4.2, "WS-Coordination and WS-Transaction."

Business processes

In order to compose Web services into a structured workflow, a standard vocabulary is required. The Business Process Execution Language for Web services provides a process description vocabulary that can be compiled into runtime scripts, executable by middleware products that support orchestration. BPEL4WS, along with other business process vocabularies, brings Web services into the realm of enterprise integration.

For more information, see section 4.3, "Business Process Execution Language for Web Services (BPEL4WS)."

Security

Probably the largest gap in the first-generation Web services platform was an absence of any real security standards. Consequently, organizations were reluctant to expose business processes over the Internet.

The WS-Security framework institutes a thorough security model consisting of a stack of complementary standards. It establishes security measures to protect SOAP messages throughout a message path, and supports the creation of policies and the unification of trust boundaries. The core WS-Security specifications are further supplemented by a series of established XML security standards.

For more information, see section 4.4, "WS-Security and the Web services security specifications."

Reliable messaging

In order for a solution to be truly robust, its communications framework must be fail-safe. Within service-oriented architectures, this requires a system for the guaranteed delivery of a message, which includes a way of communicating delivery failures. WS-ReliableMessaging provides such a system, along with a set of policies that can be used to support delivery-related business rules.

For more information, see section 4.5, "WS-ReliableMessaging."

Policies

Within a service-oriented enterprise, it would be useful to be able to abstract high-level business rules, security rules, and descriptive properties so that they can be applied to groups of services as policies. The WS-Policy framework consists of a set of specifications that allow for the description of such policies, as well as a standard means of attaching them to Web services.

For more information, see section 4.6, "WS-Policy."

Attachments

The messaging-centric communications framework introduced by service-oriented environments provides an efficient and flexible data transport system. The use of SOAP as a message format standard, however, can limit the type of data that can be transported. The WS-Attachments specification supplements SOAP by supporting the delivery of additional data formats and files as encoded SOAP message attachments.

For more information, see section 4.7, "WS-Attachments."

4.1.2   The second-generation landscape

Figure 4.2 expands the relationship model provided in Figure 3.1 by explaining the relationships and dependencies between first- and second-generation specifications.

The fact that Web services standards exist as independent modules allows them to be composed in unique combinations. This "composability" is a key architectural aspect of the Web services platform, especially in relation to second-generation specifications. It allows for the design of individual services to be highly efficient, targeted, and customized to their respective roles within an application environment.

This affects the application design on a number of levels. For example:

- The application is only required to use the set of Web services specifications necessary to perform its tasks.
- The application logic within a Web service needs only to incorporate the parts of a specification it requires to perform its intended function.
- Only header blocks relating to standards used by a Web service for the execution of a given function need to be represented within its SOAP messages.

Additionally, Web services developers are required only to be proficient in the usage of standards required by a given application. The composable nature of the Web services platform will become increasingly significant as new standards continue to emerge. Regardless of how large the technology set grows, you will always be able to streamline application designs to use only what is actually required. To stay on top of trends and developments in relation to these standards visit www.specifications.ws.

NOTE

Many of the specifications discussed in this chapter are implemented using SOAP header blocks. You will also hear these standards referred to as *SOAP extensions* or *SOAP features*.

SUMMARY OF KEY POINTS

- Second-generation Web service specifications establish an extended service-oriented architecture that supports enough advanced business functions to rival traditional distributed platforms.
- The second-generation Web services platform is structured around the concept of composable specifications.
- The range of functionality provided by these standards continues to grow, as do vendor implementations of the specifications.

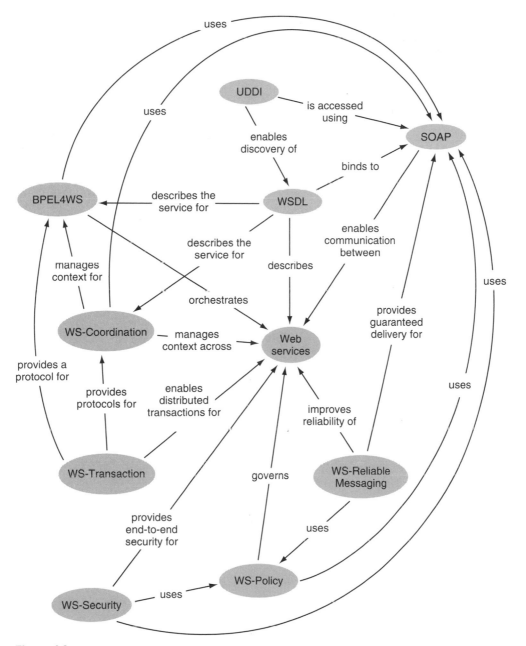

Figure 4.2
High-level relationships between first- and second-generation standards.

4.2 WS-Coordination and WS-Transaction

The loosely coupled nature of Web services requires an approach to maintaining a persistent activity context that differs from traditional distributed environments. In order to preserve the integrity of an activity, a context management service is required. To apply this context for the management of transactions, structured protocols are required to dictate behavioral aspects of services that participate in the activity.

For this reason, the WS-Coordination and WS-Transaction specifications were developed. The former provides a framework for context management, and the latter supplies two specific transaction protocols that utilize this framework.

4.2.1 Concepts

When a group of Web services collectively interact to execute a unit of programming logic, it will often be required for these services to share a common context. By doing so, the task or activity receives an identity that is propagated to each participating service. This context not only defines the runtime existence of the activity, it also establishes a level of control over how the task being executed can be processed (see Figure 4.3).

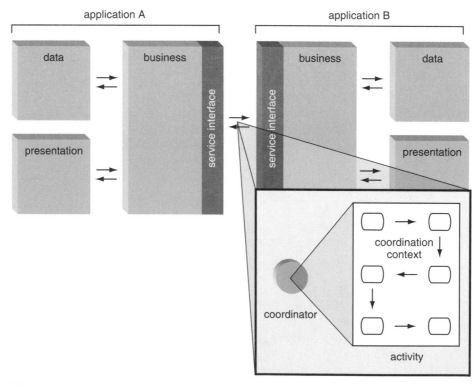

Figure 4.3
A WS-Coordination service keeping track of an activity's coordination context.

The WS-Coordination specification provides a standard mechanism for services to distribute and register for the context definition that represents an activity. It accomplishes this by introducing a standard coordination service model, consisting of individual services that provide dedicated operations for the following functions:

- context creation
- registration for coordination contexts
- protocol selection

These three services are represented collectively by a coordination service, also known as a *coordinator* (shown in Figure 4.4).

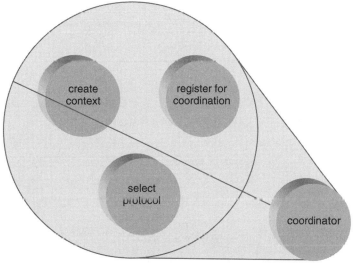

Figure 4.4
A coordinator service used to manage a coordination context.

Other Web service specifications can implement this framework by providing *Coordination Type* definitions. The WS-Transaction specification defines two coordination types, one for short-term, or *atomic transactions*, and another for long-running *business activities*.

NOTE

The atomic transaction part of the WS-Transaction specification is superseded by a separate standard titled WS-AtomicTransaction. Similarly, the planned WS-BusinessActivity standard will replace the corresponding coordination type definition within WS-Transaction. See www.specifications.ws for more information.

Atomic transactions

Traditional ACID-type[1] functionality is provided by the atomic transaction type. It implements the well known commit and rollback mechanisms, where the activity either successfully completes as a whole, or is returned to its original state.

A service participating in an atomic transaction can register for different types of atomic transaction *coordination protocols*. The following are defined by WS-Transaction:

- The *Completion* protocol provides the standard commit or rollback function. The service that initiates the transaction typically registers for this protocol.

- A variation of the Completion protocol is *CompletionWithAck*. It provides the same functionality, but requires that the coordination service remain after the transaction completes, until an acknowledgement is received.

- Two-phase commit type transactions (that allow for the transaction scope to span resource managers) are supported through the use of the *2PC* protocol.

- Registering for *PhaseZero* simply allows a service to be notified prior to the start of a two-phase transaction.

- Any service that takes part in a transaction can register for *OutcomeNotification*, so that it can be notified of the transaction completion status.

Chapter 9 introduces a service model based on this coordination type, called the Coordination Service for Atomic Transactions (or Atomic Transaction Coordinator).

Business activities

During the execution of an atomic transaction, resources involved with the activity are often locked, and remain in suspension until the transaction finishes. Since the lifecycle of this type of transaction is typically short, this will not tend to tax a system's resources. What if, though, you needed to keep track of an activity that could take hours or even days to complete?

WS-Transaction provides the business activity coordination type that allows context to be preserved for long-running transactions. Even though context information is maintained, resources typically are not locked.

This establishes an important distinction in how atomic transaction coordinators and business activity coordinators deal with activity failures. The atomic transaction coordination type responds to a failure condition with a standard ACID rollback.

---

1.   ACID represents the following four standard transaction properties: atomicity, consistency, isolation, and durability.

The business activity coordinator, however, supplies a separate *compensation* process that kicks in when the original process activity cannot complete as expected. A compensation is different from an exception handling routine, as the compensation can introduce a process activity of its own, which may require separate exception handling.

WS-Transaction provides the *BusinessAgreement* and *BusinessAgreementWithComplete* coordination protocols for business activity transactions. These allow a service to self-determine or be notified when it has completed its tasks for the activity.

The Business Process Execution Language for Web services relies on the business activity coordination type to manage context throughout the duration of a business process. Chapter 10 provides a service model based on the use of BPEL4WS and this coordination type, called the Coordination Service for Business Activities (or Business Activity Coordinator).

4.2.2   Syntax

The following example shows the message used to request the creation of a coordination context from the CreateContext service (also known as the *Activation* service).

```
<CreateCoordinationContext>
  <ActivationService>
     <wsu:Address>
          http://www.examples.ws/activation
     </wsu:Address>
  </ActivationService>
  <RequesterReference>
     <wsu:Address>
          http://www.xmltc.com
     </wsu:Address>
  </RequesterReference>
  <CoordinationType>
       http://schemas.xmlsoap.org/ws/2002/08/wstx
  </CoordinationType>
</CreateCoordinationContext>
```

Example 4.1   A message construct used to request the creation of a context

The `ActivationService` element defines the address of the service that will create (activate) the context. The `RequesterReference` element contains the address to which the response message should be sent.

The `CoordinationType` construct indicates which type of coordinator we would like to create. The use of the `http://schemas.xmlsoap.org/ws/2002/08/wstx` URI indicates that we are requesting an atomic transaction coordination type, as specified in the WS-Transaction specification.

For more information about the WS-Coordination, WS-Transaction and WS-Atomic-Transaction standards, visit www.specifications.ws.

SUMMARY OF KEY POINTS

• WS-Coordination provides a framework for context management.

• WS-Transaction supplies coordination types that utilize the WS-Coordination framework to provide atomic transactions and business activities.

• BPEL4WS relies on the use of WS-Coordination and WS-Transaction for the management of context using the business activity coordination type.

4.3 Business Process Execution Language for Web Services (BPEL4WS)

The ability to compose legacy and contemporary resources into coordinated sequences allows for the design of sophisticated business automation solutions, such as those traditionally provided by EAI products. Process integration into a service-oriented architecture, however, is best facilitated by a service-oriented process.

4.3.1   Recent business process specifications

A number of business process dialects have emerged over the past few years. IBM released the Web Services Flow Language (WSFL), and Microsoft provided the XLANG standard. Sun and Oracle collaborated to produce the Web Service Choreography Interface (WSCI), and both IBM and Microsoft went on to combine their efforts and created a successor to both WSFL and XLANG, called BPEL4WS.

Subsequently, the Organization for the Advancement of Structured Information Standards (OASIS) formally announced their support for BPEL4WS by forming a governing body called the OASIS Web Services Business Process Execution Language (WSBPEL) technical committee. Although competing standards are still in use, we will focus on the BPEL4WS specification in order to demonstrate how business process logic can be encapsulated within a Web service.

4.3.2   Concepts

The Business Process Execution Language for Web Services provides a comprehensive syntax for describing business workflow logic. It allows for the creation of abstract processes that can describe business protocols, as well as executable processes, that can be compiled into runtime scripts.

As illustrated in Figure 4.5, an executable process encapsulates the process description within a Web service. The BPEL4WS document essentially describes the sequence and logic behind other services managed by the process. Middleware server products use orchestration engines to implement executable process descriptions within vendor-specific platforms.

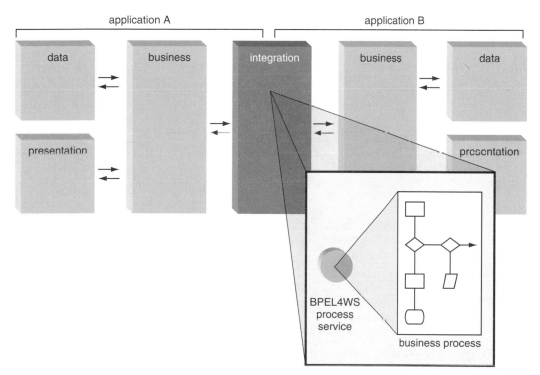

Figure 4.5
Two applications integrated and managed through the introduction of a BPEL4WS process service.

BPEL4WS and WSDL

A BPEL4WS process description incorporates numerous language constructs that can accommodate most traditional workflow requirements. The WSDL document representing the BPEL4WS process contains interfaces (previously portTypes) for the process service itself, as well as any additional services involved with the execution of the process.

Unlike regular WSDL documents, however, the service definition for a BPEL4WS process provides no binding information. It is intentionally implementation-neutral so that the process can remain mobile, reusable, and independent from changes to the technical deployment environment.

BPEL4WS and WS-Coordination/WS-Transaction

BPEL4WS relies on WS-Coordination to provide a fundamental context-management framework. The business activity coordination type, as defined by WS-Transaction, is utilized to establish a standard mechanism for managing long-running activities.

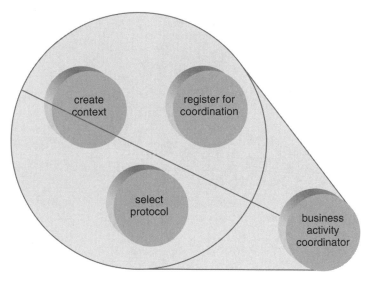

Figure 4.6
A coordination service used to manage a coordination context for long running business activities.

The business activity coordinator service model displayed in Figure 4.6 is explained in Chapter 10.

BPEL4WS and other specifications

BPEL4WS relies on the following additional standards:

- XPath as a standard location syntax, for which BPEL4WS also provides two extensions
- WS-Addressing for standardized address format representation
- XML Schema Definition Language, providing data types that can be used for BPEL4WS variables, and definitions for each primary BPEL4WS construct

Partner services

A BPEL4WS process can relate to other Web services in two ways:

1. The process service can be invoked or accessed by services external to the process, as shown in Figure 4.7.

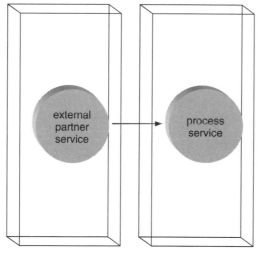

Figure 4.7
An external partner service accessing a process service.

2. Alternatively, the process service itself can invoke and interact with services that participate in the execution of a process, as demonstrated in Figure 4.8.

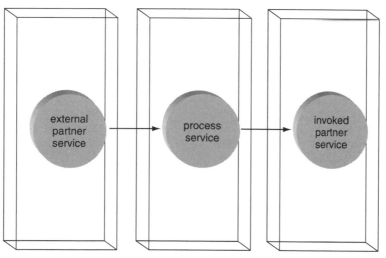

Figure 4.8
After being accessed by the external partner service, the process service invokes another service.

Services that participate with a process are referred to as *partner services*, and are defined within the process description.

Process instances

Once a BPEL4WS process has been invoked, an instance of this process remains in existence until execution has completed. Therefore, two interaction scenarios exist between the process services and external partner services:

- the partner service can invoke a new instance of a process
- the partner service can interact with an existing process instance

The latter scenario is accomplished through message correlation.

Process descriptions

A BPEL4WS *process description* defines a workflow consisting of a sequence of events based on predefined conditions and embedded logic. Each step within a workflow is implemented through the use of a *basic activity* or a *structured activity*.

Basic activities

Basic activities provide primitive workflow functions. Examples include:

- receive
- invoke
- reply
- throw
- wait

The first three (*receive*, *invoke*, and *reply*) enable interaction between a process service and partner services, as explained in the "Service interaction" section.

When certain conditions are encountered by the process, exception handling routines can be executed. The *throw* activity forces a fault condition that shifts processing to the corresponding logic.

A form of scheduled execution can be provided using the *wait* activity. It essentially suspends processing of the overall activity for a specified amount of time, or until a certain date or time is reached.

Structured activities

BPEL4WS also supplies a set of structured activities that allow for the creation of workflow logic.

- sequence
- flow
- switch
- while

Structured activities essentially determine how basic activities are utilized. The order in which they are to be executed can be set using the parent *sequence* activity. This establishes a construct hosting a list of other activities that are launched in the sequence in which they appear. In contrast, the *flow* activity construct contains a list of activities that can be executed concurrently.

The *switch* and *while* activities provide conditional logic constructs, similar to the traditional select-case statement and the do-while loop, respectively.

Service interaction

Illustrated in Figure 4.9 is a simple scenario involving an external partner service, the BPEL4WS process service, and an additional service invoked by the process.

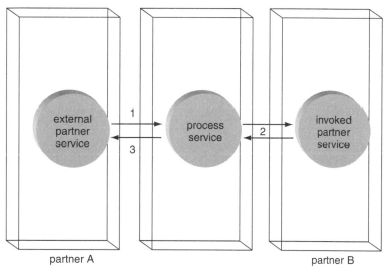

Figure 4.9
Basic activities involved in a simple interaction scenario.

1. An external partner service contacts the BPEL4WS process service by sending it a message. The receive activity within the process description establishes an entry point for a message from this partner (A).

2. The logic within the process description then reacts to the arrival of this message by applying the invoke activity to interact with another partner service (B).

3. Once the invoke activity has completed, the process service responds to partner A's original request using the reply activity.

4.3.3   Syntax

Let's take a closer look at a the internal structure of a process description.

Process element

This process root element hosts the entire process definition:

```
<process name="MyProcess"...>
  <partnerLinks>
    . . .
  </partnerLinks>
  <variables>
    . . .
  </variables>
  <faultHandlers>
    . . .
  </faultHandlers>
  <sequence>
    . . .
  </sequence>
</process>
```

Example 4.2   A skeleton BPEL4WS process definition

A process definition can consist of collections of the following constructs:

- partnerLinks
- variables
- faultHandlers
- sequence

Let's discuss each of these individually.

partnerLinks element

The partnerLinks collection of partnerLink constructs is used to represent partner services. This element assigns services a name used within the context of the process, and also allows for the allocation of roles.

```
<process name="MyProcess"...>
  <partnerLinks>
    <partnerLink name="OrderEntry" ...>
      ...
    </partnerLink>
    <partnerLink name="InventoryControl" ...>
      ...
    </partnerLink>
  </partnerLinks>
</process>
```

Example 4.3 Definition of service partners within a BPEL4WS process description

Variables element

Many business processes will involve long-running tasks, often due to various intermediate conditions that must be met before the execution of the process can continue. In order to support lengthy process lifespans, a state information management system is required. For this purpose, BPEL4WS provides the `variables` element.

Within this construct you can establish variables with different scopes using individual variable element declarations. Variables that are global can be accessed from anywhere in the process definition. Variable values typically consist of messages that contain some piece of state information.

```
<process name="MyProcess"...>
  <variables>
    <variable xmlns:ORD="http.//www.examples.ws/"
      name="OrderStatus"
      messageType="x:OrderStatus"/>
  </variables>
</process>
```

Example 4.4 A variable declaration within the variables construct

faultHandlers element

When a long running business activity fails, a business process will typically revert to a compensation process — a form of exception handling that is encapsulated within the `faultHandlers` construct.

Using nested `catch` constructs, you can define different responses for various error conditions.

```
<process name="MyProcess"...>
  <faultHandlers>
    <catch faultName="x:condition1" faultVariable="err001">
      ...
```

```
      </catch>
       <catchAll>

         ...

      </catchAll>
    </faultHandlers>
  </process>
```

Example 4.5   The faultHandlers construct consisting of nested catch constructs

Sequence element

Finally, let's revisit our original interaction scenario that demonstrates the use of the receive, invoke, and reply activities. We'll nest each activity construct within the sequence element in order to establish the order of execution.

```
<process name="MyProcess"...>
  <sequence>
    <receive partner="partnerA">

      ...

    </receive>
    <invoke partner="partnerB">

      ...

    </invoke>
    <reply partner="partnerA">

      ...

    </reply>
  </sequence>
</process>
```

Example 4.6   The sequence parent construct establishing the order of nested basic activities

Figure 4.10 positions the constructs within our sample scenario. Note the use of the partner attributes. Partner interaction is predefined within process workflows.

SUMMARY OF KEY POINTS

- BPEL4WS provides a comprehensive language for describing business processes that can also be compiled into executable scripts.

- The workflow logic within a BPEL4WS process consists of a series of basic and structured activities.

- BPEL4WS process services are based on the use of business activity coordinators, as defined within WS-Transaction.

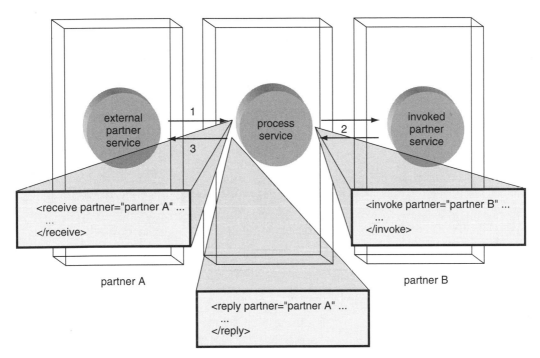

Figure 4.10
Basic activities involved in a simple interaction scenario.

To learn more about BPEL4WS, visit www.specifications.ws.

4.4 WS-Security and the Web services security specifications

As the complexity and sophistication of application and business logic within Web services increases, so does the risk associated with putting a corporation's business intelligence "out there." An increased level of service-oriented application functionality leads to more integration opportunities with external business partners. Although this guide is focused primarily on integration solutions within the enterprise, security is still an important consideration for any SOA.

The purpose of this section is to create an awareness of the many aspects of Web services security, with an emphasis on the WS-Security framework. Issues and strategies associated with the integration of some of these technologies are further discussed in Chapter 11.

4.4.1   General security concepts

While the security framework established by the many specifications that provide standards for XML and Web services is relatively new, most of the principles behind these standards are not. The fundamental characteristics of a primitive security architecture are just as relevant to service-oriented environments as they are to traditional distributed applications.

Here's a quick recap of these established concepts:

Identification

The recipient of a message needs to be able to identify the sender (Figure 4.11).

Figure 4.11
The identification of the sender by the recipient.

Authentication

The recipient of a message needs to verify that the claimed identity of the sender is valid (Figure 4.12).

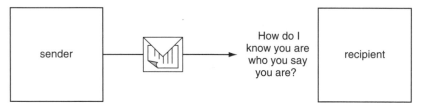

Figure 4.12
The authentication of the sender by the recipient.

Authorization

The recipient of a message needs to determine the level of the sender's security clearance (Figure 4.13). This can relate to which operations or which data the sender is granted access to.

Integrity

A message remains unaltered during transmission, up until actual delivery (Figure 4.14).

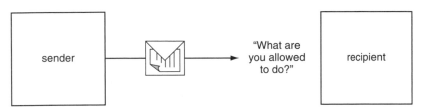

Figure 4.13
The recipient assesses the authorization level of the sender.

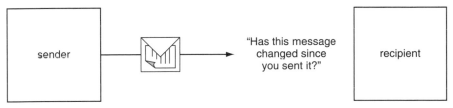

Figure 4.14
Tho integrity of a message is questioned by the recipient.

Confidentiality

The contents of a message cannot be viewed while in transit, except by authorized services (Figure 4.15).

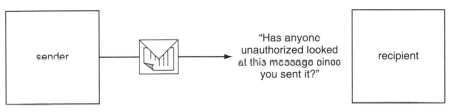

Figure 4.15
The confidentiality of a message is questioned by the recipient.

4.4.2   Specifications

To understand how service-oriented architectures deal with these security requirements, we need to take a look at the ever-evolving world of Web services and XML security specifications.

Listed in Table 4.1 are some of the more important standards, organized by how they relate to the fore-mentioned security requirements. (Note that the WS-Security Framework represents a collection of specifications, described later in this section.)

These and other specifications form building blocks that can be assembled to create service-oriented security (SOS) models. Let's take a brief look at each one.

Table 4.1   Web services security specifications and their roles

Identification	WS-Security Framework
Authentication	Extensible Access Control Markup Language (XACML)
Authorization	Extensible Rights Markup Language (XrML)
	XML Key Management (XKMS)
	Security Assertion Markup Language (SAML)
	.NET Passport
Confidentiality	WS-Security Framework
	XML-Encryption
	Secure Sockets Layer (SSL)
Integrity	WS-Security Framework
	XML-Digital Signatures

4.4.3   XML Key Management (XKMS)

XML Key Management establishes a standard means of obtaining and managing public keys. Even though XKMS is compatible with a number of public key infrastructure (PKI) technologies, it does not require any of them, and removes the need for integrating proprietary PKI products.

The XML Key Management specification consists of two complementary standards: the XML Key Registration Service and the XML Key Information Service specifications. Together, they allow for the integration of a number of security technologies, including digital signatures, certificates, and revocation status checking. For instance, XKMS can enlist XML-Digital Signatures to protect the integrity of XML document content.

4.4.4   Extensible Access Control Markup Language (XACML) and Extensible Rights Markup Language (XrML)

The XACML specification consists of two related vocabularies: one for access control and one that defines a vocabulary for request and response exchanges. Through these languages, the creation of fine-grained security policies is made possible.

It is important not to confuse XACML with the WS-Policy specification, which also can be used to define policies, and is considered part of the WS-Security framework. An additional specification that may be relevant to your environment, if you transport files with different digital formats, is the Extensible Rights Markup Language (XrML).

4.4.5   Security Assertion Markup Language (SAML) and .NET Passport

Single sign-on technologies help address an administration problem that has emerged when an enterprise environment consists of applications that independently control user access lists. If a single sign-on system is not already in place, adding Web services can contribute to the decentralized proliferation of user credentials. By opening up new integration channels, more users may be required to access applications. This can lead to an ever-increasing maintenance effort.

Popular technologies for single sign-on include the Security Assertion Markup Language (SAML) and the .NET Passport. SAML provides mechanisms for both authentication and authorization processes. Both request and response message formats are defined to facilitate the transmission of necessary credentials within a Web service activity. Microsoft's .NET Passport is a competing technology, and relies on proprietary protocols for handling authentication. It also introduces a centralized management system for user credentials, which differs from SAML's decentralized approach. Interoperability options between the two technologies do exist, and continue to improve.

4.4.6　XML-Encryption and XML-Digital Signatures

These two key specifications protect the actual content within XML documents.

The XML-Encryption specification contains a standard model for encrypting both binary and textual data, as well as a means of communicating information essential for recipients to decrypt the contents of received messages.

XML-Digital Signatures establishes a standardized format for representing digital signature data. Digital signatures establish credibility within a message, as they assure the recipient that the message was in fact transmitted by the expected partner service. It also provides a means of communicating that the message contents were not altered in transit, as well as support for standard non-repudiation. As with the XML-Encryption standard, XML-Digital Signature also supports binary and textual data.

To see XML-Encryption and XML-Digital Signatures in action, refer to the examples provided in the "Strategies for integrating Web services security" section of Chapter 11.

4.4.7　Secure Sockets Layer (SSL)

A common response to addressing WS-Security requirements is: "We'll just encrypt it with SSL." Many assume that this is a valid security measure, because they associate the Internet-based communication between Web services with the traditional interaction between a browser and a Web server.

The Secure Sockets Layer (SSL) technology enables *transport-level* security. Accessing a secured site using a browser is a fairly safe procedure, when communication is encrypted. That is because the connection is exclusive to the client browser and the Web server that acts as the gateway to internally hosted application logic.

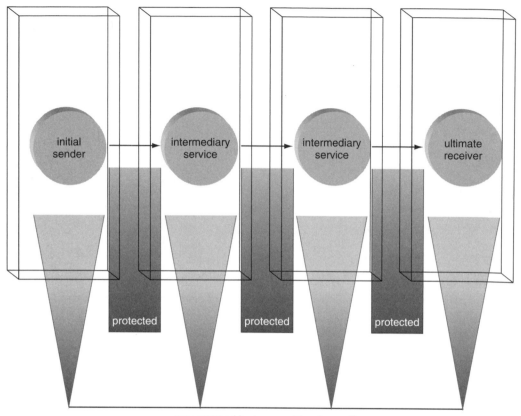

not protected by transport-level security

Figure 4.16
A message path with multiple intermediary services representing gaps in the protection
provided by transport-level security.

Once a Web service transmits a message it does not always know where that message will be traveling to, and how it will be processed before it reaches its intended destination. As shown in Figure 4.16, a number of intermediary services may be involved in the message path, and a transport-level security technology will protect the privacy of the message contents only while it is being transmitted between these intermediaries.

In other words, SSL cannot protect a message during the time that it is being processed by an intermediary service. This does not make SSL unnecessary within a service-oriented communications framework, it only limits its role. A number of additional technologies (discussed throughout this section) are required to facilitate the message-level security required for end-to-end protection.

4.4.8   The WS-Security framework

This important document establishes fundamental and conceptual security standards, and also defines a set of supplementary specifications that collectively form a Web service-centric security framework. WS-Security (also known as the *Web Services Security Language*) can be used to bridge gaps between disparate security models, but also goes beyond traditional transport-level security to provide a standard *end-to-end* security model for SOAP messages.

End-to-end and message-level security

As explained in the previous section, service-oriented environments sometimes require that intermediaries be involved with the delivery of messages. An end-to-end security model is therefore needed, so that the contents of SOAP messages remain protected throughout a message path. This is different from the traditional point-to-point model, for which transport-level security has generally been sufficient. In fact, you could view a message path involving intermediaries as a series of point-to-point connections, as illustrated in Figure 4.17.

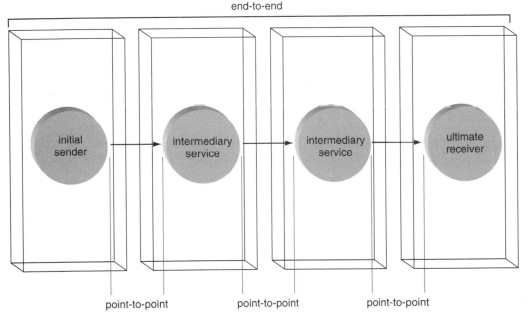

Figure 4.17
The scope of end-to-end versus point-to-point security.

To secure a message path from end-to-end, WS-Security implements security measures through the use of SOAP header blocks that travel with the message.

Specifications

Although the WS-Security framework complements a number of the specifications described earlier in this section, it is supported further by a series of supplementary standards (listed in Table 4.2).

Table 4.2   An overview of WS-Security specifications

WS-Security Framework		
WS-Policy	WS-Trust	WS-Privacy
WS-SecureConversation	WS-Federation	WS-Authorization

The first layer below the framework is frequently referred to as the *Policy Layer*, as it provides a number of building blocks for the creation of trust and privacy policies. The next row, known as the *Federation Layer*, builds on these policies to unify disparate trust domains.

Each of these specifications is briefly described in the following sections.

WS-Policy

Though not limited to providing security-related policies, this standard is a key part of the WS-Security framework. Existing corporate security polices can be expressed through policy assertions that can then be applied to groups of services. To learn more about this specification, refer to the "WS-Policy" section, later in this chapter.

WS-Trust

This specification establishes a standard trust model used to unite existing trust models, so that the validity of exchanged security tokens can be verified. WS-Trust provides a communications process for requesting the involvement of third-party trust authorities to assist with this verification.

WS-Privacy

Organizations can use WS-Privacy to communicate their privacy policies and check to see whether requestors intend to comply to these policies. WS-Privacy works in conjunction with WS-Policy and WS-Trust.

WS-SecureConversation

Various security models can be supplemented with WS-SecureConversation, which establishes a standard mechanism for exchanging security information between Web services. It provides formal definitions for the creation and exchange of security contexts and associated session keys.

WS-Federation

There are numerous ways of integrating different trust domains (or realms) when utilizing the WS-Security, WS-Policy, and WS-Trust standards. The WS-Federation specification provides a series of standards and security models for achieving a *federation* — an environment where a level of trust has been established between disparate trust domains.

WS-Authorization

WS-Authorization provides a standard for managing information used for authorization and access policies. As part of this standard, the manner in which claims are represented within security tokens is established.

4.4.9 Concepts and syntax

Due to the vast diversity of security specifications, we don't have the luxury of delving into the concepts and language syntax of each of the standards we've discussed so far. To give you a glimpse into what a SOAP header block containing security information looks like, though, I've provided a brief example that demonstrates two fundamental parts of the WS-Security framework.

Claims and security tokens

When a service requestor makes a request of a service provider, it asserts a *claim* regarding its security clearance. It is then up to the service provider to validate this claim. A service requestor may provide a number of claims in order to communicate different aspects of its security status. This set of claims is contained within a *security token* (see Figure 4.18).

Security tokens can *signed* with a signing authority, allowing them to be further verified by the recipient of the message containing the token. *Unsigned* security tokens often consist of login credentials supplied by the service requestor.

The following parent `Security` construct establishes a WS-Security header block that consists of a token with login information.

```
<Security ...>
  <UsernameToken>
    <Username>
      Terl
    </Username>
    <Password>
      onedaytherewillonlybeonesecurityspec
    </Password>
  </UsernameToken>
</Security>
```

Example 4.7 The security construct hosting a security token

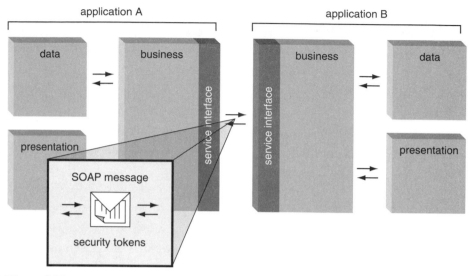

Figure 4.18
WS-Security allows for claims to be represented within standard security tokens.

The `UsernameToken` construct contains `Username` and `Password` elements that represent the credential's claim.

Additional information about the many specifications associated with the WS-Security framework can be found at `www.specifications.ws`.

SUMMARY OF KEY POINTS

- A security architecture for Web services involves technologies based on a series of specifications designed for XML and second-generation Web services.

- Web services add a new dimension to securing information due to the sometimes unpredictable nature of distributed message paths.

- The WS-Security framework addresses security issues specific to Web services environments by providing a model for message-level security.

- Features from WS-Security and XML security specifications can be assembled into a custom service-oriented security (SOS) model.

4.5 WS-ReliableMessaging

"The check's in the mail, I swear!" How can you argue with that? If someone tells you a document has been mailed, then all you can do is wait to see if it's true. And, if it doesn't arrive, you need to consider the possibility of it being lost in transit.

With a mechanism for guaranteeing the delivery of a message, though, business correspondence would be much more reliable. You would be assured that messages will either be delivered as expected, or that a notification would be sent out advising you of a failed delivery attempt.

WS-ReliableMessaging establishes standard processes for the acknowledgement of successful message deliveries and the notification of transmission failures. It can be used in conjunction with other specifications, such as WS-Security, WS-Policy, WS-Coordination, and WS-Transaction.

> **NOTE**
>
> WS-ReliableMessaging should not be confused with the competing WS-Reliability specification.

4.5.1   WS-Addressing

When discussing reliable messaging, the WS-Addressing specification is worth mentioning. It provides a standard way of representing Web service endpoints in messages, as well as numerous additional addressing characteristics. Typically, addressing information is determined or set by the transport technology used to transmit the message. WS-Addressing establishes a standardized addressing syntax, independent of the protocol used for transport. Other specifications, such as BPEL4WS, also utilize WS-Addressing.

4.5.2   Concepts

The focus of the WS-ReliableMessaging framework is relatively narrow, when compared to other specifications. Its primary concern is the guaranteed delivery of SOAP messages. This relates to the actual arrival of a message at its intended destination, but can also involve a guarantee that messages are delivered in the order in which they are sent.

WS-ReliableMessaging establishes a standard method of notifying the message sender of the success or failure of the delivery. This notification is accomplished through an *acknowledgement* (see Figure 4.19) that is sent either as a separate message, or as an embedded construct within the response message generated by the original message recipient.

Sequences

To implement a system for the reliable delivery of messages, WS-ReliableMessaging requires that SOAP header blocks be embedded with a number of message attributes hosted within a container called a *sequence*. The information within a sequence is used to identify and process messages.

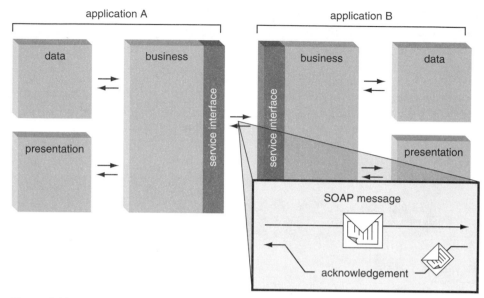

Figure 4.19
The WS-ReliableMessaging mechanism for communicating the successful delivery of
a SOAP message.

Delivery assurances

To enforce certain polices relating to the required reliability guarantees, WS-Reliable-
Messaging uses *delivery assurances*.

There are four types of delivery assurances that can be issued:

- The *AtMostOnce* assurance guarantees that a message can only be delivered once or
  not at all (Figure 4.20).
- The *AtLeastOnce* assurance allows a message to be delivered multiple times, but
  ensures that it is delivered at least once (Figure 4.21).
- The *ExactlyOnce* delivery assurance requires that a message be delivered once only
  (Figure 4.22).
- The *InOrder* assurance can supplement any of the preceding by also guaranteeing that
  messages will be delivered in the sequence in which they were sent. In the scenario
  portrayed in (Figure 4.23), for example, the initial delivery of message 2 failed. It was
  then resent, as the sequence must be completed, as per the assurance rule.

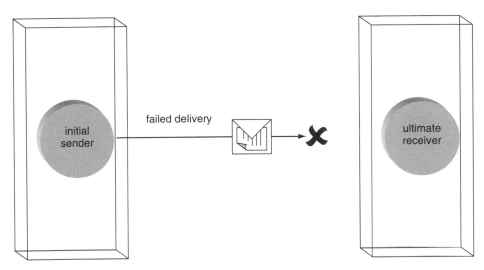

Figure 4.20
In this scenario, the AtMostOnce delivery assurance allows the failed delivery of a
message that is not followed up with another transmission attempt.

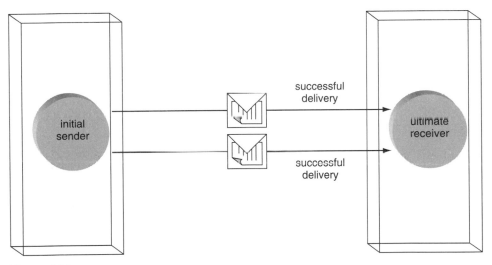

Figure 4.21
The AtLeastOnce assurance allowing a message to be sent twice.

4.5.3   Acknowledgements

For the receiver of a message to notify the sender as to whether the messages within a
sequence were successfully delivered, it responds using acknowledgement messages
(Figure 4.24).

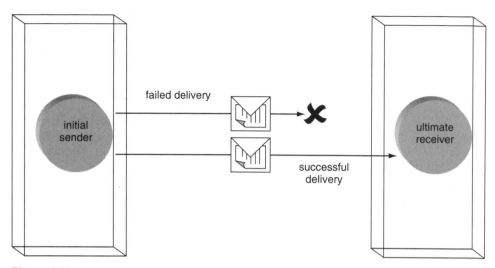

Figure 4.22
Here, a failed delivery is followed by another delivery attempt, which this time succeeds.

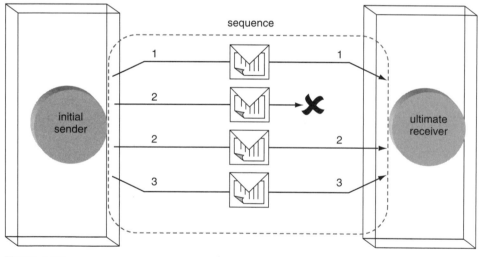

Figure 4.23
A set of messages being transmitted in a predefined sequence.

One acknowledgement can be sent for each message received. Alternatively, you can opt to have the receiver wait until the sequence has completed, before responding with just one acknowledgement for all received messages within a sequence (Figure 4.25).

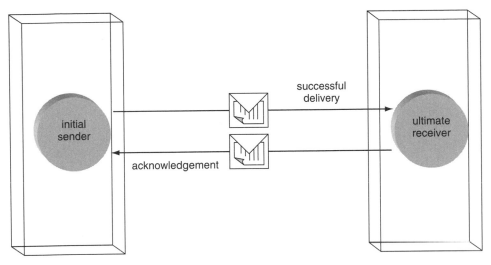

Figure 4.24
The successful delivery of a message being confirmed with an acknowledgement.

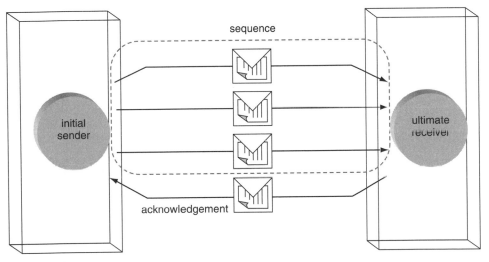

Figure 4.25
Only one acknowledgement is sent in response to receiving a number of messages in
the same sequence.

4.5.4   Syntax

Reliable messaging exists within SOAP header blocks, which are processed by SOAP
receivers along a message path.

Sequence

The parent `Sequence` construct implements reliable messaging information, as follows:

```
<wsrm:Sequence>
    <wsu:Identifier>http://www.examples.ws/</wsu:Identifier>
    <wsrm:MessageNumber>2</wsrm:MessageNumber>
    <wsrm:LastMessage/>
</wsrm:Sequence>
```

Example 4.8   The sequence construct

In the preceding example, our `Sequence` header construct uses the `Identifier` element to assign a unique URI to the sequence. The `MessageNumber` element determines the position of the current message within the overall sequence order. This number increments with each subsequent message sent as part of a sequence. Finally, the `LastMessage` element identifies this message as the last one to be delivered.

A `Sequence` construct also can contain an optional `Expires` element that limits the validity of the sequence to a date and time value. Note that there can be only one `Sequence` construct in a SOAP message.

Though this example establishes a fundamental sequence header, there is still one part we have not yet addressed: the delivery assurance. This characteristic is implemented as a policy assurance, and then associated with the message as part of a policy attachment. We therefore demonstrate this portion of the example in the "WS -Policy" section.

Note that other policy assertions can be attached to a sequence message header, including:

- sequence expiration
- inactivity timeout
- retransmission interval

SequenceAcknowledgement

An acknowledgement construct can be sent in a separate message, or as part of a response message. The parent `SequenceAcknowledgement` element hosts the same `Identifier` value, as well as the `AcknowledgementRange` element. This construct tells the original sender which of the messages in the sequence were delivered successfully, by specifying a range that corresponds to the number of messages in the sequence.

```
<wsrm:SequenceAcknowledgment>
  <wsu:Identifier>http://www.examples.ws/</wsu:Identifier>
```

```
  <wsrm:AcknowledgmentRange Upper="6" Lower="1"/>
</wsrm:SequenceAcknowledgment>
```

Example 4.9   A SequenceAcknowledgement construct providing a list of successfully delivered messages

In this example, all six messages were successfully delivered.

If, however, one of the messages in the sequence failed to arrive, the Sequence-Acknowledgement construct may need to host a number of the Acknowledgement-Range elements to identify only those that were delivered. Gaps in the sequence are considered failed deliveries.

```
<wsrm:SequenceAcknowledgment>
  <wsu:Identifier>http://www.examples.ws/</wsu:Identifier>
  <wsrm:AcknowledgmentRange Upper="3" Lower="1"/>
  <wsrm:AcknowledgmentRange Upper="6" Lower="5"/>
</wsrm:SequenceAcknowledgment>
```

Example 4.10   The SequenceAcknowledgement construct hosting multiple AcknowledgementRange elements to communicate what parts of a sequence were delivered

In our revised example, the SequenceAcknowledgement construct uses two AcknowledgementRange elements to communicate that messages 1, 2, 3, 5, and 6 were delivered. By omission, the delivery of message number 4 is assumed to have failed.

To review the original WS-ReliableMessaging standard, visit www.specifica-tions.ws.

SUMMARY OF KEY POINTS

- WS-ReliableMessaging establishes a system for communicating the successful delivery of a message and the notification of a delivery failure.

- Rules around the delivery and sequence of deliveries are provided through the use of delivery assurances.

- WS-ReliableMessaging has a close relationship with WS-Policy through which delivery assurances (and other types of assurances) can be implemented.

4.6 WS-Policy

Policies help organize and apply rules and properties of Web services within diverse application environments. The WS-Policy standard establishes a series of conventions that are further extended through the WS-PolicyAssertions and WS-PolicyAttachments specifications. Collectively, these standards form the WS-Policy framework.

4.6.1   Concepts

Policies are defined through individual *policy assertions*. Each assertion can communicate a particular preference, rule, capability, or requirement of service logic. A policy assertion is implemented syntactically through a *policy expression*.

Whatever part of the service to which a policy expression is applied to is referred to as the *policy subject*. *Policy attachments* are used to bind policy expressions to policy subjects.

To demonstrate a use for WS-Policy, let's continue with the example from the WS-ReliableMessaging section.

4.6.2   Syntax

The first message we assembled in the original example contained a `sequence` construct that provided information used for identification and sequencing purposes.

```
<wsrm:Sequence>
    <wsu:Identifier>http://www.examples.ws/</wsu:Identifier>
    <wsrm:MessageNumber>2</wsrm:MessageNumber>
    <wsrm:LastMessage/>
</wsrm:Sequence>
```

Example 4.11   The sequence construct from the WS-ReliableMessaging example

To this base set of reliable messaging data we now want to add one of the predefined delivery assurances.

Through the use of WS-Policy, WS-PolicyAssertions, and WS-PolicyAttachments features, we can:

1. establish a policy expression using the `policy` construct
2. establish the delivery assurance value as a policy assertion within this expression
3. attach the expression to the existing `sequence` construct as a policy attachment

Essentially, we need to establish a policy based on the chosen delivery assurance, and then attach it to the `sequence` header block we created in the WS-ReliableMessaging example.

We begin with the `PolicyAttachment` parent construct that hosts the policy assertion to be attached to our sequence.

```
<wsp:PolicyAttachment>
  <wsp:AppliesTo>
    <wsrm:SequenceRef>
      <wsu:Identifier>http://www.examples.ws/</wsu:Identifier>
```

```
      </wsrm:SequenceRef>
    </wsp:AppliesTo>
    <wsp:Policy>
      <wsrm:DeliveryAssurance Value="wsrm:AtLeastOnce"
        wsp:Usage="wsp:Required"/>
    </wsp:Policy>
    ...
  </wsp:PolicyAttachment>
```

Example 4.12   The PolicyAttachment construct establishing a policy and linking it to the sequence

Here we identify the sequence to which we want to attach the delivery assurance, using the `SequenceRef` construct. The delivery assurance policy itself is then defined within the `Policy` construct.

For more information about the WS-Policy standard, visit `www.specifications.ws`.

SUMMARY OF KEY POINTS

- Policies allow you to apply business and security rules to groups of Web services.

- The WS-Policy framework relies on the WS-PolicyAssertions and WS-PolicyAttachments specifications as a means of defining and associating a policy assertion to a message.

- Other standards, such as WS-Security and WS-ReliableMessaging, depend on the use WS-Policy features.

4.7 WS-Attachments

To transport payload data outside of the SOAP body, a standard for encoding this data as an attachment to the message is required. Figure 4.26 illustrates a SOAP message with a DIME (Direct Internet Message Encapsulation) attachment being passed between applications.

There are two situations where payload data delivered by a SOAP message is better represented as an attachment:

- A binary file, such as an image. Here the processing involved with encoding and decoding of the binary data makes it undesirable as content hosted within the SOAP message body.
- An XML document (or a part of an XML document) not easily represented within the standard SOAP body construct. For example, XML documents that use a different encoding standard than the message itself.

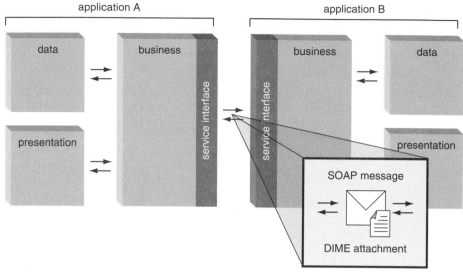

Figure 4.26
A SOAP message delivering a set of data as an attachment.

Either of these scenarios can also cause processing problems with a number of industry parsers.

The WS-Attachments specification introduces a *compound SOAP structure* consisting of a *primary message part* (the base SOAP message) and *secondary message parts* that represent the attachments. It also provides a mechanism for primary parts to reference secondary parts (using the standard `href` attribute), and for secondary parts to reference each other.

Finally, WS-Attachments specifies DIME as the attachment description format. Although not as popular as MIME (Multipurpose Internet Mail Extensions), DIME provides a lightweight encapsulation format that was deemed more suitable for SOAP message documents.

Note that MIME is the format description standard proposed by the SOAP Messages with Attachments (SwA) specification. A brief description of this competing standard follows.

SOAP Messages with Attachments (SwA)

SwA introduces a standard and extensible message structure, called the *SOAP message package*. A message package consists of the primary SOAP message and additional entities that reference and allow for the encapsulation of external files (binary or otherwise). SwA is based on the use of the MIME encoding format to describe and delimit attachments.

It is worth being familiar with both the WS-Attachments and the SwA specifications, in case your business requirements demand a specific encoding format for message attachments.

For a look at available messaging attachments standards for SOAP, visit `www.speci-fications.ws`.

SUMMARY OF KEY POINTS

- WS-Attachments provides a standard means of attaching binary and textual data to a SOAP message.

- WS-Attachments relies on DIME as the encoding format for attachments.

- The competing SOAP Messages with Attachments specification provides support for MIME encoding.

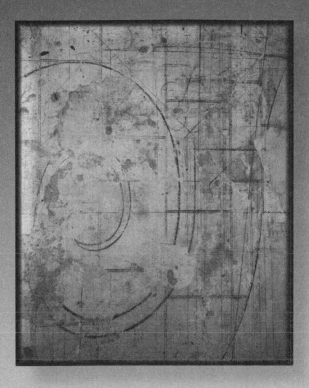

Integrating technology

Creating a contemporary service-oriented architecture requires that numerous layers of new technologies be integrated into traditional application designs. Many of these layers build upon each other, and as dependencies increase, so does the level at which these technologies entrench themselves into your technical environment.

It is important, therefore, to get it right when building this foundation. It all begins with the integration of select XML technologies that establish a data management chassis for your future applications. The quality of the application logic you deliver within service-oriented architectures will be highly reliant on the quality of the underlying XML architecture you are building upon.

Equally significant, though, is the proper integration of Web services technologies and service-oriented design principles. These represent the subsequent foundation layers that will ultimately define the extent to which business logic can be automated, expressed, and shared as services.

The next set of chapters supply a structured series of independent integration strategies, guidelines, and recommendations on how to manage a multitude of common XML and Web services integration scenarios. They will assist you in making a number of strategic design decisions to help you build a solid foundation architecture for your service-oriented solutions.

NOTE

The scope of these chapters is limited, for the most part, to the integration of technology into application environments. This differs from Part III, where we focus exclusively on the integration of applications using these technologies.

Integrating XML into applications

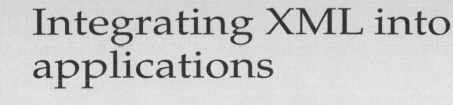

A conversation once heard at a preliminary project team meeting:

PM: "We're scheduled to begin development next month, so I just wanted to go over the task assignments I have so far. Jenny, you're in the midst of finalizing the requirements..."

Jenny nods.

PM: "And John, you're learning about this XML technology we need to incorporate this time around. How's that going?"

John: "It's pretty straightforward. We need to add some new tags to our data."

PM: "So it shouldn't affect our timeline too much?"

John: "Naw, I'm a fast typist."

Chuckles all around.

PM: "OK, and Mark, you're setting up the workstations...."

When adding a new product or technology into an established development environment, a concise research effort is often enough to understand the technical implications and the subsequent impact on the project. For the XML technology set, however, the lack of understanding expressed in the earlier dialogue will, with certainty, lead to serious architectural flaws (many of which will surface only after the application has been built). Worse yet, it will result in a missed opportunity to create a superior solution with the best data representation platform currently available.

The main reason behind this is because XML represents more than just a technology. It introduces:

- a new way of thinking about data
- a new way of representing data
- a new way of representing business rules
- a new architectural platform
- a new way of designing applications
- a new way of programming data access

Adding XML to the mix will affect the project in almost every aspect. From how it is planned and staffed, to the manner in which the application is designed, developed, tested, and (eventually) the extent to which your application will be able to interoperate with others.

There is no situation in which you will have a greater amount of freedom to dictate the technology and process of a project than when you build a custom solution from the ground up. If you are in control of your design, you will be in control of how your application manages data. That, in turn, will allow you to integrate XML technologies effectively, thus laying a solid foundation for a service-oriented architecture.

> **NOTE**
>
> This chapter focuses exclusively on integrating XML technology. References to Web services and service-oriented design are intentionally minimal, so as to not create any premature dependencies. Almost all of the strategies provided here, therefore, can be fully utilized without any requirement for the involvement of Web services technologies.

5.1 Strategies for integrating XML data representation

XML as a data representation technology is a core part of contemporary integration solutions. It therefore plays a fundamental role in both operational and conceptual aspects of an integrated architecture. Current integration platforms have embraced the core family of XML specifications, to the extent that most have become integral parts of third-party products as well as custom solutions.

This integration guide does not teach you about XML data representation — that topic has been covered extensively over the past few years. If this is new to you, take some time to review the XML tutorial in Chapter 2 before continuing. (Further recommended resources are provided at `www.serviceoriented.ws`.)

What we do cover in this section is how to best integrate XML data representation into your application environment. As previously discussed, introducing XML requires that architects and developers conceptualize and implement data differently than before. Reading a few white papers and completing a tutorial, though, will not adequately prepare you for a successful integration. Nothing replaces hands-on experience. However, the strategies provided in this section are the next best thing.

5.1.1 Positioning XML data representation in your architecture

The most important step to properly integrating XML's data representation features is in understanding how they can benefit both application and integration architectures. This will allow you to strategically position XML documents within the layers of your application environments. How you incorporate XML at this level not only affects inter-component and cross-tier communication, but also lays the groundwork for future cross-application data exchange.

XML as a data transport format within applications

Data that flows within and between the various layers of a multi-tiered architecture is frequently hosted by XML documents (see Figure 5.1). This establishes XML as a standard transport format for application data, embedding it as a core part of application architecture.

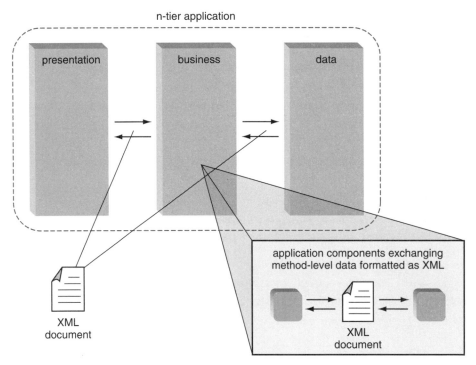

Figure 5.1
XML can establish a standard data transport format within and between application tiers.

XML as a data transport format between applications

When integrating applications, XML documents are also used to represent and transport data to and from public application interfaces. Although Part III of this book covers inter-application integration, facilitating future interoperability is an important consideration when developing single application environments. Figure 5.2 illustrated how XML documents can be passed within and across applications.

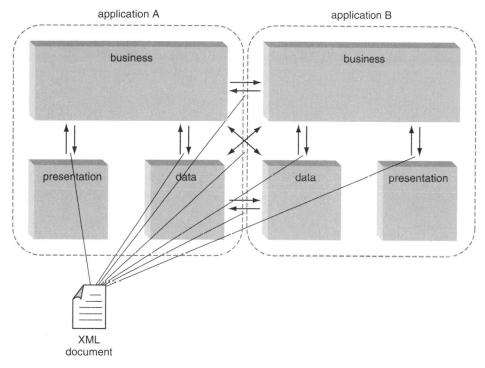

Figure 5.2
XML documents can be used as the standard data transport throughout
integrated environments.

Web services are often used to represent these application endpoints, especially
when the integration architecture is unifying disparate platforms. Within a Web services framework, XML documents are generally transported through the use of
SOAP messages.

NOTE
The integration layer that is part of a typical Web services architecture is not illustrated in these diagrams. See Chapter 3 for a description of how Web services change traditional distributed architectures.

XML as a data bridge within applications
Incorporating XML data representation allows analysts to close gaps between disparate
data and business models, as shown in Figure 5.3. This can introduce a number of challenges, especially when representing data from repositories that store data in dissimilar
formats and structures.

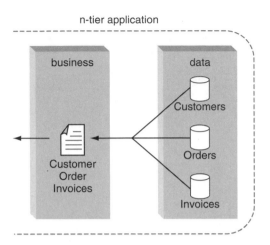

Figure 5.3
An XML document capturing data retrieved from three data sources in a unique
business context.

XML *as a data bridge across applications*

Figure 5.4 demonstrates how creating a custom data view, unique to the context of the
information exchange enabled by the solution, establishes the data model introduced
by the XML document schema as an accurate representation of the currently executing
business task.

> **NOTE**
>
> It is the standardization achieved by positioning XML as a data transport for-
> mat within applications (as illustrated in Figure 5.1) that supports the integra-
> tion scenario shown in Figure 5.4.

5.1.2   Think "tree" (a new way of representing data)

If a tree falls on an XML developer and no one else is around, does it still make a
sound? A seasoned XML professional will avoid creating unstable tree structures for
XML documents. However, for those "new to the woods," the most significant adjustment will be in visualizing data in a strictly hierarchical manner.

The XML data model is nothing new to the IT world. Directory structures used by
technologies such as the Lightweight Directory Access Protocol (LDAP) have been
organizing information into tree views for many years. Only, their use was almost
always specific, often intrinsic to an application, and rarely required the level of integration of XML.

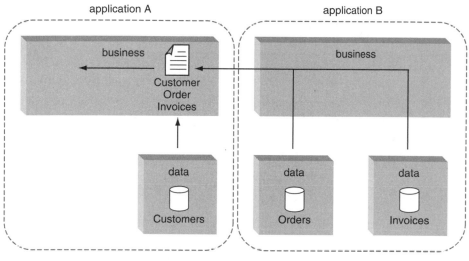

Figure 5.4
An XML document capturing data retrieved from three data sources across
two applications.

Even though there's power in its simplicity, there are also limitations that you need to be aware of before finalizing your document structures. For instance, data cannot easily be appended to an XML document, the way it can to a delimited flat-file. Also, though XML documents can easily provide traditional one-to-one and one-to-many relationships between data elements, they will not be as accommodating with many-to-many relationships (as documented in Chapter 7).

5.1.3   Easy now… (don't rush the XML document model)

Once, at an application design meeting attended by both developers and DBAs, the topic of XML document structures came up. It was given all of five minutes discussion time, during which a simple document model was thrown together. It occurred to me that the overall perception was that the processing of XML was simply an issue of file I/O. XML documents were being looked upon as standard delimited files with perhaps a few bells and whistles, but still "just" file I/O.

I halted this meeting before the team was able to get into the next agenda item, and proceeded to the white board. There I wrote the following:

> *XML Document = Database*
>
> *XML Document Structure = Data Model*

I then went on to state that:

- A great deal of the code we are about to write will involve an element of XML document parsing.
- If we choose to change our document structure after completing development, we will break the existing code.
- The data represented in the XML document will very likely grow and evolve the same way data does in our corporate databases.

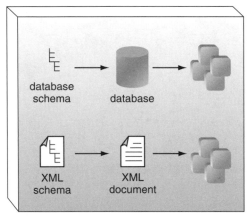

Figure 5.5
XML documents and databases both represent
data for applications, using schemas.

The group was able to draw their own conclusions from these statements, and we spent the rest of the hour revising the original structure of that document.

This simple redefinition of terms clearly communicated that:

- XML document modeling is every bit as important as and comparable to database modeling (Figure 5.5).
- Application code that performs XML parsing is as dependent on the structure of an XML document as traditional data access code is on a database's data model.
- Investing in a more serious modeling effort up front minimizes the chances of a document structure having to be altered in the future.

5.1.4   Design with foresight

By simply representing your application data in XML documents, you open the door to a number issues that, if not addressed at design time, will come back to haunt you.

Every time you model an XML document, you may be required to make strategic decisions that take the following factors into account:

- performance
- security
- extensibility
- reusability
- data access

These considerations relate not only to how XML represents data, but also to any supplementary XML technologies you are planning to use.

For instance, the XML document structure you define will determine:

- the bandwidth requirements for transmitting instances of this document
- the processing requirements for parsing this document using a programmatic API
- the structure of the document's corresponding schema definition
- the processing requirements for validating this document by the corresponding schema
- the design of corresponding transformation style sheets
- the processing requirements for corresponding transformation style sheets
- the security requirements relating to the nature of data being hosted by the document
- the ability of the document structure to be extended as the data model evolves over time
- the ability of the document (or parts of the document) to be shared within the application
- the quality of data representation for use by application components and end-users

If you take these factors into account, following the strategies provided in this chapter, you will be well on your way to designing a solid XML foundation.

> **NOTE**
> Many of the issues raised in the preceding list are explored in subsequent sections.

5.1.5   Focus on extensibility and reusability

As with any application, underlying business and data models may change over time. Building a flexible document structure that can be extended to accommodate these changes will pay off in the future.

Here are some fundamental guidelines:

- Unless you are certain further nesting will never be required and performance will not be impacted, use child elements instead of attributes when defining the document structure.

- Use generic element-type names. Avoid incorporating company, department, or product names, as these may change.

- Create a series of modular XML schemas to partition large document structures into reusable substructures (where each substructure is based on a logical context).

- Don't always hardcode namespace references. Where appropriate, bind XML documents to namespaces dynamically at runtime.

- Avoid or limit element recursion. If elements are allowed to be nested within themselves, you may lose control as to how many levels of nesting will occur. Research alternatives to extending your document structure before allowing recursion.

- Incorporate the `any` XSD schema element to preserve future extensibility options.

5.1.6   Lose weight while modeling! (keeping your documents trim)

If there's one thing you can count on, it's that your XML documents will get around. In a fully XML-enabled application environment, streams of structured data will constantly be flowing through your application layers. The manner in which you represent this data will be a major factor in determining how efficient your data flow will end up being.

"Travel light" should be your motto when defining document structures, especially when receiving data from external sources. More often than not, developers allow their application components to relay documents containing a great deal more data than their application actually requires. This excess baggage is carried around everywhere the documents go, and this, of course, can add up when application usage increases.

As illustrated in Figure 5.6, applying XML transformation at the point when messages or documents are first received will allow you to extract the subset of data relevant to your application. The processing involved in this initial step will soon reap dividends, as it will reduce subsequent bandwidth, memory, and parsing requirements.

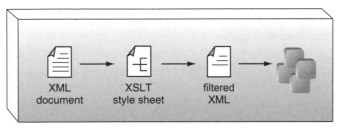

Figure 5.6
XML document is filtered by an XSLT style sheet.

Of course, the best way to avoid any of these issues is to model XML documents as accurately as possible from the start.

5.1.7   Naming element-types: performance vs. legibility

The fully customizable nature of XML allows for documents to be modeled into elegant, self-describing data repositories. This is a tempting model, especially when project teams are still getting used to the conceptual data representation of the tree structure. Allowing the contents of an XML document to be communicated clearly at a glance can improve maintainability and can also avoid (human) misinterpretation.

Having so concisely explained this aspect of XML data modeling, you must be wondering why there are eight more paragraphs in this section. Well, there is a dark side to self-descriptive XML documents: they can be HUGE. Long element-type names result in significantly larger sized files, when documents are required to host a great deal of repetitive data structures.

Just imagine the extent to which you are bloating an XML document that contains a list of a thousand inventory items, each of which is represented by an element named `InventoryItemCodeNumber`. The document is clearly legible, but there is enough redundancy here to make a data analyst cry. The size of XML documents not only affects standard parsing functions, it impacts the performance of the transformation processor.

Once it has been designed and deployed, an XML document will often never be seen by human eyes again. Knowing this in advance, you can consider modeling your documents for processing efficiency by keeping the names of elements likely to be repeated (such as detail and line items) to a minimal length.

To support the maintenance of these optimized documents, you can insert comments directly into each document, providing descriptions for abbreviated element names, or elements that are simply named after a series of codes. You could even supplement your document design with a `Legend` element that contains descriptions of other document elements with non-descriptive names.

When naming element-types that require descriptive labels, the element name lengths can greatly be reduced by relying on parent elements to establish a parent context. Returning to our previous example, assuming the `InventoryItemCodeNumber` element has a `InventoryItem` parent element, it should simply be renamed to `Code-Number`, or even `CodeNo`.

Another option worth mentioning is the incorporation of a compression technology. This can dramatically reduce the size of XML documents for transmission purposes, and may be an acceptable compromise for allowing descriptive element names in large documents. Just be aware of the extra processing steps imposed by this approach, which are required to compress and decompress documents every time they need to be accessed.

Finally, if you are creating a generic API that outputs XML for use outside of your application, you may want to consider providing two methods for each output function. The first can output a set of XML formatted data with human-readable element tags, the other with a short code-based element naming convention. Although this will increase the maintenance requirements of your API, it gives the developer the option of working with self-describing or optimized XML documents. (Alternatively, you can consolidate these two methods into one by adding a separate output format parameter.)

Despite the emphasis on optimizing document structure in this section, the importance of having self-descriptive XML documents should not be overlooked. It is one of the fundamental benefits of this data format. The key is in striking the right balance in your document design between usability and performance.

5.1.8   Applying XML consistently

You've probably heard this before: "Consistency is a key factor in achieving a standardized application design." A very true statement, but for some reason, one that frequently gets ignored when working with XML. I think we should revise this statement in all methodology publications to read: "Inconsistency is a key factor in achieving a nervous condition, along with an uncontrollable twitch in your right eye."

The point is, taking the time to ensure that XML is being applied in a standard manner across your entire application will avoid a maintenance nightmare down the road.

Here are some guidelines:

- If you've defined how XML documents will be processed and delivered within the execution of a business task, try not to deviate from that approach. This means incorporating validation and transformation steps in the same sequence, and establishing a standard data flow process. When performance requirements demand that you alter this process, try to apply these optimizations to each data flow scenario (to whatever extent this makes sense).

- On a lower level, implement design standards that determine how application component APIs process XML input and output. Each custom-developed component in your application will expose a programmatic interface with methods that provide input parameters to receive information, and output parameters for transmitting data. XML can be incorporated in different ways. For instance, a method parameter could be designed to receive a large text string, capable of containing an entire XML document. Alternatively, a parameter might only want a specific piece of data that the component will then incorporate into an XML format of its own.

There are many more ways in which you can achieve consistency. It is not about specific recommendations as much as it is about a mindset you develop when making decisions on how to incorporate XML.

Note that Chapter 12 provides a set of best practices specifically for XML standardization.

5.1.9 Choosing the right API (DOM vs. SAX vs. Data Binding)

The traditional programming interface provided by the World Wide Web Consortium (W3C) for XML documents, has been the Document Object Model (DOM). One of the most common complaints about the DOM has been the requirement that the entire XML document be loaded into memory. This allows the DOM to provide full accessibility to a complete tree view of the information. When dealing with large data sets, this can cause serious performance problems.

It was these challenges that sparked the idea for the Simple API for XML (SAX). SAX evolved from an XML mailing list discussion into a full-blown specification, providing an alternative "lightweight" API for XML documents. The best way to compare the two APIs is to associate them with database cursors. DOM is more like a static record-set allowing updates, inserts, and deletions, whereas SAX is more comparable to a directory-like, read-only cursor, for efficient data access.

There is an amicable relationship between these APIs, in that SAX can be used to create or read portions of a DOM tree. This flexibility has made SAX a valuable addition to the XML family of technologies, which is why many major XML vendors have added support for SAX to their products.

Now, enter the world of XML data binding APIs. Both the DOM and SAX provide structure-centric interfaces into an XML document. Although there is nothing flawed with this approach, it can become burdensome, especially when working with document models that are relatively static. Additionally, building programming routines around parsing code can be a substantial departure from the more business-oriented view of data traditionally provided by object-oriented classes.

Data binding APIs address these issues by offering data-centric interfaces into data bodies that are automatically marshaled into XML documents. While contemporary development tool vendors offer many different types of data binding features, most allow for an XML document to be expressed through a series of business classes. As you write routines to interact with these classes, you will notice that you will tend to produce much less code than you normally would have, to accomplish the same tasks using DOM or SAX.

Many additional data binding features exist. Some APIs allow for the dynamic conversion of any class-represented data into new XML documents, whereas others provide design-time binding to XML schemas (for the auto-generation of classes from XML schema models). Even though this type of functionality is attractive, it often comes with limitations (mostly related to the quality of XML markup output by the API methods).

So how do you decide which API to use? Here are some guidelines:

Use the DOM:

- for small to medium-sized XML documents (under 1,000 elements)
- for modifying the document structure at runtime
- when your application requires immediate access to preloaded XML document information, without performing file I/O

Use SAX:

- for large documents (over 1,000 elements)
- for documents with a limited amount of nested elements
- when the DOM is too slow
- when you need to use only a fraction of the total document data

Use data binding APIs:

- when working with static XML documents
- when requiring a class-oriented interface to XML documents
- to simplify data access programming logic

- to preserve the object-oriented nature of your programming logic
- once you are sure that the API will properly represent and process your XML documents

5.1.10 Securing XML documents

XML formatted data can travel through various tiers of a typical e-Business solution and can even venture beyond your internal environment, into the outside world (and all the way back again). If the nature of your data is sensitive, or if altering any part of an XML document potentially could harm your organization, then you need to understand where, within its path, vulnerabilities exist.

Listed here are some of the more common security issues:

- If externally referenced schemas and DTDs are ever maliciously altered, it could affect applications all over the world. Requiring XML documents to incorporate validation rules hosted outside of your environment (and outside of your control) may be unacceptable, especially if you are running critical services. If you are not confident that the remote site hosting these files is sufficiently secure, then host a copy of the referenced schema locally, within your internal environment. This will, however, require that someone in your organization keep local copies in sync with the originals.
- Many firewalls still aren't designed to question the integrity of XML markup. In fact, they generally ignore it, allowing it to freely pass through. This can result in a dangerous scenario, where XML document data can be replaced with values that could cause problems. Outside of introducing content-aware firewalls into your environment, the best way to mitigate this risk is to build very robust validation routines that thoroughly check the content of each element and attribute.
- XML parsers and XSLT processors will generally assume the security context under which they were invoked. This can lead to authentication problems when an application requires more restrictive control over the availability of parser and processor functions.
- Regardless of whether XML documents require element and attribute length restrictions, check the length of values anyway. By overloading elements or attributes, hackers can bring down the parser as well as related application components.
- Treat errors generated by the XML parser and XSLT processor as you would any other programmatic error. Provide complete exception handling routines that can gracefully deal with anticipated error conditions.

Technologies used to implement security measures are covered in Chapter 4 and Chapter 11. Security standards for XML are grouped with Web services standards to support the creation of an enterprise security model.

5.1.11 Pick the right tools

Seeing the words "Supports XML" on the cover of a development product reminds me of the controversy that surrounded the "Low Fat" label used by food manufacturers. Advertising a food product as being low fat established no reference as to what extent its fat was reduced. The same goes for XML. A product can support XML in many ways. To what degree this support is relevant and useful to your development project is something you must investigate.

Take a close look at the underlying mechanics of any product you evaluate, but don't expect to find a lot of "behind-the-scenes" documentation. It will often be up to you to dig into the files used and generated by the product.

Here are some specific things to look out for.

Review auto-generated markup and code
A current trend is to hide a lot of the syntax from the developer by providing user-interfaces that, at the click of a button, auto-generate XML, schema, or XSLT markup and code. This may or may not be what you want. My first question when I encounter this type of functionality is always, "can I edit the auto-generated code?" The answer is often "no" or an uncomfortable "yes, but you really shouldn't..." This can severely limit your application design. A serious XML-enabled application will typically need to allow uninhibited access to code and markup text.

Identify proprietary markup and code
Another problem with tools that produce all the code and markup for you is that they will often insert proprietary extensions. Many tool vendors are weary of allowing their product to produce purely generic output that could easily be migrated to a different tool set. As a result, these extensions will not only create a dependency on the product itself, they tend to unnecessarily bloat the size of the document, schema, and style sheet files being generated.

Look for proprietary file types
Many products generate new files to store various types of information relating to whatever tasks you're using the tool for. Some may be harmless, but others may deepen your dependency on the product, possibly even restricting your ability to move your work to other product platforms.

Understand the orientation of the tool

XML editors are often geared toward providing a visual interface to documents of a specific type, mainly content or data-centric documents. Editors designed for data-centric XML documents will tend to provide a GUI that facilitates the viewing of document contents in a tabular format, with rows and columns. Those editors intended for the content management crowd will provide more of a word processor-like interface. Some XML tools provide adequate views for both types of documents. Make sure you spend some time working with an editor before you commit to using it.

Assess the quality of conversion features

Schema generation and conversion have become standard features with a number of XML tools. You are able to have the tool auto-generate a DTD or XSD schema from an XML document instance, or you can convert between different schema formats. In both cases, the markup that's generated often requires further manual changes. These can be time-saving features, but always check the output.

Evaluate functional features

When managing and editing large documents, being able to effectively locate specific parts of the document can be important. Most editors support full-text searching, many allow for element and attribute-based queries, but some even provide limited or full XPath support. This can be an especially convenient way of trying out XPath queries without modifying the document source.

Understand programmatic extensions

Some tools come equipped with comprehensive APIs, allowing them to become integrated administration front-ends to XML-driven applications. This can spare you a great deal of programming, because many systems, such as messaging and document management applications, require hands-on maintenance of XML documents.

Look for quality feedback

A key feature often overlooked when assessing XML tools is feedback. You will often be relying on these tools to tell you what is wrong with any particular document you are working with. Whether you are trying to put together a well-formed XML document or a valid DTD or XSD schema file, your editor will notify you of any violations relating to the respective specification. The quality of this feedback is very important. An editor notifying you that there is a validation error on line 38 is practically useless. However, descriptive messages that clearly indicate the nature of the error, or perhaps warn you of borderline violations, are extremely useful and can significantly increase productivity.

Consider existing toolsets

You may want to give special consideration to tools already in use by your IT department. Many established tools (especially those used for modeling), have added support for XML, allowing you to leverage an existing skill set.

5.1.12 Don't try this at home (fringe optimization strategies)

So far we've covered the "good" (recommendations and techniques), the "bad" (pitfalls to avoid), and now we turn to… you guessed it, the ugly side of XML architecture.

What would you do if you were already stuck with a poorly designed XML system, desperately in need of a performance boost? Others in that position have been forced to come up with creative ways of improving performance. Some of these approaches are about as elegant as bolting an airplane engine to the roof of your car. That engine might propel you forward for a while, but eventually it would just tear off the roof, leaving you behind sitting in a badly damaged vehicle, worse off than before. These strategies may get the job done, but only at the expense of further weakening an already poor foundation.

Obligatory disclaimer: *I do not recommend any of the strategies listed here.* In fact, the purpose of this book is to provide you with enough insight so that you will never have to resort to these tactics.

Write your own, stripped down XML parser or XSLT processor

Is your XML being processed or transformed too slowly? Why not just remove unnecessary validation checking performed by standard XML parsers and XSLT processors, and build your own "light" version? Well, even though this may reduce processing cycles, the day the related specification changes, you will be stuck with a proprietary implementation. Also, you better be sure that every validation rule you remove will not impact the integrity of your current and future data. Instead of taking that route, try researching some of the new, enterprise-level parsers and processors instead, including hardware accelerators specifically designed for XML.

Custom program everything

I've seen situations where developers have become so frustrated with XML technologies that they've just ripped them all out, and replaced parsing, validation, and transformation functions with custom programming routines executed by application components. In the end, this turned out to be a very costly move, and only resulted in the developers reclaiming control of their environment from a technology platform they did not understand.

There are certainly times when adding custom programming routines is necessary to fill in some of the gaps that still exist in the XML world. By avoiding XML technologies altogether, though, you would be missing out on the most important advancements in application architecture, since the introduction of the Web itself.

Remove validation

If a set of documents remains fairly static, and you've successfully validated them once before, why bother doing it every time they are processed by your application? I guess this "optimistic" approach is kind of like driving without wearing your seatbelt. Things may work out most of the time, if not all of the time, but what if...

If you are considering an approach similar to this, first learn about granular schema updates (as discussed later in this chapter). At the very least, perform some periodic (perhaps daily) validation of your document set.

SUMMARY OF KEY POINTS

- Understanding how and where XML documents can host and represent your corporate data is the most important step in your integration effort.

- XML data representation introduces the concept of XML document modeling. This is different, but no less important than defining traditional data models for corporate repositories.

- A common mistake is to underestimate the significance of an application's initial XML data representation. As with any data model, an application will develop programmatic dependencies that will be difficult and expensive to change.

5.2 Strategies for integrating XML data validation

The following sections explore some of the more common validation technologies, and provide a number of strategies for how to best implement a validation framework for your application.

5.2.1   XSD schemas or DTDs?

DTDs, originally created for SGML and used with HTML and XML, represent an established, traditional approach to XML data validation. The XML Schema Definition Language (XSD) is a more recent innovation, which has matured and gained wide industry support. XSD schemas provide a sophisticated set of features allowing for the creation and validation of complex XML documents. Compared to the XSD, the features offered by the DTD language are severely limited. That doesn't mean, however, that DTDs are obsolete quite yet.

When to use DTDs instead of XSD schemas

Some of the reasons DTDs may be more suitable than XSD schemas (Figure 5.7) include:

- If the structure of your XML documents is relatively simple, and you are confident it will not change, DTDs provide an easy-to-use syntax that can efficiently be incorporated into an application.

- DTD files tend to be smaller in size than XSD schemas. If your validation code needs to be transmitted across distributed environments, DTDs may provide a lightweight, bandwidth-friendly alternative.

- If proprietary tools or products are part of your fixed application environment, they may not yet support XSD schemas. If integration with these products is a project requirement, you may be forced to work with DTDs.

- Since DTDs have been around much longer, it is more likely that some of your existing developers will already have some expertise. This may be a factor, considering that the learning curve imposed by the XML Schema Definition Language is significant.

- More ready-made DTDs are available for purchase and reuse (although, this is rapidly changing).

- XSD schemas have more processing overhead because they are more complex, larger in size, and contain links that need to be resolved at runtime.

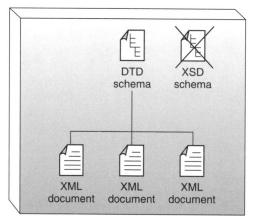

Figure 5.7
Using DTDs instead of XSD schemas.

When to use XSD schemas instead of DTDs
Reasons to choose XSD schemas over DTDs (Figure 5.8) include:

- XSD schemas are the future. If you are starting from scratch, with no predisposition or prerequisites, you are better off building your application design on XSD schemas. Industry support is strong and rapidly increasing.

- If the structure of your XML documents is complex and can benefit from multiple data type support as well as highly customizable validation rules, then XSD schemas will be required.
- XSD schemas can facilitate complicated data representation requirements, and are more suited for tighter integration with relational databases.
- Only XSD schemas are supported natively by the Simple Object Access Protocol (SOAP). Because SOAP is the primary messaging protocol used by Web Services, this is a critical consideration.
- XSD schemas have far more extensibility options than DTDs.
- Better data-binding libraries (such as Castor and XmlSerialization) build on top of XSD, rather than DTDs.

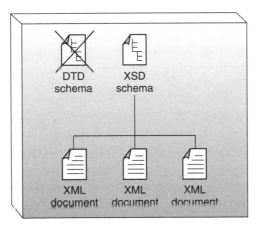

Figure 5.8
Using XSD schemas instead of DTDs.

Another option: use both (side-by-side)
DTDs and XSD schemas can successfully coexist within an application architecture, as shown in Figure 5.9.

The most common reasons they are used together are:

- XSD schemas can act as the master validation part of an application, and DTDs can abstract a subset of the XSD schema validation rules. DTDs can then be used as a lightweight validation mechanism for messaging purposes.
- An existing application may already use DTDs, but extensions to this application introduce XSD schemas.

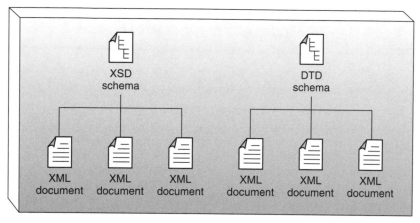

Figure 5.9
Using XSD schemas alongside DTDs.

In either case, the challenge lies in keeping the DTDs and the XSD schemas in alignment. This maintenance effort can be aided by tools that provide DTD-to-XSD migration and conversion features.

Another option: use both (together)
DTDs and XSD schemas can be used to validate the same documents, as illustrated in Figure 5.10. This may be an option when an existing base of XML documents is already using DTDs, but new validation requirements come along, which can only be fulfilled by the XML Schema Definition Language.

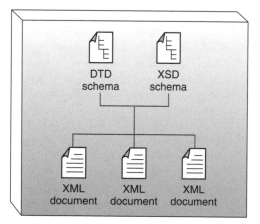

Figure 5.10
Combining the use of DTDs and XSD schemas.

Supplementing established DTDs with XSD schemas is an acceptable transition strategy. It may be cost or time prohibitive to replace all DTDs with XSD schemas at once, especially when your current application requires increased validation functionality only within a subset of your XML document set.

Another option: use neither
Both DTDs and XSD schemas have limitations that may not allow you to implement your application's business rules and validation requirements fully (Figure 5.11). A number of alternatives are discussed later in this section.

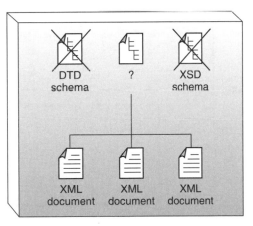

Figure 5.11
Using an alternative schema technology.

5.2.2   Positioning DTDs in your architecture

DTD files will often accompany an XML document as it travels between application components and across physical boundaries (see Figure 5.12). When XML is stored within or dynamically output by relational databases, application logic can associate corresponding DTDs for runtime validation purposes. Alternatively, DTD schema definitions can be stored alongside XML documents in special repository structures.

Frequently, individual applications demand distinct data formats for which a more powerful data representation and validation technology is required. It is therefore less common to utilize DTDs when integrating disparate applications.

The primary reason for considering the use of DTDs within contemporary integration environments (Figure 5.13) is performance. DTDs tend to be smaller in size than those created using other schema languages. This may make them more suitable when performance requirements are very narrow, and a lightweight alternative is required.

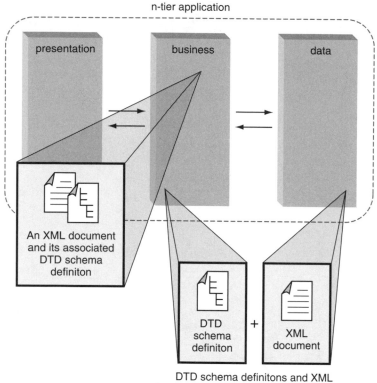

Figure 5.12
XML documents and associated DTD schema definitions within an n-tier
application environment.

5.2.3   Positioning XSD schemas in your architecture

The most fundamental role XSD schemas fulfill at runtime is the validation of XML
document instances. Data validation, however, is just the beginning. The numerous features and adaptive characteristics of the XSD language allow integration solutions to
utilize it in many creative ways.

XSD schemas as a validation layer within an application
XSD schemas can reside in any application tier. They can be stored or even invoked
within the data access layer. As illustrated in Figure 5.14, they are most commonly used
to validate incoming XML documents within a business tier.

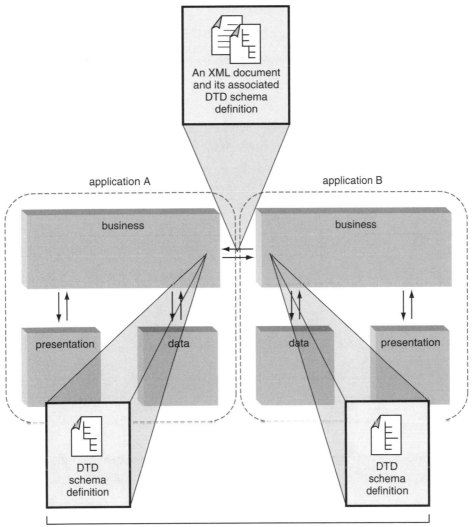

Figure 5.13
Some areas where DTD schema definitions may be found within integration architectures.

XSD schemas as a validation layer for cross-application communication
A wide variety of data transfer channels can exist in legacy and contemporary integration solutions. Some are established through custom application logic, others by the use of database platform extensions.

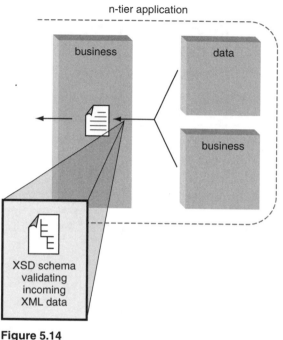

Figure 5.14
XSD establishing a validation layer.

XSD schemas can be deployed in many of these configurations (Figure 5.15), depending on how XML-friendly the application hosting environments are. Sometimes, schemas are created dynamically. In this case the schema resides in memory, with a limited lifespan and consisting of auto-generated markup.

When exchanging data between applications with different data format requirements, XSD schemas typically are enlisted to protect the integrity of the data represented by the respective formats (Figure 5.16).

XSD schemas as an ancillary data technology

As explained in Figure 5.17, the utilization of XSD can go far beyond providing data validation functionality. Many contemporary XML and Web services specifications incorporate XSD schema definitions natively as a standard data type and data model format. As a result, XSD schemas show up in numerous integration scenarios, acting as both a primary and ancillary technology.

5.2.4   Understand the syntactical limitations of XSD schemas

The previous section established that DTDs provide basic validation functionality, and the advent of the XML Schema Definition Language opened the door for the creation of sophisticated XML document structures with complex validation requirements.

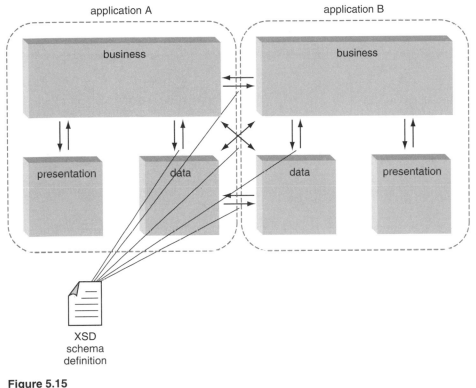

Figure 5.15
XSD schemas can establish and validate XML data models throughout integration
architectures.

Even XSD schemas, however, have limitations. Before committing to XSD as the sole
means of expressing and enforcing your application's business rules, take the time to
understand its boundaries, as they relate to your requirements.

XSD schemas have limited or no support in the following areas:

- conditional constraints
- inter-element dependencies
- cross-document validation
- null values for attributes
- validation of large numeric data values

The XML Schema specification currently is being revised, and many of these issues will
likely be resolved. In the meantime, however, you will need to turn elsewhere if you hit
a wall while trying to design a pure XSD-based validation layer.

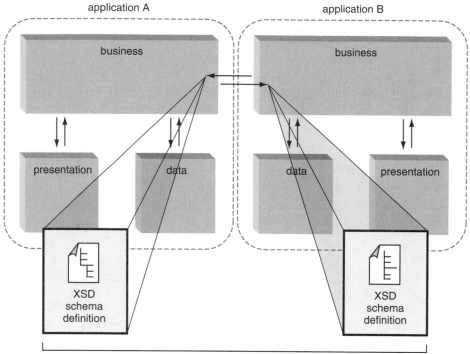

Figure 5.16
XSD schemas validating incoming data for each application endpoint.

5.2.5   Understand the performance limitations of XSD schemas

One of the primary challenges with integrating XSD schemas, especially in larger applications, relates to the sheer complexity of XSD markup. Many find the syntax excessively verbose, and the resulting schema files too large and unwieldy (Figure 5.18).

The maintenance effort can be, of course, alleviated with a good editing tool. The size problem, however, could lead to performance challenges when schemas are required to accompany XML documents through multi-route transmissions.

Additionally, the larger XSD schema files can be very processor-intensive, which could lead to scalability limitations in high-volume multi-user environments.

5.2.6   Other fish in the sea (more schema definition languages)

The previous sections have established the following potential problems with integrating XSD schemas:

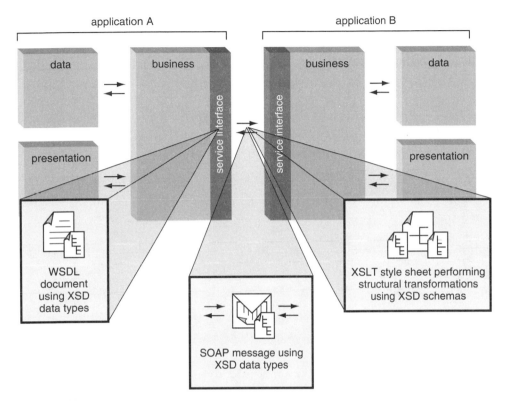

Figure 5.17
XSD features used by WSDL, XSLT, and SOAP.

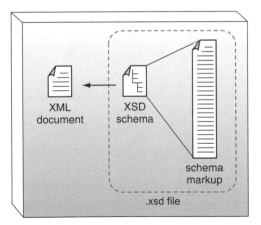

Figure 5.18
Typical XSD schemas require a great deal
of markup.

- limitations of the language
- effort of maintaining complex code
- significant runtime processing requirements
- transmission of potentially large files

There is a very good chance none of these issues will affect your application, in which case you can introduce a complete XSD-based validation layer to your application design. However, should you run into (or be concerned about) any of these problems, read on.

Vendors and working groups have targeted the weaknesses of XSD schemas by providing the following alternative and supplementary XML schema definition languages and frameworks:

- Schema Adjunct Framework (SAF)
- Schematron
- RELAX and RELAX NG
- Schema for Object Oriented XML (SOX)
- Document Schema Definition Languages (DSDL) Interoperability Framework

These, along with several other proprietary initiatives, have emerged in recent years, and are continuing to evolve and adapt to the industry demand for a more flexible XML-based validation platform. You can use these resources to:

- supplement XSD schemas in order to fill validation requirement gaps
- assist in the maintenance of your validation code, by allowing a subset of your validation requirements to be managed by a more user-friendly or performance-centric technology
- provide a viable alternative and perhaps even replace XSD schemas altogether

> **NOTE**
>
> If you need some of the functionality offered by these validation resources, but would still like to make XSD schemas a central part of your application architecture, then consider partitioning your XML validation requirements into specific functional zones. Create a custom integration framework for addressing each area with the most suitable validation approach.

5.2.7   Supplementing XSD schema validation

One final option for overcoming the limitations of XSD schemas is to simply custom program the validation rules yourself, using one of the following approaches.

Use XSLT to enforce validation

This is not its primary purpose; however, the XSLT language has a number of useful validation features. When style sheets process XML data, they will generate a series of errors when validation fails. These error conditions can be trapped and processed by the application.

Custom program validation routines within application components

Obviously, this is what we are trying to avoid by using XML validation in the first place, however, if unique validation requirements come your way (for which the XML validation technology set cannot provide a solution), you will need to embed this functionality in the application.

Another situation in which this approach may be suitable is if runtime performance requirements demand a response faster than your XML processor is capable of providing.

Application-specific annotations

By supplementing your schemas with annotations, custom application routines can look for and process this extra data as though they were validation rules. Still not perfect, but at least all of your validation rules are in one place.

Even though the components in your application are enforcing these particular rules, they still are separated from the compiled code, and therefore can be maintained independently, along with the rest of the XSD schema markup.

Note that the XML Schema Definition Language provides two separate elements for annotations: the `documentation` element intended for arbitrary comments by the schema author, and the `appinfo` element, reserved for custom application processing instructions.

5.2.8   Integrating XML validation into a distributed architecture

Since a distributed application consists of a series of components that reside on a number of application servers, it may be convenient to deploy copies of validation schemas on each server (as shown in Figure 5.19). This approach, however, is undesirable, because it:

- Makes for a poor application design, by creating redundancy and imposing additional maintenance effort.
- Introduces a potential security risk by making more copies of schemas available, while offering less control of schema content. The potential risk is in the increased physical availability of the schema content. Schema documents can contain business rules and formulas that may be confidential to an organization. By deploying physical copies of a schema across multiple physical servers, you increase the availability of these files.

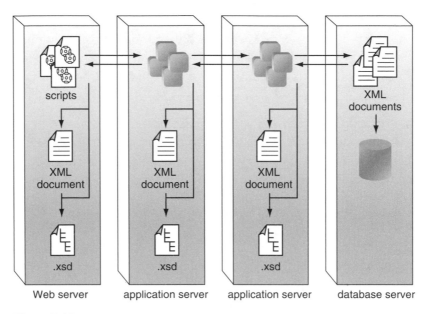

scripts

XML
document

.xsd

XML
document

.xsd

XML
document

.xsd

XML
documents

Web server   application server   application server   database server

Figure 5.19
A physical architecture with redundant schema files.

An alternative is to accompany each transmitted XML document or stream with its own schema. This tactic, however, comes with performance trade-offs that could become unacceptable for applications with high-volume requirements or limited infrastructure resources.

So how do we deal with these challenges? Here's a good strategy for avoiding many of the problems introduced when attempting to integrate XML validation into distributed environments:

1. Store the schemas within the application database.
2. Upon application start-up, retrieve the most commonly required schemas into memory on each application server.
3. Design the application to access the schemas in memory, whenever required.

See Figure 5.20 for an illustration of this option.

To implement this design, follow these guidelines:

• Build component routines that invoke validation in such a way that if a requested schema is not found in memory, it is automatically retrieved from the database.

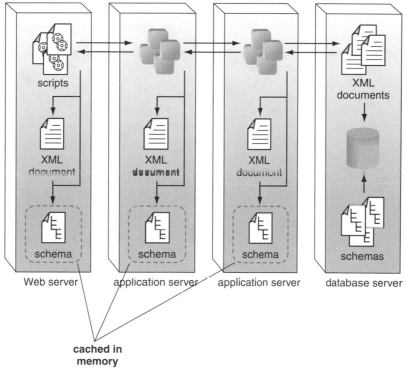

Figure 5.20
A physical architecture illustrating schemas stored in memory.

- If you have a middle-tier state management repository (also known as an In-Memory Database) already in place, it may be a preferable alternative to storing the schema elsewhere.

5.2.9   Avoiding over-validation

When moving sets of data around within an application, it is customary to validate the information prior to its transmission. Deciding on where data validation occurs is a key design issue when integrating XML documents into a typical application architecture.

Regardless of how schemas are referenced by the application, another pitfall is potential over-validation of XML documents. It is common for application components to ensure the integrity of data upon sending or receiving information. When that data consists of entire XML documents, validation could occur every time the document is transmitted and received (within or between physical application layers), regardless of whether any modifications were made (see Figure 5.21).

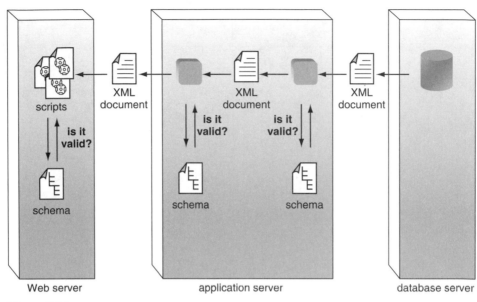

Figure 5.21
An application design wherein XML documents are over-validated.

To minimize this processing overhead, one strategy is to add a `Validated` element (or attribute) to every XML document. Similar to the traditional "IsDirty" tag used with data entry forms, the value of this element can be reset to "no" every time changes to the document are made, and then back to "yes" when the modified document is again validated.

As long as routines that process the XML data consistently use this approach (perhaps through the use of a shared subroutine), validation will occur only when necessary, and performance will improve. Figure 5.22 illustrates this design approach.

5.2.10 Consider targeted validation

By identifying the sections of an XML document that remain static throughout certain stages of its processing, granular XSD schemas can be used to validate only the parts of the document that do change (as shown in Figure 5.23).

This can significantly reduce the amount of processing traditionally required to validate whole documents. The only caveat here is that the entire document should always be validated at some point during the execution of the business task.

Targeted validation is best applied within application routines that alter XML document instances, and then validate the modified parts prior to forwarding the document itself.

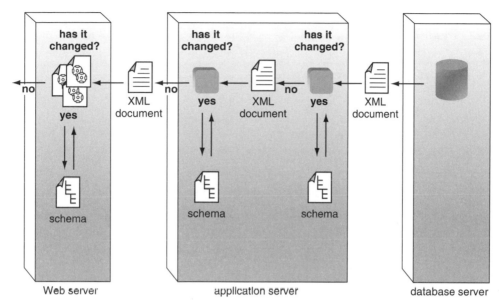

Figure 5.22
Before validation, XML documents are checked to determine whether they were altered since the last validation.

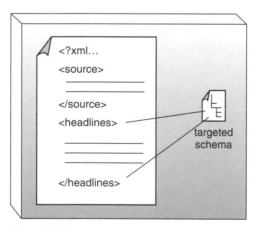

Figure 5.23
A schema designed to validate only a specific part of an XML document.

5.2.11 Building modular and extensible XSD schemas

The ability to assemble a schema from multiple different schema documents is one of the most powerful features of the XML Schema Definition Language. Enterprise applications often demand this level of flexibility, in order to respond to unpredictable runtime conditions requiring validation. As shown in Figure 5.24, sophisticated programming logic can take advantage of schema modules to support the creation of flexible document instances.

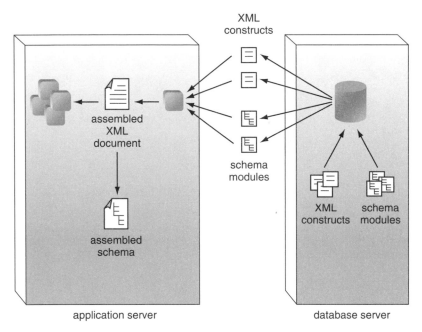

Figure 5.24
An application builds an XML document and the associated schema at runtime.

Furthermore, an application design based on modular schemas will lead to a highly normalized data model. This establishes a desirable level of extensibility that will benefit the overall technical environment, beyond the current project. Creating granular schema modules will also lead to reusable schema documents. In other words, schemas can represent data entities that can be used in different types of XML documents.

XSD enables one schema to include another through the use of the `include` and `import` elements. The latter allows the schema to reference other schemas in different namespaces. Additionally, it provides the `redefine` element, with which one schema document can actually override elements and attributes of another.

Another aspect of XSD schemas that provides some flexibility in terms of how schema files can adapt to different data models is the `any` element. Through its use, schema definitions can be extended with others.

5.2.12 Understand the integration limitations of your database

Although Chapter 7 is dedicated to the topic of integrating XML with databases, here we take a high-level look at the common technical boundaries you may encounter within contemporary database platforms.

Databases with no XML support

Discontinued products, and those with vendors not interested in supporting current trends, will have no notion of XML. In these environments you will be limited to working with XML documents as raw string values. Depending on the extent to which you want to support XML documents within your database, you will need to design creative data models to mirror the XML structures, and the relationship between documents, schemas, and other supporting documents, such as style sheets.

Databases for which third-party products provide XML support

Some software vendors have discovered a market for third-party products, such as connectors, adapters, gateways, and bridge components. These products fill integration gaps by performing dynamic conversion between XML and legacy data formats.

Though they can still affect runtime performance, using these products often can save a great deal of development effort. This is especially true for add-ons that work with very old repositories for which development expertise may be rare and/or expensive.

Third-party vendors need to be evaluated carefully to ensure that their products are robust and scalable enough to meet expected usage requirements. Generally, third party products don't undergo the quality assurance rigor of the database solutions from major vendors.

Databases with XML extensions

Again, this environment will limit you to the functionality provided by a proprietary platform. The upside, however, is that the XML extensions are supplied by the same vendor as the database. This generally results in a more reliable solution, because the extensions should be built with the same level of scalability for which the database was designed.

Databases with native XML support

There are native XML databases, but there are also relational databases that provide native XML support. This is obviously the most desirable solution. If you are able to simply upgrade your existing repository to a new version that provides XML-aware storage, retrieval, and querying of XML documents, then you've addressed many common integration challenges.

SUMMARY OF KEY POINTS
• XML data validation technologies are used to define the structure of an XML document, establish rules around its data, and enforce those rules.
• The functionality provided by XML data validation is essential to an application relying on XML data.
• Key integration challenges include relating validation technologies to existing databases, encapsulating complex business rules, and preventing performance impacts.

5.3 Strategies for integrating XML schema administration

Allowing different parts of your IT department to create their own schemas independently is the equivalent of deploying a UNIX server in one area, an NT server in the next, and topping it off with a Linux server somewhere else. Knowing full well these environments will need to interoperate in the future, this would not make a lot of sense.

5.3.1   XML schemas and the silent disparity pattern

The ad-hoc creation of schemas, however, is a common problem in many organizations. The main reason is simply a lack of understanding as to the importance of schema standardization.

Many organizations find themselves iterating through this common cycle:

1. Build an application that uses XML.
2. Create schemas as required.
3. Attempt to integrate the application with another.
4. Realize there is an overlap or incompatibility between the respective schemas.

At this point, you could choose to address this problem by:

- remodeling one of the two schemas
- introducing a transformation layer between the two environments
- proceeding with the integration despite the irregularities in the data models

None of these solutions is particularly desirable. The first option will require revisiting application logic and reestablishing data models. The second approach adds a new layer of processing. The last option requires that the integration application be built upon a poor foundation. That can only lead to more problems in the future, and perhaps even result in a failure of the integration solution itself.

This is only a sample of the type of problems that can be caused by two applications being built independently. Now magnify these issues to encompass the array of applications that have been built, are being built, and will be built within a typical enterprise.

Though it's difficult to know which systems will need to share data in the future, by requiring that all applications use a common set of XML schemas you will avoid many potential integration problems.

5.3.2   A step-by-step XWIF process

Imagine if one set of centrally managed schemas established a common set of data models for ten different applications. Even if each of those applications was developed independently, any future integration requirements could be smoothly implemented, as interoperability is already part of the application design.

So how do we accomplish this? We need a formal process to govern the design and evolution of standard corporate schemas, related vocabularies, and namespaces. Every process will be different, as organizations are structured and run in different ways, however, the steps provided in Figure 5.25 will get you started.

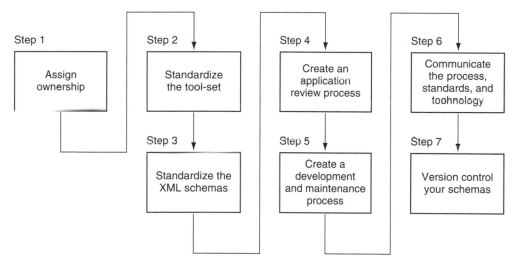

Figure 5.25
An XWIF process for integrating schema administration.

Step 1: Assign ownership
Tell your developers to stop scheming! To avoid creating disparate and redundant XML document representations, centralize the maintenance of all validation code by assigning ownership to an XML Data Custodian. This role, introduced by the XWIF framework, establishes a controlled approach to evolving document structures and XML data models.

Overall, XML Data Custodians are responsible for:

- ownership of XML vocabularies
- determination of schema definition languages
- ownership of schemas
- ownership of schema standards
- namespace domain administration

For a detailed description of this role and advice on how best to incorporate it into a typical project team, refer to Chapter 12.

Step 2: Identify sources of auto-generated schemas and standardize the relevant tool set
Probably the biggest reason that XML schemas are implemented independently and differently are front-end tools that auto-generate schema markup. Development tools, XML editors, data converters, and data mapping tools frequently provide an option to create a schema document based on an existing data model or XML document instance.

Besides almost never being accurate, these auto-generated schemas can lead to many problems. Once you have identified products that generate markup and code, document how each creates a schema and where those schemas are being used. The tool you end up using to maintain the schema markup should ideally be the same one used by development projects to author schemas.

Step 3: Standardize on official XML schemas
A standard requiring project teams to incorporate official schemas needs to be implemented, in order for the organization to gain control of schema usage. This should be classified as a formal standard on par with any standards related to modeling database schemas.

Step 4: Create an application review process
When new (XML-based) application projects emerge, the application design should be reviewed by the XML Data Custodian.

This will allow that person to:

- avoid any duplication of data models between existing data models and ones introduced by the application
- align new schemas with the format of existing schemas, based on naming and structure conventions

- identify opportunities for reuse of schema modules
- look for ways to modularize proposed new schemas

Step 5: Create a development and maintenance process

XML schemas represent corporate data. The majority of this data is likely already defined, managed and overseen by various entities in your organization. In order for your XML schemas to be kept in alignment with current data models, a process typically will be required.

This type of process generally consists of communication and authorization steps through which legacy schema owners are notified of changes to XML data models.

Step 6: Communicate the process, standards, and technology

To effectively establish new processes and roles within your organization, education is vital. Publishing standards and process descriptions on a local intranet can be useful, but the key is to educate those most affected by the standardization of XML schemas.

Step 7: Version control your schemas

As with a relational data model, applications that begin to depend on XML schemas will need to be considered when changes or extensions are required. Preserving the integrity of existing schema models, therefore, is key.

Fortunately, the XSD schema specification provides features that allow core schemas to be extended and even overridden. This can be very useful, but it requires a great deal of foresight and modeling effort. Using such features therefore should become part of your schema modeling standards.

NOTE

Some organizations use namespaces for version control, however this is not recommended in environments where namespaces are better utilized to represent organizational or technical domains.

SUMMARY OF KEY POINTS

- The most common mistake in development projects is letting the developers design the validation schemas.

- As much as databases belong to the DBA, schemas belong to a new organization role, the XWIF XML Data Custodian.

- Standards and maintenance processes are key to evolving a central, normalized set of XML schemas within an organization.

5.4 Strategies for integrating XML transformation

Being able to transform XML documents into multiple output formats has become a key part of contemporary XML architectures. Armed with the ability to provide conditional logic, parameters, procedures, and other data manipulation features, XSLT has become the foremost (and practically unrivaled) technology to supply this important function.

Adding XSLT to the mix of XML technologies within your architecture opens up a whole number of new integration opportunities. Provided here are a collection of strategies and guidelines that explore transformation.

5.4.1   Positioning XSLT in your architecture

XSLT style sheets are commonly utilized within an n-tier architecture as translation mechanisms for document and repository-based data. Essentially, wherever XML-compliant data streams exist, XSLT can add value by acting as the data's manipulation agent. The potential application of XSLT is therefore very broad.

XSLT as a transformation technology within an application

An application can use XSLT internally for a number of structural data manipulation functions, such as the conversion of data received from disparate application data sources, and the dynamic filtering (or trimming) of oversized data sets retrieved from proprietary APIs or database products.

When learning about XML transformation, most of the emphasis tends to be on the transmission of data from the server toward the client. This is natural, since we tend to see the primary function of an application as delivering data to some destination.

XML transformation, however, is equally useful for translating data formats and document structures received by the application (Figure 5.26). For instance, information provided by a user in an HTML form can be posted back to the Web server and serialized into an XML document that is then processed by server-side application components.

XSLT as a presentation unifier for a single application

When new output mediums are required (for instance, to facilitate a new user demographic), XSLT can be utilized to support various presentation renditions, with the help of supplemental technologies (Figure 5.27 displays an example).

In order for XSLT to support the translation of application data into one or more presentation output formats, separate style sheets are generally created. This allows for the abstraction of presentation logic into an aesthetic transformation layer.

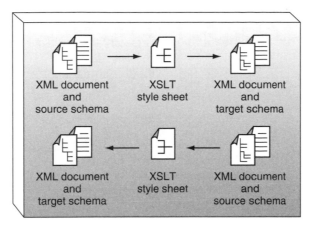

Figure 5.26
XSLT is used to transform XML documents to and from
different types.

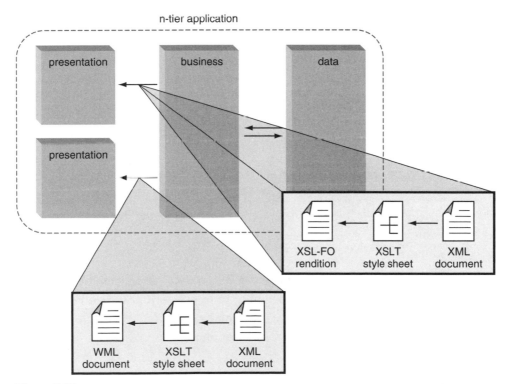

Figure 5.27
An application using XSLT style sheets to support two different aesthetic output formats.

XSLT as a transformation technology between applications

The two-way transformation model has become especially popular with EAI and B2B solutions, where data interchange is enabled by allowing XSLT to act as a central translation engine between multiple applications and organizations.

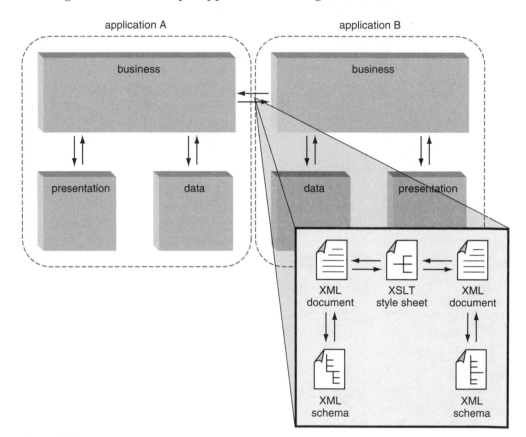

Figure 5.28
XSLT can perform dynamic structural transformations.

As shown in Figure 5.28, style sheets created at design time are enlisted by the application to dynamically convert an XML document from one format to another, based on existing schema definitions. Many EAI broker products rely on this XSLT feature to enable communication between disparate application platforms.

XSLT as a presentation unifier for multiple applications

When integrating applications that need to share data used by their respective clients, XSLT can enable the dynamic translation of a single XML document into different output formats. This, for instance, would allow an application facilitating wireless devices to be integrated with an application that produced print media, as shown in Figure 5.29.

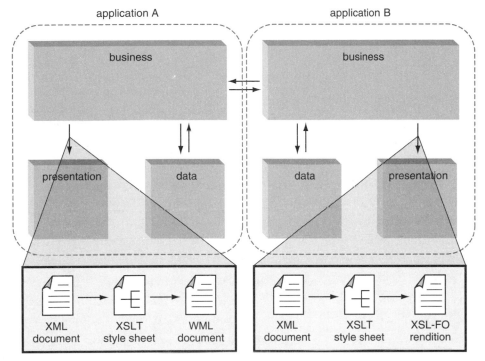

Figure 5.29
Presentation centric transformations can be incorporated to output data for different mediums.

5.4.2   Pre-transform for static caching

Transformation is a processor-intensive task directly related to the complexity of the document structures and the volume of data involved in the formatting of the final output. When transforming content that does not require real-time delivery, you may be able to introduce a caching system.

By periodically pre-transforming certain bodies of data to static documents stored on disk or in memory, you can optimize the transformation process by eliminating a great deal of runtime processing.

If you pursue this approach, make sure you take the following considerations into account:

- If the data is considered sensitive, then caching introduces a potential security risk.
- A garbage collection routine will likely be required to remove out-of-date content from wherever it is being stored.

5.4.3   Create dynamic XSLT style sheets

Like any other XML documents, XSLT style sheets can be created on the fly. This is especially useful when mapping XSLT functionality to business rules that rely on real-time access to outside data sources.

Style sheets do not need to be created completely from scratch. XSLT also supports parameters that can be set at runtime.

5.4.4   Simplify aesthetic transformation with CSS

XSLT likely will be responsible for the bulk of your data structure transformations. You are not obligated, however, to use it for the presentation of your XML data. Traditional CSS style sheets can be used to a limited extent.

There are a number of reasons why you may want to consider this option:

- CSS style sheets are much easier to author and maintain. Many (non-technical) Web designers are proficient with CSS, and they may be the ones who want to retain control of an application's presentation logic.
- CSS style sheets can be rendered by just about all browsers, allowing the processing of presentation information to be delegated away from the servers. (Browser support for XSLT is expected to eventually become commonplace, but isn't quite there yet.)
- CSS requires much less syntax and results in smaller style sheet files. If your presentation formatting information needs to travel with your XML documents, this may be a consideration.

5.4.5   Understand the scalability limitations of XSLT

XSLT processors are built for mainstream usage. When deployed in enterprise environments with high volume processing requirements, they may deliver inadequate performance, or fail to perform at all.

As with DOM-based XML parsers, XSLT processors load entire XML documents into memory before they begin processing the contents. This can slow down your application, while loading up your server's resources. Additionally, when working with complex document structures you may run into a memory allocation size limitation that can grind your transformation process to a painful halt.

You can alleviate some of these processing demands by:

- introducing a queue system to control transformation throughput
- modeling your XML documents into manageable sizes

For serious high-volume environments, you may be forced to seek an alternative to standard XSLT processors, such as enterprise transformation engines or XML hardware accelerators. Finally, you may also need to consider building a custom application component using XPath or SAX to execute some transformation functions.

5.4.6 Strategic redundancy

One of the drawbacks of a standard XML architecture is that it does not provide a native indexing mechanism to expedite data manipulation processing. As a result, the performance of applications that require different views of the same data will be impacted if the application attempts to generate this information at runtime.

Although you can investigate the use of several products that provide database-like indexing and querying features, there may be a simpler and less expensive alternative. If you know in advance the different data views an application will require, you can pre-generate those views and store them as separate XML documents. Your application will then be required to update redundant data automatically, whenever information in a related document is altered.

This may go against established data modeling principles, but there are times when you need to denormalize a database in order to improve performance, and this really is no different. I'm not saying that this strategy should become part of your development methodology, but you can see it as a means to an end that can dramatically increase performance at the cost of a slightly more convoluted back-end.

Here are some guidelines for assessing and implementing this strategy:

- Attempt this only if you can keep the amount of redundant documents to a minimum. Too many inter-dependent documents will impose unreasonable maintenance requirements, and will result in too much runtime processing.
- Keep all documents containing redundant data in one logical group. Do not allow any cross-over from other logical groups. In other words, don't let one group of documents contain redundant data from another.
- The goal here is to avoid inefficient runtime processing. An example of where this strategy may be consistently appropriate is when summarizing information from multiple document sources into one.

5.5 Strategies for integrating XML data querying

Once data is represented by XML it conforms to a standard format that allows it to be searched and manipulated using a standard query language. This implies that the

> **SUMMARY OF KEY POINTS (Section 5.4)**
>
> • The structural and aesthetic transformation features provided by XSLT can be utilized within single and multi-application architectures.
>
> • As with XML parsers, many XSLT processors will "overheat" when faced with high-volume processing scenarios.
>
> • Pre-transformation and the creation of redundant data views can be effective strategies for improving application performance

extent to which you standardize XML data representation within your organization will determine the level of data access unification you can achieve across your corporate intelligence.

This section explores the XQuery language as a technology for the standardized querying of XML data. While XQuery is still considered a second-tier XML technology, its anticipated usage has significant implications on how the next generation of XML architectures will be designed.

5.5.1   Positioning XQuery in your architecture

On a fundamental level, XQuery can unify multiple data sources with single statement queries. This can simplify and optimize data access architectures.

XQuery as a query technology within an application
An XQuery expression can be used to search multiple XML data sources (or proprietary data sources with XQuery support), returning a single view of the collectively queried data in a unique context (see Figure 5.30).

XQuery as a query technology across application data sources
Figure 5.31 shows how integrated environments can utilize XQuery by allowing a single expression to query data sources across application boundaries.

5.5.2   Multi-data source abstraction

XQuery can be leveraged to effectively abstract multi-source data access from application logic, as illustrated in Figure 5.32. This level of abstraction can provide an extremely useful and efficient access point, centralized to unify disparate platforms and query languages.

By establishing a centralized data access layer, the application logic responsible for data access can also be standardized, as it can be limited to XQuery expressions. Furthermore, a fundamental benefit of XQuery is its ability to allow one query expression to

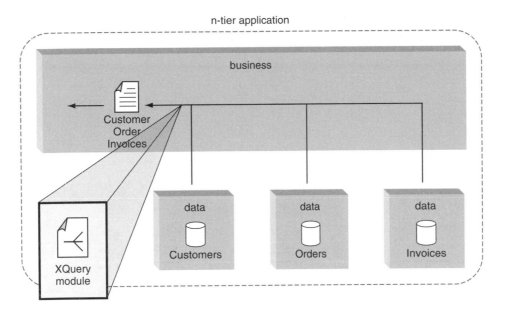

Figure 5.30
An XQuery module positioned to query multiple data sources within a single application environment.

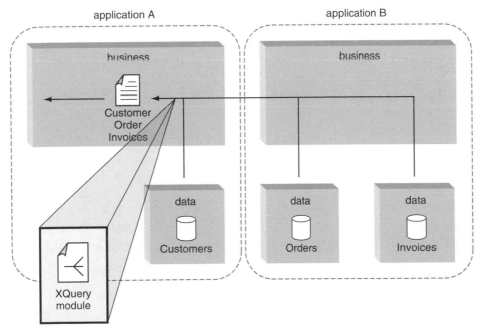

Figure 5.31
An XQuery returning results from multiple data sources across application domains.

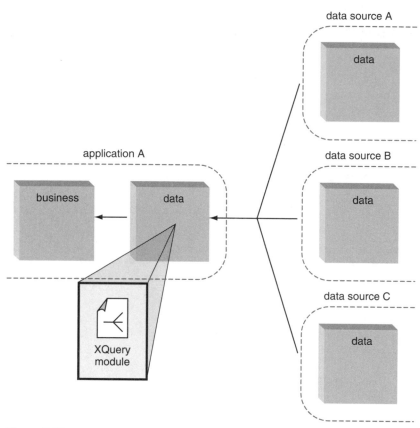

Figure 5.32
XQuery providing a central data access point for legacy repositories in support
of a single application.

search multiple data sources. This can increase standardization, while also simplifying
data access logic.

5.5.3   Establishing a data policy management layer

If properly scaled with a suitable processing engine, single query access to a collection of
legacy repositories can result in a powerful information and data policy management
layer (see Figure 5.33). This enables a variety of unique data representation combinations.

When integrated to this extent, XQuery enables a core part of enterprise architecture. By
achieving a level of centralization that facilitates multiple applications and data sources,
organizations will be able to gain a high degree of control over their data access logic.
This will allow for the creation of polices that can be applied to one layer, but are enforced
across all related applications and repositories.

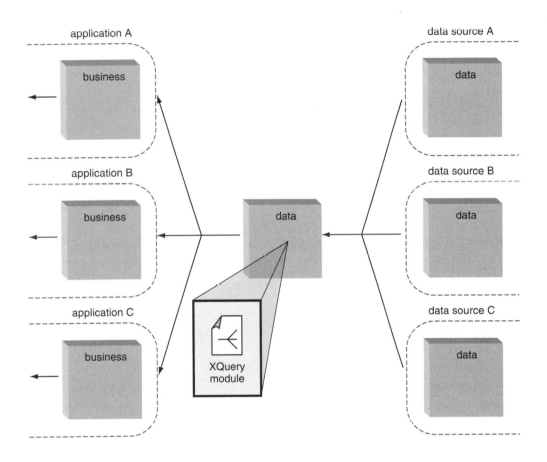

Figure 5.33
XQuery establishing a central data management layer for a number of applications.

5.5.4   Unifying documents and data

Standardizing on XML as an application data representation technology establishes a consistent format that represents data originating in corporate repositories. As previously stated, XQuery can be used to issues sophisticated searches against these XML data sources.

Imagine, though, if you also standardize on XML as a meta language that structures and categorizes your corporate documents. This would essentially allow you to create a global information framework with a common data classification and management platform.

First, let's look at how most organizations currently access their corporate information (Figure 5.34). For instance, let's say the data used by your organization's applications and reporting tools is typically kept in relational databases. Access to this environment is standardized via a set of supported data access protocols (such as ODBC) and a standard query language (such as SQL).

Documents, on the other hand, usually reside on the local LAN, accessed via shared folders or intranet sites. Indexing engines provide full-text searching, and some search products offer limited meta query parameters that are often based on high-level meta information, such as author, title, data modified, etc. In this environment, it is not possible to run a query targeting specific types of data within documents, as data is not classified at a granular level.

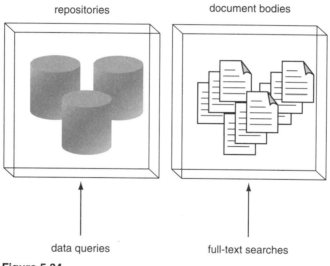

repositories   document bodies

data queries   full-text searches

Figure 5.34
Traditional information segregation.

It is also difficult — if not impossible — to run a single query across both sets of information. If you did want to search databases and documents, you'd probably need a specialized tool, or you'd have to resort to writing two separate queries, and then merging the results with a custom application routine.

How does XQuery change all this? By restructuring your documents using XML, you have turned every one of your corporate documents into a mini-repository, as searchable as any standard relational database (Figure 5.35).

Applications that can access the corporate documents over a local intranet can perform queries based on specific data elements (as opposed to the standard full-text searches), while also executing searches across databases.

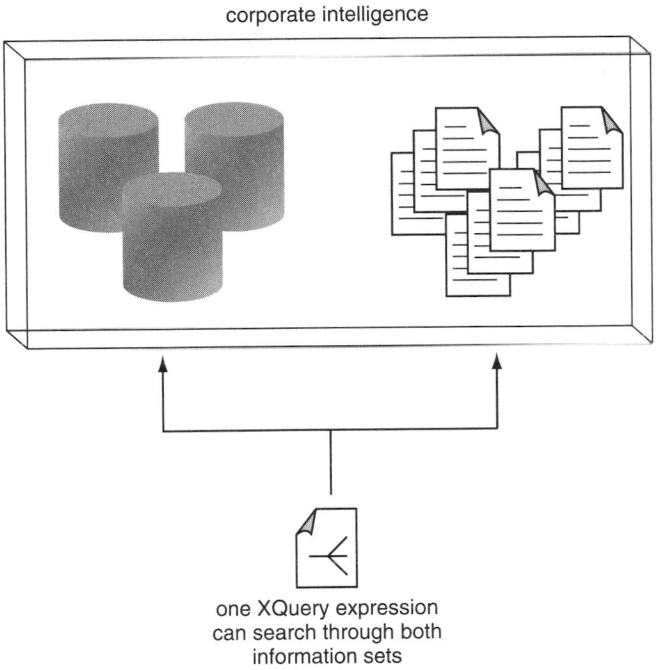

corporate intelligence

one XQuery expression
can search through both
information sets

Figure 5.35
Unified information access architecture.

SUMMARY OF KEY POINTS

- XQuery can unify disparate data platforms, by establishing a central location for data access logic.

- XQuery can centralize data access logic to an extreme extent, giving it the potential to become a core architectural component within an enterprise.

- XQuery can search XML-compliant documents and data, unifying an organization's collective intelligence.

Integrating Web services into applications

The revival of the service-oriented design paradigm, coupled with a number of widely supported Internet technologies, have resulted in a platform shift comparable with (but not equal to) that of XML. Since the architecture introduced by Web services consists solely of XML technologies, this new service-oriented platform can be considered a continuation of the XML movement.

The most common and valuable use of Web services is to enable inter-application and inter-organization communication, by abstracting proprietary technology and establishing a universal integration framework. This is why the bulk of the integration strategies for Web services is provided in Parts III and IV of this book, where we broaden our scope to cross-application and enterprise-wide integration issues.

This by no means lessens the importance of incorporating Web services technology (and accompanying design concepts) within your current application development project. In fact, having to focus on only a single application environment will give you a great deal of freedom as to how you approach this integration challenge.

Web services not only affect how you design an application, they can impose a variety of strategic and technical factors. This is because Web services introduce:

- a new way of building application architecture
- a new way of exposing application functionality
- a new way of partitioning and representing business logic
- a new way of achieving interoperability
- a new communications framework
- new opportunities for application reuse

NOTE

If you are new to the world of Web services, read through the tutorials provided in Chapters 3 and 4 before continuing with this chapter.

6.1 Service models

Described here is the basic set of XWIF design models for Web services (referred to as *service models* from here on). Each model has a specific role and a common set of characteristics.

6.1.1   Utility services

Due to their autonomous nature, Web services are often utilized to encapsulate functionality so generic in nature that it can be reused both within and between applications.

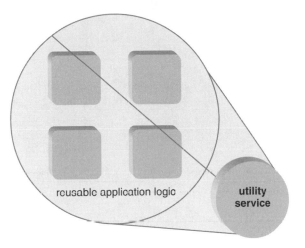

Figure 6.1
The utility service model.

Creating *utility services* (Figure 6.1) is much like building reusable components, except that they can be deployed and accessed outside of platform boundaries (Figure 6.2).

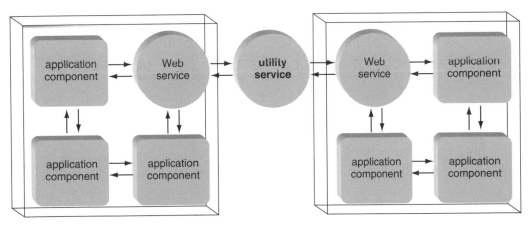

Figure 6.2
A utility service being shared by other Web services.

This model has opened up a whole new third-party marketplace. If you find a ready-made service that fits the bill, then it just might make good sense to purchase or lease it for your application.

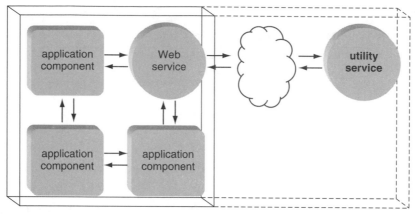

Figure 6.3
A remote third-party utility service being incorporated by an application.

However, if the service is only available "for rent" via the Internet, then you need to evaluate the risks associated with availability and security before relying on it as part of your permanent application design. Third-party services hosted at vendor sites (Figure 6.3) need to provide a great deal of value in order to justify the expense, and offset the risks and performance impact they can introduce.

Examples of useful utility services include:

- A service that encapsulates data conversion using XSLT or custom code. This service could provide a generic interface to various transformation routines that provide runtime conversion of XML documents or other file formats. These types of in-house utility services can become extremely useful in EAI environments, and can be utilized by (or even bundled with) integration brokers. (The section, "A guide to middleware" in Chapter 8 discusses integration brokers and other EAI technologies.)

- A service exposing a cached data store. Imagine if a number of your applications require regular access to a common set of relatively static data. Instead of each application accessing and perhaps caching this information individually, a central service could provide a single point of contact for a variety of global information.

- A service that performs a calculation. A currency converter is a classic example. Not only could such a service convert various currency values, it could access up-to-date rates at runtime, and even provide historical rate information.

Every service model description in this book provides a summary of common characteristics. Use these as points of reference when first designing Web services, and deviate as necessary. Typical characteristics of the utility service model are provided in Table 6.1.

NOTE
Message types can be either document- or RPC-centric. This relates to the two message formats supported by the Simple Object Access Protocol.

Table 6.1 Typical characteristics of utility services

Typical service characteristics	
Anticipated usage volume	High to very high. For remote third-party services, usage requirements need to be assessed carefully prior to their incorporation within an application.
Interface design characteristics	Generically named coarse-grained operations with multiple parameters that support arrays, if necessary. Since utility services tend to be deployed outside of application boundaries, round-trips need to be minimized. Therefore, standard distributed computing conventions apply, promoting the transfer of as much data as possible with every request and response.
Message types	Document-centric.
Deployment requirements	Depending on the nature of the service, and the range of its anticipated requestors, utility services may need to reside on a dedicated server. This will allow them to be shared without the need for redundant implementations. However, usage demands may require services to be replicated.

6.1.2 Business services

A service designed to represent a specific business function.

Business services (Figure 6.4) consolidate existing functionality into unique business contexts, and can play key roles in the support of new business processes. A service-oriented architecture will almost always contain a number of pure business services. Common characteristics of this service model are provided in Table 6.2.

6.1.3 Controller services

Multiple services can be composed to represent the execution of a high-level business task. Collections of services utilized this way are referred to as *service assemblies* (discussed in more detail later in this chapter).

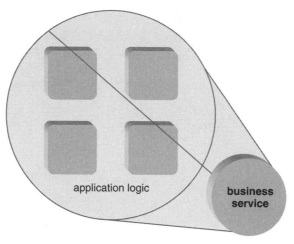

Figure 6.4
The business service model.

Table 6.2   Typical characteristics of business services

	Typical service characteristics
Anticipated usage volume	Medium to high. The usage of the service will relate to how often the particular business function it represents is executed.
Interface design characteristics	Fine- to coarse-grained. Business service interfaces need to be optimized in order to best support the application logic they expose. Redundant service operations are sometimes provided to offer fine-grained functionality to local requestors, and coarse-grained operations to remote requestors.
Message types	Document-centric.
Deployment requirements	For performance and security reasons, business services are generally deployed close to the application components with which they need to interact.

Controller services (Figure 6.5) encapsulate and coordinate an assembly of Web services, and can contain all of the necessary logic to complete a business function. Therefore, a controller service also can be classified as a type of business or process service, as shown in Figure 6.6. Table 6.3 also lists the most common characteristics of this service model.

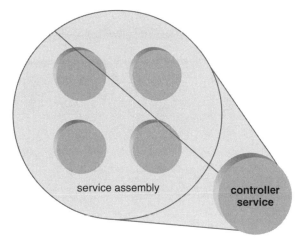

Figure 6.5
The business service model.

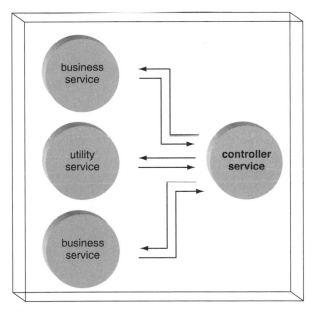

Figure 6.6
A controller service interacting with various other services
to execute a business function.

Table 6.3   Typical characteristics of controller services

	Typical service characteristics
Anticipated usage volume	Medium to high. The usage of the service will relate to how often the particular business function it represents is executed. As the central contact point for other services, overall usage tends to be higher.
Interface design characteristics	Coarse-grained. Controller services typically consolidate existing service interfaces into a small set of business function-specific operations.
Message types	Document-centric.
Deployment requirements	The physical location of controller services can vary, depending on how many services they represent. If the services under a controller service are distributed across multiple physical boundaries, and if usage volumes are relatively high, a controller service may be located on a central server.

SUMMARY OF KEY POINTS

• Service models classify types of Web services with common characteristics.

6.2 Modeling service-oriented component classes and Web service interfaces

You'll find yourself asking many questions when you first look at integrating Web services into your application design. Once you gain an understanding of the technology, there still remains the issue of actually modeling your application in such a way that it can facilitate the Web services integration layer.

You will be required to make a number of strategic decisions, including:

• To what extent does the application actually need Web services?

• What kind of business logic should be encapsulated within each service?

• How much application functionality should be executed by each service?

• What type of application functionality should not be represented by a service?

• What are the technical limitations of the available Web services development and deployment platforms?

- How can application components be optimized to accommodate services?
- How can component classes be designed to best facilitate future interaction with Web services?
- How should the service interface be designed?

To help you gather the information required to answer these questions, the following two XWIF processes are provided:

1. Designing service-oriented component classes
2. Designing Web service interfaces

Completing either of these processes not only will assist you in making important design decisions, they will allow you to gain an insight into the common changes a traditional application architecture needs to undergo in order to accommodate the service integration layer introduced by the SOA.

6.2.1   Designing service-oriented component classes (a step-by-step XWIF process)

Before we get into the details of this process, let me first share with you the reasons why I included it in this guide. Although the IT industry remains in a period of transition where Web services and service-oriented principles are gradually being adopted, I've witnessed the emergence of three types of application development projects:

- those that incorporate Web services to a full extent
- those that incorporate Web services to a limited extent
- those that do not incorporate Web services at all

Service-oriented design issues are high on the list of priorities in the first type of project, since Web services form a key part of the application architecture. If Web services, however, only supplement a traditional distributed application, or if they are not part of the application design at all, service-oriented principles are rarely taken into consideration.

Even now, when awareness of the importance of the Web services technology platform is at an all-time high, projects delivering applications based on traditional distributed platforms do so with complete disregard for any future extensibility with Web services.

There are a number of reasons as to why this trend is so common:

- A lack of understanding as to what Web services are. Many view Web services as a new-generation technology platform that will eventually replace current distributed environments. Therefore, there is no need to take this technology into consideration now.

- The Web services technology set and service-oriented modeling principles are complex and confusing. Therefore, incorporating support for this new framework now will increase project costs and skill set requirements with no foreseeable justification.
- The Web services platform is immature and still far from being relevant. Therefore, it is best to continue with an established and proven approach.

These are all dangerous assumptions. If you are building a new application and choose to ignore the fundamental design characteristics of service-oriented architectures, you will likely be faced with the following problems in the not-so-distant future:

- significant performance challenges when adding service interface layers to your application
- a less than ideal design, since Web services eventually will be required to compensate for incompatible legacy design characteristics within your application
- additional cost and effort to redesign your application to improve performance and provide a better fit for a service interface layer

Much of this can be avoided with a speculative design approach. Note that a comprehensive knowledge of Web service technologies is not required, because this process is specifically for distributed applications that are being designed *without* the use of Web services.

Also, the process makes no assumptions with regards to how or to what extent you will be using Web services. It simply introduces some very fundamental design principles that allow you to model your component classes in such a way that they can (eventually) be best exposed through Web service interfaces. Hence, we are creating *service-oriented component classes*.

Obviously, you will not end up with an application fully optimized for use within service-oriented architectures. For that, we'd need to know your requirements for Web services up-front. What you will be achieving, however, is an environment that will drastically reduce the performance and design problems frequently encountered when adding Web services after the fact.

Incidentally, much of this guide preaches designing applications for a future state. See the best practice, "Build toward a future state," in Chapter 13 for more information.

Now, back to our process. As previously mentioned, a primary benefit to designing components with future service interaction in mind is performance.

By creating streamlined component interfaces you will be able to:

- reduce runtime processing overhead by keeping application logic lean
- eliminate the transmission and filtering of excess information by establishing concise input and output streams

The ultimate goal of this process is to produce a set of refined and optimized components, capable of efficiently responding to service requests. We accomplish this by first building the application design in a traditional manner. We then assess various aspects of the class interfaces, and continue on to remodel the classes using service-oriented design principles.

> **NOTE**
> A number of the following process steps (Figure 6.7) discuss the need to accommodate functional gaps in the mainstream Web services framework. Many of these issues are being addressed through the second-generation Web services specifications. Depending on the extent to which your development and operating platforms support these standards, you can adjust this process accordingly. You should therefore use it as a "worst case" approach that can be customized to accommodate the Web services features (or lack thereof) within your environment.

Step 1: Take inventory of business component classes

If you haven't designed the layer of business classes for your application yet, then first do so, the way you normally would. If Web services are new to your environment, it is easier to identify relevant parts of business logic within an existing application model rather than try to build service-oriented component classes from scratch.

Once you have your component classes defined, put them in a list along with their respective public interfaces. Choose one of the classes for your first run through this exercise.

Our sample classes (Figure 6.8) make up a simple accounting application. For the purpose of this exercise, we will continue with the ProcessInvoice class.

Step 2: Identify logic for which Web service support is limited

There are functional areas for which industry standard support may be sparse for Web services. This is where you may encounter problems when you want to represent and expose a piece of functionality residing in a traditional component.

The best way to make this determination is to study the documentation of your existing development platform. You will likely discover that some areas of Web services functionality are supported through the use of either non-standard programming extensions, third-party add-ons, or perhaps even not supported at all.

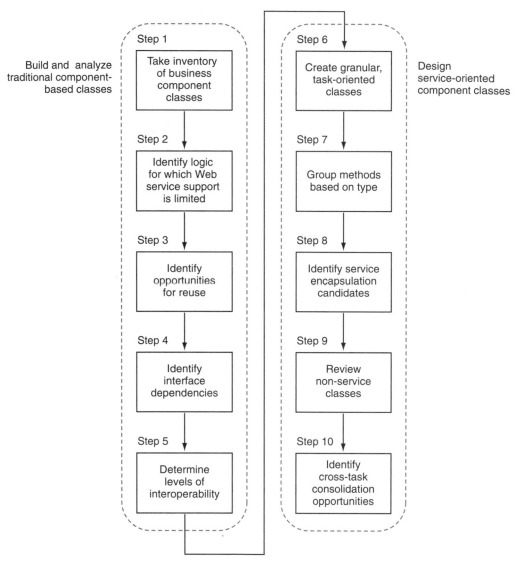

Figure 6.7
An XWIF process for modeling service-oriented components.

Even though this step can be time consuming, it is important to identify these potential limitations early in the process, because they can affect the design of your component classes. Once you've investigated your current development and application hosting platforms for features or extensions related specifically to the nature of the functionality provided by the current component class, you should identify any parts (methods) of that class that are of concern.

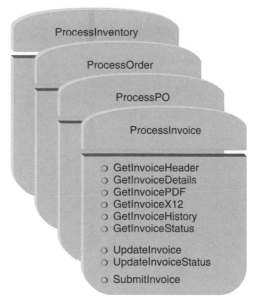

Figure 6.8
The planned set of application classes.

The purpose of this step is not to eliminate functionality, but only to flag pieces of application logic that may or may not end up being difficult to represent within a Web service.

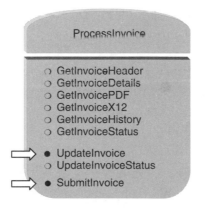

Figure 6.9
Two methods have been identified.

In reviewing our ProcessInvoice class (Figure 6.9), we've identified the UpdateInvoice and SubmitInvoice methods as potentially requiring application logic that may be difficult to encapsulate and express within a Web service. For instance, they may require distributed transaction support but there is no indication that the current development platform will offer this support anytime in the near future.

If functionality provided by a class or a method involves the use of a security model or security-related technology that may be difficult to support by potential service requestors, then that piece of application logic should also be identified. (Again, we are only flagging methods or classes at this stage.)

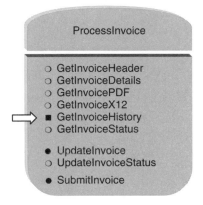

Figure 6.10
The GetInvoiceHistory method is
tagged with a different icon.

In our example (Figure 6.10), only the GetInvoiceHistory method requires a different authentication model than the other class methods.

Step 3: Identify opportunities for reuse

A service-oriented architecture opens the door for new reuse opportunities. Analyze each of the routines within your class methods and try to locate those that may be useful to other parts of your application (or, potentially, to other applications within your organization).

After reviewing the functionality in our class (Figure 6.11), we've determined that the GetInvoicePDF method could be reused by other applications.

Step 4: Identify interface dependencies

Quite often, publicly exposed methods will have internal dependencies. These may consist of one method having to call the other in order to complete its task, or it may be that two or more public methods share the same set of private methods or properties. These types of situations create inter-dependencies that may require the methods to remain in one class (unless they are remodeled).

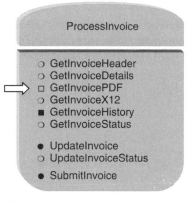

Figure 6.11
A reusable class method is discovered
and labeled.

Review your routines (or pseudo code) in order to identify methods with significant dependencies. Group these methods together in your class diagram.

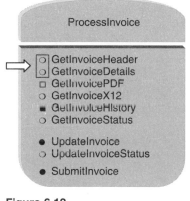

Figure 6.12
An internal dependency between class
methods is highlighted.

Both the GetInvoiceHeader and GetInvoiceDetails methods (Figure 6.12) rely on the same set of private routines. To avoid the deployment of redundant programming logic, it is preferable for these methods to remain in the same class.

Step 5: Determine levels of interoperability
The driving motivation behind introducing any service-oriented principle within an application design is to improve some form of interoperability. For the purpose of this exercise, we are most interested in grouping methods according to the extent to which

they need to share data across internal and/or external boundaries. A method used to exchange data between application services is interoperating at a different level than one that can be accessed by an external requestor.

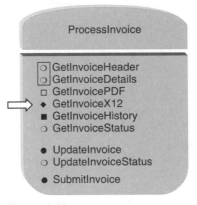

Figure 6.13
A method that will most certainly be involved in an external data interchange is identified.

The GetInvoiceX12 method (Figure 6.13) supplies a version of the invoice document in the X12 EDI format. We've highlighted this method, because it is intended for data exchange with an external system.

Step 6: Create granular, task-oriented classes
A key part of service-oriented business modeling is composing services into logical groups that support a business process. In order to realize the conceptual design of a service-oriented business process, Web services need to be designed in such a way that they can properly implement each step within the process logic. (Chapter 14 explores service-oriented business modeling principles in detail.)

If any of your classes contain a number of methods that collectively perform multiple business tasks, then you should consider grouping them into smaller sized classes, with more focused functionality. Depending on how granular your classes are to begin with, this step may or may not be necessary.

Note that this is not an attempt at changing the way you design components. You will only be subdividing application logic in order to determine which pieces of functionality are potentially suitable for incorporation within Web services. Anything you disassemble here can still be reassembled later.

Our GetInvoice class was fairly coarse in that it provided functions for retrieving, updating, and submitting invoices. As a result, we've split it into three smaller, more task-oriented classes (Figure 6.14).

Figure 6.14
The methods in the original class have been distributed into three smaller classes.

Step 7: Group methods based on type

Depending on how you've categorized methods so far, you may now be able to partition this functionality further into separate, even finer grained classes. To best support the service integration layer, it is often beneficial to introduce more granularity by narrowing the functionality delivered by each overall task.

As a starting point, simply group methods into new classes, based on the icons you used to identify their characteristics.

We've removed three methods from the GetInvoice class into three separate classes, each with its own specialized task (Figure 6.15). Note that the names of these new classes are no longer specific to invoice processing, and we've distinguished them with a different color. The relevance of this will be clarified later in the process.

Step 8: Identify service encapsulation candidates

At this stage, enough information has been gathered to determine which of our new set of classes would be most suited for encapsulation within Web services.

Answering the following questions may help you determine whether classifying a class as a potential service is justified:

- Will other applications ever need to access the functionality provided by the class?
- Can other applications potentially reuse any of the functionality provided by the class?
- Are you seriously considering standardizing on a service-oriented architecture in the foreseeable future?

Without understanding more about the implications of an SOA and related Web services technology, it may be difficult to answer these questions accurately. If you can't, it

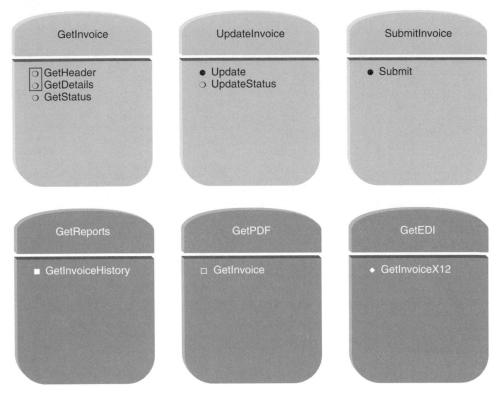

Figure 6.15
Three more classes now represent the original collection of methods.

won't prevent you from completing this exercise, as you are only identifying candidates at this stage. You are not committing to anything more.

Note that just because a class is a candidate, however, does not mean that it is necessarily suitable for use within a Web service. All we have established here is a system for filtering out the parts of your application logic that comply with service-oriented modeling requirements.

We've determined that the GetInvoice, GetReports, GetPDF, and GetEDI classes provide application logic suitable for potential future service encapsulation (Figure 6.16).

Step 9: Review non-service classes
Classes that currently do not seem to qualify as Web service candidates can be consolidated back into a single coarse class, or remain as a set of granular classes.

In our example, we could group the Update, UpdateStatus, and Submit methods back into a coarse class, and revive our original class name of ProcessInvoice. However, we decide to leave it the way it is, since it establishes a consistent level of interface granularity.

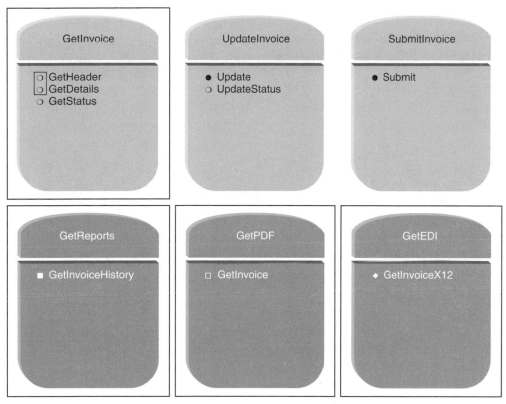

Figure 6.16
Four candidates have been identified.

Step 10: Identify cross-task consolidation opportunities

As you iterate through this process for your remaining application classes, look for methods that have compatible requirements (i.e., equal authentication or interoperability levels) and consider placing these into existing generic classes.

Consolidating similar methods will not always be appropriate. There are a number of factors to take into account, with each new method you consider:

- If any of these methods are not equally generic to the others, then they may be better off in separate classes. This will allow each group of methods to evolve independently.

- There will be a performance impact to loading a larger component into memory, when only a portion of it will be required to complete a given task. In high-volume environments, however, where services are shared at runtime, grouping similar methods will not significantly impact memory requirements (as components are typically cached).

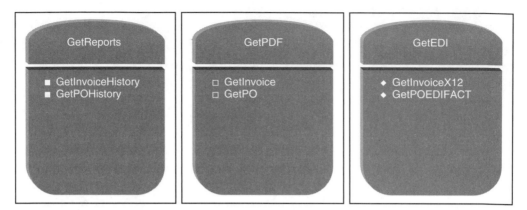

Figure 6.17
Methods have been added to utility service candidates.

After completing the past ten steps for the ProcessPO class, we identified three methods that could be grouped into existing classes (Figure 6.17).

6.2.2 Designing Web service interfaces (a step-by-step XWIF process)

As Web services become more commonplace in your environment, they begin establishing an ever-broadening interoperability framework. Enterprise application logic becomes encapsulated through service interfaces that create endpoints for numerous potential service requestors.

The emergence of these service-oriented architectures evolve into an intrinsic extension to your IT infrastructure. The effort you put into designing Web service interfaces eventually will become a primary factor in determining the quality of this environment and, ultimately, the extent to which your organization can transition towards a service-oriented enterprise.

NOTE
Before you read through the following process description, study the WSDL tutorial in Chapter 3, and reference the best practice, "Design against an interface (not vice versa)," in Chapter 13.

The XWIF process provided here (Figure 6.18) establishes a structured system for analyzing and designing consistent and extensible service interfaces.

Use this process as a starting point for:

- standardizing the manner in which services are modeled
- establishing the criteria used to define service characteristics

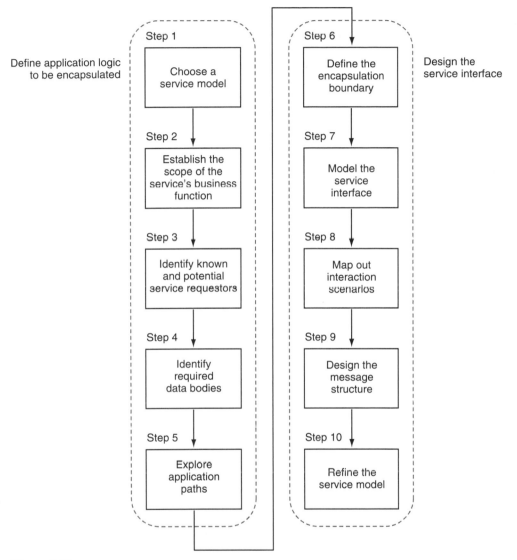

Figure 6.18
An XWIF process for modeling service interfaces.

Also, feel free to customize individual process steps as required.

Step 1: Choose a service model
Identify which model best describes the planned content of your service. The service model classification is important as different models typically have different usage and deployment requirements. From a modeling perspective, this type of classification

provides a functional baseline that communicates the overall purpose of a service. Remember that services can belong to more than one model. For instance, a business service can also be a controller service.

It may be difficult to assess the potential for reuse this early in the design process. If you are building a business service, but believe there is an opportunity for it to be reused by other applications, still classify it as a business service until you know just how generic the functionality will end up being. Services are best classified as utility services, once it has been confirmed that their overall purpose is to be shared and reused.

Reference the following suggested service model descriptions:

- utility services (Chapter 6)
- business services (Chapter 6)
- controller services (Chapter 6)
- proxy services (Chapter 9)
- wrapper services (Chapter 9)
- coordination services for atomic transactions (Chapter 9)
- process services (Chapter 10)
- coordination services for business activities (Chapter 10)

Step 2: Establish the scope of the service's business function

Here's where business and utility services go in separate directions. Accurately defining the function of a service is very significant to the overall quality of a service-oriented environment. A clear distinction between what a service does and does not encompass will allow it to be effectively utilized, shared, and potentially distributed.

More importantly, it will avoid costly redevelopment efforts in the future. Vaguely defined services may have a primary purpose, but supplementary and related functions might creep into the service scope. Such a service may meet immediate requirements, but the day you want to expand your service framework, you will find that you probably need to remove some of the secondary functions from your original service into a new one. Either that, or you will end up with redundant functionality, present in both.

At this stage you should also take into account any technical limitations imposed by your development platform that may affect the functionality planned for your Web service. The extent to which standard Web services specifications are supported may set the boundary within which you can define the business functionality that your Web service is capable of encapsulating.

Step 3: Identify known and potential service requestors

It is common for services initially to be geared toward fulfilling the requirements of a single application. However, it is possible that, at some point, they will be discovered and utilized by other requestors as well. It is therefore important to spend some time speculating as to what types of potential requestors this service may need to interact with.

Take the following types of service requestors into consideration:

- parts of your application that may be encapsulated into services in the future
- other applications that may become service-enabled in the future
- other services that may want to encapsulate your service as part of a service assembly
- external organizations that may be allowed access to the part of your application represented by the service

Supplement this list with details about how you foresee these requestors using your service. It is easy to spend a great deal of time speculating at this point. Limit your effort to realistic scenarios.

Step 4: Identify the required data bodies

Once you've defined the scope of the service's business function, list each set of data that the service will need to access. Separate data bodies managed by the service interface from any pieces of data the service accesses internally.

For instance, a lookup table referenced by a service component to complete the validation of a submitted piece of data based on a business rule, would be listed separately from the parameter data that was originally submitted.

Step 5: Explore application paths

At this point you should have a good understanding of your service's functional scope, as well as what data (existing and new) will be affected and accessed by the service. This step provides you an opportunity to discover alternative methods of interfacing with your application.

When looking at the components your service will need to involve in order to complete its business function, there may be some obvious candidates. It is always useful to explore alternatives to ensure that the path your service will take when navigating through your application is optimal.

If you are building a custom solution from the ground up then you may not need to complete this step. If, however, you are integrating a service within an existing application (perhaps as part of an extension), then evaluating different avenues for completing the service's business function is worthwhile.

For instance, if you've determined that the nature of your data access does not always require the layers of processing imposed by the legacy application interface, then it may make sense to allow a service direct access to data cached by components on the application server.

Step 6: Define the encapsulation boundary

Time to secure the perimeter. Once you know what part of an application your service will interact with, you are essentially defining its physical scope.

The best way to make this determination is to draw all component classes that directly interact with the service in a diagram (Figures 6.19 and 6.20). If possible, establish the sequence in which component classes are called.

Figure 6.19
The utility service boundary encapsulates one
component class.

Step 7: Model the service interface

The most important step in this process is the design of the public service interface. All of the information you've collected so far should give you a good understanding as to the overall function, expected usage, and anticipated requestors of the service.

Use this information, along with any modeling standards you may have, to define a clear, concise, and consistent service interface (Figures 6.21 and 6.22). Remember,

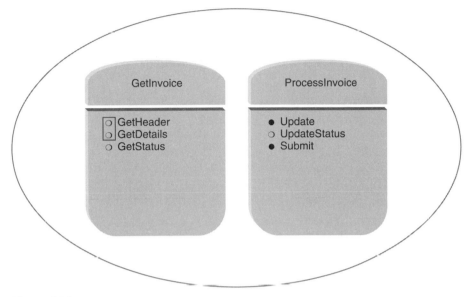

Figure 6.20
The business service boundary encapsulates two component classes.

you are creating more than a programmatic interface, you potentially are defining infrastructure.

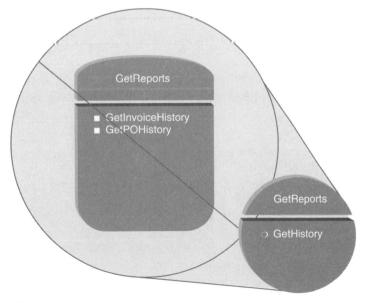

Figure 6.21
A utility service interface evolving out of its encapsulated functionality.

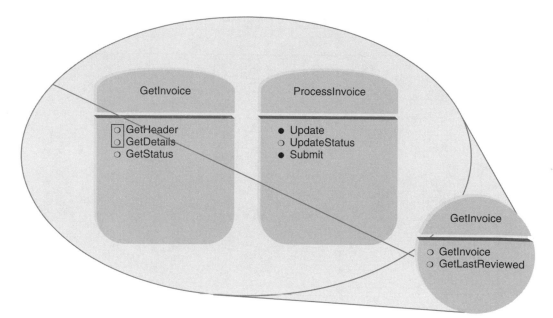

Figure 6.22
A business service interface representing two component classes.

Step 8: Map out interaction scenarios
More often than not, a service will have to manage multiple component (and service) interactions. Depending on how many variations exist within the execution of your service's business task, you may be interacting with different components during each invocation of a service operation.

By mapping out all of the possible interaction scenarios ahead of time you will not only gain a solid understanding of the processing involved with each situation, you will also be creating usage scenarios that easily can become the basis for future test cases (Figures 6.23 and 6.24).

Step 9: Design the message payload
Finally, you will need to model XML documents to represent both incoming and outgoing data delivered by messages sent between the service provider and requestor operations.

Begin with a simple message format for now, and expand it as necessary. Apply the modeling techniques provided in Chapter 5, and read through the section, "Strategies for integrating SOAP messaging," later in this chapter.

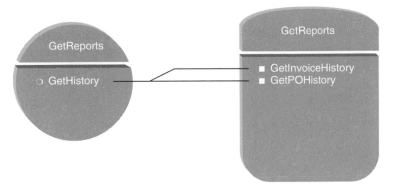

Figure 6.23
Executing the GetHistory operation requires interaction with the GetReports
class' GetInvoiceHistory and GetPOHistory methods.

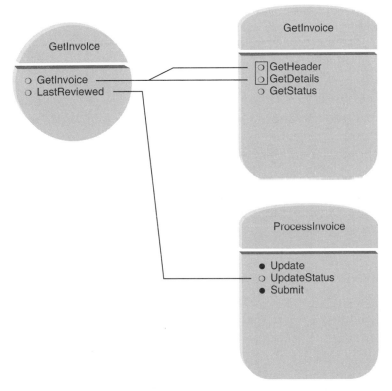

Figure 6.24
The GetInvoice operation interacts only with the GetInvoice class, whereas
the LastReviewed operation interacts with the ProcessInvoice class.

Step 10: Refine the service model

Revisit the list of available service models, and verify that the model you originally chose for your Web service is still accurate. Proceed to the following sections of this chapter:

- Strategies for integrating service-oriented encapsulation
- Strategies for integrating service assemblies
- Strategies for performance optimization

The strategies and guidelines provided in these sections will allow you to refine your service model further. They supply additional opportunities for increasing the sophistication of your Web service by:

- standardizing interface characteristics
- improving performance
- maximizing accessibility
- factoring in assemblies
- covering other common design issues

Finally, visit the section, "Best practices for designing service-oriented environments," in Chapter 13 and incorporate any relevant recommendations. Coupling select strategies and best practices with your new service design will allow you to take advantage of the highly modular and thoroughly analyzed service interfaces you've been building.

6.3 Strategies for integrating service-oriented encapsulation

If you are adding Web services to an already distributed and component-based environment, the idea of object modeling will not be foreign to you. Many of the concepts dealing with how to split up application functionality, business logic, and business rules, apply to functionality encapsulated within Web services as well. The concepts are similar, but the rules are not.

The primary motivation behind integrating Web services is to foster interoperability. To accomplish this, much of the criteria concerning how application functionality is partitioned and represented within a service relates back to its ability to effectively share data.

6.3.1 Define criteria for consistent logic encapsulation and interface granularity

Essentially, this means approaching your interface design the same way each time you model a service. Using a process like the XWIF example provided in the previous section is extremely useful for establishing standard service interface designs. Without such a process, the danger of ending up with a myriad of model designs is quite high. Uncontrolled modeling will eventually lead to a poor enterprise integration architecture.

Note that this does not mean you should be advocating that all Web services be created with the same level of granularity. Based on the service model you choose, and the expected usage and deployment environment your service will be subject to, the appropriate granularity levels may vary. It is just recommended that you apply a standard set of criteria, implemented in a standard process, which allows the service designer to determine the characteristics of the service interface (including its granularity) in a consistent manner.

6.3.2 Establish a standard naming convention

This may seem like a trivial issue at first, but inconsistent interfaces can snowball into a significant problem once you begin building and relying on more services.

For example, let's take an application with a Web service that provides an operation for retrieving an invoice, and another service that contains an operation for retrieving a purchase order. The first operation should not be called GetInvoice if the second is named GetPOInfo, since both operation names should follow the same name structure. If both GetInvoice and GetPOInfo operations exist, it would be easy to assume that the latter provides only meta information about the document.

Make sure you read through the naming convention best practice provided in Chapter 13 for more information.

6.3.3 Parameter-driven vs. operation-oriented interfaces

Depending on how and by whom your Web service will be used, the programmatic interface can be designed in different ways (Figure 6.25). Although not elegant by any means, it is common to see a group of similar functions represented by a series of operations, each identified with a label consisting of the standard verb+noun format used by component methods. This operation-oriented design model provides a naming convention with the benefit of clearly communicating the purpose of an operation at a glance.

An alternative is to streamline this interface by consolidating similar operations and adding one or more parameters to provide context to the operation call. In the next example, for instance, the second version of the Web service's GetInvoice class provides a single operation that accepts a parameter identifying which piece of the invoice information it should retrieve.

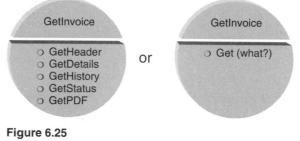

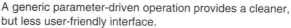

Figure 6.25
A generic parameter-driven operation provides a cleaner,
but less user-friendly interface.

The advantage here is that the interface is highly extensible, because new functions can be added without necessarily impacting the interface.

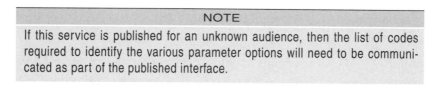

NOTE

If this service is published for an unknown audience, then the list of codes required to identify the various parameter options will need to be communicated as part of the published interface.

6.3.4   Designing for diverse granularity

When designing Web services, a great deal of focus is placed on interface granularity (Figure 6.26). Coarse-grained services that encapsulate more functionality within a single operation can improve overall performance by minimizing service invocations and the associated amount of processing overhead.

Fine-grained services, on the other hand, can establish a more flexible, agile, and responsive service-oriented architecture. Within such an environment, operations are focused solely on detailed business tasks or even subtasks. There are situations where this approach can also improve performance, in that data transport sizes are kept small.

Instead of choosing between design models, you can incorporate both within one service interface (as shown in Figure 6.27). This may create some redundancy, but will establish a model that can facilitate a range of interaction scenarios with diverse requestors.

For example, it can facilitate remote invocations (where coarse operations are preferable), or it can participate in local activities, such as being a child service within an assembly (where fine-grained operations are more suitable).

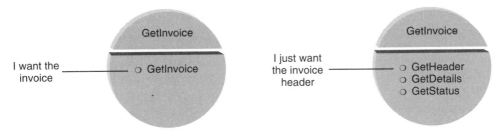

Figure 6.26
Examples of coarse- and fine-grained service interfaces.

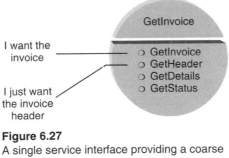

Figure 6.27
A single service interface providing a coarse
operation and several fine-grained operations.

The trade off to this design approach is keeping the operation redundancy in alignment throughout future changes to the service interface. Services of this nature are best maintained under strict modeling standards.

6.3.5 Utilize generic services consistently

Even if you don't use a standard Web service modeling process, it is highly advisable that you incorporate a formal review or approval of service designs in order to identify opportunities for potential reuse. Services that provide some form of generic functionality can greatly optimize an application architecture and increase the overall productivity of application development projects.

This is possible, though, only if redundant pieces of programming logic are abstracted, consolidated, and made available to others. By assigning ownership of utility services to a central resource, that person can be responsible for "catching" reusable functionality by being involved with the review of service designs (prior to development). The Service Library Manager role description in Chapter 13 provides a profile of the responsibilities and prerequisites of this position. Keeping an eye on opportunities for reuse, will allow you to work toward a relatively normalized SOA.

6.3.6   Establish separate standards for internal and external services

I know what you're thinking. Why would you want to have a separate set of standards for internal and external Web services, when, given the potential of an SOA, your internal services could one day become externally accessible? That, of course, makes sense, and if you can apply one set of design standards to all of your Web services, then you are certainly better off. There are, however, some practical considerations you should first take into account. But, before we do, first let's define what we mean by *internal* and *external* services.

Internal services

Service providers containing interfaces accessed by service requestors within an organization boundary are considered internal services. This, however, does not necessarily relate to the end-user demographic of the Web service. An internal service can be invoked indirectly by an external user. For instance, a visitor to your corporate Web site may request a Web resource that, in turn, enlists a Web service to dynamically calculate and deliver some data, which is subsequently rendered on a Web page. The service interface is never exposed to anyone outside of the organization, so it is still considered an internal service.

External services

An external service is one that does make its service interface (along with anything else provided in the service description) available to users, partners, and customers outside of the organization boundary. Third-party utility services available for lease or purchase are classic examples. Types of external service more relevant to enterprise environments are services that enable inter-organization or B2B integration by allowing outside business partners to interface with enterprise applications.

Structuring enterprise standards

Take these common issues into consideration when putting together design standards for enterprise Web services:

- Assuming that design and development standards already exist within your organization, any new standards for internal services should be kept relatively aligned with what you already have. If you've made a decision to begin supporting Web services, and perhaps even move towards an SOA, you will likely not have the freedom to change existing design and development standards.

- The types of external Web service requestors can vary. For instance, some may be anonymous, whereas others may require authentication. Some may require your service for a short time, and others may access it repeatedly. Either way, the general focus on service interfaces designed for external consumption is for them to be highly generic and to provide explicit clarity. This affects both naming conventions and the data manipulation of operation parameters (messages).

- How, and to what extent a Web service will be used, is generally more predictable with internal services deployed and invoked within a controlled environment. Usage volumes of external services (and internal services that can participate in business tasks initiated by external requestors) will often require some guesswork. These types of services, therefore, frequently demand a higher level of built-in scalability in order to establish a comfortable usage range.

- Depending on the nature of your external services, you may be required to register them with a discovery agent, such as a public UDDI registry. This will make the service available for discovery by new potential customers or business partners. Unless an enterprise has amassed a large amount of services, service descriptions for internal Web services can be provided through a manual publishing process, without the need for dynamic discovery.

- Because the user-base of external services is not always known, they are more likely to be supplemented with the option to output user-interface information.[1]

- Because they need to be designed for the unknown, external Web services usually will be outfitted with elaborate validation and exception handling routines.

Another circumstance you may encounter is for a service originally developed as an external service to be identified as being useful for internal usage. In this situation you have two options. You can bring the external service into your internal environment and live with a bit of interface and behavioral inconsistency, or you can add an internal interface to your external service. The latter option may be especially desirable if you find new ways of representing the functionality encapsulated by the service to better facilitate the related internal business processes.

6.3.7   Considering third-party Web services

As the market for reusable Web services opens up, it will become worth checking to see what's out there before building something that may already exist. Just a few words of caution, though. If you find a service you want to buy, make sure that:

- The service was built by a company with a focus on manufacturing shrink-wrapped products. Anybody can register a Web service and make it available to

---

1.   See the section, "Strategies for enhancing service functionality," for more guidelines relating to out-putting user-interface data from Web services.

the general public. Unless it was developed with some form of quality control, and designed with sufficient generic functionality, it will likely not be useful to an enterprise-level application.

- The service is compatible with your environment. An open communications platform is different from an open development platform, and Web services achieve only the former. If you are bringing the service in-house, then it will need to comply to your existing environment. Services hosted by the service merchant should, of course, be accessible to any standard requestor. Providers of externally accessed services also need to meet requirements imposed by second-generation standards, such as WS-Security.

- The service will be reliable. Third-party services accessed via the Internet will need to guarantee the degree of availability and robustness required by your application. Assuming that clients other than your application also will be using the service, it will need to be designed with an optimum level of scalability. Try to get the service provider to sign a Service Level Agreement (SLA) guaranteeing your required level of reliability.

It is worth scanning the market to see what vendors are offering, but be sure you don't spend more time evaluating third-party Web services than it would take to develop your own.

SUMMARY OF KEY POINTS

- How you partition your application logic, and what you end up encapsulating within your services will define the quality of your architecture.

- The scope of Web service interfaces tends to be smaller and more focused than the interfaces exposed by traditional component classes. This increased modularity has many benefits, but also introduces new integration challenges.

- Speculative modeling is an important part of designing a Web service. It allows the service designer to prepare the service for a range of probable interaction scenarios.

6.4 Strategies for integrating service assemblies

The ability to compose multiple (and disparate) Web services is a key, albeit long-term, benefit of moving towards a service-oriented architecture. It is an aspect of service design that can only be effectively realized, however, if you are designing your services with an assembly model in mind.

6.4.1 Everything in moderation, including service assemblies

Being able to reuse and combine a collection of services into unique configurations has an inherent appeal. It's an ambitious modeling principle that can result in sophisticated application designs. It is also, however, a technique that easily can be overused (or misused), to the point where it becomes a detriment.

Here are two primary design considerations.

Dependencies

Service assemblies consisting of too many services introduce too many potential dependencies. With dependencies come limitations and a loss of flexibility.

It is easy to take a step backward when building service assemblies. Without even realizing it, you can take a progressive service-oriented architecture and move it into the rigid realm in which many traditional component-based designs found themselves. Having stated that, though, there is a place for assembled services. The remaining sections explore some of the more appropriate uses of the controller service model and composed assemblies.

Performance

Each Web service will introduce processing overhead associated with the transfer and parsing of SOAP messages. Multiply this by the amount of services in your assembly, involved during a typical execution of a business task. If you're introducing more than two services, you may start running into noticeable performance trade-offs.

Unless your application hosting environment provides a form of process sharing or service caching that can reduce the amount of runtime processing involved between native collections of Web services, you may need to restrict your assemblies to a set level of services.

6.4.2 Modeling service assemblies

Service assemblies are most efficient when participating services are designed to be light and agile. This requires a granular design that results in a tendency to break business tasks down into multiple subtasks, each represented by a separate service, and each relatively independent.

This level of granularity and loose coupling also fits nicely into the overall service-oriented architecture ideal. In the real world, however, this design approach often results in the following dilemma:

- Loosely coupled Web services require more runtime processing in order to achieve the dynamic binding between services and service requestors.
- The granular interface design established by Web services often requires service requestors to make multiple calls to the same service in order to complete a single application function.

Add to this the serialization overhead introduced by SOAP messages, and you could end up with a significant amount of latency, especially in a highly distributed environment.

A common way of addressing these performance concerns is to introduce a layer of coarse controller services that encapsulate specific operations from one or more granular services (see Figure 6.28). This parent service layer then becomes the new contact point for service requestors.

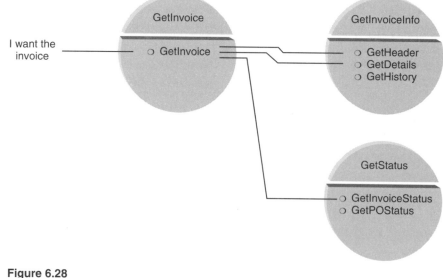

Figure 6.28
With a coarse parent service, the requestor requires only one call to retrieve the invoice.

So, have we solved the problem? Not quite. The remaining issue with this approach is that if all you want is just a piece of the invoice, then using the coarse service returns more information than you actually need (as in Figure 6.29).

The solution is simply to make both parent and granular services accessible to service requestors. This allows the requestor to choose a coarsely or granularly defined operation, as shown in Figure 6.30.

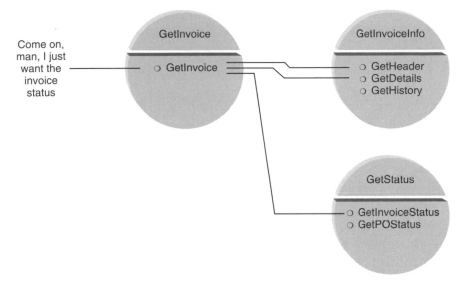

Figure 6.29
A service requestor needing only the invoice status also receives the invoice header and details.

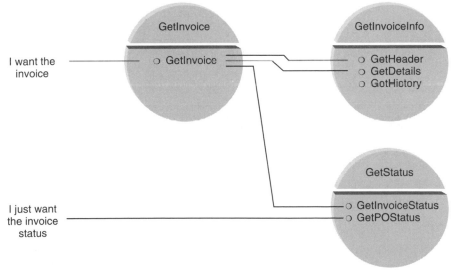

Figure 6.30
Each service requestor receives only the data it needs.

This design approach imposes more maintenance effort in order to keep the parent controller service layers in alignment with the (more granular) child services they represent.

However, the result is a flexible design that preserves service-oriented principles, while improving runtime performance.

Finally, one alternative that should be mentioned is a parameter-driven[2] service operation design that can facilitate both coarse and granular data requests.

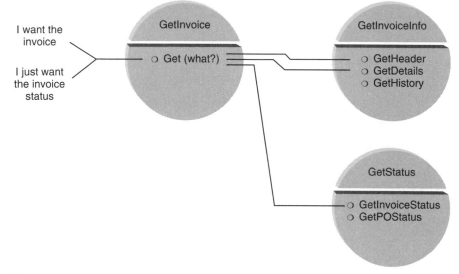

Figure 6.31
An assembly fronted by a parameter-driven controller service interface.

As illustrated in Figure 6.31, this option still forces all service requests to pass through the controller layer. Using a parameter-drive design can be a legitimate approach, especially if the controller is also a process service that needs to maintain control of the involvement of other services.

6.4.3   Compound service assemblies

In the previous section we introduced an approach where a group of Web services (and components) were used to provide different levels of functional granularity for performance reasons.

This concept can be taken further to extend to the encapsulation of entire business functions, within an assembly of Web services. A compound Web service typically is based on a combination of a controller and business service. It provides a coarse interface that delivers business functionality by using a series of services that can be

---

2.   See the "Parameter-driven vs. operation-oriented interfaces" section for more information on this option.

based on disparate (coarse and granular, business and other) models. Figures 6.32 and 6.33 provide some examples.

SUMMARY OF KEY POINTS

- Service assemblies can be useful, but should be carefully utilized to avoid architectural dependencies.

- Different assembly configurations are possible to provide a balance of granular and coarse functionality.

- Performance is a key consideration, due to the inherent processing overhead imposed by any Web service invocation.

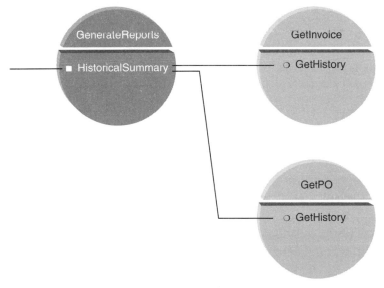

Figure 6.32
A service assembly, where a service enlists services or components from different businesses processes.

6.5 Strategies for enhancing service functionality

6.5.1 Outputting user-interface information

Web services typically are classified as providers of server-side programming logic. They can, however, assist service requestors with the presentation of data, and the overall user experience. External services, especially, may be required to further equip data intended for front-end presentation with user-interface markup.

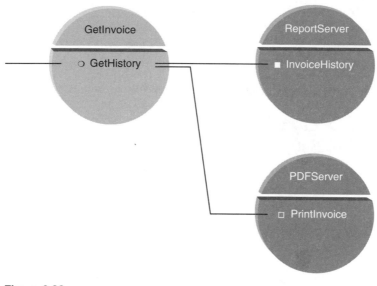

Figure 6.33
A service assembly, where a business service utilizes generic services or
components.

Examples of this include:

- The service possesses a solid understanding of the characteristics and validation
  requirements of the business data it is managing. It can therefore provide requestors
  with an operation or operation parameter that allows them to request a block of HTML
  markup that will accurately represent the data on a standard form. This markup can be
  supplemented with client-side scripts that properly validate form input.
- The service can supply an option that will allow a set of report data to be returned,
  preformatted in an HTML table. This saves the requestor from having to assemble or
  transform the data.
- The user-interface information provided by a Web service can be requested just once,
  at design time by the developer. It can then be embedded into the application to
  spare repeated transfer of the same information. If this becomes common practice,
  then the service provider could even associate a version to the user-interface,
  allowing the requestor to check for updates periodically.

6.5.2   Caching more than textual data

Chapters 9 and 11 discuss integration architectures configured to cache data in various
ways. These architectures are designed to retain commonly accessed pieces of data in

memory to save the processing overhead of repeated requests and retrieval of this information. Most discussions around data caching focus on this aspect, however there is more that you can do with caching.

Here are some examples:

- When working with mixed content, especially if the Web service also is providing user-interface information, caching various binary resources, such as images and even documents, can be an effective way of optimizing performance.
- Caching business rules and formulas can benefit a variety of business functions that rely on the runtime interpretation and processing of data.

6.5.3   Streamlining the service design with usage patterns

Once your application has been up and running for a while, you will be able to analyze how it is being used. Various analysis tools will allow you to derive trends and patterns from your usage logs. This information will then provide you with the opportunity to refine the caching functionality of your Web services in the following ways.

Anticipated caching

Knowing in advance what the user will request, based on common navigation patterns, will allow you to preload the information required for the (typical) subsequent request. This type of preemptive data retrieval can lead to highly responsive service designs.

Process refinement

Deviations or premature exiting from predefined processes can be analyzed and may lead to changes in the default process currently provided by a process service.

Reducing usage errors

Application errors can be captured in event logs, from which common points of error can then be identified. The service can address these problem areas with supplementary information or perhaps a different design altogether to reduce the occurrences of errors.

Usage patterns for service requestors

So far we've discussed usage patterns only within the context of an end-user interacting with our application. This approach to optimization is equally useful when analyzing usage in inter-application scenarios. Utility services used by a wide variety of service requestors can also benefit from a better understanding of how they are being used.

SUMMARY OF KEY POINTS

• Web services can supplement data with user-interface information to ensure proper representation and validation.

• Web service performance can be streamlined through caching techniques.

• Usage patterns can further optimize service designs.

6.6 Strategies for integrating SOAP messaging

Integrating SOAP into what has traditionally been a binary-driven communications environment introduces some unique challenges. This section is dedicated to providing strategies to counter these issues.

NOTE

Chapter 3 provides an introductory tutorial that explains the SOAP language, as well as the SOAP technology platform.

6.6.1   SOAP message performance management

XML documents can be large, but wrapping them in SOAP messages makes them even larger. Being an XML-based language itself, SOAP inherits XML's verbosity, and therefore SOAP messages tend to be much bulkier than their binary counterparts. The additional overhead imposed on message transmissions will demand more bandwidth and additional CPU power to efficiently serialize SOAP messages at runtime.

A way of mitigating this performance impact is simply to make every message count. Especially if your SOAP messages are traveling across the Internet, or perhaps multiple internal server boundaries look for ways to consolidate the content of messages to minimize the amount of roundtrips required for a given business task. This, of course, also relates back to the service design model you are using. Having a coarse layer of compound services, for instance, will facilitate this approach.

6.6.2   SOAP message compression techniques

An effective strategy is required to apply compression properly so that it is truly effective in countering the performance impact of larger sized SOAP messages. Since this approach adds the extra processing steps of compressing and decompressing content, you will need to ensure that you are indeed reducing the amount of runtime processing.

The performance benefits of compressing SOAP messages is related directly to their size. Messages containing larger documents will be processed significantly faster with compression, whereas the performance increase of smaller-sized messages will be negligible, or even non-existent.

If you take a look at the types of messages that tend to be involved in request and response message exchange patterns, you will likely encounter the following:

A request for data, resulting in the following two messages (Figure 6.34):

1. A message from the service requestor to the service provider, containing a command with query parameters.
2. A message from the service to the original service requestor, with a payload of the requested data.

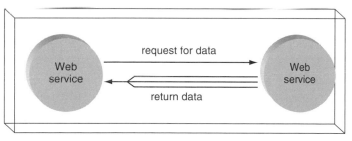

Figure 6.34
The message size for the data request is much smaller than the response message containing the data.

A submission of data, resulting in the following two messages (Figure 6.35):

1. A message from the service requestor to the service provider, containing the submitted data.
2. A message from the destination service to the original service requestor, consisting of a code indicating the success or failure of the data submission.

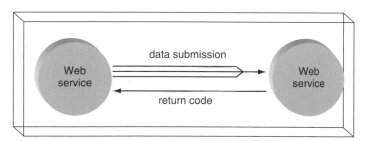

Figure 6.35
The message size for the data submission is much larger than the response message containing a return code.

In either of these scenarios, we have a small and a large SOAP message. This is common with SOAP transmissions, and allows us to create a simple and effective deployment strategy for compression technologies, as shown in Figures 6.36 and 6.37.

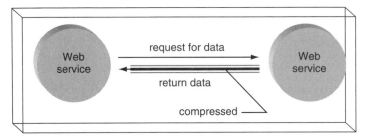

Figure 6.36
Only the response message is compressed.

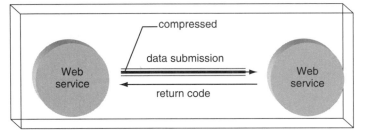

Figure 6.37
Only the data submission message is compressed.

Essentially, only large messages are compressed, meaning that compression will often be utilized one-way, in a two-way SOAP interchange.

6.6.3   Security issues with SOAP messaging

XML opens the door to sharing data, and Web services can open it even further by exposing your business logic to known or unknown users via SOAP messaging. Provided here is some guidance as to where and when you should wedge in that door stop, and gain control over who gets access to what.

SOAP messages are XML documents, and as such, exist as plain ASCII text. Though there are benefits to the simplicity of this format, there are also a number of precautions that need to be taken into consideration when using SOAP as a container for your corporate data.

Following are some of the more common security issues you may need to be aware of:

- Due to its plain text format, SOAP messages are inherently more vulnerable. Serious e-business solutions will almost always encrypt SOAP transmissions, even when the nature of the data does not necessarily require it. The constant encryption and decryption can impact performance, which is especially relevant, given that SOAP already requires more runtime processing than traditional inter-component communication technologies.

- One of the benefits of SOAP is that it, when used via HTTP, can transmit serialized data via port 80 of your firewall. Port 80 is the standard entry point for all Web content, and therefore no additional ports need to be opened to pass through the XML syntax of a SOAP message. The danger here is that the text being delivered by the SOAP envelope may have been altered since its original transmission. You may need a content aware firewall that can actually analyze and verify the integrity of data values within an HTTP stream. This, though, will add yet another layer of processing.

SSL solves most common transport-related security issues by protecting the information used for authentication or identification of the client and server. However, it will not address message-level security. The WS-Security specification deals specifically with message-level security models, including the management of security tokens and the persistence of a security context throughout a service activity.

Before finalizing your security architecture, make sure you understand both the features, and the level of industry support for alternative and supplementary security technologies, such as XML Key Management, XML Encryption, SAML, XACML, XML Digital Signatures, and others. (Read through the section, "WS-Security and the Web services security specifications," in Chapter 4 for more information.)

6.6.4 SOAP data types

If you are unable to work with version 1.2 of the SOAP specification, you'll find that one of the more challenging parts of integrating SOAP messaging is fitting RPC-centric data into SOAP data types. Transporting documents will not be much of an issue, because they will likely be self-contained within the SOAP message body, or as an attachment. (In the case of XML documents, they will be accompanied by schema definitions.)

When your SOAP message transmits commands, however, you may run into some issues. Whatever programming language you used to develop your Web services, you will probably have a much richer set of data types from which to choose. Command information, including parameter data, needs to be slotted into a subset of XSD data types, which may require an adjustment to how the data is represented in the native programming code.

An incompatibility between a programming language's data types and those used by SOAP can cause a number of problems, including:

- inconsistent validation of data

- inconsistent data type boundaries or values

- hard to trace errors

These issues can be resolved by adding more validation code within the Web service routines, to ensure an alignment between native and SOAP data types. Such routines will always need to enforce the lowest common denominator values.

Another approach is to avoid SOAP data types altogether, by using only text elements to host all command data, and to supplement each element with a data type identifier. This will allow the Web service routines to understand the "type context" of a piece of data and assign the appropriate native data type. It is, however, an unconventional approach that may not be conducive to creating generic services for public use.

If supported by your platform, your best alternative is to upgrade to SOAP 1.2, which provides full support for XSD schema data types.

6.6.5   Easing into SOAP

Since this chapter is about integrating Web services, we've focused exclusively on the utilization of SOAP within a service-oriented environment. If you don't have a pressing need to incorporate Web services at this stage, but are interested in exploring the technology behind a SOAP-driven messaging framework, then there is one transition strategy you can consider.

As we've learned so far, SOAP is simply a messaging transport language for XML documents. It does not care whether those documents contain RPC commands for Web services, data retrieved from corporate repositories, or static content for a Web site. The document is simply placed in the SOAP envelope's body, and information related to where it is going and how it will be processed populates the optional envelope header area.

You can upgrade your existing XML architecture by adding a SOAP layer to communication channels used to transport XML documents. Remember, SOAP is just more XML. It can add value by providing a consistent location for routing information, and additional meta information describing the document being transmitted.

This approach has the following benefits:

- It will allow you to accurately assess the impact of the SOAP messaging framework on your current environment.

- It will provide an opportunity for you to measure the performance requirements of the SOAP messaging layer.

- You will get a first-hand look at the SOAP language, and the intricacies of the SOAP message structure.

- You can focus on the integration of service-oriented messaging, without also having to contend with the new technologies and design requirements introduced by Web services.

SUMMARY OF KEY POINTS

- One way to counter the performance impact of larger sized SOAP messages is through the use of compression technologies.

- A SOAP-based messaging architecture will bring with it a number of security challenges. The WS-Security framework and supplementary security standards address these issues.

- Adding SOAP to a non-service-oriented XML architecture allows you to phase into the Web services technology set.

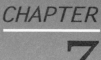

CHAPTER

7

Integrating XML and databases

When talking about XML to DBAs and data analysts in the past, my enthusiasm frequently was greeted with a level of suspicion that often made me feel like I was trying to sell undercoating on a used car. XML's acceptance in the overall IT mainstream has since increased dramatically, because it has become a relatively common part of database environments. Still, there is a significant lack of understanding as to how or why XML can or should integrate with traditional corporate repositories.

One of the obstacles to both conceptualizing and realizing the integration of XML formatted data with traditional databases is simply the fact that XML was not designed with databases in mind. XML's origins lie in document meta tagging, and the XML language was developed to infuse structure and meaning into the vast amount of presentation-oriented content on the Internet.

Now that it has evolved into a core application development technology, it is being used for a variety of sophisticated data representation and transportation purposes. It has found a home in just about every layer of application architecture, except... the relational database tier. Here it fits less comfortably (Figure 7.1).

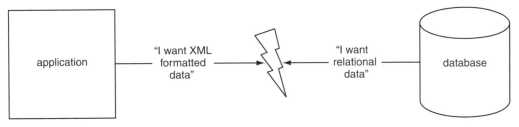

Figure 7.1
Application components and databases have different data format preferences.

XML documents and relational databases represent and structure data in very different ways. This draws an invisible border between the two environments, and getting these data platforms to cooperate efficiently can be as challenging as negotiating a treaty between two very different cultures. And guess what — you're the arbitrator.

7.1 Comparing XML and relational databases

Before creating any sort of data integration strategy, it is important to first understand the fundamental differences between relational databases and the XML technology set,

> **NOTE**
> Though important to designing a robust service-oriented architecture, integrating XML and databases does not require or depend on the presence of Web services. As a result, there is little reference to Web services in this chapter, allowing you to apply the architectures and strategies to environments outside of SOAs.

and their respective relationships to your corporate data. This section covers some of the major areas of data management, and contrasts how they are addressed by each platform.

> **NOTE**
> We are not making this comparison to provide a choice between the two platforms. We are only assessing the features of each to gain an understanding their differences.

7.1.1 Data storage and security

The most basic feature of any data management system is its ability to securely store information. This is where relational databases provide an unparalleled set of features, barely comparable to XML's simple file format (see Table 7.1).

Table 7.1 Data storage and security comparison

	Databases	XML
Physical storage	Highly controlled storage environment.	Plain text.
Security	Proprietary security, or a security system integrated with the operating system. Provides granular control over most aspects of the data and its structure.	No built-in security. Access control is set on a file or folder level, or is managed by the application.

7.1.2 Data representation

XML documents and relational databases approach the representation of data from different ends of the spectrum. XML documents introduce a cohesive, structured hierarchy, whereas RDBMSs provide a more flexible relational model (see Table 7.2).

These two platforms face significant integration challenges because XML document hiearchies are difficult to recreate within relational databases, and relational data models are difficult to represent within XML documents.

Table 7.2   Data representation comparison

	Databases	XML
Data model	Relational data model, consisting of tabular data entities (tables), with rows and columns.	Hierarchical data model, composed of document structures with element and attribute nodes.
Data types	A wide variety of data types typically are provided, including support for binary data.	XSD schemas are equipped with a comparable set of data types.
Data element relationships	Column definitions can interrelate within and between tables, according to DDL rules.	References can be explicitly or intrinsically defined between elements.

Understanding these simple limitations is the most important part of creating an effective integration strategy.

7.1.3   Data integrity and validation

In Table 7.3, we look at how data management systems provided by databases and XML preserve the integrity of the data they represent.

7.1.4   Data querying and indexing

Next, in Table 7.4, is a comparison of generic searching and indexing features.

7.1.5   Additional features

Rounding up this high-level comparison is Table 7.5, providing a list of features found in both database and XML technologies, most of which are exclusive to their respective environment.

SUMMARY OF KEY POINTS

- XML and relational databases are fundamentally incompatible data platforms, created for different purposes.

- The requirement to integrate these two types of technologies stems from XML's popularity in application environments.

- An understanding of how XML documents differ from relational databases is required in order to devise effective integration strategies.

Table 7.3   Data validation comparison

	Databases	XML
Schema	The loose structure of relational schemas provide a great deal of flexibility as to how data entities can exist and interrelate.	XML schemas are more rigid in that they are restricted to an element hierarchy. More sophisticated schema technologies, such as the XML Schema language, provide functionality that can achieve detachment of elements.
Referential integrity	Extensive support is provided to ensure that relationship constraints are enforced. Typical features include the ability to propagate changes in related columns via cascading deletions and updates.	Although references simulate inter-element relationships to an extent, no comparable enforcement of RDBMS-like referential integrity is provided. Additionally, while relational databases enforce referential integrity at the time data is altered, a separate validation step is required by the XML parser.
Supplemental validation	Validation can be further supplemented through the use of triggers and stored procedures.	XSD schemas can be designed to validate elements and attributes according to custom rules. Additional technologies, such as XSLT and Schematron, can be used to further refine the level of validation.

7.2 Integration architectures for XML and relational databases

As you look through each of the upcoming architecture diagrams, it is worth remembering that there is no one standard approach. The many different integration requirements organizations tend to have in this part of the application architecture demand a flexible set of integration models that will vary in design and scope.

If you are already using XML within your application, or if you already have an application design, follow this short process to best assess the suitability of an alternative architecture:

1. Describe the role XML currently plays within your application. Make sure you have a clear understanding as to how and why XML is being utilized.

Table 7.4   Data querying and indexing comparison

	Databases	XML
Query languages	Most commercial RDBMSs support the industry standard SQL. Many add proprietary extensions.	Single XML documents are most commonly queried via the DOM and SAX APIs, or by using XPath expressions. The XML technology most comparable to SQL is XQuery, which provides a comprehensive syntax that also supports cross-document searches.
Query result manipulation	SQL provides a number of output parameters that can group, sort, and further customize the query results.	XSLT and XQuery can be used to manipulate the output of XML formatted data. Both languages can group, sort, and perform complex data manipulation.
Querying across multiple repositories	Several database platforms allow multi-data source queries, as long as each repository supports the protocol used to issue the query.	XPath cannot query multiple XML documents, however XQuery can. XSLT can also query multiple documents (using the document function).
Indexing	Sophisticated indices are supported, customizable to the column level. RDBMS indices can be fine-tuned for optimized querying.	The XML technology set does not support a comparable indexing extension. XML document indices are often created and maintained by custom applications.

2. Pick a primary business task and map the processing steps between the application components. Show how and where XML data is being manipulated and transported.

3. When you reach the database layer, identify how the XML-formatted data currently is being derived, where inserts and updates are required, and how often the same body of data is reused.

4. Review each of the integration architectures in this section, and identify the one closest to your current or planned design.

5. Study the pros, cons, and suitability guidelines to ensure that your current architecture provides the best possible integration design for your application requirements. If it doesn't, consider one of the alternatives.

6. Finally, if no one architecture adequately meets your requirements, pick the one that is the closest, and modify it to whatever extent you need to.

Table 7.5   Comparison of various additional features

	Databases	XML
Transactions	Most databases provide transaction and rollback support, and most support the common ACID[a] properties. Some RDBMSs also come with two-phase commit capabilities, extending transaction support across multiple databases.	The XML platform does not yet provide an industry standard transaction technology (although support for ACID properties is provided through the use of the WS-Coordination and WS-Transaction second-generation Web services specifications).
Multi-user access, record locking	To preserve the integrity of data during concurrent usage, most databases provide a means of controlling access to data while it is being updated. RDBMSs typically support either page-level or row-level record locking, as well as different locking models (e.g., pessimistic, optimistic).	Access to XML documents existing as physical files is essentially file I/O controlled by the application via the XML parser. There are no comparable locking features.
Platform dependence	Relational databases are commercial products that impose a vendor-dependent storage platform. However, data generally can be easily migrated between databases from different vendors.	The family of XML specifications are open industry standards and are not dependent on any commercial platform.
Schema dependence	Schemas are a required part of a database. The schema features are provided by the database software.	Schemas are an optional part of XML documents. If used, one of several available schema technologies can be chosen.
Schema reuse	The schema is bound to the database instance. Schemas can be encapsulated with DDL, but not easily reused without the help of modeling tools.	The schema exists as an independent entity. Multiple documents can use the same schema.
Nesting	Table columns generally do not provide intrinsic nesting.	XML elements can contain nested child elements.

a.   ACID represents the following four standard transaction properties: atomicity, consistency, isolation, and durability.

7.2.1   Storing XML documents as database records

This approach simply places entire XML documents into dedicated database tables, putting the responsibility of validating and processing these documents on the application (Figure 7.2). The new tables are separated from the current data model, and therefore will likely not affect the existing relational data.

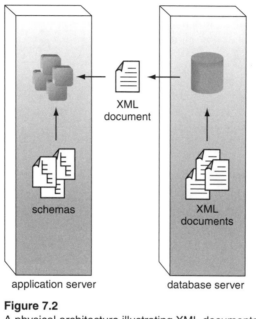

application server   database server

Figure 7.2
A physical architecture illustrating XML documents
being stored and retrieved from a relational database.

Corresponding schemas can be stored (and cached) with the application, and linked dynamically upon retrieval of the document. Alternatively, schemas can be placed in the database with the XML documents, where they can be retrieved together, as illustrated in Figure 7.3.

To accommodate this architecture, schemas and XML documents can be placed in separate tables, united by a simple one-to-many relationship. If a single XML document can link to multiple schemas, then this will require a many-to-many relationship.

If XML document and schema constructs (modules) are supported, then additional tables would need to be added in order to support one-to-many relationships between the tables hosting the master XML documents and schemas, and their respective constructs.

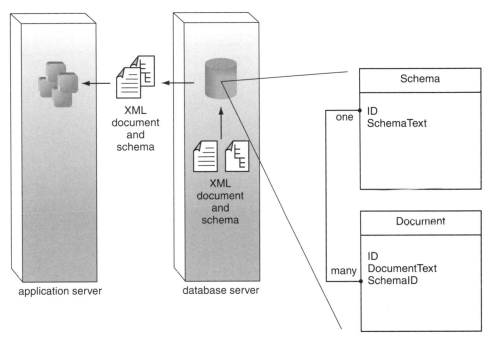

Figure 7.3
A variation of this architecture, where schemas are stored alongside XML documents, within the database.

Also, it is advisable for the primary and foreign key values used by the database to be represented within the document and schema content (perhaps as embedded annotations). This will allow you to efficiently reference the source record of an XML document or schema being processed by the application.

Suitable for:

- Redundant storage of legacy data, preformatted in XML. This would require some method of synchronization, depending on how static the data remains.

- Storing new application data that does not relate to existing legacy data. If there's any chance that this information will need to tie into your existing legacy data, then this may not be such a great idea. However, in situations where you simply want to store complete XML documents that are fully independent of the existing legacy repository, this provides a simple way of adding XML support without having to worry about mapping.

- Storing state information. Session data that needs to be temporarily (or even permanently) persisted fits perfectly into this model. The data may require only a simple database table to store the document within a single column.

Pros:

- XML data is mobile and easily detached. Alternatively, should integration with the existing data model be required, it can still be performed by simply removing the new tables.

- Allows for an easier migration to a native XML database, as these database systems tend to store XML documents in their entirety as well.

- Existing data models will likely not be affected.

Cons:

- Queries against these new tables may be limited to full-text searches, which are notoriously slow.

- Even when using full-text searches, many databases are not XML-aware (cannot distinguish tags from data). This translates into poor search results that require further processing to be useful.

- This design will introduce a level of data modeling disparity.

- If the option to store schemas with XML documents is chosen, more runtime processing will be required to retrieve a single document. (This can be mitigated by introducing an application caching strategy that retrieves the schema periodically.)

7.2.2   Storing XML document constructs as database records

Similar to the previous architecture, this design approach (illustrated in Figure 7.4) also introduces a loosely coupled model that does not affect the existing legacy data. The difference is that here an XML document is divided into logical constructs (decomposed into smaller XML chunks), each of which is stored independently.

To accommodate this architecture, schemas can be divided into multiple granular schemas. These schema modules can also be assembled dynamically into a composite schema instance that matches the structure of the generated XML document (as shown in Figure 7.5). For more information about modular schema design, see the "Building modular and extensible XSD schemas" section in Chapter 5.

Suitable for:

- Object-based or class-based application interfaces.

- New application data requiring flexible document structures that are determined at runtime. This type of requirement typically is encountered when supporting parameter-driven business rules.

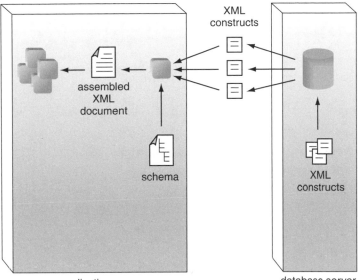

Figure 7.4
A physical architecture where XML constructs are stored independently in a
relational database, and then assembled into a complete XML document at
runtime by the application.

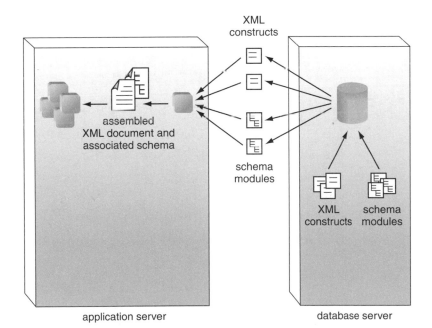

Figure 7.5
Schema modules are stored and assembled alongside XML document
constructs in the database.

Pros:

- Establishes a highly reusable data platform.
- Existing data model likely will not be impacted.

Cons:

- Introduces a potentially complex data model extension, and places the burden of document assembly on the application.
- Can complicate validation, as creating and maintaining schemas for all possible construct combinations may become an unwieldy task.
- All of the cons listed under the previous section.

7.2.3   Using XML to represent a view of database queries

This model allows for dynamically created views of database queries, represented as XML documents. The resulting architecture (shown in Figure 7.6) is most common when working with the proprietary XML extensions provided by database vendors.

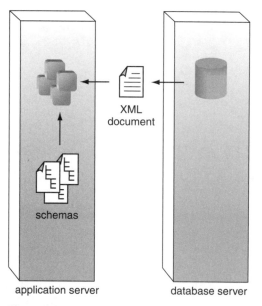

Figure 7.6
In this physical architecture, the requested data is returned in the format of an XML document by the database.

Suitable for:

- Dynamically created XML documents with a limited lifespan. In other words, for when XML is used as a transport format for legacy data.

- XML documents auto-generated by proprietary database extensions. Most database vendors provide a way of outputting legacy data into an XML format.

- Lookup tables and static data retrieved and stored in memory at runtime, by the application.

Pros:

- If using proprietary database extensions, this architecture is relatively easy to implement.

- Does not affect existing legacy data model.

Cons:

- When using proprietary database extensions, the degree to which this output format can be utilized is limited to the features of the database product. Some databases output unrefined (and sometimes cryptic) XML markup. These documents often require further processing and filtering by the application. (See the "Database extensions" section later in this chapter for more information.)

- Proprietary database extensions tie you to a database platform, and much of XML's mobility is lost.

7.2.4   Using XML to represent a view of a relational data model

In this architecture, XML documents are modeled to accurately represent portions of the legacy data model (see Figure 7.7). This approach requires the most up-front design work to properly map relational data structures to XML's hierarchical format.

Suitable for:

- Applications requiring an accurate representation of select relational data entities.

- Applications that need to perform granular updates of legacy data hosted in XML documents.

Pros:

- Establishes a highly flexible and mobile data transport mechanism that accompanies data with a self-contained data model.

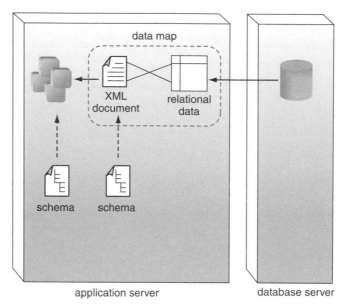

Figure 7.7
A physical architecture illustrating the use of a data map to represent relational data within an XML document.

- RDBMS-comparable support for inserts and updates.
- Focus on XML parsing provides a comprehensive abstraction of RDBMS data access.

Cons:

- Complex to design and maintain.
- Sophisticated approach, but still does not remove the need to perform queries against the database.

7.2.5 Using XML to represent relational data within an in-memory database (IMDB)

XML actually can be utilized to increase application performance by caching relational data on the application server. This architecture can be combined with others, depending on how you want to represent and map the relational data bodies to XML documents, and whether you need to preserve inter-table relationships.

Once you've defined how XML is to represent your data, you can have a utility component retrieve the information once, upon the start of an application, or periodically, based on preset refresh intervals. As explained in Figure 7.8, this component can then parse and load XML documents into a globally accessible memory space.

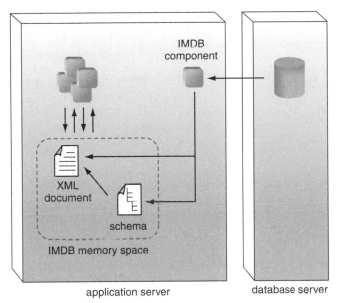

application server   database server

Figure 7.8
A physical architecture in which XML data is cached in memory.

Suitable for:

- Applications with high-usage volumes.
- Relatively static data, such as lookup tables.

Pros:

- Shifts processing load from database to application server, which can dramatically increase performance.
- Cost-effective method of scaling an application (memory is cheaper than database licenses).

Cons:

- May introduce vertical scaling requirements.
- Although faster, the overall architecture is less robust (memory space is more volatile and environmentally sensitive than a hard drive).

7.3 Strategies for integrating XML with relational databases

Section 7.4 is dedicated to data mapping, and provides numerous techniques for overcoming the inherent differences between XML and relational data models. Before you

SUMMARY OF KEY POINTS (Section 7.2)

- There is no one standard integration architecture for XML and relational databases.

- Architectures often will need to be designed around the features and limitations of the proprietary database platform.

- The storage of XML documents may vary from the storage of schemas. Sometimes XML documents are auto-generated, and need to be linked dynamically to existing schema files.

delve into the mysterious world of data maps, relationship pointers, and relational hierarchies, here are more high-level integration strategies to keep in mind.

7.3.1   Target only the data you need

There is one simple design principle that you should take to heart: Whenever possible, restrict application data to the context of the current business task. In other words, only encapsulate the pieces of data and the parts of the data model relevant to the immediate application function.

There are two reasons this one design point is important:

Performance

Keeping the data model on the XML side of your architecture lean is a crucial step to designing performance optimization into your application. It is very easy simply to take the results of a query and stuff them into a generic or dynamically generated document structure, especially when working with database extensions that already do this for you.

Designing XML documents to represent too much data is a surprisingly common pitfall, which almost always results in eventual performance challenges. It's more effort to discern the parts of data you really need from those that can be discarded. The time you invest in order to put together a proper document model design up-front is nothing compared to the effort required to redesign and re-implement a new document model once the application has been deployed. (See Chapter 5 for many XML document modeling guidelines and standards.)

Task-oriented data representation

Your legacy repository may not have been designed to accommodate your current or future application tasks. Each task performed by an application represents a business function that involves a subset of your corporate data within a unique context.

By the mere fact that your application architecture is already XML-enabled, you have the opportunity to model your documents so that they can best represent only the data relevant to the business task at hand. This means that you can custom-tailor your data representation (while still preserving its validation and relational rules) to establish a data view that relates to the requirements of the application function currently being executed.

This moves into the area of object- or class-based data mapping, but we'll call it task-oriented data representation for now. All that I recommend is that you present the data in such a way that it can easily be consumed and processed by the application, while also being associated with a business task.

Task-oriented data representation also can improve application maintenance. Since your data is uniquely identified with a specific business task, it can be more easily traced and logged.

7.3.2 Avoiding relationships by creating specialized data views

If you are repeatedly working with the same sets of legacy data, you can save a great deal of integration effort by pre-consolidating this information into a database view. Instead of having to map to, extract, and assemble multiple tables every time, you can simply map the one view of data to one or more XML documents.

Additionally, if your database provides XML support, and your column names are self-descriptive, you can have the database auto-generate relatively optimized XML markup, on demand.

Finally, you can supplement this approach by creating XSD schemas or DTDs in support of each view. Do this, however, only if you are certain that the views are fairly permanent. Also, note that views are often read-only. In this case, view-derived documents would not be suitable for updates and inserts, as your data will not be accompanied by the necessary data model rules.

7.3.3 Create XML-friendly database models

If you are in a position to build a brand new database, you can take a number of steps to streamline the integration process with XML documents. Here are some suggestions.

Avoid granular tables and relationships
This isn't to suggest that you should compromise the integrity of your data model, but if you do have the choice between creating a series of larger tables and a multitude of smaller joined tables, you will save yourself a great deal of mapping effort by cutting down on inter-table relationships.

Support preformatted XML views
Consider adding tables to store for XML documents representing redundant views of static legacy data. Your database may provide support for automatically generating and synchronizing these views, via the use of stored procedures, triggers, or other extensions.

Consider descriptive column names
If you will be using proprietary XML extensions provided by your database, you may be subjected to auto-generated XML documents based entirely on your existing DDL syntax. By having self-descriptive column names, you will end up with more self-descriptive XML documents. Consider this only if you actually need your XML documents to contain descriptive element-type names. Read through the section, "Naming element-types: performance vs. legibility," in Chapter 5 to learn more about the implications of using self-descriptive element-types.

Avoid composite keys
If you will be mapping your data to DTDs, avoid composite keys. For the purpose of mapping relationships within XML documents, it is preferable to uniquely identify a record by adding a primary key rather than by defining a key based on a combination of multiple column values. If you are working with XSD schemas, however, recreating composite keys will be less of an issue.

7.3.4   Extending the schema model with annotations

Regardless of the schema technology you end up using, a hierarchical data representation can only reflect the complexities of a relational data model to a certain extent. You often will find yourself compensating for gaps by writing application routines that supplement the schema validation with custom data rules and processing.

A classic example is the enforcement of referential integrity. A relational database will typically allow you to propagate and cascade updates or deletions to column values involved in a relationship. Deleting an invoice record, for instance, automatically will delete all associated invoice detail records.

Even though this type of rule enforcement will need to be processed by the application, it is often preferable for these rules to still exist within the schema file itself, as opposed to residing independently in application components. This is where schema annotations are very useful.

By creating a standard set of codes to represent common processing rules, you can embed processing statements as comments or annotations within each schema file. Especially when using the `appinfo` element in XSD schemas, these annotations are easily parsed, retrieved, and processed by the application at runtime. (For more information on annotating XSD schemas, refer to the "Supplementing XSD schema validation" section in Chapter 5.)

7.3.5   Non-XML data models in XML schemas

Continuing from the previous section, let's take this technique a step further. If your application environment consists of a mixture of data formats, you could place validation rules and processing instructions within your schema annotation that apply to non-XML formatted data. In this case, a schema would typically be related to a business task, and could then encompass the validation rules of any data involved in the execution of that task, regardless of format.

By centralizing all data-related rules into one file, you retain the mobility and extensibility of the XML application model. By creating standards around the code syntax, you also establish a loosely coupled relationship between the application and your data model.

7.3.6   Developing a caching strategy

Retrieving and composing XML documents at runtime can be a processor-intensive task, especially if you need to perform some form of dynamic linking. To minimize the amount of times a particular body of application data is generated this way, develop a caching strategy to hold an XML document in memory as long as possible.

The in-memory database architecture (as illustrated in the "Using XML to represent relational data within an in-memory database (IMDB)" section) demonstrates the performance benefits of caching legacy data on the application server within XML documents. XML data is very well suited for storage in memory, and even if you don't build a formal architecture around the use of an IMDB, you should consider developing a strategy for caching documents (or perhaps constructs) whenever possible.

Suitable types of data include:

- static report data
- lookup tables
- state and session information
- application configuration parameters
- processing instructions and validation rules

...and pretty much any other piece of (relatively static) information that will need to be accessed throughout the lifetime of an application instance. Note that security requirements and memory limitations may restrict the type and amount of data you can place in memory.

7.3.7   Querying the XSD schema

When working with XSD schemas, the data model established by the schema is open to be queried and parsed, as any other XML document. This gives developers a standard API into the structure, constraints, and validation characteristics of any piece XML formatted data (see Figure 7.9).

By querying schema files at runtime, applications can dynamically retrieve the data model. This facilitates the development of highly intelligent and adaptive application components that can respond to changes in auto-generated schema files.

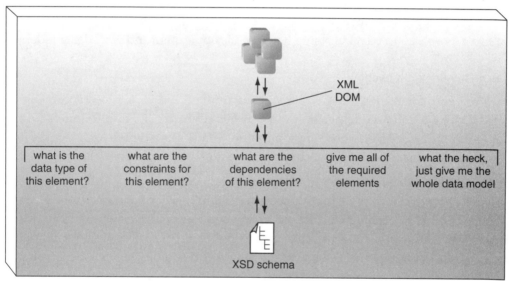

Figure 7.9
Application components can query the XSD schema file as they would any other XML document.

> **NOTE**
> If you have an XML processing library that supports a schema object model, you can also interface with an XSD schema programmatically. This would allow you to modify or even generate schema data models dynamically.

7.3.8   Control XML output with XSLT

One of the limitations of any hierarchy is that the order in which items are structured is generally fixed. If you are mapping table columns to elements or attributes within your

XML document, you may be limited to the sequence in which these elements or attributes are declared within your schema.

XSLT can provide a convenient way to:

- alter the document structure
- change the sorting order (as in Figure 7.10)
- introduce a series of logical element groups

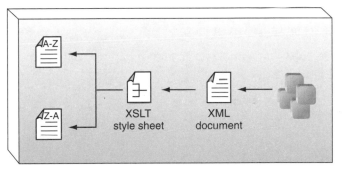

Figure 7.10
The structure of an XML document is transformed to represent different sort orders.

By dynamically creating structure-oriented XSLT style sheets and associating them with your newly populated XML documents, you can build a flexible data manipulation system that can accommodate a number of different output formats from the same data source.

7.3.9 Integrate XML with query limitations in mind

It's no secret that querying XML documents can be a slow and inefficient means of data retrieval. Where RDBMSs have indices they can utilize for nearly instant access to key pieces of data, XML parsers are forced to iterate through the document nodes in order to locate the requested information.

It is therefore preferable to have the database do as much of the querying prior to subsequent application processing of the data. If you are considering preserving relationships and other aspects of your relational data within XML documents, then try to incorporate specialized views that pre-query the data you want to represent.

If you are unsure of how data will be queried once it is returned to the application, try to model your XML documents into granular sections that can be searched faster.

7.3.10 Is a text file a legitimate repository?

After establishing the limitations of XML documents as a storage medium for corporate data, is there a point in ever considering XML documents as a valid repository? The answer is "yes, but only to a limited extent."

XML never aspired to replace the data storage capabilities of traditional databases. When XML was originally conceived, it was intended to host document-centric Web content in a structured manner, supplemented by descriptive and contextual meta information. Within an application architecture, its strength is providing a highly flexible and mobile data representation technology that can be applied in many different ways throughout a technical environment.

There are a number of situations when it may be appropriate to persist XML documents as physical files, including:

- static report data
- lookup tables
- state and session information
- application configuration parameters
- processing instructions and validation rules

If this list looks familiar, it's because it's identical to the list of data recommended for use with an IMDB. Although you may not necessarily need to load all of the data kept in physical XML documents into memory (or vice versa), the general rules apply for each approach, because your data is being hosted on the application server either way.

One additional item that can be added to this list is a configuration file in support of IMDBs, in which refresh-and-upload intervals are stored.

7.3.11 Loose coupling and developer skill sets

One of the often-overlooked benefits of abstracting data access from the database to XML is that developers no longer need to concern themselves (as much) with vendor-specific data access technology.

Once you've built an integration architecture that accomplishes a high level of independence from platform-specific technologies, you will create an environment where developers can concentrate on the management and manipulation of data with only the XML technology set. Web services can play a key role in achieving this level of platform detachment. (Read Chapter 9 for more information.)

> **SUMMARY OF KEY POINTS**
>
> • Performance is, as always, an important consideration when integrating and modeling XML data representation. Caching is a key strategy to overcoming potential bottlenecks.
>
> • Since relational databases are typically an established part of a legacy application environment, most of the integration focus is on designing XML documents around the existing relational data model. Relational databases, however, can also be "adjusted" to contribute to an improved integration.

7.4 Techniques for mapping XML to relational data

Perhaps the most challenging and awkward part of integrating relational databases with XML documents is trying to recreate relationships between database tables within the hierarchical model of XML documents.

Especially when trying to integrate complex and extensive data models, it will often feel like you're forcing a round peg into a square hole (many times over). Well, life isn't always easy, and integration projects are no exception. The point — there's a hole, there's a peg, let's grab that hammer and deal with it.

7.4.1 Mapping XML documents to relational data

To integrate a relational data model with XML, some form of data map generally will be required. This map will associate the relevant parts of your legacy data model with the corresponding parts of your XML schema.

There are several tools that can assist this process, some of which even auto-generate the XML schema files for you. You will find, however, that more often than not, an accurate mapping requires hands-on attention and manual changes to the schema markup.

There are several approaches to mapping data, depending on the nature of your data model and the design of your application components. Here are some guidelines for devising a mapping strategy.

Table-based mapping
Mapping tables to parent elements within XML documents is the most common approach. Depending on the nature of the data, columns can be represented as child elements or attributes to the parent record elements.

Template-based mapping
This is a popular alternative, supported by several middleware products. The design provides an effective means of generating XML formatted data, by embedding SQL statements in "hollowed" XML document templates. These statements

then are processed by the product at runtime, the database is queried, and the document is populated dynamically.

Class-based mapping

A less frequently used approach, class- or object-based mapping may become more common once Web services establish themselves as a standard part of application architecture. The format of a class-based XML document allows data to be mapped according to class objects and their attributes or method parameters.

7.4.2 The Bear Sightings application

Throughout section 7.4 we will be referencing a simple data model (Figure 7.11) for an application used to keep track of bears that roam into mining camps in the Yukon. This is a common problem with placer mines located in remote areas of the wilderness, and the information gathered by such an application can assist in broadcasting alerts to camp sites, especially if bears exhibiting dangerous behavior are encountered.

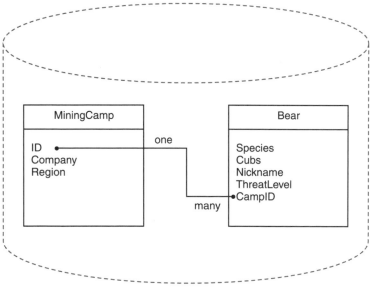

Bear Sightings Database

Figure 7.11
The application data model of the Bear Sightings database consists of two simple, related tables.

7.4.3 Intrinsic one-to-one and one-to-many relationships with XML

The hierarchical XML document structure provides natural one-to-one and one-to-many relationships, where single or multiple instances of a child element can be nested within one parent element. As long as the child element requires only a single parent element, you need to do nothing more than define this parent-child hierarchy as you would any other.

Any schema you use should be able to easily enforce a one-to-one relationship. DTDs enable this via the "?" symbol (or the absence of a symbol) within the element declaration, and XSD schemas use the maxOccurs attribute.

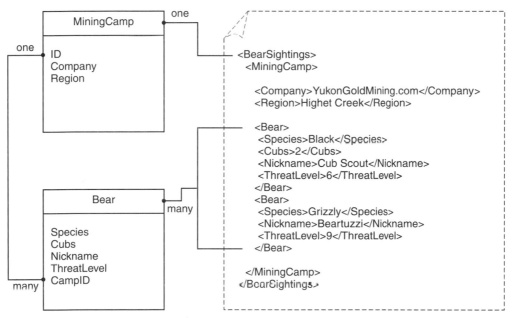

Figure 7.12
An intrinsic one-to-many relationship established within an element-centric XML document instance.

The example in Figure 7.12 illustrates an element-centric one-to-many relationship, where table columns are represented as child elements. Columns of the MiningCamp table are mapped to child elements of the MiningCamp element, and columns of the Bear table are mapped to child elements of the Bear element. Figure 7.13 shows the same data represented in an attribute-centric model.

The point at which this intrinsic relationship becomes insufficient is when you need to represent a child element that requires more than one parent element in the same document. That's when it's time to roll up your sleeves and delve into the world of DTD or XSD schema pointers. The following two sections will show you how.

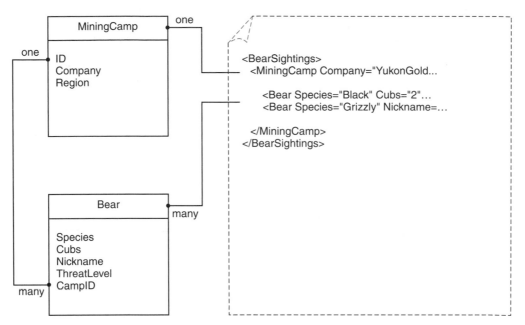

Figure 7.13
An intrinsic one-to-many relationship established within an attribute-centric XML document instance.

7.4.4 Mapping XML to relational data with DTDs

Provided here are techniques to accomplish rudimentary relational functionality within DTDs.

> **NOTE**
> XSD schemas provide more advanced relationship mapping features, as described in the "Mapping XML to relational data with XSD schemas" section.

Basic table mapping with DTDs

Put simply, you can map tables to individual DTDs, or group tables logically into one DTD. A deciding factor is whether or not you also intend to represent relationships between tables. If you do, all tables involved in a relationship will need to be contained within one DTD schema.

As the next few sections thoroughly explore, DTDs generally rely on a series of attributes that simulate pointers, and those pointers apply only within the boundary of an XML document.

Let's begin by revisiting our previous data model, and associating it with a basic DTD.

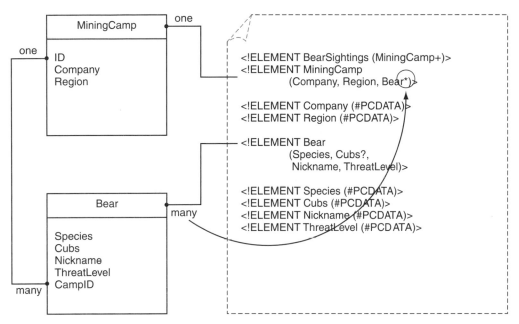

Figure 7.14
A DTD containing a parent element for each table.

As the example in Figure 7.14 demonstrates, the one-to-many relationship is established by the nesting of the `Bear` element. The asterisk symbol in the `MiningCamp` element is used to enable multiple occurrences of the `Bear` child element.

> **NOTE**
>
> If you are not mapping relationships, you have the flexibility to control the granularity of your DTDs and their corresponding XML documents. This will allow you to accommodate application performance requirements. High data volumes and complex document structures can justify distributing a relational model across multiple document types.

Data type restrictions with DTDs

A significant limitation to representing a relational data model within a DTD is the inability of DTD schemas to type data properly. The DTD language supports only four types of data: ANY, EMPTY, PCDATA, and element-only content.

Most of the time you will find yourself lumping your database columns into elements that are of type PCDATA. This places the burden of figuring out the nature of your data on the application.

One method of countering this limitation is to annotate the DTD with data type information for each element. Alternatively, you can add custom attributes to elements that identify the native database data types, as demonstrated here.

```
<ThreatLevel DataType="integer">9</ThreatLevel>
```

Example 7.1   An element instance with a custom attribute identifying the original data type

The problem with these types of workarounds is that they introduce a non-standard solution to a common problem. Outside of applications that are aware of the purpose behind the custom attributes, this solution is not useful.

Null restrictions with DTDs

DTDs have no concept of null values, which can turn into another challenge when wanting to accurately represent the data values found in databases. Since at least some of your database tables will likely allow and contain null values, you need to establish a way of expressing them within your DTD schemas.

Here are some suggestions:

- Nulls can be represented by an absence of a child element or attribute. Essentially, if the element or attribute is present and empty, it is displaying an empty value. If the element or attribute is not included in an instance of the parent element, then that indicates a null value.

- The value of null can be represented by a keyword. You can create a standard code, say "NULL," that your application can look for and interpret as a null value, as shown in this example.

```
<ThreatLevel>NULL</ThreatLevel>
```

Example 7.2   An element instance indicating a null value through the use of a pre-assigned code

As with using custom attributes to represent non-DTD supported data types, these solutions are non-standard. If your application will need to interoperate with others, the implemented method of null value management will not be evident, and may very well be ignored.

Representing relational tables with DTDs

Using the ID, IDREF, and IDREFS attributes provided by the XML specification (and further explained in subsequent sections), DTDs can define and enforce the uniqueness of an element, as well as constraints between elements.

If database tables are represented as separate XML constructs within an XML document, DTDs can simulate basic inter-table relationships, as well as the use of primary and foreign keys. When using DTDs for this purpose, however, you are restricted to representing database tables involved in relationships within one XML document.

> **NOTE**
>
> In order to achieve cross-document relationships you may need to consider using XLink and XPointer. With these supplementary technologies, the ID attribute can still be used to identify the element being referenced.

Primary keys with DTDs

The XML specification provides the ID attribute to allow unique identifiers to be assigned to XML elements. This can be useful to the application parsing the XML document, because it can search for and identify elements based on this value.

In the following example, we declare an attribute of type ID and also call it "id" (we could just as easily call it "ReferenceID" or "MiningCampID").

```
<!ELEMENT MiningCamp (Company, Region, Bear*)>
<!ATTLIST MiningCamp id ID #REQUIRED>
```

Example 7.3   An element type declaration with an ID attribute

For the purpose of establishing relationships, the ID attribute can simulate a primary key for an element construct that represents a database table.

There are two major limitations when using the ID attribute:

- The attribute value cannot begin with a number. Since database tables frequently use incrementing numeric values for keyed columns, you will often need to programmatically modify this data before placing it into the ID attribute.
- ID values need to be unique within the entire XML document, regardless of element type. Since you are restricted to representing all the tables involved in a relationship within the scope of one XML document, you may run into ID value collisions. (Incidentally, this makes the ID attribute useful as an element index value.)

The easiest way to solve both of these issues is to prefix your key values with a code that relates the ID value to its associated table.

For instance, imagine you are representing both Invoice and PO tables within one document. In your database, each table's primary key is a column called "Number," which uniquely identifies a record. An Invoice record that has a Number value of 1001 and a

PO record that also has a Number value of 1001 are legitimate within a database, however they are not within a DTD-validated XML document.

To incorporate Invoice and PO Number keys as ID attributes within an XML document, these values could instead be represented as "INV1001" and "PO1001." This is obviously not an accurate representation of table data, but it does achieve the functionality required to simulate primary keys (to an extent).

For the purpose of our example, we are prefixing the MiningCamp table's numeric ID values with the word "Camp." Our sample mining camp therefore has an ID value of "Camp1."

```
<MiningCamp ID="Camp1">
```

Example 7.4   A primary key represented by the ID attribute

Foreign keys with DTDs

The XML specification enables cross-element referencing of the ID attribute by providing the IDREF and IDREFS attributes. An element can assign the ID value of another element to its IDREF attribute, thereby establishing a relationship between the two, similar to the relationship between a primary key and a foreign key within a database.

```
<!ELEMENT Bear (Species, Cubs?, Nickname, ThreatLevel)>
<!ATTLIST Bear CampID IDREF #REQUIRED>
```

Example 7.5   An element type declaration containing a foreign key reference

The IDREFS attribute is identical to IDREF, except that it allows you to reference multiple ID values. One element, therefore, can have references to multiple others.

Since XML documents typically represent a portion of a database's relational model, they will often evolve. If the scope of your application grows, you may find your DTD expanding as well, as it needs to represent more relationship information. You can therefore use the IDREFS attribute, even if you are referencing only one value initially. This way you can add references as required without changing the original element definition.

> **NOTE**
>
> The XML schema language also supports attributes of type IDREF and IDREFS. However, since XSD schemas introduce more sophisticated ways of establishing relationships between elements, these attributes are rarely used. The subsequent section in this chapter is dedicated to relationship mapping with XSD schemas.

Relationships with DTDs

The pointing mechanism established in the previous sections (using the ID, IDREF, and IDREFS attributes) provides you with the ability to set up a series of sequential element constructs within a DTD. This allows you to identify how these elements relate, and enables you to simulate various database table relationships. All of this can lead to the creation of a relatively normalized DTD schema.

The intrinsic one-to-many relationship illustrated in the "Intrinsic one-to-one and one-to-many relationships with XML" section can be recreated using DTD pointers, as illustrated in Figures 7.15 and 7.16.

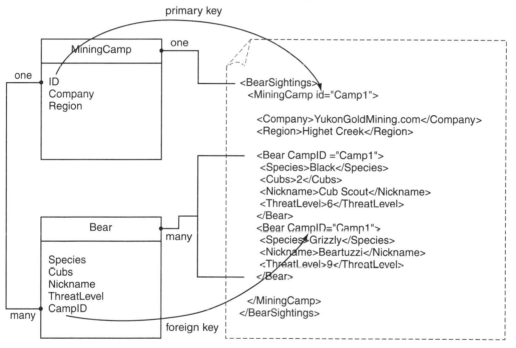

Figure 7.15
A one-to-many relationship using ID and IDREF.

This example may be interesting, but it's not really that useful. We have not gained anything over representing the one-to-many relationship without the use of pointers. The real power of DTD pointers is realized when you have a set of child elements that are required to relate to multiple parent elements.

In the example provided in Figure 7.17 the Bear elements are not explicitly nested within the parent MiningCamp element. Instead, they exist as separate constructs and

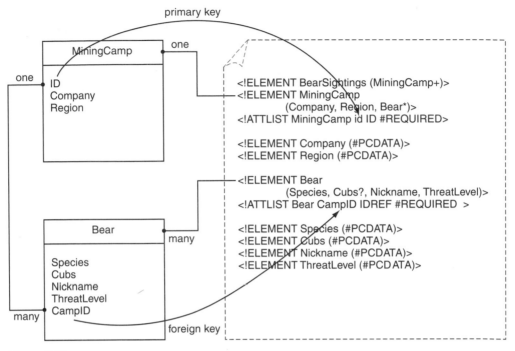

Figure 7.16
A DTD establishing ID and IDREF attributes.

reference the corresponding ID attribute (the primary key of the MiningCamp table), using their own IDREF attribute (which acts as the foreign key of the Bear table). Figure 7.18 provides the corresponding DTD.

When defining a one-to-one relationship, ensure that the declaration syntax allows a maximum of one instance of the child element within the parent element construct. This is accomplished by using the "?" symbol in the declaration statement, as shown here.

```
<!ELEMENT Bear (Cubs?)>
```

Example 7.6   An element type declaration restricting a child element to zero or one occurrence

Alternatively, you can also establish a one-to-one relationship by embedding the column values of the database record into the element as a series of attributes.

Referential integrity restrictions within DTDs
When using IDREF and IDREFS, a DTD cannot enforce an erroneous occurrence of these attributes. For instance, let's say an element representing a Country Code lookup table contains an IDREF value that corresponds to a valid Invoice ID value, like

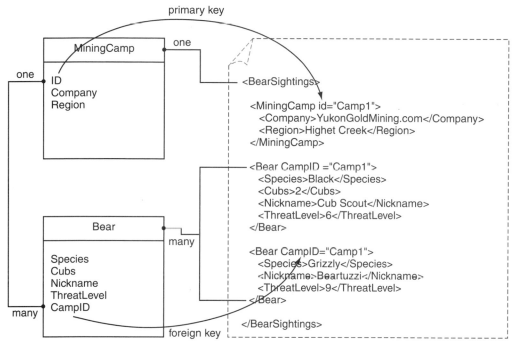

Figure 7.17
A different one-to-many relationship using ID and IDREF.

"INV1001." In databases we can set up constraints to enforce foreign key relationships between two tables. If no such relationship exists between the Invoice table and the Country Code table, the Country Code table cannot reference a primary key value from the Invoice table.

In an XML document, however, the DTD has no concept of explicit relationships between two types. It simply keeps track of ID and IDREF/IDREFS attributes, and makes sure that all IDREF and IDREFS values consist of valid ID values somewhere in the document. It doesn't matter where the IDREF or IDREFS values are located, as long as they are present and the value is unique.

It is therefore important to understand that DTDs cannot provide true referential integrity. DTDs allow for a system of pointers that can be utilized to simulate database table relationships to a limited extent.

7.4.5   Mapping XML to relational data with XSD schemas

The XML schema language provides a number of features that are very useful for representing relational data. One notable difference in how XSD schemas approach the

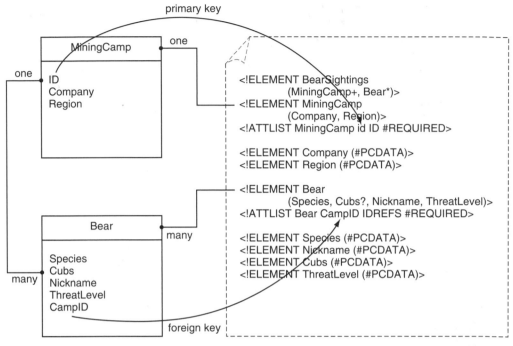

Figure 7.18
DTD providing ID and IDREFS attributes.

definition of keys, is that they incorporate XPath statements to address the shortcomings of DTDs we just discussed.

Although XSD schemas do still support the ID, IDREF and IDREFS attributes discussed in the previous section, here we focus on the parts of the XML Schema language that were added specifically to address relational data mapping requirements.

Basic table mapping with XSD schemas
When mapping database tables to XSD schemas, you generally represent tables as elements with complex types, where each column exists as a simple type element (or as a nested complex type element, when required).

```
<element name="Bear">
   <complexType>
      <attribute name="Species" type="string" />
      <attribute name="Nickname" type="string" />
      <attribute name="ThreatLevel" type="integer" />
   </complexType>
</element>
```

Example 7.7   An element declaration representing three columns from a relational table

Null restrictions with XSD schemas

Even though the XML schema language supports the null value, it does so only for elements. Attributes cannot contain nulls, and therefore any table column to which you map an attribute should not allow nulls to avoid validation conflicts.

> **NOTE**
>
> If you really do need to map a null-allowed column to an attribute, refer to the "Null restrictions with DTDs" section for customized null value management techniques that can also be applied to XSD schemas.

Primary keys with XSD schemas

Elements within XSD schemas can be exclusively identified using the `unique` element. Similar in nature to the `ID` attribute, this element provides more flexibility, and uses XPath to define the scope of its uniqueness.

```
<unique name="MiningCampID">
  <selector xpath=".//MiningCamp" />
  <field xpath="PrimaryKey" />
</unique>
```

Example 7.8   The XSD schema unique element

For the purpose of representing relational data, however, the `key` element is more suitable. As with `unique`, the `key` element enforces a level of uniqueness among the elements or attributes returned by an XPath statement.

```
<key name="MiningCampPrimaryKey">
  <selector xpath=".//MiningCamp" />
  <field xpath="PrimaryKey" />
</key>
```

Example 7.9   The XSD schema key element

The `key` element is specifically intended to be referenced by the `keyref` element. This establishes a primary-to-foreign key relationship.

> **NOTE**
>
> Unlike the `ID` attribute in DTDs, `key` element values can be numeric.

Foreign keys with XSD schemas

Elements that need to reference other elements can use `keyref`. This element defines a foreign key that points to a primary key, based on the `key` element just explained.

```
<keyref name="MiningCampForeignKey" refer="x:MiningCampPrimaryKey">
  <selector xpath=".//Bear" />
  <field xpath="ForeignKey" />
</keyref>
```

Example 7.10   The XSD schema keyref element

As with the `unique` and `key` elements, `keyref` relies on XPath statements to define the region of an XML document to which it applies.

Composite keys with XSD schemas

Databases allow for the creation of composite keys, which derive the key value from a combination of table columns. As long as that combination is unique throughout the table, the key is valid.

XSD schemas provide the same functionality. Whether declaring `unique`, `key`, or `keyref` elements, you can define multiple elements or attributes by adding a `field` element for each.

```
<key name="BearKey">
 <selector xpath=".//Bear" />
 <field xpath="Nickname" />
 <field xpath="Species" />
</key>
```

Example 7.11   A composite key created by multiple field elements

Note that composite keys can consist of elements with different data types.

Relationships with XSD schemas

Intrinsic one-to-one and one-to-many relationships are adequate for when child elements have only one parent. For a more flexible schema that allows an element to be referenced by multiple others, you will need to use the `key` and `keyref` elements explained in the previous sections.

By establishing the primary key of your child element with a key value, you will be able to add a corresponding `keyref` element to each parent that needs to reference it. You can set the `maxOccurs` indicator to control how many instances of the child element you want to allow.

Figure 7.19 provides an example that demonstrates an XSD schema-based constraint. Note that we have named the elements representing table keys "PrimaryKey" and "ForeignKey," respectively.

Next are the contents of the corresponding XSD schema file, followed by the diagram in Figure 7.20 that illustrates the relationship between the schema and table keys.

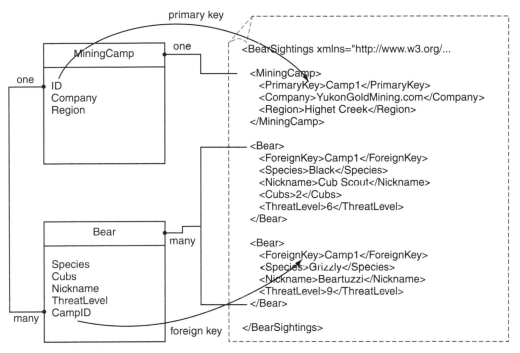

Figure 7.19
A document instance with a one-to-many relationship enforced by an XSD schema.

```
<xs:schema xmlns:xs="http://www.w3.org/2001/XMLSchema"
elementFormDefault="qualified">
 <xs:element name="BearSightings">
 <xs:complexType>
  <xs:choice maxOccurs="unbounded">

  <xs:element name="MiningCamp">
   <xs:complexType>
    <xs:sequence>
     <xs:element name="PrimaryKey" type="xs:string" minOccurs="1" />
     <xs:element name="Company" type="xs:string" />
     <xs:element name="Region" type="xs:string" />
    </xs:sequence>
   </xs:complexType>
  </xs:element>

  <xs:element name="Bear">
   <xs:complexType>
    <xs:sequence>
     <xs:element name="ForeignKey" type="xs:string" minOccurs="0" />
     <xs:element name="Species" type="xs:string" />
```

```
      <xs:element name="Nickname" type="xs:string" />
      <xs:element name="Cubs" type="xs:integer" minOccurs="0" />
      <xs:element name="ThreatLevel" type="xs:integer" />
    </xs:sequence>
   </xs:complexType>
  </xs:element>
 </xs:choice>
</xs:complexType>

<xs:key name="MiningCampPrimaryKey">
  <xs:selector xpath=".//MiningCamp" />
  <xs:field xpath="PrimaryKey" />
</xs:key>

<xs:keyref name="MiningCampForeignKey" refer="MiningCampPrimaryKey">
  <xs:selector xpath=".//Bear" />
  <xs:field xpath="ForeignKey" />
</xs:keyref>

</xs:element>
</xs:schema>
```

Example 7.12   An XSD schema enforcing constraints with key and keyref

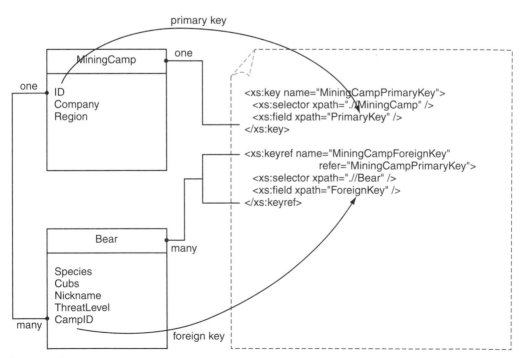

Figure 7.20
A one-to-many relationship using key and keyref.

As with the one-to-many relationship, you can easily define a one-to-one relationship by creating a parent-child association between two element declarations within the schema. The one-to-one relationship can be enforced by setting the maxOccurs indicator to "1" on the child element declaration.

For one-to-one relationships where the child element will have multiple parents, you can use the key and keyref elements as you would in a one-to-many relationship.

SUMMARY OF KEY POINTS

- XML provides natural (intrinsic) one-to-many and one-to-one relationships through its hierarchical nesting structure.

- DTDs can supply basic data mapping functionality by simulating primary keys, foreign keys, and various relationships.

- XSD schemas are equipped with more sophisticated features designed specifically for relational data mapping requirements.

7.5 Database extensions

Chances are, one of the first places you'll look for XML integration features is to your existing database. IBM, Microsoft, Oracle, and just about every other major database vendor are providing some level of XML support. Very few, however, have made any attempt to make these new features anything more than proprietary enhancements that further tie you to their platform.

This is not to say that your database's XML features are not useful or should not be used. It is just important to integrate proprietary extensions with an awareness of how they may limit you in the future.

Following are some common ways in which database products extend their data access to XML.

7.5.1 Proprietary extensions to SQL

Some database vendors simply add XML-specific commands to their version of SQL. An SQL query, for instance, can be formulated with an extra parameter indicating that the query output should be an XML document, instead of the traditional result-set format.

Embedding proprietary SQL statements into your application code will likely make your application no less independent than it was before. However, you will be missing out on one of the fundamental benefits of an XML-enabled environment: an abstraction of data access. Keeping the XML aspect of your application architecture generic establishes a foundation for many interoperability opportunities.

Encapsulating proprietary extensions in a separate component layer or within a Web service can protect your application from becoming too dependent on the database platform. (Chapter 9 is dedicated to exploring the use of Web services within numerous legacy architecture models.)

7.5.2   Proprietary versions of XML specifications

Database vendors that create proprietary versions of XML specifications tend to be pretty up-front about it. Even to the extent of creating new acronyms for their unique implementations. Building on vendor-driven standards may be a better solution than providing non-XML-based extensions altogether, but it will still tie you to a product platform.

7.5.3   Proprietary XML-to-database mapping

Some databases provide data mapping facilities that allow you to associate XML documents to existing relational data models. Data maps can be generated through either a front-end tool or a programmatic API.

Regardless of how they are accessed, proprietary data maps will restrict you to the interface of the tool or API, which can often be quite limited. Additionally, a common problem here is that the map itself is stored in a proprietary format. This creates further dependencies between your architecture and a single database platform.

It is much more desirable for a mapping tool to generate its output into XML standard syntax, such as XSD schema and XSLT files. This will allow you to migrate the data maps to another product, and also gives you the freedom of editing them yourself.

7.5.4   XML output format

One of the biggest complaints relating to XML support in current databases is the format and syntax of the XML markup generated by the database extensions. Quite often, the document structure will be based on the existing relational model, resulting in creatively awkward hierarchies. Also, carrying database column names forward to XML elements can lead to cryptic naming conventions. Add to that a slew of proprietary markup and annotated commands that some products also insert, and you may be hard-pressed to recognize what you requested as even being XML anymore.

Some database vendors mitigate this problem by giving the developer the option of supplying parameters to predetermine the naming of elements and the overall format of the requested XML document. For instance, you may be able to tell the database to output a query as an element-centric document, as opposed to one that is attribute-centric. This gives you more control, but it can also impose a great deal of runtime processing, directly proportional to the size and complexity of the document you are building.

The best way to assess whether a database's XML output will do more harm than good, is simply to execute a range of commands and study the markup that gets returned. Keep in mind that databases are performing this translation at runtime, so if the output is only marginally useful, it may not be worth the processing cycles it is consuming. You may very well be better off writing a custom routine to create exactly the output you want.

7.5.5   Stored procedures

If you read the technical documentation carefully enough, you might notice that a significant amount of a database's XML support may be occurring through the use of stored procedures. Database vendors simply have added a set of system stored procedures to perform the runtime manipulation of data between XML and the native data format.

From the vendor's perspective, this approach makes a lot of sense. They are simply building on their existing platform, and by adding features with new stored procedures, they are not required to make major changes to their existing database software.

Again, though, this design may have implications in terms of your architecture's dependence on a vendor-specific technology.

7.5.6   Importing and exporting XML documents

Most XML extensions provided by database vendors focus on the translation of XML to and from existing relational data. Some provide utilities for importing and exporting XML documents as a whole. There is less emphasis on this aspect, as it is moving the database into the realm of content management, an uncomfortable place for many relational databases.

Regardless of whether the database product actually provides extensions to explicitly store and retrieve XML documents, you can always alter the data model yourself to add a character or LOB (Large Object) typed column that can contain the document text.

The key issue here is that, though most databases provide full-text searching capabilities, very few actually support XML-aware querying. XML tags are considered part the data, and will therefore be included in the results of full-text searches. Traditional relational repositories can adequately store XML documents only for retrieval, as long as the querying of the document is performed by the application.

7.5.7   Encapsulating proprietary database extensions within Web services

All the issues raised in the previous section build a case for avoiding proprietary database extensions altogether. Instead, it supports the idea of building your own interface to repositories, and using only those extensions that allow for a loose coupling between application and data source.

This is an area where Web services fits in nicely. A service-oriented architecture can introduce an interoperability layer that achieves platform independence and mobility by encapsulating any code required to interact with proprietary database extensions. (Read Chapters 6 and 9 to learn more about how Web services can facilitate data abstraction.)

SUMMARY OF KEY POINTS

- Extensions to your existing database that provide XML support are tempting, because they provide a convenient way to get a limited amount of XML output from existing relational data.

- Since most extensions are highly proprietary, they will further tie your application to a specific database platform, potentially nullifying the mobility benefits of an XML architecture.

- Web Services can provide a suitable abstraction layer, by encapsulating application code to interact with proprietary extensions. The result is a data platform-independent application core.

7.6 Native XML databases

Even in XML-centric environments, many organizations continue to rely exclusively on the well-established relational database platforms that have seen them through a number of changes in architecture and development technology. When moving your applications to XML-compliant and service-oriented architectures, you will find the relational data model to still be very much a part of your core data access technologies.

There is, however, a place for native XML databases. An understanding of what these products can offer will allow you to place them strategically within your environment. This can lead to a number of improvements, foremost of which are performance and protection of data integrity. Next is an exploration of how and where native XML databases can be utilized.

7.6.1   Storage of document-centric data

This is where native XML databases can immediately impact an organization. If you've standardized a body of documents using XML, you will need a storage and retrieval system that can handle the unique characteristics of the XML data format. In fact, a number of content management products that use XML as the underlying document format, also utilize native XML databases for storage.

Native XML databases are designed to accommodate and properly manage an XML document structure independently from its content. This is an area where relational databases often fail. Being able to differentiate the actual data from markup (that can include processing instructions and entity references) is beyond the ability of typical relational database platforms. For data-centric XML documents, however, relational databases that have been extended with XML support are still the way to go.

7.6.2   Integrated XML schema models

In some of the architectures explored earlier in this chapter, we placed schema files in relational repositories as entire documents or construct fragments. This is an extremely loose form of integration. The database is not aware of the schema content, and therefore views these schema models as any other piece of textual data.

Some relational databases do provide conversion features and other extensions that support a level of DTD or XSD schema integration. Few, however, come close to the depth at which a native XML database represents and manages XML schema models. Not only are XML schemas used to validate the integrity of data, the native database can actually build an index around the schema structure itself.

7.6.3   Queries and data retrieval

Here's where some analysis can result in significant performance improvements. Native XML databases index content differently from their relational counterparts. This relates back to their respective data structures: the tree/node hierarchy versus open, tabular data entities. When working with documents, as opposed to pieces of data, queries typically will result in larger amounts of data being requested.

XML-aware indices can provide a faster data retrieval mechanism when a large amount of document data is requested. The parsing of large XML data constructs is faster than the equivalent processing required when retrieving and then assembling this information from a relational data source. This is another reason document-centric content is more suitable for native XML environments.

Additionally, the XML-aware nature of native XML databases supports query technologies designed specifically for the XML representation format. This opens the door to sophisticated query statements that would not be possible with many of the XML-enabled relational database platforms.

7.6.4   Native XML databases for intermediary storage

One popular use for native XML repositories is to supplement application environments that already rely on relational databases. A common challenge with XML-enabled applications is the constant conversion between relational data structures and XML document formats. In previous chapters we explored some strategies for mitigating the performance overhead this runtime conversion process can impose, including the use of in-memory databases for caching purposes.

If, however, you need to provide a permanent storage facility for cached, non-durable, and document-centric XML data, then what better place than a repository specifically designed to store XML in its native format. Figure 7.21 illustrates this architecture.

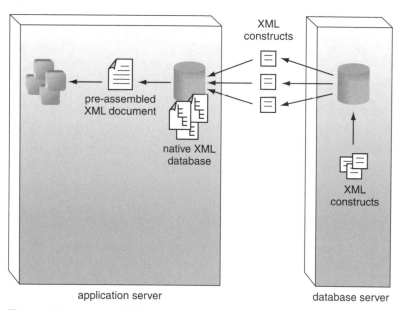

Figure 7.21   A native XML database acting as a physical cache for non-durable XML document data.

There may be situations where this architecture may even be useful for data-centric XML documents. It really comes down to what you're trading off. If you can take advantage of the integrated XML schemas, then this database can act as a pre-validator for documents that remain fairly static throughout the lifetime of the currently executing business task.

Also, if you need to cache XML formatted data for extended periods, the additional administration features offered by native XML databases may be more attractive. Finally, placing data in a native XML cache repository can open it up to a wide variety of data access opportunities that may not exist while the data is residing in a relational database.

SUMMARY OF KEY POINTS

- Native XML databases are most suitable for the storage of document-centric XML data.

- The XML-aware indices provided by native XML databases can provide faster data retrieval for large amounts of document data.

- Native XML databases can be positioned strategically alongside relational repositories.

PART

III

Integrating applications

Enabling a productive level of communication between applications can be one of the most challenging and important projects you will ever be a part of. The volatile nature of contemporary business communities, without warning, can alter the structure and philosophy of an organization.

Unpredictable requirements can emerge, demanding that you:

- connect systems that were never designed to talk with each other
- automate new business models that contrast the way the organization has been conducting business so far
- extend this automation to new business areas with different technologies, methodologies, and expectations

And, that you do all this in a cost-effective and responsive manner.

Fortunately, there is sufficient technology and intelligence that, if properly applied, can help you create the lines of communication to facilitate immediate business concerns. More importantly, you can accomplish this while transforming your enterprise's technical landscape into a haven for interoperability, where data sharing becomes second nature.

In other words, with the right strategies you can take advantage of these "involuntary changes," and use them as an opportunity to improve the technology and increase the quality of your automated enterprise.

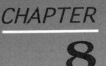

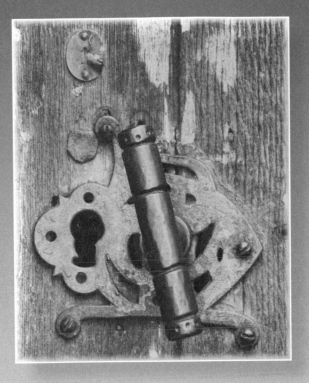

The mechanics of application integration

very integration solution is unique. As a result, integration projects often produce creative new ways of combining products, programming logic, tools, and various technologies. To help you through the often volatile nature of integration environments are sets of proven design principles and standard technologies. This chapter is dedicated to establishing these fundamental building blocks, providing a basis and a reference point for many of the strategies in subsequent chapters.

8.1 Understanding application integration

The primary motivation behind just about any form of application integration is for two or more applications to be involved in the transfer of data. The nature of this transfer can be as simple as one application retrieving a value stored in the other's repository. Or, it can be as intricate as the merging and collaboration of both applications' data, resources, and business logic, in order to support the automated process of yet another application.

8.1.1   Types of integration projects

Most integration projects can be grouped into two categories:

- those that address immediate business requirements
- those that (aim to) establish a better way of enabling integration in general

The benefit of building XML and service-oriented integration architectures is that though you may only be trying to meet your current set of business requirements, you will (perhaps even inadvertently) also be taking a step toward establishing an enterprise-wide integration standard.

That's just one step, though. Planning a migration toward a service-oriented enterprise will allow you to take full advantage of what the XML and Web services platforms have to offer. Chapter 14 provides a great deal of guidance as to how to define a long-term migration strategy.

8.1.2   Typical integration requirements

Although the variety of implementations can be endless, there is a great deal of commonality in the overall functions performed by integration solutions.

Here are some examples:

- application A needs periodic access to application B's database in order to retrieve a specific data value
- application A needs regular access to application B's database in order to perform a variety of queries
- application A needs to borrow some of application B's business logic in order to perform a computation or process a business function
- application A has collected data that belongs in application B's database (application A therefore needs to be able to submit this data to application B, which in turn, needs to validate and process this data prior to storing it in its database)
- application A needs to reference data from application B, as well as utilize application B's business logic a number of times, during the execution of a business task
- applications A and B need to share a common repository in order to avoid storing redundant data
- applications A and B need to collaborate business logic and exchange data in order to support a new or revised business process
- applications A and B each play a specific role within a larger business process (managed by application C)

Abstracting integration tasks into generic functions can be an interesting exercise. There may be opportunities to identify common characteristics in different integration approaches. This may lead you to compare the architectures of integration solutions within your environment, and determine which are more effective than others.

8.1.3 Progress versus impact

When studying the differences in how integration solutions are designed, it is tempting to want to standardize. This goes back to the two types of projects we established at the beginning of this section. The latter, more ambitious project aims to achieve such a standardization.

Typically, this includes:

- establishing an interoperability framework, or creating a building block in support of a future framework
- utilizing open, vendor-independent technologies
- introducing new design standards with an emphasis on generic accessibility, open interfaces, and data sharing

These goals may be attainable, but will, no doubt, significantly increase the cost of an integration project. Additionally, the steps required to achieving these goals may contrast to the ultimate goal of many integration initiatives, which is to achieve a new level of interoperability while minimizing the impact on existing environments.

Examples include:

- avoiding the introduction of new technologies, when solutions can be built on existing platforms
- avoiding the introduction of overly complex application logic and processing
- avoiding the creation of a fragmented environment through the introduction of business logic that resides outside of established application boundaries
- avoiding tightly bound integration channels between applications that are easily broken if either application is modified
- minimizing redevelopment of applications affected by the integration
- mitigating increased performance demands on applications affected by the integration

How then, can one establish a new, enterprise-wide integration framework, while being confined to such a level of "impact avoidance"? It's a good question, and one that turns many integration projects into a balancing act. Progress versus impact.

8.1.4   Types of integration solutions

When comparing traditional approaches to more recent methods of integration, there is a noticeable change in the underlying requirements that drive these projects. Although almost all efforts enable or enhance business automation, emphasis has shifted from just enabling automation to improving and realizing automation intelligence. Business processes have become the heart and soul of organizations, and they are demanding that technology does them justice.

The level of required business automation intelligence determines the high-level configuration of an integration solution. Most can be grouped into two categories: extensions to an existing application and new business processes.

Extensions to an existing application

An existing application is extended to support new features or a modified business process. This extension requires that the application accesses foreign data or interfaces with business logic that resides in another application. To avoid redundant data or redevelopment of existing business functionality, an integration channel connecting the two applications is required (Figure 8.1).

If both applications were developed on a common technology platform, the integration effort is generally minimal.

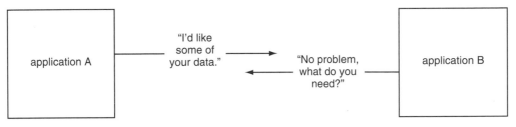

Figure 8.1
Integration in a homogenous environment.

Most challenges, however, arise when needing to connect applications based on different technologies, platforms, and operating environments (Figure 8.2). That's when the fun begins.

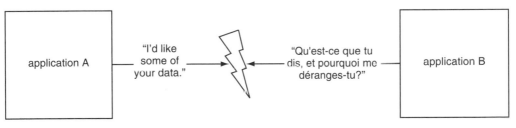

Figure 8.2
Integration challenges with disparate applications.

New business processes

Corporate mergers, organizational restructuring, and expanding service areas are only some of the reasons existing business models are being revisited, extended, or even completely replaced. These types of events can result in drastic changes to existing business processes. Some are combined, others consolidated, and often, entirely new processes are introduced (Figure 8.3).

These fundamental changes can result in huge impositions on technical environments responsible for automating the affected business areas. Incorporating new business processes introduces a whole new dimension to application integration, especially when the process requires a number of disparate applications to interoperate.

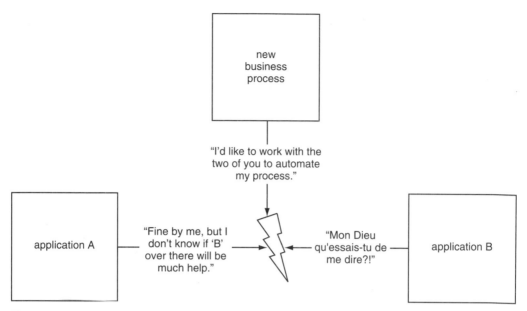

Figure 8.3
Integration challenges when imposing a new business process that involves disparate applications.

SUMMARY OF KEY POINTS

- Integration projects can have different characteristics and goals.

- There is a constant struggle to add value, while minimizing impact.

- Business process automation is driving integration technology.

8.2 Integration levels

The need for applications to talk to each other has existed ever since business processes first became automated. Initial attempts to achieve interoperability were centered around the sharing of data through replication and direct access to repositories. Interoperability trends then shifted to application or logic-oriented integration, which still achieved data sharing requirements, but also incorporated the business rules related to the shared data.

The EAI movement has built upon and evolved these traditional models to introduce a more sophisticated cross-application framework to support the integration of new business processes.

Let's take a closer look at each of the traditional levels illustrated in Figure 8.4.

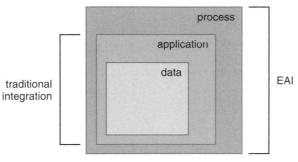

Figure 8.4
The fundamental integration levels.

8.2.1 Data-level integration

Data from one application is shared without involving its application logic (Figure 8.5). For example, if application A receives direct access to application B's database, none of application B's logic is involved in the transfer of its data.

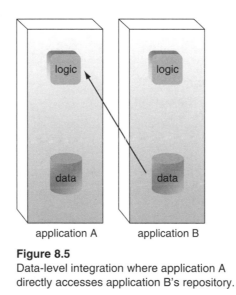

application A   application B

Figure 8.5
Data-level integration where application A directly accesses application B's repository.

Alternatively, the required data from application B's repository can be replicated to application A's database (Figure 8.6). This is another very common form of data-level integration. The one-way data transfer and central database models described in Chapter 9 are examples of this architecture.

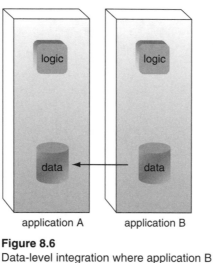

Figure 8.6
Data-level integration where application B
replicates data to application A's repository.

8.2.2   Application-level integration

Application logic within both applications govern the exchange of data (Figure 8.7). For
example, application A makes a request for information from application B by directly
interfacing with and invoking programming logic within application B. All subsequent
communication is managed through this connection, and any business logic introduced
by application B is applied to the data exchange.

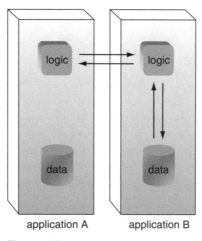

Figure 8.7
Point-to-point application-level integration.

Typically, application-level integration is required when the scope of one application is extended so that it requires access to data and/or logic managed by another application. Because the desired data is controlled and protected by layers of business logic, direct data access is no longer an option. (Many of the models explained in the section, "Web services and point-to-point architectures," of Chapter 9 operate at this level.)

NOTE

When working with disparate application platforms, an intermediate step often is introduced to translate incompatible communication protocols.

8.2.3   Process-level integration

At this level, the sharing of data or application logic facilitates a new automated business process, or the merging of two or more existing processes (Figure 8.8). This new process is realized through (but not limited to) the integration of two or more applications.

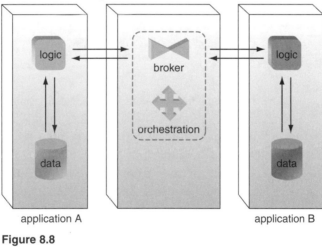

Figure 8.8
A basic EAI architecture.

Traditionally, business process-level integration has been accomplished through a variety of point-to-point integration models; however, the advent of EAI and specialized middleware have made the messaging framework model a more suitable choice.

In an EAI messaging architecture, a broker component is used to enable communication between disparate applications. A separate orchestration component then allows the management and execution of new processes. (See Chapter 10 for more information about broker and orchestration components, and for examples of common EAI messaging architectures.)

8.2.4   Service-oriented integration

It is important to understand that Web services do not provide an integration solution by themselves. Introducing Web services into an environment does not replace the need for middleware and many traditional integration technologies. Web services are not a new form of application integration or EAI, they simply add new components that can be utilized effectively in a variety of architectures.

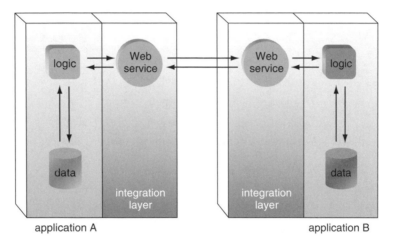

Figure 8.9
Integration layers establishing a service-oriented integration architecture.

As illustrated in Figure 8.9, the logical integration layer created by exposing legacy APIs via Web services simply offers a standard means of sharing data and programming logic. This has become a very attractive part of integration architecture and, when properly designed, establishes a foundation for a service-oriented enterprise.

SUMMARY OF KEY POINTS

- Data-level integration allows for applications to share data without necessarily involving business logic.

- Application-level integration is typically realized through point-to-point integration architectures where applications connect to and interact with each other's logic.

- Process-level integration generally is associated with EAI solutions, and most commonly facilitated by broker and orchestration components.

- Service-oriented integration introduces Web services to establish a platform-independent interoperability model within various integration architectures.

8.3 A guide to middleware

Ask ten people what middleware is, and you'll probably get a consensus that it's a pretty vague term that can mean a lot of different things. The same probably holds true for EAI. No discussion about integration fundamentals is complete without a look at the many shades of middleware technology.

8.3.1 "EAI" versus "middleware"

To some, the term "EAI middleware" may be confusing, since "EAI" and "middleware" are sometimes used to classify types of integration solutions. Thus, an EAI solution frequently is considered more contemporary than a middleware solution.

The term "middleware" is also broadly used to identify software services and products that enable inter-application communication, especially in heterogeneous environments. "EAI" can also be used as a label for a more progressive type of integration solution that utilizes some of the more recent middleware products (especially those based on messaging frameworks).

This book uses the latter definition of these terms.

8.3.2 Shredding the Oreo

An overly simplistic, but nevertheless accurate analogy is the comparison of middleware to the filling of an Oreo cookie. The hard and rigid outer ends are held together by a malleable middle layer. Who knows what combination of chemicals make up that white filling, but in the end, it does its job by connecting together the two ends, and maintaining that connection.

The same holds true for just about any enterprise environment. The term "middleware" encompasses a wide variety of software products and services that can be combined in endless configurations to enable some form of end-to-end communication. A quality connection will be robust enough to preserve a communication channel through a variety of environmental conditions.

If we limit the scope of this analogy to the confines of an application environment, the related middleware will be responsible for enabling communication between the front and back-end layers of a multi-tiered design. Let's take a step back to think outside of the cookie.

Traditional middleware has evolved from enabling a conversation between two pieces of software on different servers, to providing highly sophisticated platforms for high-volume transaction-oriented data exchange between a wide variety of different applications.

In fact, a traditional enterprise is a lot like a box of… Oreo cookies. Applications typically had fixed connections to others, but try integrating new applications, and you have to rip off one end of the cookie to fit on another.

Take that box, empty it in a blender, and hit the purée button. Now have a look at the resulting pile of crumbs. You'll see dark and white bits. The dark ones are your legacy applications, now broken down into multiple, independent services. Everything white represents a common medium of communication that connects these services (in other words, communication protocols and the middleware that utilizes them). It is through the shredded Oreo filing that XML travels.

Why did we just spend a whole page comparing middleware to cookies? Only to emphasize the need for existing environments to be completely overhauled in order to achieve a true EAI architecture. And, more importantly, to highlight the importance of choosing the right middleware products to begin with. Those already designed with EAI in mind will require a great deal less shredding.

8.3.3 Common middleware services and products

Provided here are a number of categories that represent the bulk of relevant middleware software.

Data access technology
To support the emergence of client-server platforms, data access technologies and protocols were required to allow remote clients to connect to and interact with data sources on dedicated servers.

This category includes the following technologies:

- data access protocols, such as JDBC, ODBC, and OLE/DB
- programmatic data access APIs, such as ActiveX Data Objects (ADO)
- stored procedures and database triggers (depending on the nature of the functions they execute)

Although originally developed to facilitate two-tier communication, most data access services have been refined to incorporate additional features, such as connection pooling and XML extensions. This allows them to support contemporary multi-tier architectures.

Distributed technology
This platform evolved out of the client-server model, during the period when most two-tier applications underwent a transition to three and then multi-tier architectures.

To facilitate the new physical boundaries imposed by distributed designs, applications had to be developed differently.

Included within this category are the following technology platforms:

- Custom-developed software components used to enable application integration. Component-based software is typically tied to a proprietary development platform.
- Remote invocation protocols, such as Remote Procedure Call (RPC), used to connect components on different servers. Different RPC-based implementations exists for each proprietary component platform. Examples include DCOM and CORBA.
- Adapters (also known as connectors, gateways, and bridge components) used to enable communication between application logic residing on different platforms, as well as various legacy applications and specialized software products. (For more information about the role of adapters within integration architectures, see Chapter 10.)
- Object request brokers and other software services that provide runtime environments for distributed applications. Again, these products typically are tied to a proprietary platform.

Even though the integration layer introduced by Web services reduces the need for some of these technologies within inter-application environments, they remain an important part of application architecture. (Chapter 10 explores how many traditional architectures utilizing distributed technologies are affected by the introduction of Web services.)

Message queues and message-oriented middleware
RPC-based communication is synchronous by nature, which makes it ideal for component communication required to execute most application business functions. Even though asynchronous communication eventually was supported by some RPC implementations, it is still a less suitable protocol for the publish/subscribe type functionality required in many enterprise environments, especially in cross-application solutions.

To accommodate this need for asynchronous functionality, message-oriented middleware (MOM) products introduced a combination of messaging concepts and queue services. The messaging and routing structure provided by MOM solutions heavily influenced the messaging framework that has become the basis of most current EAI message brokers.

Application servers and transaction monitors
Perhaps the broadest category of middleware, application servers consist of server products providing server-side application hosting and supplementary middleware

services. Transaction processing monitors, legacy servers, and Web application servers fall into this category. Even object request brokers could be classified as application servers.

Integration brokers

Consider this the EAI category of middleware, since these products are what currently typify an EAI solution. Integration brokers, also known as message brokers, can include the following types of services and features:

- business rule management
- orchestration and workflow management
- rules-based and content-based message routing
- transaction support
- schema mapping and dynamic transformation

8.3.4   A checklist for buying middleware

If you just want to get from A to B (and maybe back to A again), you don't need a top-of-the-line vehicle, and you certainly don't need a lot of extra options either. Maybe you don't need a car at all.

Many integration products are designed with an entire enterprise environment in mind, and therefore would be overkill for a cross-application integration project. Others, however, may be suitable and affordable enough to assist your efforts, while laying a foundation for future interoperability requirements.

Understand the range of supported integration models

Some middleware products have a fixed, built-in integration model. It is important that you don't get bound to a such a product (and its one model). If you do, the evolution of your enterprise architecture could be severely inhibited.

Therefore, it is imperative that the products you consider support a range of models, and allow for a flexible migration between them. Such a solution will not only facilitate extensions and changes to your overall integration architectures, its adaptive nature also will allow you to more easily incorporate it into your existing environment.

Beware industry-specific middleware solutions

Some middleware products emerged out of custom application development projects that were focused initially on a set of specific business requirements. As a result, those solutions can be industry specific. The problem is that they may not advertise themselves as such.

Adding a few generic interfaces to a product that was built with just one industry in mind will not make it suitable for general use. The best way to investigate this is to find other customers in your industry, who have successfully used the product.

Make sure the product manufacturer is progressive

A typical integration solution will never stay the same. Progressive vendors will constantly be refining their products to stay current with technology trends and platform shifts. Most important for service-oriented solutions is the support of second-generation Web services specifications.

Once you are tied to a middleware product, you will be forced to submit to the pace at which the vendor decides to update product features and characteristics. The best way to choose a suitable product is to check the history of its vendor. For instance, you can investigate how responsive a vendor is to important industry developments by reading past press releases, or learning about how feature sets have evolved through past product releases.

Business process mapping features are critical

Business process automation enabled via EAI solutions is becoming more and more common. The advent of orchestration that allows for embedded workflows to coordinate message routing and incorporate complex business rules (and other forms of dynamic processing) has become a key part of enterprise environments.

The extent to which your middleware supports orchestration functionality is extremely important. This is because the level at which you will be able to express the logic of your business process will be determined by the quality of the process mapping functionality provided by the product vendor.

The best way to assess the orchestration features is to try them out. Let your business analyst come up with a range of scenarios that you can try to express and implement with the product's orchestration designer. When you run into a wall, make notes and later use these as decision points for determining which product is worth buying. So much attention usually is placed on the back-end mechanics of a middleware solution that this critical piece of front-end functionality is often overlooked.

It is also important that your middleware solution supports a standard business process definition language, such as BPEL4WS. If, however, it does not provide an adequate front-end tool, then you may want to consider replacing it with a more suitable third-party tool also capable of generating BPEL4WS markup.

Deployment and integration effort

Implementing a middleware solution almost always turns into a full integration project. Not only will you be installing the middleware product vendor's shrink-wrapped software, you will be using it to connect two or more of your applications.

This will frequently involve tasks such as:

- installing and configuring communications software
- establishing and testing new communication channels
- modeling XML documents used for message transports
- creating data maps for runtime transformation
- configuring various security settings

The effort and associated cost of this deployment needs to be added to the purchase cost when comparing middleware products. Round the assessment off by getting answers to the following questions:

- Can it be rolled out in a phased manner?
- How much external assistance will be needed?
- Is there any custom coding required?

Maintenance considerations

Once you've got the solution up and running, you need to understand what it will take to keep it that way. Enterprise applications can be high maintenance, demanding a surprising amount of attention and administrative effort.

Typical maintenance tasks include:

- general configuration changes
- security settings
- version control
- performance optimization
- monitoring and logging
- tracing and auditing
- troubleshooting
- business rule maintenance

The ease at which a solution allows you to perform these tasks is a very significant consideration. The best way to understand what's involved in being a middleware-based solution administrator is to give it a test run. Arrange an evaluation implementation with your vendor, and think up some common scenarios you may be faced with. Then, try acting through them with the system online.

An important aspect of maintaining a server product is the required skill set. If you find yourself depending on external consultants to help you through common administrative tasks, not only will maintaining a solution be cumbersome, it will be expensive. Additionally, it will increase response times for change requests and troubleshooting.

Another (often critical) consideration is the availability of the solution's runtime. If common changes to configuration settings or business rules require you to shut down all or parts of the environment, then you need to seriously assess the operational impact of that inconvenience.

Usability of administration tools are important
Related to the maintenance process imposed by middleware solutions is the quality of the administrative tools provided by the product. Your ability to run an enterprise environment effectively will often be limited to the usability and functionality of the administrative front-end.

Usability is especially important in EAI middleware, because these solutions are frequently utilized to represent and encapsulate:

- business logic
- business rules
- business processes

You need to feel comfortable that you can express these aspects of your applications properly. Your middleware product can actually become a virtual application, in which case it needs to accurately facilitate the nature of your business automation.

Finally, another important aspect of maintenance tools is their ability to allow remote administration. Decentralized access to the many different configuration and business-related settings will give you a great deal of flexibility. You should, however, also be able to restrict the amount of remote access allowed.

Scalability considerations
Think ahead when looking at middleware products. Especially when beginning with a small to medium-sized project, it is important that you understand the capabilities of your solution beyond the project's immediate scope.

Some major considerations include:

- load balancing features and options
- ability to distribute middleware components
- fail-over support
- limitations of adapters (and other components that can become potential performance bottlenecks)
- availability of enterprise-level components (perhaps to replace "standard" grade components bundled with the product)

If you are confident that your solution can scale properly to meet your future performance requirements, you must then ask the next big question: How expensive are additional licenses? It is highly recommended you price out a future, maximum-scaled configuration. If your face hasn't lost its color by the time you review these numbers, then you may have an appropriate candidate.

SUMMARY OF KEY POINTS

- EAI introduces a new generation of middleware solutions.

- Middleware products have evolved to accommodate changes in application architecture.

- Purchasing a middleware solution requires careful analysis.

8.4 Choosing an integration path

Let's say your technical environment consists of a mixed bag of application platforms, glued together by various integration products and solutions. You survey the various inter-application communication channels that have been built over the years, and determine that though some have successfully united applications, others may seem more like patch jobs. You notice, though, that none (or very few) follow a consistent integration model. Each of these "traditional" integration solutions was designed to address a specific set of business requirements. Few were developed with enterprise-level interoperability in mind.

Meanwhile, the industry around you is changing. Applications are becoming XML-driven, service-oriented, and enterprise-minded. Organizations are forming enterprise-wide hubs, fueled by modern messaging frameworks, and integration challenges are being met with solutions of unparalleled sophistication.

As the quality of integration solutions becomes an increasingly prominent issue, many organizations are finding themselves in this position. If yours is one of them, then there are two options you will likely need to seriously consider.

8.4.1 Two paths, one destination

There are many ways to upgrade and improve on traditional integration designs. However, there are two specific paths most relevant to the transition from legacy architecture to service-oriented enterprise frameworks.

The first option is to build on what you already have. This involves adding Web service integration layers to legacy environments. Since Chapter 9 is dedicated to exploring this option, we'll focus more on the alternative, which is to jump directly into EAI. Let's take a closer look at some of the implications involved with this wholesale move.

8.4.2 Moving to EAI

Some of the more compelling reasons to consider replacing traditional integration environments with EAI solutions include the following.

- Upgrading to a modern EAI product that already provides an XML and Web services-compliant architecture is an attractive springboard into the most current technology platform.
- Newer EAI solutions are more geared towards enterprise integration. By plugging your legacy applications into enterprise hubs, you will enable them to participate in and contribute to new, process-oriented integration environments.

8.4.3 Common myths

Before we continue, let's first dispel a few common myths.

Myth #1: The sooner the better
The longer legacy applications remain out of the loop, the harder and more expensive it will be to upgrade them.

There may be some characteristics of particular applications that make this statement valid. Generally, though, legacy applications are a prime integration target for modern EAI products. Unless your legacy platform is completely obsolete, there is likely to be some form of adapter or connector technology available, many of which are designed specifically to support Web services.

Myth #2: If you buy, you comply
Replacing traditional integrated solutions is the only way to participate in modern XML-driven and service-oriented enterprise architectures.

This is almost always untrue. One of the major strengths of Web services and XML is their adaptability. (As previously stated, the entire next chapter discusses the use of these technologies within legacy integration architectures.)

8.4.4   The impact of an upgrade

Now let's take a closer look at some of the challenges you may be in for if you decide to move ahead with an upgrade to an EAI solution.

Upgrading integration solutions is expensive
Not only are you (to put it mildly) "affecting" two or more legacy application environments, purchasing enterprise EAI messaging products is a significant expense. Here are some common areas where cost can become a major factor:

- enterprise server licenses
- increased hardware requirements
- consulting expertise
- redevelopment of existing integration platforms
- migration of the data communications framework
- retesting old business processes in a new environment

Upgrading integration solutions is time-consuming
Depending on the existing complexity of integration, replacing the solution may turn into a lengthy project. The effort may consist of:

- programming changes to legacy applications
- requirements for new programming logic
- implementation and configuration of the new EAI product

Upgrading integration solutions is disruptive
Large scale projects of this nature may impose significant interruptions of service in your legacy environments. Integration projects are different from standard development projects in this respect.

Adding new extensions to one application can typically be achieved by the installation of new components, executables, or scripts that provide a fair degree of backward compatibility. Overhauling an integration architecture, however, often requires that you rip out existing communication channels to make room for new ones. Ideally you would migrate such a solution through testing and staging environments before deploying it in the real world. Since you are working with legacy applications for which these environments may no longer exist, adding them now would significantly inflate your project cost.

The value may not always outweigh the cost

Once you put it all down on paper, it may be difficult to justify the expense. This is because messaging-based EAI products are designed for the enterprise. They are commonly funded as part of a long-term integration strategy with the consolidation of numerous existing and upcoming applications in mind. When comparing the cost of an EAI solution to that of a straightforward point-to-point integration project, for instance, the return on investment (ROI) projections for the traditional approach will always look more attractive.

8.4.5 Weighing your options

You've collected the facts, and it's time to make a decision. Before you do, though, make sure you take one other option into consideration. Besides replacing an old solution with a new one, you can build upon what you already have. There are two reasons you may want to follow this approach:

1. Adding layers of XML and Web services onto an existing solution can provide a very cost-effective means of allowing legacy systems to participate in those parts of the enterprise already based on a service-oriented EAI architecture.
2. Careful planning and a strategic technology upgrade can pave the way for a phased migration into a full enterprise integration solution. If properly executed, this migration plan has two benefits: the ability for the solution to plug into existing architectures, and the reduced cost and effort of replacing such a solution with a modern EAI product based on a messaging architecture.

It is worth noting that many of the concerns raised in the previous section are still valid (to an extent) when upgrading legacy architectures individually. By transitioning to a service-oriented integration model in phases, however, the cost, the impact, and the magnitude of challenges become incremental, and therefore, more manageable.

By understanding how XML and Web services fit into the confines of traditional integration environments, you will be able to better understand the benefits and limitations of building on what you already have. The rest of Part III is dedicated to exploring the marriage of traditional integration architectures, EAI solutions, and SOAs.

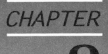

Service-oriented architectures for legacy integration

The movement toward service-oriented architectures and integration solutions is responsible for a great deal of upheaval in the traditional legacy world — much like a political uprising where masses demand change and a new way of thinking. Though I might find it disturbing to think of my Web services as a band of hippies shouting "get loose" in the face of a rigid regime of tightly bound legacy environments, there is some merit to this analogy.

The respective paradigms are in sharp contrast to each other (Figure 9.1). Their differences have been responsible for an entirely new generation of integration challenges. From a real-world perspective, the introduction of service-oriented architectures adds to the heterogeneity of already diverse enterprise environments — yet another platform bringing in new technologies, new design principles, and more complexity. Though a short-sighted view of this trend, it is an accurate assessment of what lies ahead for many organizations.

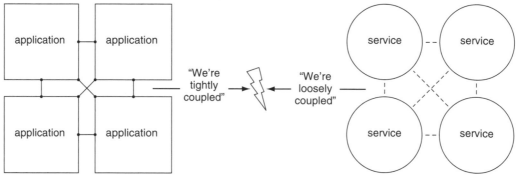

Figure 9.1
Traditional and service-oriented architectures have different integration philosophies.

Amidst the rallies and protests, it will be up to you, the integrator, to stand up and say "can't we all just get along?" Before you do, make sure you're prepared. Once someone asks "and how exactly do we accomplish that?" you'll need ideas and answers. This chapter supplies both.

9.1 Service models for application integration

The XWIF service models described here are typical of those involved in cross-application integration scenarios. Their roles, therefore, are centered around enabling and managing

---

WHAT CONSTITUTES A LEGACY?

Before we proceed, let's define the term *legacy.* Many organizations classify legacy systems as those that preceded the distributed computing platform. Even in service-oriented environments, multi-tiered applications often are not labeled with the "legacy" tag, because the Web services architecture is viewed as a continuation or extension of object- and component-based design approaches. However, in relation to service-oriented architectures, integration solutions that bridge application boundaries using proprietary remoting technologies can certainly be considered legacy.

Due to this ambiguity, we apply the word "legacy" in two ways. When discussing architectures and applications in general, it is used to distinguish pre-SOA environments from pure service-oriented solutions. (The term *traditional* is also used for this purpose.) However, when documenting pre-SOA architectures, we make it a point to distinguish component-based (or n-tier) designs from other legacy environments. This distinction is consistent with the diagramming standards used throughout this book.

NOTE

Architectural diagrams visually identify legacy application logic separately from n-tier components and Web services. Also, in this chapter arrows are used within diagrams to illustrate data flow only.

---

remote communication. Their use, however, is by no means limited to legacy integration environments. All of these service models (especially wrapper and coordination services) are just as commonly utilized in contemporary integration solutions.

9.1.1 Proxy services

This is the simplest type of service and one that often does not even require any custom development. Most development platforms provide tools that support the automatic creation of a Web service proxy. Typically, these tools generate WSDL markup, producing a service interface that mirrors that of an existing application component.

Through the use of a *proxy service* (Figure 9.2), a component can access its service interface as it would a native component interface. Proxy services are extremely easy to create, but often inefficient in design. In addition to an extra layer of processing, performance can further suffer from exposing a component interface design not optimized for Web service interaction. To learn more about optimizing service interfaces and underlying components, see the section, "Modeling service-oriented component classes and Web service interfaces," in Chapter 6. Also, see Table 9.1 for a description of characteristics most commonly associated with proxy services.

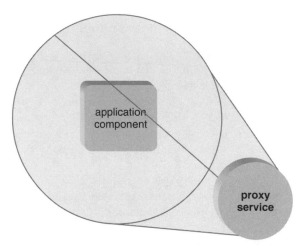

Figure 9.2
A component represented by a proxy service.

Table 9.1   Typical characteristics of proxy services

Typical service characteristics	
Anticipated usage volume	Low to medium. Proxy services typically provide little more than a service-compliant interface for a component. They therefore do not assist with the increased scalability demands that components may be subjected to, once exposed to new service requestors.
Interface design characteristics	Proxy service interfaces are usually auto-generated to represent existing interfaces, which means the service interface granularity mirrors the existing granularity of the interface from which the proxy interface was derived.
	Some development tools will supplement service interfaces with separate operations for synchronous and asynchronous communication.
	Note that a service does not need to consist of auto-generated markup and code to be considered a proxy service. A custom created Web service that accurately resembles an existing component interface is equally a proxy service.
Message types	RPC-centric.
Deployment requirements	The proxy service generally resides alongside its corresponding legacy component, in the native application hosting environment.

Proxy services can be evolved into wrapper-like services by customizing the auto-generated markup and code into a streamlined service interface.

9.1.2 Wrapper services

Wrapper services (Figure 9.3) expose specific parts of legacy applications through a service interface. This model essentially adds a facade to legacy functionality, within whatever context you choose.

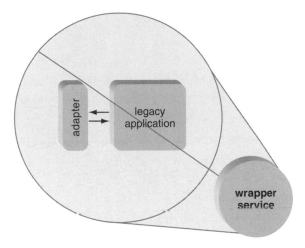

Figure 9.3
A wrapper service encapsulating a legacy application
and its adapter.

Typically, wrapper services are custom developed. Using existing interoperability tools and adapters within the current development platform, the service can interact with numerous parts of the legacy application in order to complete a function. The granularity of wrapper services tends to vary, as their functional scope relates to the amount of legacy application logic they are exposing. Table 9.2 provides a list of common characteristics for wrapper services.

Table 9.2 Typical characteristics of wrapper services

Typical service characteristics	
Anticipated usage volume	Low to medium. Wrapper services generally provide generic interfaces to a subset of legacy application functionality. Without additional logic, they may not be able to facilitate increased usage volumes. For high usage scenarios, additional business logic may be required, which means a business service would be more suitable.
Interface design characteristics	Typically, legacy functions are represented by service interfaces, streamlined for generic usage.

Table 9.2   Typical characteristics of wrapper services *(Continued)*

	Typical service characteristics
Message types	RPC-centric or document-centric.
Deployment requirements	Varies, depending on the connector technology required by the legacy application.

Another form of wrapper service is one that is supplied by a middleware vendor to accompany a specific service adapter. Such a wrapper service likely will expose the adapter's interface in a manner optimized for SOA environments. These types of Web services are also referred to as *adapter services*.

After reading through these two service model descriptions, you might ask yourself how a wrapper service is different from a business or proxy service. Here are some specific distinctions:

- Wrapper services are custom developed by the vendor or a project developer. Λ proxy service generally consists of auto-generated code and markup.

- Wrapper services are often designed to encapsulate the functionality exposed by a legacy adapter. Proxy services typically mirror application component interfaces.

- Wrapper services can be designed to expose a select part of available legacy logic. Proxy services often just duplicate existing component class interfaces.

- Proxy services typically utilize RPC-centric messaging. Messages used by wrapper service operations can be either RPC- or document-centric.

- Even though they can establish a unique interface context, wrapper services don't tend to introduce new business logic (whereas business services do).

9.1.3   Coordination services (for atomic transactions)

Used specifically to manage a coordination context, these services are an implementation of the service model defined in the WS-Coordination specification. A coordination service follows a predefined assembly model, consisting of three services that provide the following functions:

- context creation
- registration for coordination contexts
- protocol selection

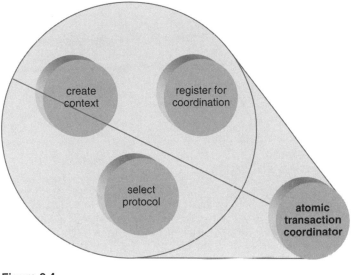

Figure 9.4
A coordination service (such as the atomic transaction coordinator) is a
controller representing an assembly of three additional services, each
with a predefined role.

Coordination services (or *coordinators*) are utilized primarily to enable atomic transactions and business activities. The WS-Transaction specification provides coordination type definitions for both of these roles, along with several coordination
protocols.

NOTE
The atomic transaction part of the WS-Transaction specification is superseded by a separate standard titled WS-AtomicTransaction. Similarly, the planned WS-BusinessActivity standard will replace the corresponding coordination type definition within WS-Transaction. See `www.specifications.ws` for more information.

The most common use of coordination services within legacy integration architecture is
to enable ACID-like transactions. Therefore, the context of this service model is for
atomic transactions only. (The coordination service model for business activities is covered in Chapter 10.) Coordination services for atomic transactions are also known as
atomic transaction coordinators (Figure 9.4). Common characteristics of this service model
are listed in Table 9.3.

Table 9.3   Typical characteristics of coordination services for atomic transactions

Typical service characteristics	
Anticipated usage volume	Medium to high. When atomic transactions are involved in service activities, coordination services are actively involved in keeping track of participants through the use of a propagated coordination context.
Interface design characteristics	Predefined by the WS-Coordination specification, but also extensible.
Message types	Document-centric.
Deployment requirements	Generally, these services are deployed along with the services they represent. They may be centrally deployed if coordinated activities consist of a large number of participants.

SUMMARY OF KEY POINTS

• Proxy services are easily created and deployed, but typically lack a quality service interface design.

• Wrapper (or adapter) services tend to be more sophisticated than proxy services, but are also limited to the legacy functionality they expose.

• Coordination services manage a context within a service activity and are used most often to coordinate transactions.

9.2 Fundamental integration components

Integration architectures that incorporate Web services are frequently accompanied by supplementary software products that facilitate connectivity and the overall communication process.

9.2.1   Adapters

An *adapter* is a specialized piece of software used to connect heterogeneous applications or application components. For most legacy integration projects, adapters are required to bridge technology gaps that exist between incompatible platforms. In fact, adapters have become such an integral part of integration solutions that many of the architectures explored in this chapter are often referred to as *adapter architectures* (see Figure 9.5).

Adapters are available for:

- legacy systems
- remoting technologies
- databases and data access protocols
- application servers
- integration brokers
- numerous proprietary solutions

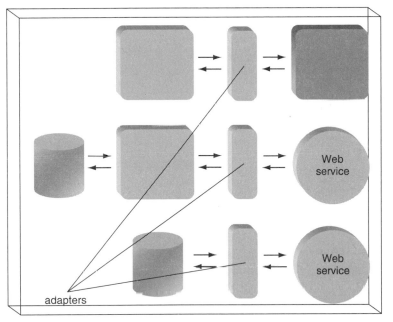
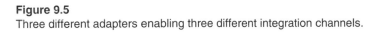

Figure 9.5
Three different adapters enabling three different integration channels.

Many vendors provide adapter products. Quite often you'll be able to choose from a number of adapters that connect the same two technology platforms.

The manner in which an adapter enables integration can also vary. Some provide a rich set of generic functionality, whereas others restrict their features to specialized implementations. A common adapter design exposes a programmatic interface that can be used to interact with the legacy environment it represents. Alternatively, adapters can achieve interoperability by translating data formats or communication protocols.

Low-end adapters tend to be inexpensive and not scalable. Licenses for enterprise-level adapters designed for high-volume environments can be very costly. Vendors frequently build useful supplementary features into the more high-end adapter components. In addition to enabling cross-platform communication, the more sophisticated (or intelligent) adapters can perform additional functions, such as:

- data transformation
- exception handling
- routing
- data caching
- event management

For the purpose of this book, gateways, connectors, and component bridges fall under the category of adapters. In fact, you could even classify Web services as a form of adapter as well. As with any of the adapters we've discussed, Web services enable one or more levels of cross-platform communication.

9.2.2   Intermediaries

The messaging framework established by Web services fully supports the notion of a multi-service message path. As illustrated in Figure 9.6, once a SOAP message is sent by the initial sender, it can be processed by numerous intermediary services, before arriving at the ultimate receiver.

The role of an intermediary is assumed by the Web service when it receives a message from a service requestor, and then forwards the message to the service provider. Within the standard Web services architecture, an intermediary is only allowed to process and modify the message header. To preserve the integrity of the message, its data cannot be altered.

The SOAP specification defines two types of intermediaries:

- *forwarding intermediaries*, which relay a message to the next intermediary or the ultimate SOAP receiver
- *active intermediaries*, that process the SOAP message prior to forwarding

Forwarding intermediaries are also referred to as *passive intermediaries*, because they don't perform any significant processing actions on or in response to the SOAP message itself. SOAP routers are a form of forwarding intermediaries, even though they can provide additional features, such as protocol translation and load balancing.

Note that there are SOAP extensions available to better control the processing of a message through an intermediary-filled path. WS-Routing and WS-Referral are

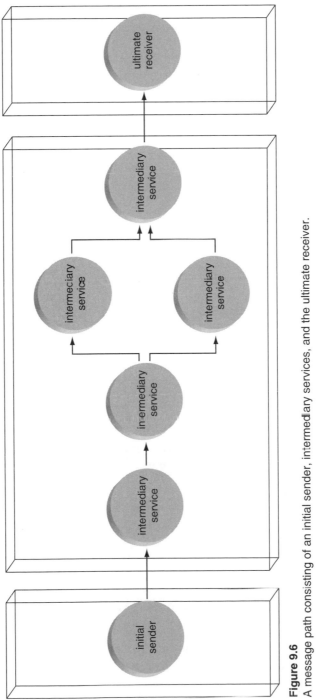

Figure 9.6
A message path consisting of an initial sender, intermediary services, and the ultimate receiver.

315

second-generation Web service specifications that provide a standard way of defining routing characteristics within message paths. (For more information regarding
these standards, visit www.specifications.ws.)

9.2.3   Interceptors

Service interceptors (also known as *SOAP handlers*) act as software agents that can pre-
process SOAP messages prior to being delivered to the destination service (see
Figure 9.7). They can also intercept and process messages transmitted by the service.

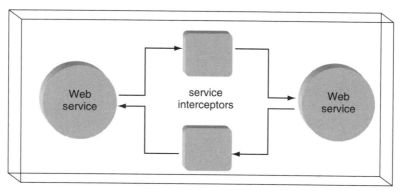

Figure 9.7
Service interceptors providing intermediary processing logic.

These software agents can fulfill a variety of functions aimed mostly at improving the
overall message processing performance. For instance, an interceptor can perform a
preliminary security check on a SOAP request. If successful, the message is passed on
to the service. If the check fails, the message is rejected, and the service is never both-
ered. Another common application is for interceptors to enable the compression (or
decompression) of SOAP messages.

Interceptor agents are different from application logic represented by a Web service.
They are not encapsulated within the service boundary, and their logic is not exposed
by the service interface. They exist as independent software components, and are
developed and deployed within proprietary development platforms.

9.3 Web services and one-way integration architectures

Even though they represent some of the most primitive attempts at achieving application interoperability, one-way integration models are still being utilized today. Simple
in design, and relatively inexpensive to implement, this loosely coupled approach can

facilitate basic data sharing requirements with minimal impact to a technical environment (Figure 9.8).

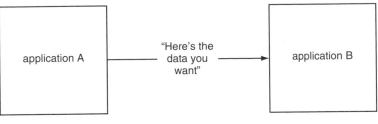

Figure 9.8
One way data transfer.

Though generally considered a means to an end, this method of single direction data transfer can be especially suitable when two applications need to only be linked together temporarily.

There are two common variations of this integration model: batch export and import, and direct data access.

9.3.1 Batch export and import

This loose form of integration simply allows for one application to export data into a certain format that is then imported by another.

Traditional architecture
The data transfer process may be somewhat automated, where application B routinely monitors a certain location, such as a network folder, for the arrival of new data files. Alternatively, the process may be manual, where an individual performs the export and import of the data, and perhaps even supplements this by converting or shaping the data format, prior to import. Data is exported and imported in batches, and commonly hosted in delimited files.

This architecture (Figure 9.9) may be suitable for applications that do not require real-time data exchange, such as those with repositories that periodically refresh a subset of the imported data. It is also appropriate for temporary or sporadic transfer of information between two disparate data sources.

Even though this approach is easy to design and inexpensive to implement, it can end up being expensive to maintain in the long-run. Regular human involvement in the handling of the transferred data increases the chance of errors. Since this model typically does not support real-time data transfer, its usefulness is severely limited within enterprise environments.

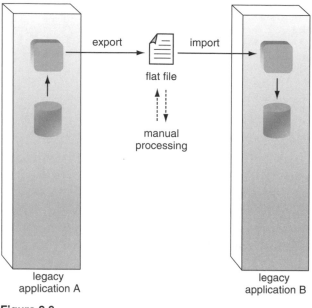

Figure 9.9
The batch export and import architecture, which can be based on
an automated or manual process.

Encapsulating import and export functions within Web services

A wrapper service can be used to abstract the export service, whereas a business service can be utilized to perform the actual data conversion and delivery to the target legacy application. Even though XML and SOAP introduce a new data transport mechanism, legacy systems can continue sending and receiving data in their native formats.

As shown in Figure 9.10, adding integration layers to represent the respective legacy applications opens up a number of interesting opportunities for extending the original architecture. For instance, in batch data transfer systems, either the exporting or importing application can initiate the transfer. The integration layer introduced by Web services can reverse the initiator and receiver roles, as required. This, perhaps, can improve the existing process but, more importantly, makes both legacy applications more able to integrate with others.

If availability is an issue with either legacy environment, its Web service can capture and place the data into a temporary storage area, such as a queue. This allows the unavailable application to complete its part in the transfer process once it is ready. (It also provides the option of establishing another integration interface — the queue itself.)

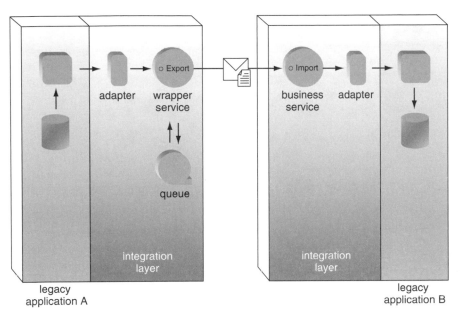

Figure 9.10
A sample batch export and import architecture where services transport legacy data
as SOAP attachments.

Architectural comparison matrix

The matrix in Table 9.4 provides a comparison of common architectural characteristics.

Table 9.4   Typical characteristics of traditional and service-enabled batch export
and import architectures

Characteristic	Traditional	Service-oriented
Data transfer	Manual or automated using a polling function.	Typically automated, but it can still be manual, if required. Polling mechanisms can also be applied.
Data conversion	Manual or automated by the importing or exporting application.	Can be automated within the integration layer, through the use of custom application logic and/or XSLT transformations.

Table 9.4   Typical characteristics of traditional and service-enabled batch export and import architectures *(Continued)*

Characteristic	Traditional	Service-oriented
Delivery of data	Delivery can be shared by exporting and importing applications. For instance, the exporting application can deliver a data file to a location that the importing application routinely checks.	Data can be embedded within a SOAP message as XML content, or as a SOAP attachment. Alternatively, legacy data can be transported in its native format as a SOAP attachment.
Data validation	Importing application will typically perform some sort of validation before accepting and processing the data file.	Integration layer can contain sufficient logic to validate data and provide various exception handling options for dealing with invalid data. The service can supplement existing validation with additional logic, without requiring changes to legacy code.
Performance	Data transfer is rarely accomplished in real time. Instead, data is exported in batches and then imported during regular automated intervals, or via a manual process.	Existing push and pull mechanisms can be reversed or combined to automate the data transfer process to whatever extent the availability of legacy applications allow.
Security	Security is restricted to the accessibility of the export function, as well as the temporary storage area for the exported data. For instance, if data is written to a network folder, the access permissions for that folder define the level of data security.	Data can be kept in memory or stored in a temporary repository, such as a state database or a queue. Data does not have to go beyond the integration layer until it is ready for import, which can increase overall security. Also, data transfer can be secured on a message level through encryption and digital signatures.
Transaction support	Transaction support may be non-existent, or limited to transactional queues.	If both export and import can be automated, then there may be an opportunity to involve these functions in an atomic transaction coordination type. The actual benefits of this, however, may be limited, as the legacy applications may not require or recognize completed transaction conditions.

Table 9.4 Typical characteristics of traditional and service-enabled batch export and import architectures *(Continued)*

Characteristic	Traditional	Service-oriented
Additional interoperability	Unless other applications can import the data format provided by the exporting application, interoperability is severely limited.	Export and import functions can be encapsulated in a separate integration layer. By isolating these functions into a separate service, you can offer a number of new output formats. This can make the data available to a variety of additional service requestors.
Extensibility	Application logic can be extended through further custom programming.	Web services can be extended individually to support new functionality for the inter-application data transfer process, or to provide generic data sharing features for other applications.

9.3.2 Direct data access

In this one-way integration model, the requesting application simply bypasses the source application's business logic, by retrieving data directly from the source repository.

Traditional architecture

As long as application A's repository allows for external access to its data, application B can use supported data access protocols to retrieve the information it needs. Although application A's code generally is not affected, its database may need to be set up to support application B as a new client, perhaps with specific permissions.

Since this model (Figure 9.11) is generally used for data retrieval only, the source application's database can further accommodate application B by providing specialized views of data, specific to the business function being executed.

Client-server applications sometimes utilize this approach, especially when direct integration with another application's logic is too difficult or complex. For instance, when the bulk of an application's programming resides as a fat client executable on user workstations, most function-level integration scenarios are unrealistic.

Further, this is an option in environments where business and validation rules are embedded within database triggers and stored procedures. If data integrity is consistently protected natively within the database, then bypassing application programming to access this data can be a viable option. If, however, relevant business rules reside within the source application logic, the retrieved data could be misrepresented.

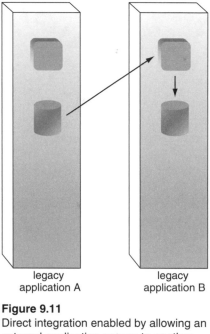

legend:
legacy   legacy
application A   application B

Figure 9.11
Direct integration enabled by allowing an
external application access to another
application's repository.

The main advantage to this approach is that one application can retrieve data from
another repository in real-time, without requiring programming changes to that repository's application. The downside is that integration is limited to data transfer only.
Also, opening up a database to a new application can sometimes overwhelm the database server and cause a bottleneck for both applications.

Encapsulating data access within a Web service
By introducing an integration layer in the source application (A), a business or wrapper
service can expose a public interface providing application-specific and generic data
access functionality (see Figure 9.12). As with the previous model, the service can be
designed to offer multiple data output formats. Application B's wrapper service simply
issues queries to application A's repository.

Architectural comparison matrix
The matrix in Table 9.5 provides a comparison of common architectural characteristics.

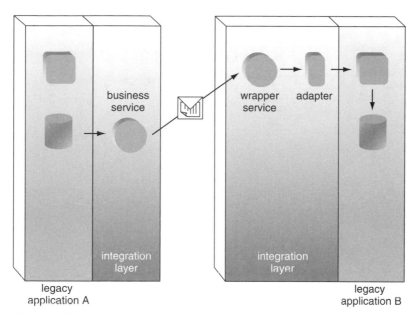

Figure 9.12
An architecture incorporating a Web service that abstracts external data access
functionality, and another that consumes it.

Table 9.5   Typical characteristics of traditional and service-enabled direct data access
architectures

Characteristic	Traditional	Service-oriented
Data transfer	Using a supported data access protocol, the requesting application retrieves data directly from the source application repository.	The service requestor issues a request for the data from the service provider. The service provider retrieves the data from the source application's repository, and responds to the request.
Data conversion	Since the query parameters are defined by the requesting application, no data conversion should be required.	Structural data transformation can be supplied if the Web service representing the source database acts as a hub for other applications that may require different output formats.

Table 9.5 Typical characteristics of traditional and service-enabled direct data access architectures *(Continued)*

Characteristic	Traditional	Service-oriented
Delivery of data	Standard database query using shared data access protocols (such as ODBC).	Retrieved data is formatted as an XML document and transported within a SOAP message. WS-ReliableMessaging may be enlisted to strengthen the robustness of the messaging framework.
Data validation	Database may provide supplementary validation via stored procedures. Data can be validated further upon successful retrieval by the requesting application.	Data can be validated at either service endpoint using an XSD schema.
Performance	Data retrieval performance is related to the complexity of the query statement and the structure of the database schema. Establishing a remote database connection can be costly, and maintaining a pool of connections can be memory intensive.	Although the query performance can be improved by issuing the query locally or by requesting XML output from the database, further processing is required to format the data properly prior to delivery. The actual transfer of data can introduce latency in relation to the size of the transmitted SOAP message. Therefore, larger message sizes may warrant the use of a compression technology. The use of an IMDB can significantly improve response times.
Security	Security is managed at the database level and authentication is performed during the creation of a database connection.	Incorporating the WS-Security framework can open up access to the service provider beyond applications that support the native database protocols. Only single message authentication is required, and credentials passed within the SOAP message can also be encrypted to secure the actual transport of the data.

Table 9.5 Typical characteristics of traditional and service-enabled direct data access architectures *(Continued)*

Characteristic	Traditional	Service-oriented
Transaction support	Since this architecture provides only data retrieval functionality, no transaction support is required.	Unless the service representing the source repository provides data access features that include inserts and updates, transaction support is likely not necessary.
Additional interoperability	On its own, the repository can facilitate other applications that support its data access protocols. Alternatively, a DBMS adapter (or gateway) can be introduced to support a greater variety of clients. A separate application component may be required to provide serious, open-ended interoperability for additional applications. This would then restrict data access communication to that component's remoting technology.	Additional business logic can be added to the service provider in this architecture, expanding its functional scope to facilitate generic data sharing. In addition to multiple data output formats, the service can monitor the most requested data and automatically cache preformatted XML documents in an IMDB.
Extensibility	There is little room for extensions to application logic. The database can be outfitted with custom views and optimized indices in order to better support external data sharing requirements. Stored procedures can also be added to respond to data access events.	The services that recreate the basic data retrieval function can be extended to support numerous interoperability scenarios. Service interfaces can contain business-specific and generic operations for fine- and coarse-grained data delivery, respectively.

SUMMARY OF KEY POINTS

- Web services can abstract legacy endpoints involved in one-way data transfer. To facilitate the limitations inherent in legacy environments, the use of a repository (such as a queue) may be required for the storage of non-durable data.

- The introduction of the Web services integration layer provides an opportunity to open up legacy functions to other applications in the enterprise.

- Web services can build on legacy application logic to extend functionality and improve the overall one-way data transfer process.

9.4   Web services and point-to-point architectures

One of the most popular integration models is the programmatic creation of a direct data exchange channel between two applications (Figure 9.13). A point-to-point architecture can establish a sophisticated level of interoperability with a great deal of control over the delivery and processing of transferred data.

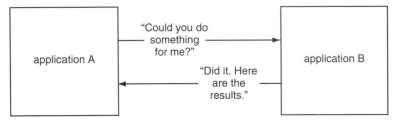

Figure 9.13
Synchronous request and response data exchange.

9.4.1   Tightly coupled integration between homogenous legacy applications

Tying together applications that share a common development technology platform is a relatively straightforward integration project. Custom extensions are built to facilitate all of the respective data exchange requirements of participating applications. This is the most tightly bound integration model, resulting in a permanent integration channel where inter-application dependencies are created and embedded on a function level.

Traditional architecture
The granular level of integration that is made possible in this architecture (Figure 9.14) can accommodate complex business processes, cross-application business tasks that require synchronous processing, data persistence, and long-running transactions.

Connecting applications in this manner gives the developer complete control over the data exchange functionality, and the transfer of data can be highly optimized. Additionally, applications can take advantage of proprietary features exclusive to their platform.

On the flip-side, though, this extent of integration can be quite expensive both to develop and maintain. Once deployed, it is not easily changed, and therefore does not foster enterprise-level interoperability. The dependencies created in point-to-point data sharing channels establish boundaries that can require significant redevelopment when faced with accommodating future cross-application communication requirements. Finally, building upon an already proprietary platform only deepens the dependency on vendor-specific technology.

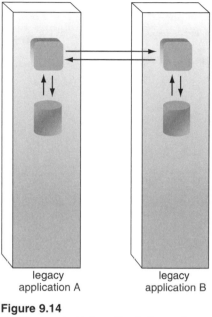

legacy
application A

legacy
application B

Figure 9.14
Tightly-coupled integration between two
homogenous applications.

Encapsulating legacy interfaces within Web services

As illustrated in Figure 9.15, introducing Web services into a homogenous integration environment can provide an opportunity for you to break away from the limitations imposed by this traditionally tight integration model. Moreover, you can accomplish this while still preserving a great deal of the original functionality.

Adapters are required for legacy environments with which the SOAP server cannot communicate directly.

Architectural comparison matrix

The matrix in Table 9.6 provides a comparison of common architectural characteristics.

9.4.2 Tightly coupled integration between heterogeneous applications

Corporate mergers and reorganizations often result in developers having to make two very different applications talk to each other. The typical integration architecture that establishes communication between disparate applications is similar to the previous model, in that a direct connection is created between the two applications. Usually, the differences in platform and technology are overcome through the use of an adapter component.

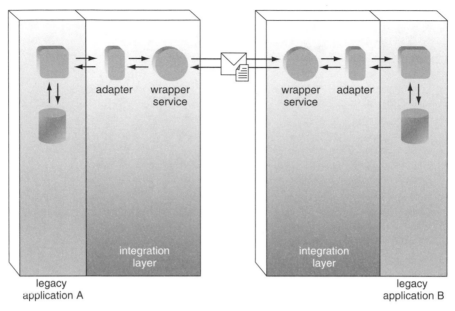

Figure 9.15
Web services representing homogenous legacy applications.

Table 9.6   Typical characteristics of traditional and service-enabled architectures for homogenous legacy applications

Characteristic	Traditional	Service-oriented
Data exchange	Inter-application connections are based on proprietary communication protocols. Integration is at a function level, and custom programming is required for each modification. Due to the tight level of integration, a great deal of control is provided over the processing and exchange of data.	Utilization of wrapper services restricts integration to whatever functionality is exposed by legacy adapters.
Data format conversion	The need for modifying exchanged data depends on how differently the applications are built. Typically, tight integration channels are customized to facilitate the exact nature of the data exchange, which means additional conversion is not a requirement.	Legacy applications will probably not be interested in XML formatted data. Web services therefore will need to serialize and deserialize transported data to and from XML.

Table 9.6   Typical characteristics of traditional and service-enabled architectures for homogenous legacy applications *(Continued)*

Characteristic	Traditional	Service-oriented
Delivery of data	Data is exchanged via proprietary logic and communication protocols.	Legacy data is formatted into an XML document that is transmitted within a SOAP message. Depending on the nature of the data, it may not be necessary to represent it with an elaborate document schema, unless supplementary validation is required. It may be sufficient to embed a data block within a set of parent tags, or as a SOAP attachment. Reliable messaging can be utilized using the WS-ReliableMessaging framework.
Data validation	Validation occurs where appropriate within the respective legacy application logic.	If legacy applications already perform sufficient validation, only minimal XML schema validation may be required.
Performance	The efficiency of data exchange depends on the quality of the proprietary legacy platforms, and on whether applications are communicating locally or remotely.	Smaller-sized XML documents (and the possible absence of complex schemas) will lessen the performance impact of message transmissions. The size of the data payload can also be reduced with a compression technology.
Security	The level of security is completely dependent on the proprietary features of the legacy platform, and the application hosting environment.	Security features are limited to those exposed by the legacy adapters. Encryption and other security measures will be required to protect authentication information transported between services.
Transaction support	Tight integration allows for distributed transaction support to the extent of the features provided by the legacy platform, as well as disparate platforms for which adapters are available.	Common transaction types can be coordinated through the use of coordination services. The coordination types defined by the WS-Transaction specification are supported by a number of transaction protocols.

Table 9.6   Typical characteristics of traditional and service-enabled architectures for homogenous legacy applications *(Continued)*

Characteristic	Traditional	Service-oriented
Additional interoperability	Restricted to legacy applications compatible with the proprietary integration platform.	Generic Web service interface designs can open up adapter functionality to other applications.
Extensibility	Requires custom programming.	Service logic can supplement legacy logic with external logic.

NOTE

Heterogeneous integration architectures for component-based applications are covered separately, following this section.

Traditional architecture

In the scenario illustrated in Figure 9.16, the adapter resides on the calling application server and takes care of all remote communication with the legacy application. Through this adapter, legacy application B exposes essential functionality via an API compatible with application A.

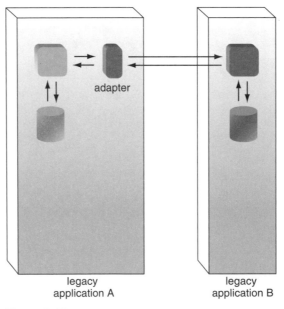

legacy application A   legacy application B

Figure 9.16
Tightly coupled integration between heterogeneous applications.

Loosely coupled integration with service integration layers

Wrapper services simply can abstract the adapter functionality of the respective legacy environments, as demonstrated in Figure 9.17.

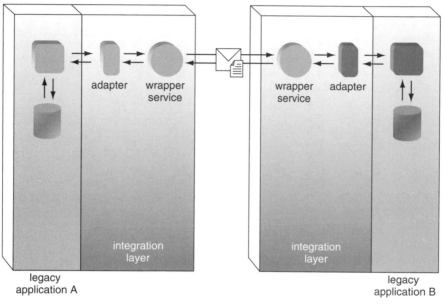

Figure 9.17
Service-oriented integration between heterogeneous applications.

Further isolating the integration layer allows one Web service to represent multiple legacy adapters, as shown in Figure 9.18. This extended abstraction model can lead to a sophisticated service interface that combines and streamlines legacy data and logic.

Notice how the first architecture (Figure 9.17) demonstrates the transfer of the data payload as a SOAP attachment, whereas the second diagram (Figure 9.18) suggests a regular, document-centric SOAP message. The extended architecture utilizes a business service that can combine data from multiple sources in a unique context. This task-oriented view of data is better represented by an XML document. Data, preformatted for consumption by a legacy application can simply be transmitted as is. The target legacy application likely will not support data formatted within an XML schema.

Architectural comparison matrix

The matrix in Table 9.7 provides a comparison of common architectural characteristics.

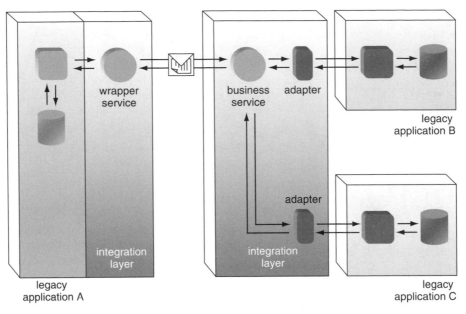

Figure 9.18
A business service interacting with multiple legacy adapters.

Table 9.7   Typical characteristics of traditional and service-enabled architectures for heterogeneous legacy applications

Characteristic	Traditional	Service-oriented
Data exchange	Remote communication can be controlled by adapter technology. Data exchange between an application and an adapter often is restricted to the functionality exposed by the adapter. Other forms of protocol translation products, such as more specialized adapters, may also be available.	Integration layers provide services that interact with respective legacy adapters. Inter-service communication is based on a standard request/response message exchange pattern.
Data format conversion	The need for format conversions depends on the features offered by the adapter interface. Intelligent adapters often will contain built-in transformation features.	The data format may or may not need to change, depending on the functional requirements of the receiving application. For instance, if services are only used to enable delivery (and do not contribute any business logic), then data can simply be packaged as a SOAP attachment.

Table 9.7 Typical characteristics of traditional and service-enabled architectures for heterogeneous legacy applications *(Continued)*

Characteristic	Traditional	Service-oriented
Delivery of data	Transfer of data is managed by proprietary (adapter-controlled) communication.	Data retrieved from adapter functions is placed in XML documents for transport via SOAP. The payload data can be bundled as a SOAP attachment. Delivery of messages or failure conditions can be guaranteed using WS-ReliableMessaging.
Data validation	Any validation requirements are fulfilled within legacy application routines.	Additional data validation typically will be needed when services expose legacy functionality for generic use by new applications. Especially when pure XML output is requested, the service may be required to perform validation prior to sending response messages.
Performance	Directly related to the quality and scalability of the legacy environments and their respective adapters.	Also highly dependent on the legacy adapters, but often slower than a pure legacy integration. The latency imposed by the additional parsing and communications processing can be somewhat alleviated through the use of caching techniques.
Security	Limited to the security models supported by both legacy environments, and the security functions provided through their adapters.	WS-Security features may be required to compensate for differences in authorization and authentication technologies and models.
Transaction support	Legacy transaction processing monitors may allow for cross-platform transactions, including the support of the two-phase commit protocol.	Various middleware solutions will assist service integration layers in preserving existing transaction features, while also allowing for the scope of these transactions to extend to new service activities.

Table 9.7 Typical characteristics of traditional and service-enabled architectures for heterogeneous legacy applications *(Continued)*

Characteristic	Traditional	Service-oriented
Additional interoperability	New interoperability participants will require legacy adapters compatible with their respective platforms.	Adapter functions exposed by service interfaces can be accessed by new service requestors.
Extensibility	Integration architecture can be modified and extended through custom programming. Extensibility is limited to adapter functionality, unless a custom adapter is developed.	Services can introduce new logic or access external legacy functions through the use of additional service adapters.

9.4.3   Integration between homogenous component-based applications

Data exchange between multi-tier applications typically relies on a distributed computing model, utilizing a platform standard remote invocation technology.

Traditional architecture

A component-based application (A) can interact with a remote component belonging to another application (B), by invoking a proxy stub. This stub exposes the same interface as the remote component, but it is installed on the requesting application's server.

The calling component does not know or care that the component it is invoking is on another machine. The proxy stub assumes ownership of the communication, and marshals the request across server boundaries using an RPC-based protocol. This distributed inter-application architecture (Figure 9.19) is identical to the distributed architecture within an application boundary, where application components can be deployed across multiple servers.

Connecting homogenous applications in a tightly bound manner can lead to a highly efficient and scalable integration platform. This point-to-point model provides each application a great deal of control over the other. So much so, that communication boundaries can become blurred. Once autonomous applications with distinct features are merged to form a single, larger solution.

This level of integration, however, can lead to a great number of dependencies. Applications become intertwined and established communication channels are difficult to change or extend. These problems can be somewhat mitigated by the fact that

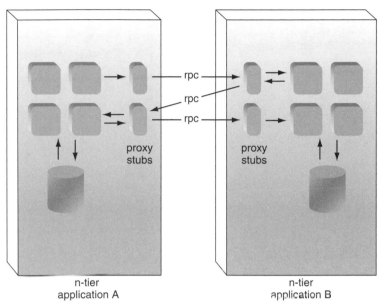

Figure 9.19
Homogenous component-based applications relying on an RPC protocol for remote communication.

component-based design in general promotes reuse and object-oriented principles, such as inheritance and polymorphism. Granular component designs can accommodate tight integration architectures by providing abstraction layers that isolate some (technology and business logic) dependencies.

Component-based architecture with Web services
Figure 9.20 shows how the remote communications framework, including the proxy stubs, is replaced completely by the Web service integration layer.

Although performance may not be optimal (or even comparable to the original RPC environment), adding integration layers that introduce proxy services will break many of the original dependencies, empowering applications to take advantage of new interoperability opportunities. If required, the proxy services can be extended into other service models. This will lead to a more streamlined interface and performance-friendly messaging framework.

Architectural comparison matrix
The matrix in Table 9.8 provides a comparison of common architectural characteristics.

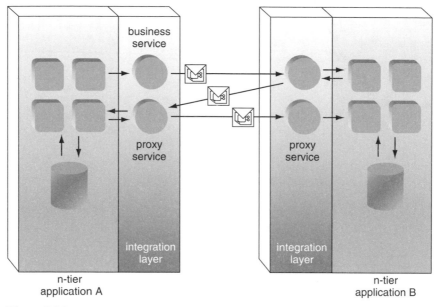

Figure 9.20
Homogenous component-based applications relying on RPC-style SOAP
messages for remote communication.

Table 9.8 Typical characteristics of traditional and service-enabled architectures for homogenous component-based applications

Characteristic	Traditional	Service-oriented
Data exchange	Synchronous request and response patterns are typically provided by a common RPC protocol. Components interact with local proxy stubs that support the programmatic interface of the remote component.	RPC-style SOAP messages can duplicate the characteristics of remote procedures via a TCP/IP-based protocol, most likely HTTP.
Data format conversion	Not required due to common platform.	Traditional component-based environments may not welcome XML formatted data, which may require the service to serialize and deserialize the contents of the SOAP message.
Delivery of data	Binary remoting protocols provide method-level delivery of parameter data.	RPC-style SOAP messages also provide method-level data delivery. Each set of input and output parameters is packaged in a separate message.

Table 9.8 Typical characteristics of traditional and service-enabled architectures for homogenous component-based applications *(Continued)*

Characteristic	Traditional	Service-oriented
Data validation	Custom application routines perform any required validation.	Validation beyond the intrinsic schemas within the service definition is generally not performed by proxy services.
Performance	Good performance can be achieved, although it is dependent on the quality of component class interface designs.	The extra processing overhead introduced by the integration layer reduces runtime performance. The increased size of SOAP messages increases bandwidth requirements. Compression technologies can be used to reduce message sizes, but performance will still tend to be much slower than a pure RPC-driven solution. As with component-based solutions, the interface quality will influence the performance of the application.
Security	Industry standard security protocols are supported by major distributed computing platforms. The degree of delegation across physical boundaries can vary. Remote communication usually can be encrypted as well. The use of firewalls can limit the utilization of RPC-based protocols.	Message-level security can be established in order to support most existing security models. Further, transport-level security, such as encryption, can be added to ensure privacy. (Service intermediaries, however, are not subject to transport-level security measures.) SOAP messages used over HTTP are generally firewall-friendly. However, newer XML-aware firewall products may be required to protect an application from malicious content. Polices can be introduced to better manage security rules.
Transaction support	ACID-compliant, distributed transaction support is very common with component-based platforms, including two-phase commit transactions with legacy repositories.	Atomic transactions, as defined by the WS-Transaction specification, can provide many common transaction features (including the two-phase commit protocol).

Table 9.8   Typical characteristics of traditional and service-enabled architectures for
homogenous component-based applications *(Continued)*

Characteristic	Traditional	Service-oriented
Additional interoperability	Interoperability between other homogenous applications is achieved easily by adding new components or extending existing ones.	A comparable level of interoperability is provided by the service integration layers; however, the integration potential is expanded to disparate environments also exposed through service interfaces.
Extensibility	If using an interface versioning system, components typically can be extended while maintaining backward compatibility to existing interface dependencies.	The level of interface abstraction that can be realized through the use of Web services also promotes a high degree of impact-free extensibility. It does not, however, eliminate interface dependencies altogether.

9.4.4   Integration between heterogeneous component-based applications

Component-based architectures evolved into three major platforms: COM, CORBA, and RMI. Each relied on a proprietary technology set, which made cross-platform communication challenging.

Typically, a special adapter component establishes a cross-platform bridge that allows one application (A) to interact with a component of another (B).

Traditional architecture

Depending on the extent of integration, adapter components may be required in one or both applications environments. The diagram in Figure 9.21 illustrates the former scenario, indicating that application A is driving most of the cross-application interaction.

When integrating disparate component-based applications, the use of an adapter component layer provides a relatively simplified cross-RPC protocol design. Since all communication runs through adapters, they do introduce a new point of failure. The extra layer of translation processing can also result in significant latency.

Component-based architecture with Web services

The architecture illustrated in Figure 9.22 looks a great deal like the service-enabled architecture that replaced the homogenous component-based environment in the previous section. It is actually very similar, the only difference being that separate technology platforms are hosting the respective applications' services.

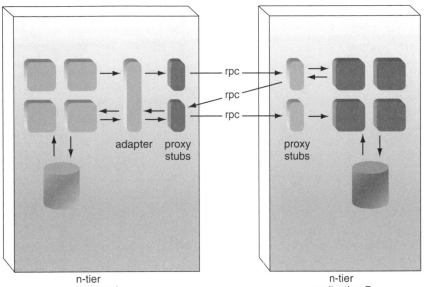

Figure 9.21
Heterogeneous component-based applications utilizing an adapter component for RPC protocol translation.

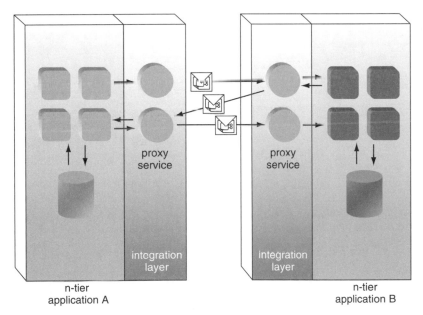

Figure 9.22
Heterogeneous component-based applications relying on proxy services for remote communication.

As explained in Figure 9.23, SOAP servers (or listeners) installed on each application platform effectively replace the need for a protocol adapter. They fulfill this role by marshaling requests and responses to the individual application's native component protocol.

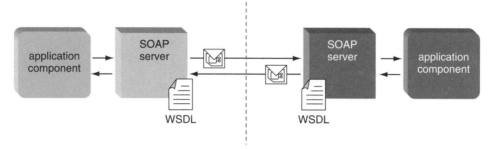

Figure 9.23
SOAP servers act as a form of protocol adapter between SOAP messaging and native component technology communication.

Architectural comparison matrix

The matrix in Table 9.9 provides a comparison of common architectural characteristics.

Table 9.9   Typical characteristics for traditional and service-enabled architectures for heterogeneous component-based applications

Characteristic	Traditional	Service-oriented
Data exchange	Although different component platforms are involved, one remoting technology is used to provide synchronous data transfer.	Synchronous data exchange can be simulated with RPC-style SOAP messages. The use of Web services introduces the option to extend this message framework with an asynchronous, document-centric messaging model.
Data format conversion	The receiving application typically enlists an RPC adapter to convert the format of the requested data from one remoting protocol to another.	RPC communication has been replaced by SOAP messaging, so inter-RPC protocol translation is no longer required. SOAP servers hosting respective application Web services translate RPC commands delivered by SOAP messages to native component protocols.
Delivery of data	Method parameter data is delivered using the chosen remoting technology.	SOAP messages can deliver RPC or document-style data payloads.

Table 9.9   Typical characteristics for traditional and service-enabled architectures for heterogeneous component-based applications *(Continued)*

Characteristic	Traditional	Service-oriented
Data validation	Custom programming routines perform validation where appropriate.	SOAP message payloads can be validated using accompanying schemas. Additional levels of validation can be introduced at the integration layer level.
Performance	While still using efficient remoting technologies for data transport, the protocol conversion processing imposed by the RPC adapter can add significant latency.	The service integration layer introduces new processing and bandwidth requirements. This is somewhat mitigated by the fact that the RPC adapter is no longer required.
Security	Although security models between disparate component platforms may be compatible, they still need to be expressed successfully through the RPC adapter.	WS-Security features can be used to bridge gaps between different security models. Message-level security measures will typically need to be applied, especially when intermediary services are involved along the message path.
Transaction support	Different component-based platforms can participate in transactions with the support of interoperability extensions and transaction coordinators.	Coordination services can be implemented with a number of atomic transaction protocols. The feature set offered by the WS-Transaction specification can accommodate most transaction requirements.
Additional interoperability	Further interoperability between disparate component platforms is, again, dependent on the availability and quality of suitable adapters.	Interoperability opportunities are immediately opened to other applications providing service integration layers.
Extensibility	Careful maintenance of component interfaces can allow component logic to be extended with minimal impact to the existing application environment.	Service interfaces are sufficiently abstracted to allow for functionality to be effectively extended. Interfaces can be equipped with fine- and coarse-grained operations to support traditional RPC-style communication, as well as document-centric message exchanges.

9.5 Web services and centralized database architectures

A less common but still ambitious approach to achieving application interoperability is for two or more applications to share a common repository (Figure 9.24). In this design, a single database provides a comprehensive data model that represents data used by multiple applications.

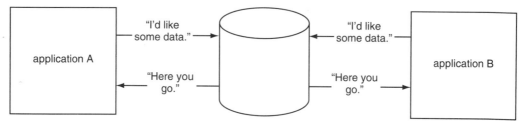

Figure 9.24
Two applications sharing a common repository.

9.5.1   Traditional architecture

Individual applications with significant common data requirements can benefit from sharing a repository (see Figure 9.25). This is feasible in environments where data-related business rules are also stored within the shared repository

Some designs centralize only data common to both applications, in order to avoid redundancy. In this case, data specific to each application can be hosted in supplementary repositories.

Other approaches place all corporate data in one repository. While still reducing the risk of data redundancy, this design burdens one database with the entire processing load of two applications. Future data sharing requirements are simplified through the use of open data access protocols.

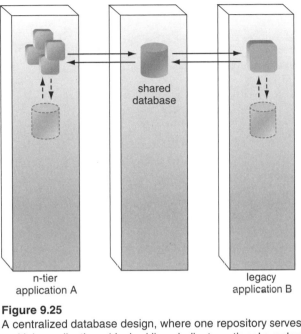

n-tier
application A

shared
database

legacy
application B

Figure 9.25
A centralized database design, where one repository serves data to
multiple applications (dashed lines indicate optional supplementary
databases).

Regardless of the design, a shared database is always at risk of becoming a performance bottleneck. Therefore it must be scaled carefully to accommodate potential application loads.

Since the level of coupling between applications and the database can be excessively tight, the centralized schema can become increasingly complex. Finally, since this model only facilitates data exchange, it does not assist in business automation-driven integration.

9.5.2   Using a Web service as a data access controller

Figure 9.26 shows how a Web service can be positioned as the central access point for the database. This removes the dependency on the database platform, and establishes a generic data access layer.

Architectural comparison matrix
The matrix in Table 9.10 provides a comparison of common architectural characteristics.

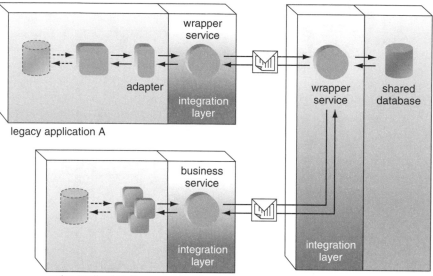

Figure 9.26
A centralized database architecture utilizing a Web service to represent external
data access to the shared database.

Table 9.10 Typical characteristics for traditional and service-enabled centralized database
architectures

Characteristic	Traditional	Service-oriented
Data exchange	Typically accomplished through the use of common data access protocols. If a component is used to represent the shared repository, that component's remoting technology will establish the communication framework for the exchange of data.	The service used to represent the shared repository establishes the standard XML and SOAP messaging framework. It may need to interact with the database using a data adapter (such as a DBMS gateway).
Data format conversion	Generally, no data format conversion is required. Data is retrieved according to the query parameters specified by the requesting application.	Although data is retrieved locally by the repository's wrapper service, it can be offered in multiple output formats.
Delivery of data	If interacting directly with the database, a standard data set is returned, as specified in the original query statement. A controller component may further format or relay this data set.	The wrapper service representing the repository will serve document-centric SOAP messages.

Table 9.10 Typical characteristics for traditional and service-enabled centralized database architectures *(Continued)*

Characteristic	Traditional	Service-oriented
Data validation	Validation will likely occur within the application, but can also be implemented on the repository-level through the use of stored procedures or triggers.	Data can be pre-validated by the repository service provider; however, it likely will be further validated by the receiving application.
Performance	This architecture does introduce a potential bottleneck, because data access performance will be determined by the scalability of the repository and the volume of runtime usage. Additionally, the creation of database connections can be expensive. Unless security requirements demand individual database connections, a pool of connections will likely be provided. This still can affect performance once usage exceeds the amount of connections in the pool.	The use of Web services does not alleviate the database from its processing demands. However, it does introduce a potentially more efficient means of transporting data to and from the repository. It can also abstract proprietary database details. Binary data access protocols create a great deal of network traffic requiring several system calls to perform a single data access function. Coarse-grained service interfaces allow for the one-time delivery of a single set of data to and from the repository. All data access is then performed locally between the wrapper service and the database. Use of encryption during message transport can noticeably impact the delivery of large data sets. However, compression can be applied to counter this effect.
Security	The security models supported by the database determine how authentication and authorization can be implemented. If connection pooling is required, security measures may be limited. The use of an application component to represent the repository can affect the authentication process.	Depending on the security models used by applications accessing the repository, various security measures can be implemented to provide message (data) level and transport level security.

Table 9.10 Typical characteristics for traditional and service-enabled centralized database architectures *(Continued)*

Characteristic	Traditional	Service-oriented
Transaction support	Standard ACID transaction support is expected in this architecture.	Atomic transaction functionality can be provided through the use of WS-Transaction defined coordination types.
Additional interoperability	Shared repositories can be further supplemented with replicated data from other databases. The use of a utility component that represents the repository can increase interoperability by providing a generic data access interface. (Some development platforms already provide ready-made utility components of this nature.)	By exposing a public data access interface to an existing repository, the wrapper service can make the data available to outside service requestors.
Extensibility	A data server can be introduced to effectively represent multiple databases as a single data source. This could simplify the architecture, distribute the processing load, and allow for better maintenance of logical corporate data sets.	A wrapper service would not inhibit the use of a data server. Additionally, the interoperability opportunities introduced through a service integration layer can potentially allow the repository wrapper service to access additional repositories for supplementary data processing.

SUMMARY OF KEY POINTS

- An integration layer can introduce a Web service that assumes ownership of data access to a shared data repository.

- The use of Web services in this environment opens up the availability of the shared repository to other applications that may not have originally supported the database's native data access protocols.

9.6 Service-oriented analysis for legacy architectures

The architecture diagrams provided throughout the previous sections depict the logical interaction between the primary parts of application environments involved in various integration architectures. Don't let their simplicity fool you. To focus on concepts relevant to service integration, these diagrams intentionally hide the nasty details floating just beneath the surface of typical integration solutions.

In real life, legacy integration environments consist of multiple technology layers, each introducing its own level of complexity. Supplanting these environments in order to introduce a service-oriented integration mechanism no doubt will generate a variety of unique challenges.

The following XWIF process (Figure 9.27) provides a step-by-step feasibility analysis for service-enabling traditional integration architectures. Specifically, this exercise will guide you through a structured process of information gathering that will allow you to:

- better assess the technical and organizational impact of upgrading a traditional architecture with service integration layers
- identify key decision points
- more accurately define the scope of the required integration project
- verify that the project itself will deliver enough value to be justified

Step 1: Define business requirements and expectations

The best place to begin any analysis of this sort is first to understand what it is you are trying to accomplish; in other words, the problem your planned integration project is going to solve. This may be easy to document, since your project may be limited to simply service-enabling functionality that already exists in a traditional integration solution.

Start by listing the actual requirements for your integration project. Make sure you group immediate and short-term business requirements separately from long-term goals. Define each requirement with as much detail as possible, accurately representing expectations related to each requirement.

For instance, let's assume there's a requirement for the payroll system to retrieve employee timesheet history information from a separate legacy repository. There may be associated expectations, such as:

- the data retrieval process must consistently complete within two seconds
- the availability of the timesheet system must be equal to that of the payroll application

These expectations essentially broaden the scope of the functional requirement, as well as the functionality that will need to be delivered by the integration solution.

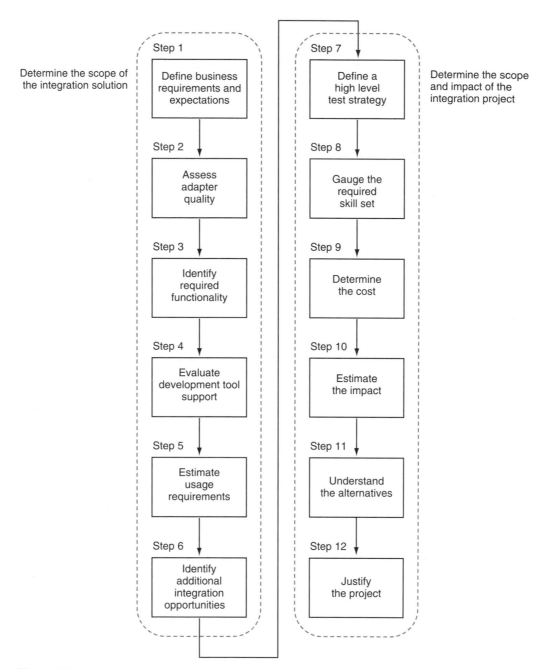

Figure 9.27
An XWIF process for analyzing the feasibility of service-enabling traditional integration architectures.

Step 2: Assess adapter quality

It is highly advisable that you understand the capabilities and limitations of the technology available to you as early as possible in any integration project involving legacy environments. Specifically, you need to understand the intricacies of adapter technology.

Adapters are a key part of both traditional and contemporary integration environments. The features provided by adapters are invaluable for enabling connectivity. A quality design, though, is an adapter product's most important feature.

Adapter products come in many shapes and sizes, and are manufactured by a wide range of vendors. It is not uncommon for an adapter to be involved in every single cross-application task executed by every user of the application.

A quality adapter will:

- effortlessly handle large amounts of concurrency
- gracefully respond to various exception conditions
- allow itself to be scaled, as required

An adapter lacking these capabilities could easily become the weakest link in your communication channels.

To fully understand how good an adapter product is, you will need to install it and perform some hands-on testing. Ideally, you could deploy it within a variety of usage scenarios. If you do encounter severe limitations, as a last resort, you can explore the option of custom developing your own adapter.

Once you (and any technical staff that assisted in this evaluation) are convinced that the product you've chosen is sound, then file those research notes and proceed.

Step 3: Identify required functionality

Did you think we were done with adapters yet? Sorry, but you're going to get to know your adaptive pal even better. If you are working with an application adapter that exposes an API, perform a detailed analysis of the programmatic interface. Ensure that the business requirements you intend to meet in your target service-oriented architecture actually can be realized through the functionality exposed by the adapter.

Here are some further guidelines for this step:

- The focus here is not only on functionality, but also performance. For instance, application adapter APIs utilized in distributed environments (in other words, APIs required to make remote calls back to the legacy system) are notoriously slow. Once you've tested various functions, make sure you can live with the response times.

- Another factor you may need to take into account is transport security. It may not be a requirement, but if it is, further encryption or additional authentication processes that involve the adapter can add a whole new layer of processing overhead to a simple function call.

The more time you spend learning about the adapter's capabilities now, the less surprises you'll encounter later on, once the integration project is underway. Note that this analysis should be at the function or method level.

Step 4: Evaluate development tool support

Despite the level of abstraction an adapter can provide, your actual legacy code may still require changes. It may be time to dust off and re-familiarize yourself with the old tools originally used to program the legacy applications. Before you do, though, check to see if new versions of these tools have been released.

It is not uncommon for a "re-integration" project such as this to result in the introduction of new, more sophisticated legacy application hosting environments. Upgrades to the application server, operating environment, and the legacy development tools may even open the door for improving other (non-integrated) legacy functions.

Step 5: Estimate usage requirements

Back to the performance issue. It's time to estimate how many users you are expecting in your newly service-enabled architecture. The main consideration here is the *potential* concurrency.

Depending on the size of your enterprise, you may not be able to speculate what applications (existing or new) will want or need to interact with your newly service-enabled legacy application. Any information you can gather at this point, however, is valuable. For instance, if, after an investigation, you've determined that there is a fair degree of interest in the logic or data you'll be exposing, you will likely need to look beyond the usage requirements of your immediate project.

Legacy systems may very well not be designed to accommodate a greater amount of concurrency than they already do. If this is the case, you need to either programmatically enhance the affected parts of the legacy application, or explore various data caching and optimization techniques within the integration layers.

Which brings us to another key consideration: the performance impact imposed by the addition of service integration layers. Data exchange between Web services has its own set of performance challenges. In your testing phase, ensure that your legacy functions still operate with the more latent responses they will likely be subjected to.

Step 6: Identify additional integration opportunities

While gathering information to estimate future performance requirements, you (hopefully) were able to get a better idea as to the types of applications that might be connecting to your legacy system in the future. This information is valuable, because it can help justify the project.

It also will affect the way you design your service interfaces. For instance, if you are relatively confident that five other applications will be integrating with your legacy system's wrapper service over the next six months, you will probably be inclined to design a much more generic set of service operations, and perhaps even add a few more than your current integration project requires. Document any potential integration and interoperability opportunities separately from your performance estimates.

Step 7: Define a high level test strategy

When replacing the entire communications framework upon which applications have relied for years, there needs to be an emphasis on testing the many different data exchange scenarios this new framework will have to support.

When determining the scope of a project of this nature, a high-level test strategy can be extremely useful. It can lead to the identification of many technology issues, along with a better estimated functional testing effort.

Step 8: Gauge the required skill set

You've got a good idea as to the scope of your integration project, including short and long term interoperability requirements. This scope determines the effort and expertise required to deliver the integration solution. Effort is time, but assembling the required expertise to carry out this effort can be challenging. Your project may need a blend of development resources, ranging from legacy programmers to Web service designers and intelligent adapter specialists.

List the various roles and associated skills required by your project, and separately group those positions for which you will need to seek external help. Often vendors can supply consultants with niche expertise in proprietary technologies. These resources can be very helpful, but will also likely be the most expensive members of your project team.

Step 9: Estimate the impact

Uprooting established integration solutions will tend to shake things up. Once you have a good idea as to the effort and resources required to physically transition production applications to your target architecture, you should be able to determine what the overall impact of this upgrade will be. Specifically, estimate the duration of the following project phases:

- deployment (custom and purchased application components)
- configuration (data formats and middleware products)
- testing (functional and volume)

Now, determine how the execution of these phases will affect your organization. Here are some potential areas to consider:

- disruption of service
- training and mentoring
- administration and maintenance processes

Step 10: Determine the cost

You've assembled enough information for some of the fundamental expenses, and now it's time to round off your budget with the additional costs. Here are some common items to look out for:

- adapter licenses
- current legacy development tools
- Web service developers and architects
- consultants with legacy expertise
- Web service hosting infrastructure
- hardware upgrades for legacy environments

Also, don't forget to include the cost of performing this analysis as well. The steps that involve research and testing can require the involvement of a number of your technical resources.

Step 11: Understand the alternatives

Generally, when faced with building a service layer on top of a legacy architecture, you have two alternatives:

- Don't do it. Simply extend the existing legacy environment to whatever extent necessary to meet your current business requirements.

- Upgrade the integration architecture to an EAI solution. This may or may not involve replacing parts of the legacy application altogether. It is, though, an attractive option, especially when considering the sophistication of current EAI products and architectures.

If you are seriously considering the latter option, make sure you read through the "Choosing an integration path" section in Chapter 8.

Step 12: Justify the project

Time to review all of the information you've collected, and weigh the good against the items in your notes surrounded by large red exclamation marks. If you're satisfied that you've achieved a clear understanding of the scope, impact, and cost of this project then you should be in a good position to determine whether or not it makes sense to proceed.

SUMMARY OF KEY POINTS

- Service-oriented integration architectures are inherently different from traditional integration approaches.

- Before making the transition to a new cross-application integration architecture, it is important to understand the cost and impact this migration will impose.

- A key part of researching an integration project is understanding the technology behind available adapter products.

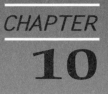

Service-oriented architectures for enterprise integration

With the broad acceptance and popularity of XML and Web services as a technology platform, and EAI as a strategic remodeling of business infrastructure, it's hard to say how these respective trends affected each other as they emerged.

One could argue that the EAI initiative was rejuvenated with the infusion of XML-enabled technologies and service-oriented architectures, as the introduction of these complementary platforms resulted in an overhaul of EAI architectures. As a result, the quality and sophistication of EAI products has never been better.

On the other hand, the momentum behind the EAI trend could very well have been a major contributor to the popularity of XML, and especially to Web services. The increasing need to reduce the costs of integrating disparate environments led to the ubiquitous requirement for a standard data sharing platform, independent of ties to vendors and existing technologies. XML provided a standard data transport which empowered Web services with the ability to effectively abstract proprietary platforms in support of utilizing this transport standard to communicate over previously non-standard boundaries.

Perhaps both claims are true, and really, it's not of much consequence anymore. XML and Web services have become key enabling technologies within the world of EAI, and EAI products are being built from the ground up in support of the XML and Web services technology platforms.

10.1 Service models for enterprise integration architectures

The process-oriented nature of EAI solutions has driven the requirement for service models that can execute and manage various aspects of enterprise business. EAI middleware is typically involved with the creation and hosting of these services; however, it is not uncommon for custom-developed integration solutions to provide these types of services independently. Either way, an understanding of their roles and underlying technologies is vital when designing an enterprise integration architecture. The following XWIF service models are distinctive of service-oriented EAI environments.

10.1.1 Process services

When coordinating the message exchange pattern involved in the execution of a business task, it is often necessary to encapsulate the interaction between Web services into a dedicated business process. This provides a central source of business logic that determines the rules, conditions, and exceptions relating to the workflow scenarios that can occur within a solution.

A number of business process dialects have emerged; however, the BPEL4WS specification has received the broadest industry support. It is complemented by the WS-Coordination and WS-Transaction standards to provide a framework for building sophisticated and fully managed business workflows.

A BPEL4WS *process service* (Figure 10.1) exists as a Web service composed from numerous language constructs that can facilitate most traditional workflow requirements. The WSDL document representing the BPEL4WS process contains interfaces (or portTypes) for the process service itself, as well as any additional services involved with the execution of the process.

Unlike regular WSDL documents, however, the service definition for a BPEL4WS process provides no binding information. It is intentionally implementation-neutral so that the process can remain mobile, reusable, and independent from changes to the technical deployment environment.

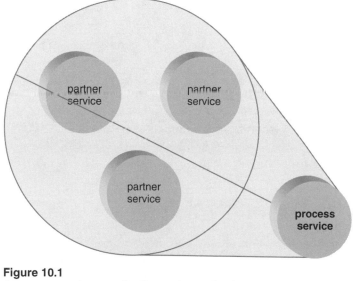

Figure 10.1
A process service coordinating and exposing functionality from three partner services.

As illustrated in Figure 10.2, process services can expose BPEL4WS processes to manage a variety of activity scenarios, involving numerous partner services (typically based on the business service model).

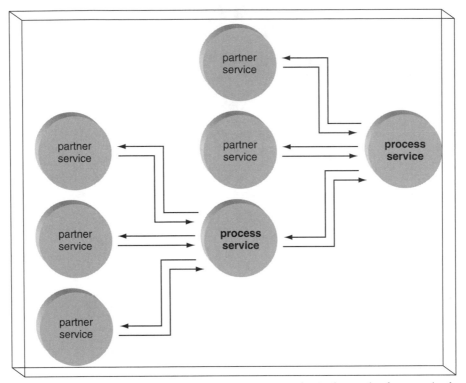

orchestration engine from vendor A

Figure 10.2
A process service assembly interacting with a nested process service assembly.

Various forms of service composition are realized through the use of process services, as shown in Figure 10.3. Generally, the interaction between process and partner services is managed by an orchestration engine. For a list of common service model characteristics, see Table 10.1.

10.1.2 Coordination services (for business activities)

WS-Coordination is closely associated with the WS-Transaction specification, which defines two distinct coordination types, both of which are relevant to enterprise integration environments. The first, atomic transactions, enables the management of ACID-like transactions. The service model for atomic transaction coordinators is established in Chapter 9; it is the most common type of coordination service used in legacy integration architectures. The second coordination type provides a model for long running transactions, and is represented as part of the *coordination service model (for business activities)*.

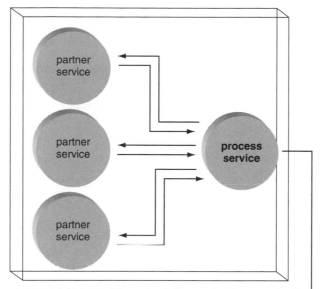

process A (managed by orchestration engine from vendor A)

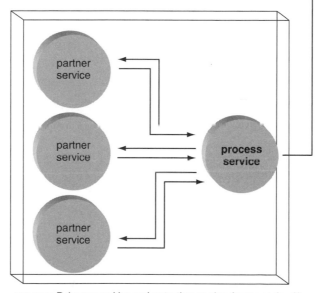

process B (managed by orchestration engine from vendor A)

Figure 10.3
Compatible process services interoperating across platform
boundaries.

Table 10.1 Typical characteristics of process services

	Typical service characteristics
Anticipated usage volume	High to very high. Since the service will be involved with each step executed by a process, it can be highly utilized.
Interface design characteristics	The WSDL definition of a process service can differ from regular Web services. When using BPEL4WS, for instance, the service definition can remain implementation-independent so that it can express a generic process description that can be deployed in different platforms.
Message types	Document-centric.
Deployment requirements	Typically, process services are hosted (and their descriptions executed) by the orchestration engine within the integration product's runtime.

NOTE

The atomic transaction part of the WS-Transaction specification is superseded by a separate standard titled WS-AtomicTransaction. Similarly, the planned WS-BusinessActivity standard will replace the corresponding coordination type definition within WS-Transaction. See `www.specifications.ws` for more information.

Business process integration is a typical characteristic of EAI solutions, which is why coordination services for business activities are utilized exclusively for the management of long running business activities.

This service model (also known as the *business activity coordinator* shown in Figure 10.4) is generally used in conjunction with process services as a means of handling success and failure conditions related to the execution of the overall process activity (see Table 10.2 for a list of common characteristics).

The WS-Coordination specification provides an assembly of services with predefined interfaces that support the management of a coordination context. Specifically, this collection of services provides separate operations for the creation of a context, the registration for a context, and the selection of a protocol.

10.2 Fundamental enterprise integration architecture components

EAI solutions centralize inter-application communication and automate new processes with the help of two core components: the *broker* component and the *orchestration*

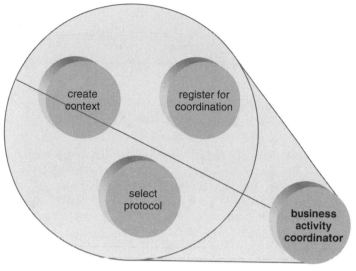

Figure 10.4
A coordination service used to manage a coordination context for long running business activities.

Table 10.2   Typical characteristics of coordination services for long running business activities

	Typical service characteristics
Anticipated usage volume	Low to high. Since business activities can span minutes, hours, or even days, the processing involved in managing the coordination context can be sporadic.
Interface design characteristics	Predefined by the WS-Coordination specification, but also extensible.
Message types	Document-centric.
Deployment requirements	It is common for EAI servers to host and manage business activity coordinators. This would imply a centralized deployment within the EAI server environment.

engine. The fundamental functions enabled by these components establish the basic EAI architecture illustrated in Figure 10.5.

To demonstrate how these components function, basic data exchange scenarios are provided in this section. Even though these examples might seem simplistic, they explain key EAI concepts. Most enterprise integration problems are solved through the use of these two core components. Incidentally, these two integration scenarios are equally common in B2Bi (business-to-business integration) environments.

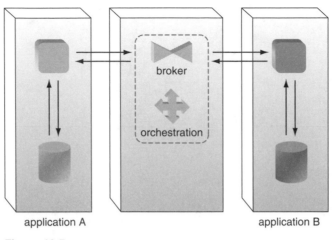

Figure 10.5
A basic EAI architecture.

10.2.1 Broker

The *broker* component is capable of performing a wide variety of runtime functions, such as:

- sophisticated data transformations
- merging documents from different sources
- supplementing received data from one application with additional information from another

The primary function of an integration broker component, however, is to ensure that data received from one source is always in the format expected by the destination (Figure 10.6).

Data exchange with a broker component

The following five-step process demonstrates the retrieval of data by application B, in response to a request from application A. (How the request is sent to application B is not relevant to this example.) Figure 10.7 provides an overview of the process steps.

Step 1: retrieve requested data from the source database (Figure 10.8)   Application A initiates a request for data that is transmitted to application B. Application B processes this request and retrieves the data.

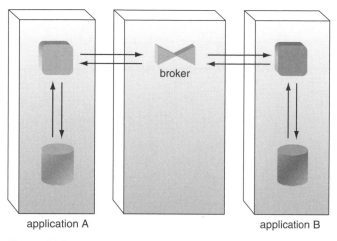

application A   application B

Figure 10.6
Application-level integration involving an application broker.

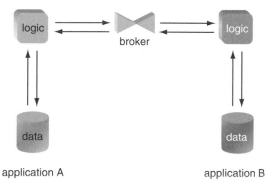

application A   application B

Figure 10.7
The key components involved in a simple data exchange
scenario with an integration broker.

NOTE
As indicated by the different shading applied to the respective application symbols, it is assumed that data between disparate applications is being exchanged.

Step 2: validate source data using source schema (Figure 10.9) At some point, the
retrieved data is validated against a schema representing the data model of the message document that will be used to transport the data outside of the application
boundary.

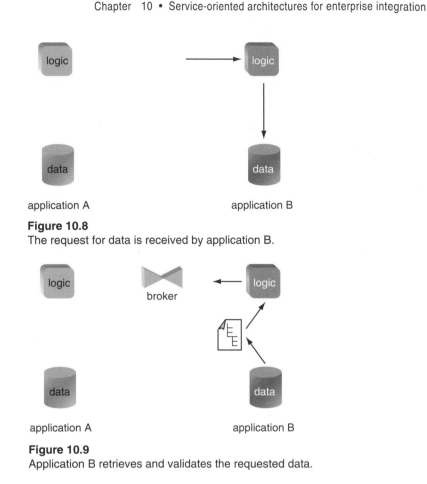

Figure 10.8
The request for data is received by application B.

Figure 10.9
Application B retrieves and validates the requested data.

This step may occur natively within the database, or it may be executed within application B's logic. The latter case is more likely if the data is retrieved from multiple data sources, in which case a unique schema for this specific representation may exist.

Step 3: broker the data format (Figure 10.10)   Finally, here's where our broker component kicks in. It will already have schemas from both applications, as well as a data map that will allow it to transform the retrieved data into the data format required by application A.

Also, in this example, it performs a dynamic lookup from an external data source in order to supplement the received data with additional information. The transformation also filters out some unnecessary data (not shown).

Step 4: validate target data using target schema (Figure 10.11)   Application A receives and validates the data contained within the response to its original request.

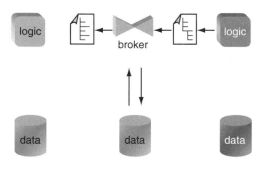

application A   application B

Figure 10.10
The broker service transforms, filters, and adds to
the received data in order to produce a response
acceptable to the requesting application.

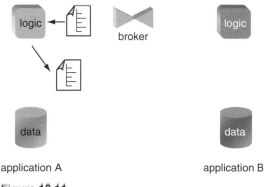

application A   application B

Figure 10.11
The transformed data is sent to application A, where
it is validated.

Step 5: insert data into target database (Figure 10.12)   Once successfully validated,
application A processes and then inserts the data in its database.

10.2.2 Orchestration

An orchestration engine is used to encapsulate and execute business process logic
(Figure 10.13). A process can introduce complex rules and workflows that often contain
new business rules, exception handling, and transaction management features, involving a number of different applications and data sources.

Orchestration can, for instance:

- integrate with other applications to retrieve additional data
- invoke the broker component for manipulation of data

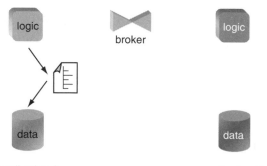

Figure 10.12
Application A accepts and stores the received data.

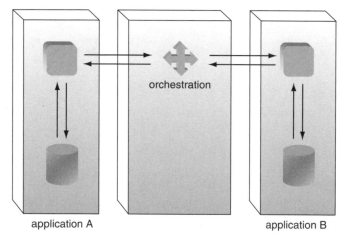

Figure 10.13
Process-level integration managed by an orchestration engine.

- use existing application logic to further process or validate the retrieved data
- reject the data if any form of validation fails

Often, the workflow behind the process managed by orchestration will have been mapped previously into a number of steps with conditional logic and content-based decision points.

Orchestration-managed messaging tends to be more sophisticated than the standard SOAP messages you may be using in simpler integration scenarios. For instance, messages processed by EAI components can contain routing and transaction information in addition to standard data structure.

Also, messages undergo various states. A message can have a *permanent state*, but also a *process state* that it may be required to assume when an incomplete process is stored as non-durable data. Also known as *hydration*, this state is temporary until the process is active again, at which time the message resumes its *active message state*.

The use of orchestration will often classify an integration solution as a *virtual application*. Abstracting process and business logic into orchestration workflows also results in elaborate service assemblies that encapsulate aggregated process logic.

Data exchange with orchestration

As with the integration broker example, this process demonstrates the retrieval of data by application B, in response to a request from application A. Figure 10.14 provides an overview of the process steps.

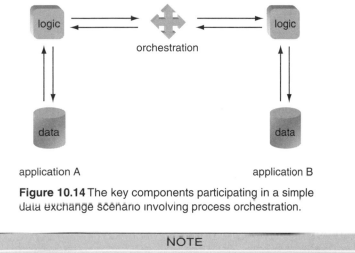

Figure 10.14 The key components participating in a simple data exchange scenario involving process orchestration.

> **NOTE**
>
> Unlike the scenario used for the integration broker process, these environments are homogenous (although this is not a requirement for orchestration).

Step 1: request data from orchestration (Figure 10.15) Application A initiates a request for data that is transmitted to the orchestration engine. A key aspect of this scenario is the fact that application A does not even need to be aware of application B's existence.

A's only point of contact for all external communication is an entry point into the process. It simply forwards requests to and receives responses from the orchestration component representing the process. This gives orchestration the freedom to fulfill those requests by using any available resources to which it has access.

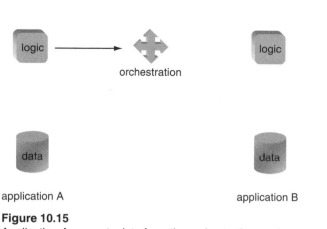

Figure 10.15
Application A requests data from the orchestration engine.

Step 2: request data from application (Figure 10.16)   Assuming that no further processing is required, the orchestration engine simply routes the request to application B, which proceeds to retrieve the requested data. (Application B's validation of the message contents is not shown.)

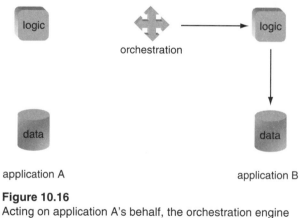

Figure 10.16
Acting on application A's behalf, the orchestration engine
relays the request for data from application B.

Step 3: return response to orchestration (Figure 10.17)   Application B forwards the retrieved data to the orchestration engine, as requested.

In this scenario, application B does not need to know where the request for this data originated. Also, it is only aware of the process instance as its sole external point of contact for all communication outside of its application boundary.

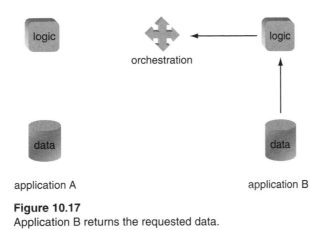

Figure 10.17
Application B returns the requested data.

Step 4: process orchestration logic (Figure 10.18)   At this point the orchestration engine can execute a wide variety of processing options, all depending on the nature of the business process it is representing.

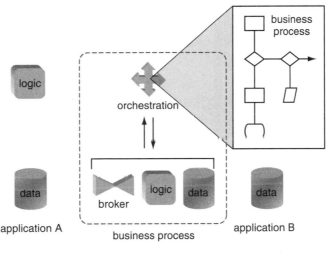

Figure 10.18
Orchestration's business process manipulates the requested data.

In our example, orchestration executes a business process that further validates the data, and then requests a security clearance before allowing it to be passed to application A. To perform these steps, it utilizes a separate data source, outside business logic, and finally the integration broker component for transformation.

Note that this step could have just as easily occurred during the initial request by application A.

Step 5: forward data to requesting application (Figure 10.19)   Assuming all required orchestration processing was completed successfully, the requested data is sent to application A, which subsequently validates and stores it in its database.

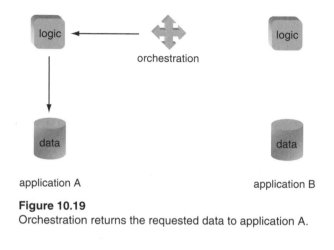

Figure 10.19
Orchestration returns the requested data to application A.

SUMMARY OF KEY POINTS

- There are two fundamental parts of an EAI solution, the integration broker component and the orchestration engine.

- The integration component broker is responsible for enabling communication between applications requiring different data formats.

- The orchestration engine encapsulates and executes business processes that can involve a variety of applications and resources.

10.3 Web services and enterprise integration architectures

Integration architectures designed for the enterprise reach beyond cross-application communication concerns. Primarily driven by business process automation, these solutions can be extremely broad in both functional and architectural scopes (Figure 10.20).

Numerous EAI solution vendors have provided sophisticated environments to accommodate ever-changing business processes. The two fundamental integration components explained in the previous section are key players in these environments, because they support the introduction of new business processes (or changes to existing processes) by unifying disparate applications to collaborate on a functional level.

Most EAI solutions rely on asynchronous messaging-based communication frameworks, and therefore open up the interaction options between the integrated participants. XML

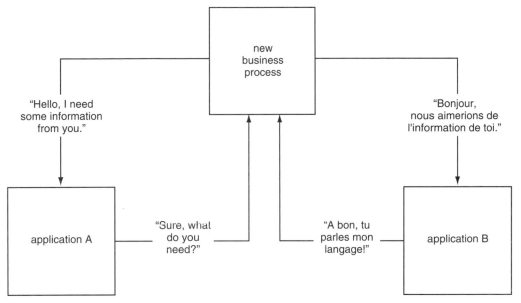

Figure 10.20
A new business process orchestrates the involvement of two applications.

is a natural fit for this framework, and has established itself as its standard data representation technology. Web services have also infiltrated traditional EAI environments, and their support has reached the point where vendors are building pure service-oriented enterprise integration products.

This leads us to a common problem with traditional EAI: interoperability between vendor platforms. Toward the end of this section we explore how this very significant issue is being addressed through a contemporary service-oriented EAI model.

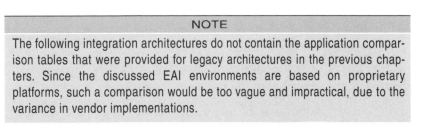

NOTE

The following integration architectures do not contain the application comparison tables that were provided for legacy architectures in the previous chapters. Since the discussed EAI environments are based on proprietary platforms, such a comparison would be too vague and impractical, due to the variance in vendor implementations.

10.4 Hub and spoke

The most popular of the traditional EAI models, this architecture promotes centralized processing through a hub that is provided by proprietary middleware. A centrally located server hosts the integration logic that controls the orchestration and brokering of all inter-application communication.

10.4.1 Traditional architecture

Through a series of adapters, a wide variety of disparate client applications can participate in data exchange as well as the orchestration workflow that resides within the hub logic. Once an application is connected to the hub, it may not even need to be aware of other applications it ends up indirectly interacting with.

Figure 10.21 shows how integrated applications essentially create point-to-point connections with the hub itself. By hiding the solution participants from each other, a level of "logic autonomy" is established.

Facilitated by broker transformation features, orchestration-enabled routing can support one-to-one, one-to-many, and many-to-many data exchange patterns. This level of flexibility can lead to a variety of creative integration scenarios. The fact that all of the data flows through a central location reduces the potential of redundant data re-entry and processing, and also makes the monitoring of communication much easier.

In addition to simplifying a number of administration tasks, this design centralizes the maintenance of the process logic, and even promotes reuse within the application components that implement the centralized orchestration workflow.

This model, however, does introduce some risks. As the busiest and most popular part of an integration architecture, the hub environment can become a potential processing hazard. Bottleneck situations are a constant danger, unless scalability is carefully planned and designed into the hub infrastructure.

Also, the hub can establish a single point of failure for a very large amount of automation. Imagine twelve different applications working together to support automated processes for five divisions of an organization. Now imagine the one point through which all data must flow going down. Not a pretty picture. Though measures can be taken, such as replication and clustering, the cost of putting together a fully scalable hub-and-spoke environment with full fail-over support may be prohibitive.

It has been theorized that one of the major reasons this model has been so heavily promoted is that it benefits the vendors more than you. Once your enterprise commits to a full-scale EAI solution, it will create a great number of dependencies on a proprietary technology. The solution will be expensive to purchase, expensive to build upon, and extremely expense to replace. A centralized hub that introduces a vendor-specific product to control all communication between your integrated applications will become deeply entrenched in your organization. For better or for worse.

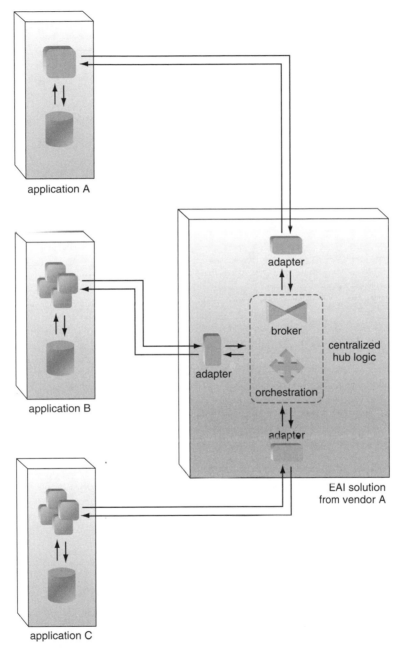

Figure 10.21
A basic hub and spoke architecture.

10.4.2 Adding integration layers with Web services

Web service integration layers are added to this environment (Figure 10.22), less to broaden its interoperability potential, but more to allow service-enabled applications to participate without the use of EAI adapters.

A service-oriented extension to traditional hub-and-spoke solutions is a nice fit for the asynchronous messaging model that is typically already established. As a result, integrated applications using Web services will often perform well in these environments.

The inclusion of service integration layers within this architecture, however, does little to address the typical problems associated with the hub-and-spoke approach. The open service interfaces do allow for supplementary processing from resources external to the integration environment. This option, however, may be considered undesirable, as it essentially introduces new integration channels that cannot be maintained and administered from the same central location as the others.

10.5 Messaging bus

Also known as the *publish and subscribe* or the *information bus* model, this architecture offers a common alternative to the popular hub-and-spoke design. The overall concept is similar, in that it consists of a central integration environment to which a number of client applications individually connect. The underlying data processing structure, however, differs.

10.5.1 Traditional architecture

The message bus architecture, as illustrated in Figure 10.23, introduces an information pipeline that acts like a kind of shuttle for incoming and outgoing messages. Applications typically are assigned the role of *publisher* or *subscriber*, which essentially translates into source and destination endpoints within an asynchronous context.

Each potential integration source is considered a publisher to which other applications can subscribe. Once a publisher transmits information, the bus broadcasts the data to each registered subscriber. As with the hub-and-spoke architecture, the messages can (and likely will) undergo various processing steps before arriving at their destinations.

Data can be transformed, routed, or subjected to conditional logic within the process orchestration workflow. Processing tends to be more partitioned, and therefore less centralized than in a hub-and-spoke environment. This lessens the risk of performance bottlenecks, and increases scalability. Another typical characteristic of this architecture is a greater tendency toward utilizing intelligent adapters. The core hub logic therefore

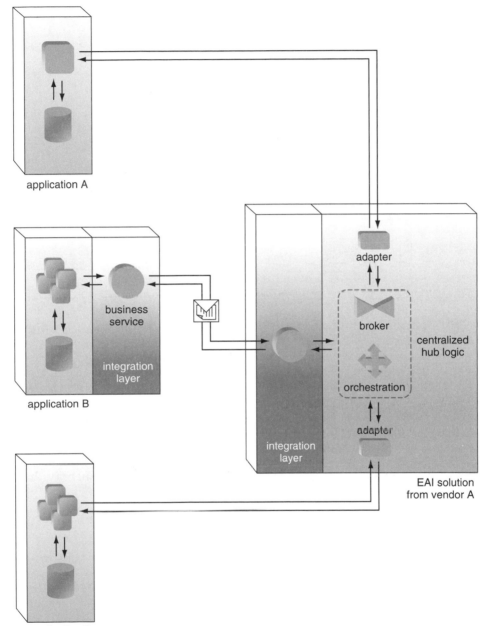

Figure 10.22
A service-enabled hub-and-spoke architecture.

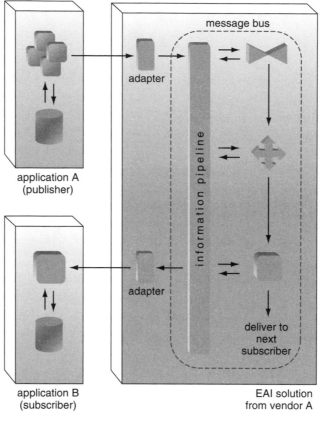

Figure 10.23
The messaging bus architecture.

is lightened by allowing adapters to distribute and perform a larger share of the pre- and post-processing tasks.

This "islands of processing" model, though, can result in significant administration effort. Maintenance and troubleshooting can also be more challenging for messaging bus implementations, as commonly used fire-and-forget transmission patterns make errand messages (and other types of error conditions) harder to trace.

10.5.2 Messaging bus solutions that utilize Web services

Service integration layers establish a more standardized communications framework within this environment (as shown in Figure 10.24), as they do in all non-service-oriented architectures. Since Web services tend to further abstract adapter technology, they can lessen the overall processing load of the messaging bus servers. This may be especially significant if the integration layer results in the physical distribution of the heavier, more processing-intensive intelligent adapters.

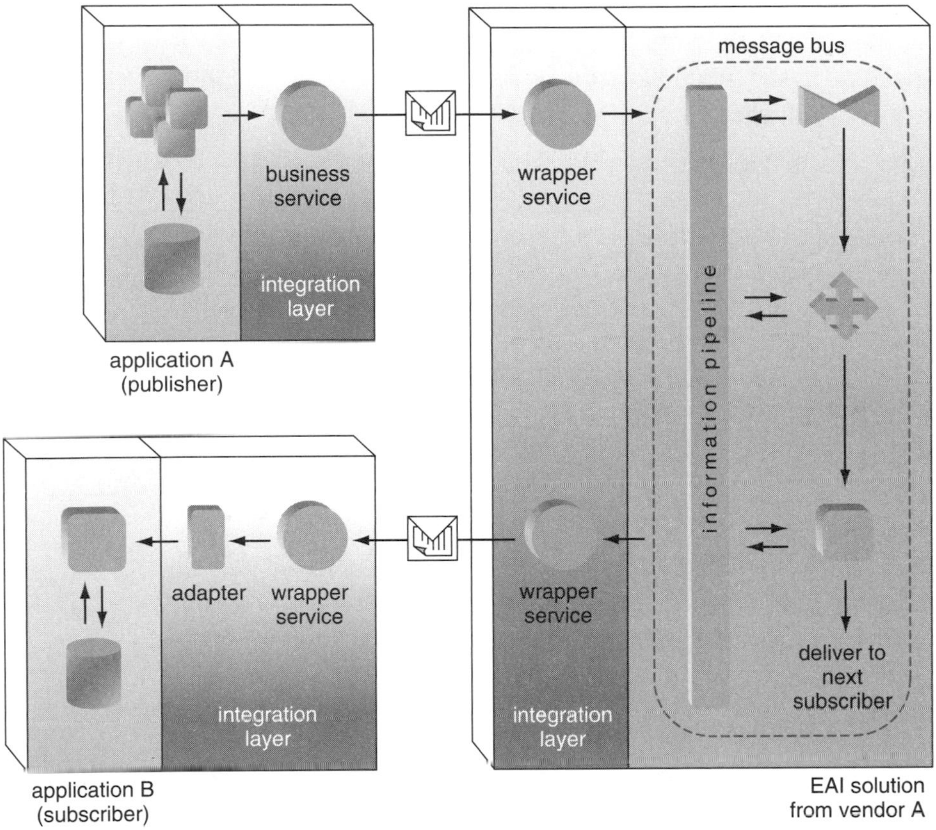

Figure 10.24
The messaging bus architecture with service integration layers.

As with other messaging-based EAI solutions, Web services complement the asynchronous message exchange models very well. Though even vanilla messaging bus solutions can be set up in such a manner that they simulate the hub-and-spoke architecture, adding integration layers facilitates this by supporting both synchronous and asynchronous messaging models, if required.

10.6 Enterprise Service Bus (ESB)

If you built a pure service-oriented architecture from scratch, you could design it in such a way that you would avoid many of the problems that have plagued proprietary EAI solutions. Your only real challenge would be the time and expense required to build an enterprise-grade integration architecture driven by an army of standardized Web services.

What if, though, someone built a platform supporting such an architecture for you. The underlying technology would still be proprietary, but would not lock you in. Every component of the solution would exist as a Web service, allowing you to exchange or upgrade it as you please. Um… do you deliver?

The enterprise service bus model is a pure implementation of service-oriented principles. Figure 10.25 shows how the core integration platform is built as a series of Web services that provide traditional orchestration and broker features as well as a number of other standard EAI functions. Don't like the service engine that came with your

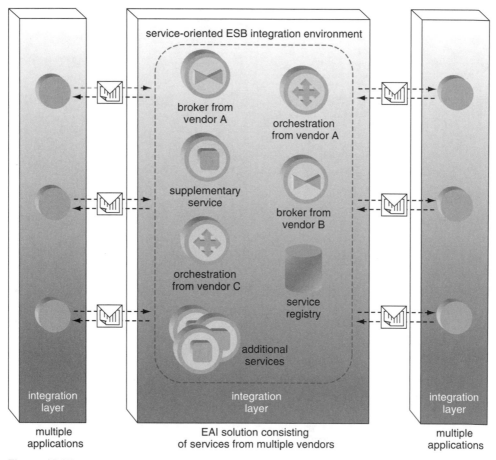

Figure 10.25
The enterprise service bus architecture (services are hosted by containers provided by the integration platform).

product? Pull it out and drop in a new one. Or, supplement it with additional services from other vendors.

ESB is a refreshing departure from the proprietary stigma often associated with traditional EAI products. Some vendors have recognized an opportunity to combine the best of both worlds, while liberating product owners from vendor dependencies.

Typical ESB architectures establish an integration platform that acts as a dynamic hosting environment for intelligent service intermediaries. Service containers can host a variety of service components. Even though the containers may be proprietary, the services they host are not. In addition to supporting interchangeable services, it also allows for the underlying hosting environment to be replaced while preserving the logic already encapsulated by these services.

One of the most significant benefits of this architecture is its ability to transcend the many obstacles of traditional inter-EAI-integration. If two ESB solutions were implemented with different vendor platforms, the open interface policy of this model would make any disparity in the service hosting environments almost irrelevant. (See Chapter 11 for a more thorough discussion of this issue.)

Service-oriented integration strategies

T he last two chapters described how common traditional integration architectures can be supplemented by and transitioned toward an SOA. Provided here are a collection of design strategies for refining and extending integrated service-oriented architectures.

Many of these strategies focus on maximizing the quality of Web services that represent the contact points for external applications. These *integration endpoint services* (Figure 11.1) are a critical part of service-oriented design within integrated environments. Each establishes a standard interface that potentially can represent an enormous amount of business automation logic. The importance of performance, robustness, security, standardization, and intelligent utilization, therefore are amplified for these Web services.

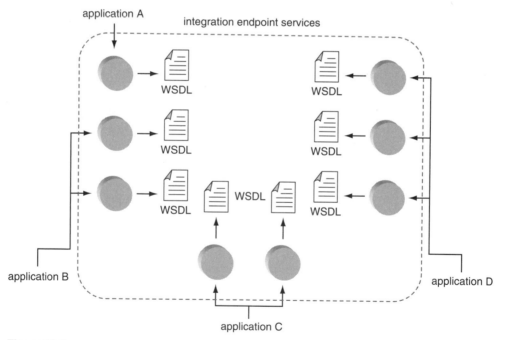

Figure 11.1
Integration endpoint services representing disparate applications.

Collectively, these integration endpoint services form a *service-oriented integration architecture;* an environment unifying a variety of applications through a set of standardized service interfaces.

> **NOTE**
>
> Although this chapter is dedicated to Web service design and architecture issues, the standardization of integration endpoint services is discussed through a series of best practices in Chapter 13.

11.1 Strategies for streamlining integration endpoint interfaces

A service-oriented integration architecture establishes a level of service interface ubiquity. This does wonders for standardizing interoperability, but in no way guarantees a quality data sharing environment. The efficiency and usability of a Web services framework relies on the design of individual service interfaces.

Application integration projects are frequently preoccupied with immediate integration requirements. When service-enabling legacy applications, these short-term objectives typically focus on accurately exposing functionality residing within the legacy application logic.

Adding an integration layer to legacy environments, however, provides an opportunity to think long term. By enhancing existing interfaces and even existing functionality, your new integration architecture can offer a variety of new features and, more importantly, can establish a better SOA design.

11.1.1 Make interfaces more generic

Many traditional applications were never built with interoperability in mind, and therefore do not provide generic interfaces. Auto-generated proxy services will frequently mirror existing component interfaces, and therefore provide no real improvement. It's up to you to do a bit of modeling work in order to make both the interface naming convention, as well as the functionality of the interface, more generic.

This can entail combining component methods into one service operation (as in the example in Figure 11.2), or splitting coarsely grained component methods into multiple service operations (see Figure 11.3). It all comes down to thinking beyond immediate integration requirements.

When splitting a coarse piece of legacy application logic into multiple service operations, it typically requires working with the parameters of the source function. For instance, a component method providing general accounting report data will probably contain a series of input parameters that it will use to define the search criteria of the report.

One of the parameters may allow you to set an accounting document type so that report information is returned only for a specific body of accounting data. You could

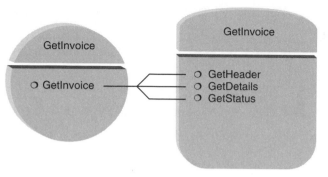

Figure 11.2
An example of a service providing a generic operation that
represents multiple component methods.

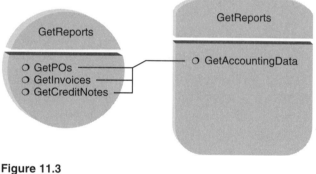

Figure 11.3
A service achieving increased usability by providing a group of
granular operations that all relate to the same component method.

represent each parameter value as a separate service operation. This not only makes
your service more generic, it also makes it easier to use.

11.1.2 Consolidate legacy interfaces

The context in which your service will be used may differ from what the legacy application logic was intended for. This often means that you can combine various pieces of
your legacy programming logic to facilitate the new context within the function of a
service operation.

This model (illustrated in Figure 11.4) not only creates a more useful service interface, it
can greatly increase performance by combining the execution of multiple legacy functions into one service operation call.

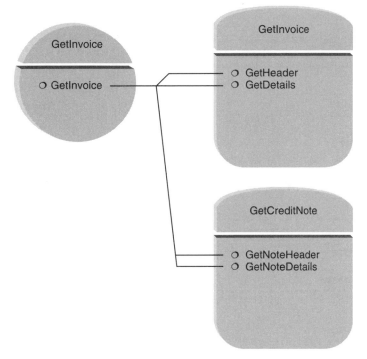

Figure 11.4
A single service operation utilizing four component methods.

11.1.3 Consolidate proxy interfaces

When Web services are first added to multi-tier applications, the components for which service interfaces are required are typically represented by proxy services, as shown in Figure 11.5. This service model offers an easy-to-create extension that allows the affected part of the application to begin immediately interacting with other service-enabled environments.

Since component interfaces were not originally created with this type of messaging framework in mind, it is recommended that the initial set of proxy services be replaced. Introducing a business service allows the integration layer designer to create an optimized service interface.

Figure 11.6 demonstrates how the context of business tasks executed by the proxy services can be accurately encapsulated by a business service. Additionally, various component interface characteristics can either be combined or expanded upon, in order to further facilitate interoperability and increase performance.

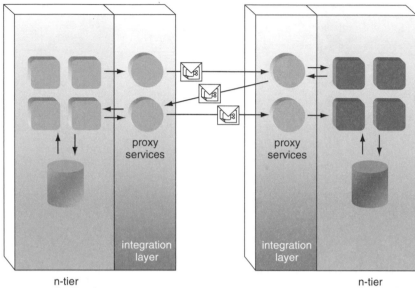

Figure 11.5
Typical out-of-the-box integration layers consisting of standard proxy services.

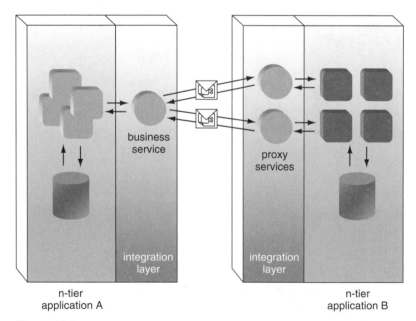

Figure 11.6
A similar design where application A's proxy service layer has been replaced
with an optimized business service.

If both applications replace the RPC-centric messaging model promoted by proxy services, they can standardize on document-centric SOAP messages. This can lead to further improvements in performance.

11.1.4   Supplement legacy logic with external logic

It is well worth investigating opportunities to incorporate application logic within other environments. This can facilitate and perhaps even broaden the usage of a service operation.

Within homogenous environments, a single service may have access to multiple applications (Figure 11.7). In this situation, the service may be able to choose the pieces of functionality that it can incorporate into its operations.

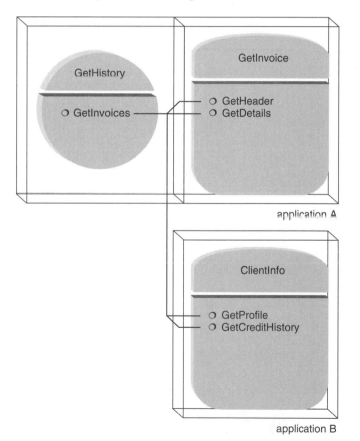

Figure 11.7
A Web service operation making use of component methods from
different applications.

In more service-oriented environments, a new service operation can simply incorporate legacy application logic already exposed through existing Web services. Figure 11.8 shows an example. (This follows the assembly model introduced in Chapter 6.)

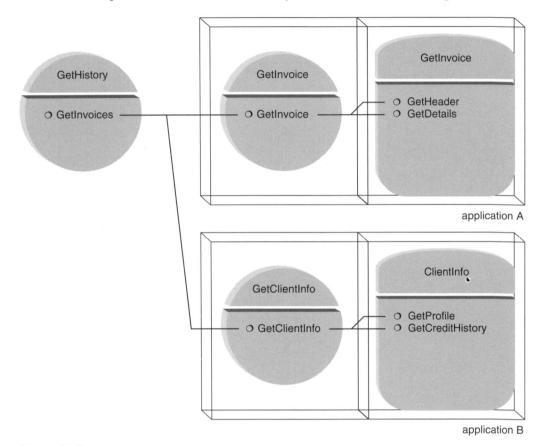

Figure 11.8
A service assembly where one controller service encapsulates functionality from business services representing legacy applications.

Incorporating external application functionality can turn into a fair amount of effort. Both up-front analysis and subsequent development may be costly. The benefits of a quality and high-performance service, however, may be well worth it.

> **NOTE**
>
> Though this design approach promotes reuse, it can generate unplanned inter-service dependencies. It may introduce the need for cross-application project interface contracts and interface maintenance processes.

11.1.5 Add support for multiple data output formats

Even if the scope of your current integration project is limited to facilitating data exchange between two distinct applications, you may still want to consider building some generic interoperability into your services by supporting multiple output formats for your data.

Though not a trivial piece of logic to simply append to an existing service design, it can greatly improve future interoperability requirements without the need to start entirely new integration projects.

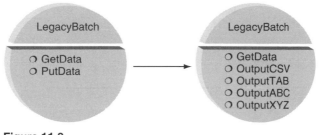

Figure 11.9
A business service extended to offer multiple output formats.

In the example provided in Figure 11.9, the original service designed to act as a hub for the batch export and import legacy architecture has been enhanced further to provide a number of additional output formats.

11.1.6 Provide alternative interfaces for different SOAP clients

It is often natural to add a service integration layer to n-tier applications that support RPC-style SOAP messages. This message format promotes the method-level data exchange already designed into traditional application components.

As your application evolves, you will likely be taking a close look at replacing this message format with document-centric SOAP messages. Especially in distributed environments, this can lead to a number of interoperability improvements, the foremost of which is performance.

Since dependencies may already exist on the RPC-style messages provided by the first set of proxy services you added, you will likely not want to overhaul you architecture until it's absolutely necessary.

You can ease the transition from RPC to document-centric SOAP messaging by supporting both formats with separate integration layers (Figures 11.10 and 11.11). If you're not comfortable with a design that consists of different access points into the same application logic, you can add another layer to abstract the different interface options into one service endpoint.

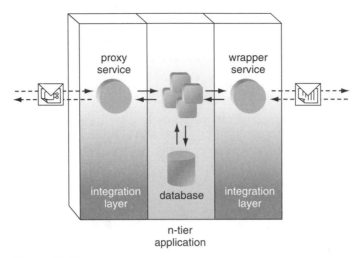

Figure 11.10
A component-based application encased by different integration layers.

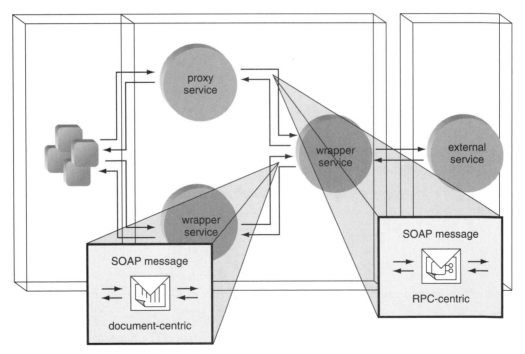

Figure 11.11
A parent wrapper service that determines which underlying service interface is most appropriate, based on SOAP message format characteristics.

SUMMARY OF KEY POINTS

- Since Web services can make existing functionality available for new interoperability opportunities, creating a generic service interface is often recommended.

- With a bit of modeling work, legacy component interfaces can be streamlined in the Web service interface.

- Legacy functionality can also be supplemented with additional external functions, while still represented by the same Web service.

11.2 Strategies for optimizing integration endpoint services

Designing quality endpoint services requires more than streamlined interfaces. How these important Web services function internally, and how they inter-relate with each other are key design considerations that affect the entire integration architecture.

11.2.1 Minimize the use of service intermediaries

When first building service integration layers on top of legacy applications, it's highly recommended that you keep the new service architecture as simple as possible (Figure 11.12). It is easy to complicate an SOA unnecessarily with complex routing logic and granular intermediary services. An overly ambitious design can lead to an unwieldy integration environment. Robustness could be compromised, and performance problems can start emerging.

If at all possible, try to limit your intermediaries to the hub-type services that act as the generic interface to service requestors outside of the integration architecture. This non-intrusive controller service performs a specific function to facilitate interoperability without adding too much complexity to existing message exchange patterns between legacy services.

Once a service-enabled integration architecture has been established, and you've had time to assess and attend to various performance, availability, and robustness issues with your new environment, you will be able to add intermediaries much more effectively.

11.2.2 Consider using service interceptors

If you are looking for ways of alleviating your Web service from routine processing tasks, service interceptors provide an alternative to delegating functionality to other Web services (Figure 11.13).

When breaking down the various functions your integration architecture will need to provide, it would be worth your while to read up on what type of interceptor or

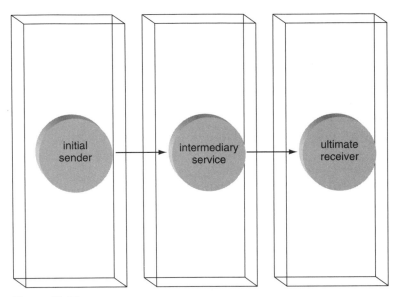

Figure 11.12
A message path containing one intermediary service.

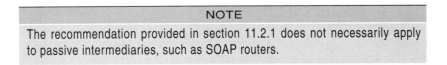

NOTE
The recommendation provided in section 11.2.1 does not necessarily apply
to passive intermediaries, such as SOAP routers.

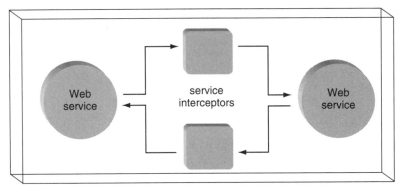

Figure 11.13
Service interceptors providing intermediary processing logic.

agent features are available in your development environment. Some middleware
products that supply hosting environments for Web services already utilize various
service interceptors to perform monitoring and administrative functions. Every time

your Web service sends or receives a message, you may be invoking a number of these software agents without even knowing it.

Here are some general guidelines for the usage of service interceptors:

- Use them to lessen the dependency between service logic and proprietary characteristics of your development platform.
- Do not place business logic or business rules within interceptors. They are most suited to providing generic, reusable functions.
- Keep them small. Interceptors tend to get a lot of use. You don't want bloated runtime components constantly hanging around your memory space and being invoked with every user interaction.

11.2.3   Data processing delegation

When Web services represent the endpoints to existing or new integration channels, they easily can become the busiest parts of your integrated environment. To avoid bottleneck situations, and to minimize hardware scaling expenses, the processing demands on endpoint services need to be trimmed as much as possible.

Wherever feasible, processing outside of the actual transmission or receipt of data by the service should be delegated elsewhere. This narrows the service focus to receiving and delivery functions.

For instance, data that a service provider needs to send in response to a request can be formatted fully, validated, and otherwise prepared by various back-end application components, prior to the service logic receiving it (as shown in the example in Figure 11.14). If there are security concerns regarding this process, then perhaps a validation code can be embedded in the document format. The service would then simply need to check this one part of the data, before packaging and transmitting the message and the data payload.

Figure 11.15 suggests that the service requestor receiving the message could perhaps perform some selective validation, before passing the data back to its application. There, a more thorough validation can be performed, as well as any other required processing.

NOTE
Although not suitable for business logic, service interceptors can also be very effective in reducing the processing load on application services. (Service interceptors are introduced in Chapter 9.)

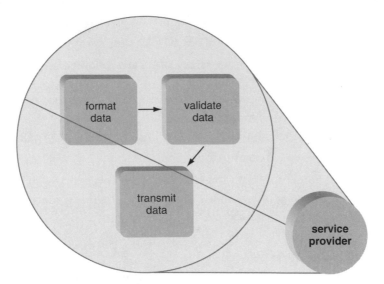

Figure 11.14
A service provider delegating data processing.

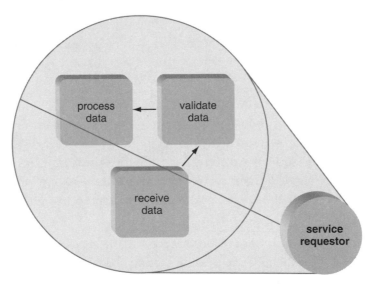

Figure 11.15
A service requestor delegating data processing.

11.2.4   Caching the provider WSDL definition

This won't be a strategy you'll hear a lot of XML academics recommend. It can be an effective way of enhancing performance, though, if properly applied. The Web services definition almost always exists as a separate file that gets interpreted and processed by the service requestor at runtime. To reduce this repetitive processing overhead, you can store the service provider's WSDL document in memory (see Figure 11.16). You can even take this a step further and embed the service definition within the application logic of a service requestor.

The latter approach obviously goes against standard practice, and cannot be applied in many situations. However, for integration connections that have been, and are expected to remain relatively static, you certainly can consider the option of caching this file.

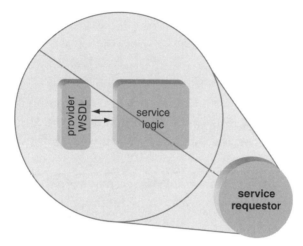

Figure 11.16
A service requestor encapsulating the provider service
definition.

A classic candidate would be the definition of a wrapper service that represents a legacy application that exposes a simple export function. This feature has been publicly available for a long time, and probably will remain so for the lifetime of the legacy environment. Applications that need to use this function in order to routinely retrieve legacy data can be represented by a Web service that caches the legacy wrapper service's WSDL information. This may speed up processing to the extent that performance gains outweigh the negative aspects of this option (which include potential limitations on maintenance, extensibility, and mobility).

> ### SUMMARY OF KEY POINTS
>
> - Performance within a service-oriented integration architecture can be tuned by properly utilizing service intermediaries and interceptors.
>
> - Performance can be further enhanced by delegating less relevant processing tasks and incorporating a caching strategy.

11.3 Strategies for integrating legacy architectures

A common pattern throughout the service-enabled architectures explored earlier in this guide has been the insertion of service integration layers as endpoints to traditional application environments. This forms the most basic type of service-oriented integration architecture.

There are numerous ways in which such an architecture can be extended, enhanced, and optimized. Provided here are a collection of strategies that may be useful to you both as potential solutions, and as a means of gaining a better understanding of where you can now take your service-oriented integration solution.

11.3.1   Create a transition architecture by adding partial integration layers

One way to phase in an SOA is to introduce a partial integration layer to already integrated environments. This approach, as illustrated in Figure 11.17, is less disruptive than replacing the entire integration framework. It does, however, result in a more convoluted design.

Although this strategy allows for services to be easily incorporated in existing environments, it is recommended only as a transition architecture. The ultimate goal should be to complete the transition by extending the integration layers to represent all cross-application communication.

11.3.2   Data caching with an IMDB

To expedite the data transfer process and improve overall responsiveness, the service integration layer can incorporate a data caching mechanism, such as an in-memory database (IMDB). One of the key benefits to this design (illustrated in Figure 11.18) is that it alleviates a great deal of processing from the source application. This is often a significant issue in legacy environments, where existing applications are designed and scaled to accommodate only their respective user base.

Even though an IMDB can coexist on the same server as the source application, it will typically be isolated to a dedicated environment. By doing so, the impact to the source application environment is minimized.

Furthermore, by caching data in memory and isolating this memory space onto a dedicated server, the data retrieval performance for the requesting application is improved as well. If data persistence is a requirement, this architecture can be extended with physical caching.

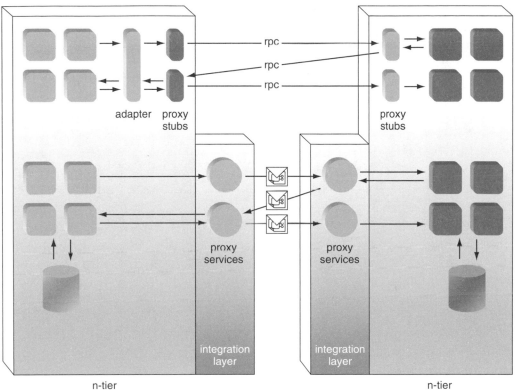

Figure 11.17
A transition architecture where components represented by proxy services coexist with components that still interact using RPC.

11.3.3 Utilizing a queue to counter scalability demands

When adding a Web services integration layer on top of existing legacy environments, use of the legacy applications may increase beyond what they were originally designed for. For instance, a component-based application that is currently serving a predetermined set of users may already be close to using its maximum allocated server resources.

Exposing this component's functionality to a new application can often require that the legacy application hosting environment either be upgraded or that the application component itself be redeveloped (or both). One relatively simple way of dealing with this type of performance challenge is to insert a queue between the Web service and the component(s) it is representing, as shown in Figure 11.19.

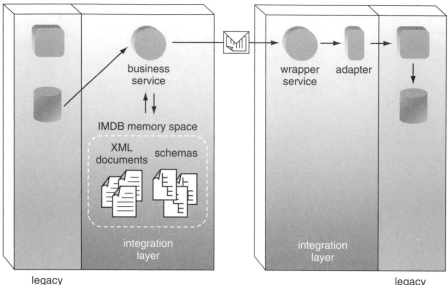

Figure 11.18
A Web service utilizing an IMDB to cache XML document and schema files.

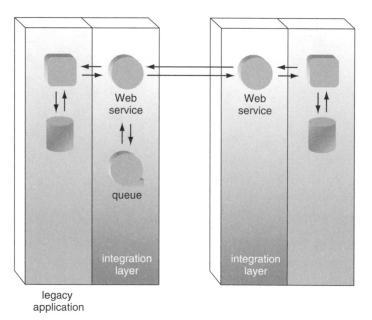

Figure 11.19
A Web service utilizing a queue to manage overflow requests for the
legacy application.

Any requests that cannot be dealt with by the component can be queued until the component is available. This will not always be a useful solution, especially for integrated applications that require real-time data interchange, but it may be a cost-effective compromise.

11.3.4   Adding a mini-hub

In many service-enabled legacy architectures, integration layers are simply added to the respective legacy applications. We can take this approach a step further by adding a third integration layer that can abstract generic functionality and provide a centralized, open access point for applications outside of the original integration boundaries.

The key benefit here is that it essentially creates a mini-hub that can be extended to facilitate potential future integration requirements. Business logic can be introduced to further process data and logic from the original legacy applications. This approach also establishes an overall cleaner design model, where each Web service has a more granular and distinct purpose.

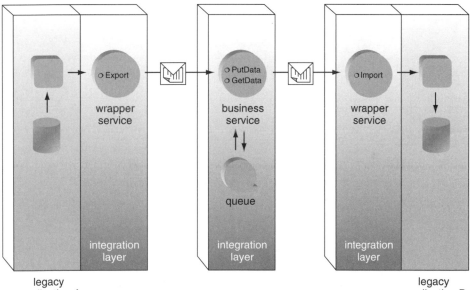

Figure 11.20
An example of the batch export and import architecture outfitted with a Web service hub.

In the diagram shown in Figure 11.20, a new service integration layer is inserted into the traditional batch export and import architecture. The new Web service encapsulates exposed legacy functions into a generic interface. It further supplements this logic with a queue that can act as a temporary repository (or cache) for exported data.

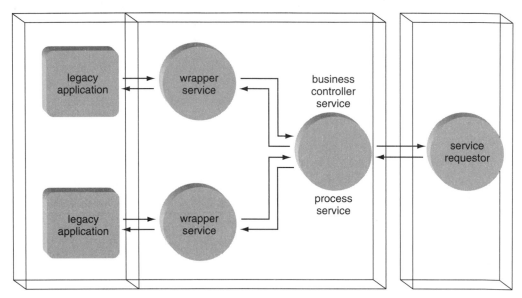

Figure 11.21
The business service acting as a controller service to outside applications could also be
a process service.

The introduction of this layer takes us into the realm of enterprise integration (Figure 11.21). You essentially are promoting the feature set of a service assembly through a new business controller service. (Without proper middleware, however, the scalability and extensibility of this model are limited. To learn more about middleware, see Chapter 8.)

11.3.5 Abstract legacy adapter technology

When working in environments where Web services are required to interact with multiple types of legacy adapter technologies, you can introduce a utility layer to remove dependencies between vendor adapters and your service business logic (see Figure 11.22).

A virtual adapter contains the logic required to interact with numerous adapters and essentially treats them as protocols representing legacy functions. This protects your core service business logic from changes and upgrades in the adapter products.

11.3.6 Leveraging legacy integration architectures

By creating a standardized integration layer with Web services, a disparate application environment becomes less of a problem. As long as applications can effectively relay

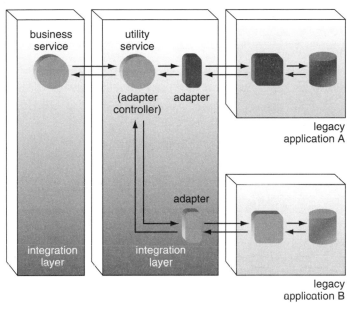

Figure 11.22
A utility service abstracting legacy adapter interaction.

their communication via the integration layer, they can interoperate with any other compliant applications in the enterprise (Figure 11.23).

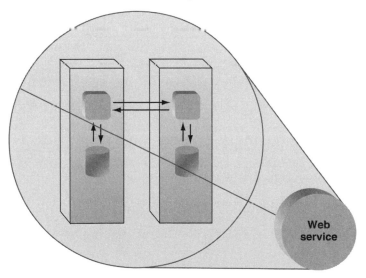

Figure 11.23
A service representing an entire legacy integration architecture.

Preserving existing integration solutions promotes diverse disparity, and may affect the way you view your heterogeneous environment. Since the need for application environments to be consistent is no longer there, the pressure to buy into and standardize on the same platforms is reduced. You can now continue to build on existing legacy environments, and pick application development and hosting platforms that are best for the application (not necessarily for the standardization of applications).

11.3.7 Appending Web services to legacy integration architectures

When looking at bringing already integrated applications into a more service-oriented environment, it sometimes makes sense to preserve the existing integration architecture. The cost of ripping out (especially tightly bound) communication channels to replace them with the Web services integration layers is not always justifiable or even necessary.

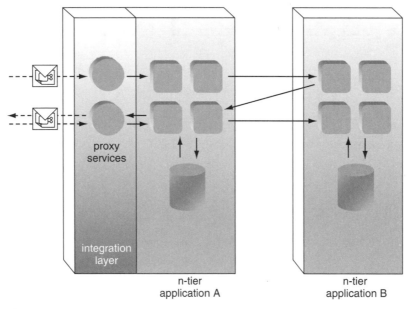

Figure 11.24
Preserving a traditional point-to-point architecture while exposing functionality
from one application with a service integration layer.

If two applications are successfully cooperating to automate an existing business process that will not be changing anytime soon, then there may be little reason to alter the status quo. If others, however, require access to one or both of the applications' programming logic or data, then an integration layer can simply be appended to the application (see Figures 11.24 and 11.25). This way application functionality is externally exposed without disrupting the existing integration architecture.

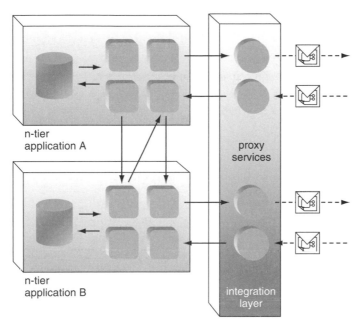

Figure 11.25
A (relatively) non-intrusive integration layer exposing functionality
from two applications already bound by a point-to-point integration
architecture.

A key consideration with this model is the performance impact on the application that
is now making its programming logic available to more users.

SUMMARY OF KEY POINTS

- By applying partial integration layers, traditional integration solutions can remain
  unchanged, and still participate in service-oriented environments.

- Strategically utilizing queues and positioning hub integration layers can facilitate future
  interoperability and improve overall reliability.

- Leveraging existing legacy logic is often preferable to replacing it.

11.4 Strategies for enterprise solution integration

An exploration of enterprise integration will undoubtedly lead to challenges. Strategic
responses to these issues are extremely important. Making the wrong decision can lead
a major initiative down the wrong path. On an enterprise-level, a wrong turn can have
repercussions that will echo through your organization for years to come.

Here are a few guidelines that address some of the more common issues.

11.4.1   Pragmatic service-oriented integration

When working with traditional EAI solutions you are subjected to a more rigid integration environment than if simply creating a platform-neutral service-oriented architecture. Even after having added integration layers that introduce a series of Web services (Figure 11.26), there may be little motivation to service-enable existing (proprietary) EAI integration channels.

Long-term interoperability considerations may be less of an immediate requirement than in less proprietary integration environments. Many EAI models are based on the expectation that all communication flows through the EAI product, where data is processed along predefined message paths.

If I'm considering upgrading an integration channel from a proprietary communication protocol to a Web service messaging channel, I have to take a few things into consideration. First, as long as I continue to use this EAI product, my application is expected to communicate exclusively with the EAI servers. What then, would be the point of building for a more interoperable tomorrow, when there will be no one else to interoperate with.

Second, the performance impact of the SOAP/HTTP approach plus the additional challenges surrounding the representation of proprietary security models via a service-oriented framework makes this effort seem even more futile.

There's nothing preventing you from adding Web services to existing EAI application clients, and there's also no rule that states you must flow all communication traffic through the EAI servers. If you branch out and begin extending your enterprise integration architecture outside of these solutions, however, you will end up with a less consistent and more fragmented enterprise architecture.

This can lead to a number of challenges, including:

- decentralized administration
- integration logic residing outside of centralized orchestration processes
- emergence of non-standardized message processing logic
- promotion of an inconsistent integration methodology

If your current EAI solution is not meeting your requirements, you are better off choosing between abandoning EAI in favor of creating a pure service-oriented architecture, or upgrading to a better EAI product.

An ESB-type solution may be your best option, since it promotes the use of Web services in all integration channels. Should you want to break away from an ESB architecture in

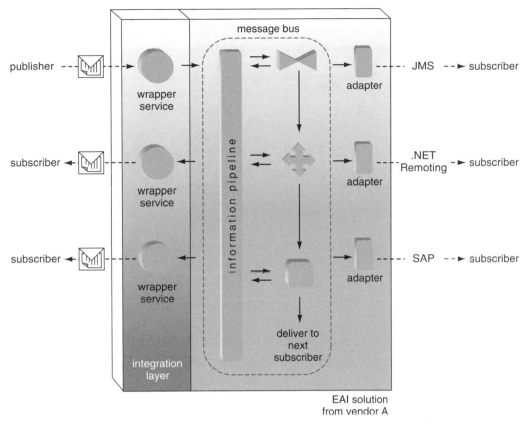

Figure 11.26
A messaging bus supporting service-oriented and proprietary integration channels.

the future, it will be much easier to do so, given that all of your applications will already have service integration layers in place.

11.4.2 Integrating disparate EAI products

Ugh! I thought EAI was supposed to make integration easier. It can, but only if you play by the EAI product vendor's rules. Try making two EAI solutions from different vendors cooperate (Figure 11.27), and you'll find yourself running back to that legacy integration project for some relaxation time.

An EAI architecture promotes standardization on a number of levels, but only within the boundaries of the solution itself. If your enterprise consists of two or more different EAI platforms (as may be the case after a corporate merger), and if new business processes require that these disparate environments exchange data, then you may be in for an uphill battle.

Most EAI products rely on adapters to establish communication with proprietary platforms. The proprietary nature of the EAI product platform itself, however, does not always have this option. EAI vendors are extremely competitive, and their solutions may not even offer an API into their product components, let alone an adapter designed to work with a competing product.

There are, of course, exceptions to this. More progressive vendors have recognized the industry demand for an open and less proprietary product platform. In response to this, they have added support for Web services and extended their product APIs.

If you are working with traditional EAI solutions, however, your options may be limited. Here are some suggestions:

- Expose whatever you can through the APIs available to you and supplement this by attempting direct integration with orchestration interfaces. Orchestration engines often offer the ability to interact openly with external resources to facilitate the automation of a given process. You can establish the integration at this level between the respective EAI product's orchestration engines and/or their direct product APIs. This is a trick that may work, but will result in some messy integration channels.

- Investigate the third-party market to see if someone out there has already done this work. If you aren't the first to require a connection between two specific EAI platforms, then there may have been sufficient demand for a vendor to create a specialized adapter. This vendor will likely have received permission from each EAI product manufacturer, and therefore will have built an adapter that goes beyond the APIs packaged with the EAI product.

- Don't look for EAI-to-EAI adapters. Instead look for EAI-to-Web services adapters. If these exist for both products, you can introduce a service hub between the two environments and bridge this gap as you would with two simple legacy applications. This may still introduce a significant effort if you need to merge orchestration processes and security models.

- Upgrade to a better EAI solution. EAI products that have been built from the ground up with Web services and purely service-oriented design concepts will give your enterprise a better foundation. Any vendor offering a product based on an SOA model, such as those that follow the ESB architecture, should be seriously considered.

11.4.3 Respect your elders (building EAI around your legacy environments)

Often, EAI solutions aim to introduce standards that will lay a foundation for short- and long-term integration projects. This would be ideal, but can be unrealistic. You can

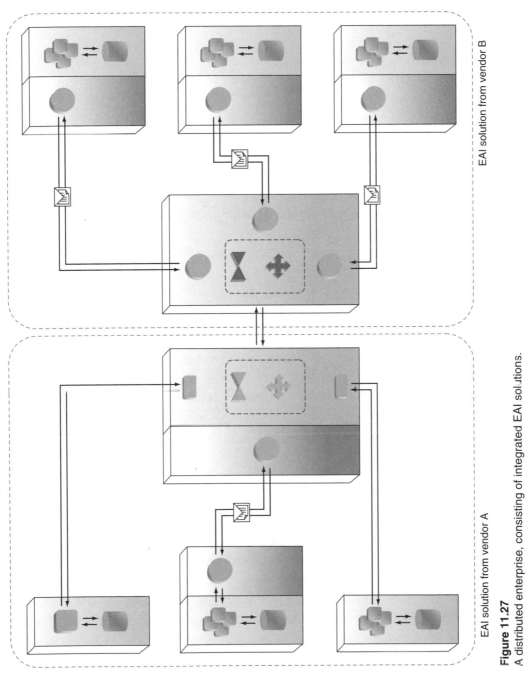

EAI solution from vendor B

EAI solution from vendor A

Figure 11.27
A distributed enterprise, consisting of integrated EAI solutions.

407

talk about standardization as much as you like, but once your listeners reach a certain age, they are not likely to change their ways that easily.

Legacy applications are often so rigid that imposing even minor changes within an environment can jeopardize stability. It is therefore a good idea to accommodate existing legacy applications to whatever extent possible. Attempting to approach legacy integration from a strictly standardized manner that places the burden of change on client applications can lead to a great deal of unnecessary disruption and effort.

11.4.4 Build a private service registry

Many of the contemporary EAI solutions already integrated with out-of-the-box Web service support will likely provide a service registry, such as a UDDI directory. If, however, you are the one adding service integration layers to your EAI environment, you should consider supplementing your effort with this piece of important infrastructure.

Keeping your service descriptions in a central location is relevant in both design and runtime situations. UDDI, for instance, provides a comprehensive model that allows a registry of services to evolve into a full-blown library. You can secure and extend an internal registry to external partners. You can even build a public registry for anonymous access.

For enterprise integration purposes, an internal private service registry will provide a dedicated container for published service descriptions. It can act as a central reference for developers in the process of building solutions, or it can accommodate application components that need to discover services dynamically, at runtime. The role of a typical UDDI registry is illustrated in Chapter 4.

11.5 Strategies for integrating Web services security

"Web services security." Say those three words to most developers and architects, and you'll see the expression on their faces change. Brows become furrowed, and smiles fade into terse, tightened lips. Say it again, just for fun, and see what other reactions you can get. Seriously, though, there are many issues that make this a complex and stressful topic.

This section, intentionally placed at the end of Part III, explores many of the common challenges that you will encounter when extending the functional scope of your service-oriented architecture. The more functionality you place into Web services, the more security becomes an issue.

11.5.1 Learn about the Web services security specifications

Just about every common aspect of security is being covered in a set of specifications designed specifically for XML and Web services. Without implementing these standards, it will be difficult to deliver enterprise applications based solely on service-oriented frameworks. It therefore will be worth your while to review and study not only the current specifications, but also emerging standards and revisions.

Some of the more important specifications include:

- WS-Security (and supplemental standards)
- Security Assertion Markup Language (SAML) and .NET Passport
- XML Key Management (XKMS)
- Extensible Rights Markup Language (XrML)
- Extensible Access Control Markup Language (XACML)
- XML-Encryption
- XML-Digital Signatures

See Chapter 4 for a brief description of each of these standards.

11.5.2 Build services with a standardized service-oriented security (SOS) model

Even though Web services may establish an operating model that can be classified as "peer-to-peer," it's really a deceiving term. As service-oriented architectures become more common, so will the use of intermediaries. It will not be unusual for a message to travel to and be processed by three or four intermediary services before arriving at its destination (an activity model that can be more accurately considered "peer-to-*").

This makes standardization of a single security model, most notably authentication, difficult. This is especially true when designing applications that intend to reuse Web services originally built for other projects. The fact that services are utilized for integration solutions may require different projects to create different security models.

Services designed for generic use should therefore be subject to standards that dictate key aspects of security. Ideally, these standards would be in alignment with existing organizational security policies.

11.5.3 Create a security services layer

One way of reducing the complexity introduced by all of the security considerations you need to take into account, is to centralize security measures into a dedicated services layer, as illustrated in Figure 11.28.

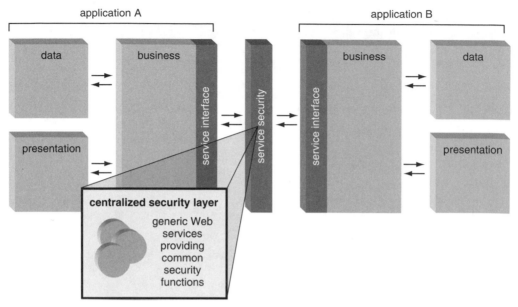

Figure 11.28
An enterprise-wide security layer.

Although this adds yet another layer of processing to your architecture, it provides many benefits, including:

- centralized administration
- increased control
- increased ability to enforce policies
- increased initial investment, but reduced long-term costs

A security layer needs to be carefully designed and deployed. It's really an all-or-nothing proposition. Poorly developed or implemented services providing security features that applications throughout the enterprise will rely on will introduce severe risks, including:

- a processing hub that can turn into a performance bottleneck
- a single point of failure that can shut down an entire enterprise

Since so many dependencies will be placed on this layer, the importance of scalability and robustness cannot be overstated. If you choose this route, do not implement a security layer until you are confident your infrastructure can adequately support it.

11.5.4   Beware remote third-party services

If you are designing an application for which a remotely located third-party service is being considered, you need to be very sure that the service does not pose a security threat. Once you send your data "out there," you lose control (Figure 11.29). As previously discussed, SSL will protect it only until it arrives at the destination, at which point other security measures will need to take effect.

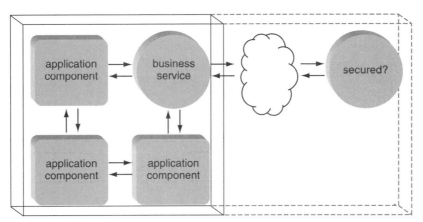

Figure 11.29
A remote third-party service assuming temporary control of your data.

If, however, the receiving third-party service does not support or acknowledge the model you are expecting it to, then interoperability will be compromised. The best way to assess this is to test third party services with a prototype that simulates the anticipated interaction scenarios.

Despite your best efforts, though, you will continue to remain at the mercy of the remote service provider. Even if an organization you've chosen to use as a service provider impressed you with its policies and guarantees, there is no way of knowing if a change in management or ownership down the line will jeopardize the quality of service they initially committed to providing.

11.5.5   Prepare for the performance impact

Security measures defined in many of the Web services specifications will demand a significantly sized layer of processing on top of the overhead already imposed by the parsing and serialization of SOAP messages.

The actual impact of these runtime technologies is often overlooked, and can result in unacceptable levels of latency, once secured business task execution times are actually

measured. Ensure that you have a good understanding of the performance requirements that will be determined by your chosen security model. Then, scale your solution accordingly, ahead of time.

Upfront analysis and testing will provide you with a great deal of data. Accelerator
technologies, such as compression, may also be able to effectively reduce some of the
processing load.

> **NOTE**
>
> The utilization of contemporary security technologies, such as those that
> allow for targeted encryption, actually can result in performance improve-
> ments. See the "Take advantage of granular security" section later in this
> chapter for examples.

11.5.6 Define an appropriate system for single sign-on

Designing the security model of your service-oriented architecture with single sign-on
in mind can establish an extremely efficient integration model. Security credentials
transmitted by services are mapped to other systems, so that the authentication process
is streamlined and administration is relatively centralized. (For more information
regarding single sign-on technologies, see Chapter 4.)

11.5.7 Don't over-describe your services

If you are making any of your Web services available outside of a controlled environment, be careful what you put into your description files. Those with malicious intent
can gather a great deal of information about your organization (such as potential entry
points) by studying the contents of WSDL descriptions, UDDI registry entries, and
unprotected SOAP messages. This is one of those areas where the self-descriptive
nature of XML can be used against you.

A recommended approach to reducing this risk is simply to audit any content you
release to the outside world. A publishing process can be established to introduce a formal approval step. This is best facilitated with a front-end tool that abstracts or differ-
entiates data from markup, as the approver may not be a technical resource.

An additional measure you can implement is the introduction of a code system that
replaces descriptive element type names. The code legend resides inside the organization, allowing for a manual or automated translation of non-descriptive XML markup
for internal usage. You would not need to encode all parts of external descriptions, but
if you've identified some potentially private pieces of information, you may want to
consider this approach.

11.5.8 Fortify or retreat integrated legacy systems

When introducing integration channels that interface with legacy environments, you are potentially subjecting established applications to new types of users and higher usage volumes.

Many legacy applications were built to provide a specific set of functions within a limited context and a restricted boundary. Sophisticated exception handling was not always high on the list of legacy developers' priorities, since the platform hosting the application was so well controlled.

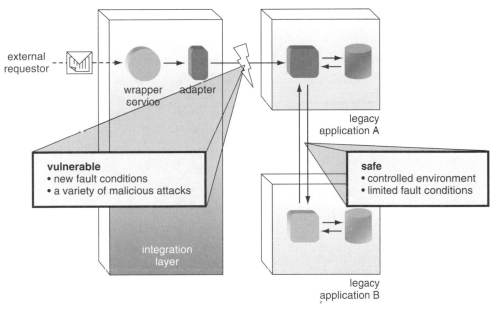

Figure 11.30
A comparison of new and established legacy communication channels.

By making these types of legacy applications participate in new processes that introduce new users, you may be imposing changes upon them for which they are not prepared. Not only will they be unable to deal with various unintentional failure conditions, they may, more importantly, be vulnerable to a wide variety of malicious attacks.

Figure 11.30 highlights how a legacy application that supports an integration architecture fronted by Web services with external clients can find its security model severely challenged. Attacks that attempt to infiltrate repositories for unauthorized access to data (or attacks that simply intend to damage or shut down the overall application framework) can be much more successful when targeted at legacy environments with few defenses.

The only effective way to prepare for these conditions is to perform a security audit on any legacy environments that will support functionality exposed externally by Web services. Each vulnerability that is identified will either need to be addressed, or may build a case for not proceeding with this part of the integration architecture.

11.5.9 Take advantage of granular security

Both the XML-Encryption and XML-Digital Signatures specifications can contribute to establishing an efficient message-level security model. They both, however, introduce processing overhead. The key to applying these technologies effectively is to protect only the essential parts of a message.

XML-Encryption allows for the granular encryption of XML document content. Similarly, XML-Digital Signatures supports the granular signing of document content. In the following example, only one element of the construct is being identified as requiring encryption.

```
<Profile>
  <Employee>
    <Name>Jim Mitchell</Name>
    <Age>36</Age>
    <EncryptedData Type='http://www.w3.org/2001/04/xmlenc#Element'
          xmlns='http://www.w3.org/2001/04/xmlenc#'>
      <CipherData>
        <CipherValue>R5J7UUI78</CipherValue>
      </CipherData>
    </EncryptedData>
  </Employee>
</Profile>
```

Example 11.1   An encrypted XML element

...only you can't tell which one, because even the element syntax itself is encrypted. Here's what the unencrypted construct would look like:

```
<Profile>
  <Employee>
    <Name>Jim Mitchell</Name>
    <Age>36</Age>
    <Income>$80,000</Income>
  </Employee>
</Profile>
```

Example 11.2   The same construct with no encryption

This granular control of message content is an important aspect of Web services security. It is not always advisable or realistic to endure the performance overhead of encrypting entire message documents, when only a fragment of the content is considered sensitive.

11.5.10 Web services and port 80

As discussed in the XML security section in Chapter 5, the concern that traditional firewalls do not monitor the traffic that passes through the standard HTTP port is amplified when working with Web services.

A content-aware firewall is an absolute must when building an infrastructure to support externally accessible Web services. Without it, service messages can deliver a wide variety of malicious content into an organization's internal environment.

11.5.11 SOAP attachments and viruses

Since SOAP messages can act as delivery mechanisms for binary and textual files, the potential to exploit this feature for malicious purposes is real. As shown in Figure 11.31, SOAP messages sent to your service provider can contain attached viruses. If your perimeter security measures do not include virus scanning, you should consider adding it.

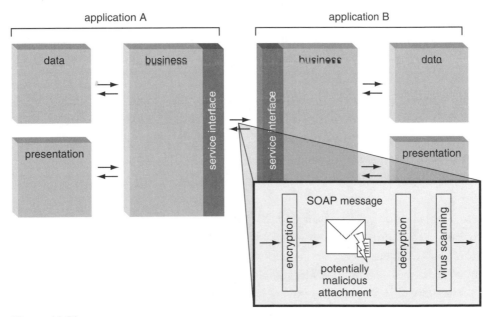

Figure 11.31
A SOAP message delivering a potentially dangerous (and encrypted) attachment.

This scenario is complicated further when encryption is applied to message contents, because it can allow a virus to escape rudimentary inspections. To counter this threat may require every service, including intermediaries, to first decrypt a message before performing the virus scan.

11.5.12 Consider the development of security policies

Policies can help organize rules that apply to various aspects of a diverse application environment. Within a service-oriented framework, policy specifications, such as the Extensible Access Control Markup Language (XACML) and WS-Policy provide a means of defining policies that determine what the service requestor can and cannot do with the requested service provider operation. A single policy can apply to a variety of applications and services.

One challenge when using policies is the enforcement of policy rules. How would you know whether a given Web service is actually checking a policy prior to allowing a service requestor access to a resource? Highly monitored environments may be able to establish this level of control, but another approach is to centralize security into a separate services layer. See the section on creating a centralized security services layer, earlier in this chapter.

11.5.13 Don't wait to think about administration

It's easy lose sight of the bigger picture when focusing on technical details. Assembling the required technologies and implementing various aspects of relevant specifications is a pretty straightforward process. All you really have to consider are the implications to the application logic and its supporting architecture.

Before you make any decisions final, though, be absolutely sure that you will be able to efficiently manage your planned security model. Looking at Web services security considerations from an enterprise perspective will place a great deal of emphasis on both infrastructure and administration. If you ignore the latter, you may end up with a sound architecture that will become difficult to control and very expensive to maintain.

Therefore, it is important that you understand the administration tasks your new security architecture will require. These tasks will likely create new roles within your organization, as well as new processes. Additionally, there will be the need for administration tools. Some may already be supplied by integration servers that provide Web service hosting features; however, you will often need to supplement these with specialized products.

One of the reasons you may be required to invest in specialized security monitoring and auditing products is to continue the enforcement of existing security polices into your service-oriented environments. Another reason simply may be that no other facilities are yet available to manage and keep track of service activities that utilize the newer technologies introduced by your Web services framework.

SUMMARY OF KEY POINTS

- Security processing can be abstracted into a dedicated security services layer.

- Many security measures will impose performance trade-offs that need to be measured carefully.

- Applying granular security technologies can reduce a great deal of security-related processing overhead.

PART

IV

Integrating the enterprise

As a matter of fact, the grass *is* greener on the other side. Getting there, though, requires some serious planning. The remaining chapters in this book provide you with a great deal of navigation. The rest is up to you. It's not a highway taking you from A to B — it's a series of paths, and each one you complete establishes a part of your foundation. Skip the paths you don't want to take, and stop at any time. There is a recommended sequence (as explained in Chapter 14), but there are no rules. You need to decide only where and how far you want to go.

Best practices and strategic processes are a great place to start. Most IT decision makers with a fundamental understanding of the concepts behind the XML and Web services technology platform will be able to appreciate how this guidance can potentially address issues and problems within the organization.

How best practices get used can vary. They can provide input for corporate visions and strategies behind long-term initiatives. They can also be applied in the short-term, to resolve immediate problems encountered during a project. Either way, they are the results of lessons learned that help shape a new enterprise.

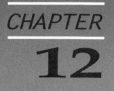

Thirty best practices for integrating XML

ntroducing XML technologies affects regions of an organization far beyond immediate technical environments. In order for XML technology to be successfully incorporated, associated concepts need to be adopted into how you build solutions and manage data. Support structures also need to be put in place to manage this new platform, and then you have to consider how your XML-enabled enterprise architecture can facilitate the entire service-oriented paradigm.

A range of best practices are provided here in order to address common integration issues, and to highlight the extent to which standardizing on the usage of XML can impact an organization.

NOTE
All best practices in this chapter are italicized and enclosed in quotation marks.

12.1 Best practices for planning XML migration projects

12.1.1 Understand what you are getting yourself into

"Determine your conceptual knowledge level of relevant XML technologies before planning a project."

Implementing a technology you don't fully comprehend will almost always lead to problems. You don't have to be a technical expert, but a solid conceptual knowledge is essential to understanding:

- how and where XML will fit into your application
- the problems it will solve once integrated

Test yourself by completing this short awareness exercise before you begin planning the involvement of XML technologies in your next project.

1. Describe how XML will help meet your project requirements. To properly define this, try relating business requirements to application functions. Then, map these functions to actual XML implementations (see Figure 12.1 for an example).
2. List the XML technologies that are being proposed for your application, and briefly describe the overall purpose of each.

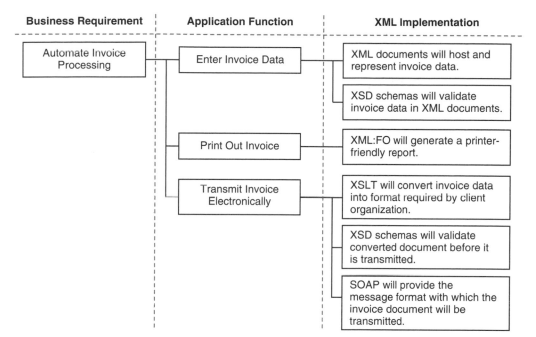

Business Requirement	Application Function	XML Implementation
Automate Invoice Processing	Enter Invoice Data	XML documents will host and represent invoice data.
		XSD schemas will validate invoice data in XML documents.
	Print Out Invoice	XML:FO will generate a printer-friendly report.
	Transmit Invoice Electronically	XSLT will convert invoice data into format required by client organization.
		XSD schemas will validate converted document before it is transmitted.
		SOAP will provide the message format with which the invoice document will be transmitted.

Figure 12.1
How business requirements can be mapped to XML features.

3. Justify how the skill set of your current project team qualifies them to work with these technologies.

4. Get a second opinion from a qualified industry professional.

Here are some guidelines:

- If an application function represents a complex task, break it into subtasks. Keep the level of functional complexity relatively consistent among each entry in the Application Function column.

- Do not focus on the details of front-end functionality. Instead of describing the steps a user would take to complete a form, for instance, simply summarize it into "user submits data."

- If you are going through this exercise for the first time, start with key business functions. Once those have been documented, finish with the secondary requirements.

- When assessing your project team's skill set against the list of required XML technologies, take into consideration any tools or products your team may be using to reduce the amount of syntactical knowledge they may require for a given XML language.

12.1.2 Assess the technical impact

Once system administrators and others in your organization responsible for maintaining the status quo begin learning about XML technologies, they will start to comprehend the magnitude of architectural and infrastructure-related changes that can be imposed by this platform. This emphasizes the need to properly scope and plan a migration.

A migration project is like a development project
"Upfront knowledge gathering will make for a quality migration project, and will empower you to mitigate and distribute the impact."

The XML technology platform does bring with it a number of significant changes. Just how chaotic the implementation of those changes has to be, though, is up to you. A common mistake is to approach a migration project from a technical perspective only. Although the technology and related logistics can be mapped out in a concise plan, that only addresses a subset of the actual issues.

The impact of each new technology or concept that you transition to will ripple across other parts of your overall environment. However, it will not always be evident what areas will be affected when focusing only on a technical migration. Therefore, it is recommended that you prepare for a migration project the way you would for a regular development project.

For instance, a development project requires a certain amount of up-front work before any actual development can begin. Before writing any code, or even documenting the application design, business analysts need to ensure that all the project requirements have been fully defined.

This often involves interviews with potential clients, incorporation of corporate strategies, and regular reviews by project stakeholders. A new or misinterpreted project requirement will be very expensive to fix, once the application has been developed. Therefore, the more time invested up-front, the less chance of anything slipping through the cracks. The same common sense holds true for an architectural migration project.

What to look out for
"Start with a corporate infrastructure view of your environment, and work your way down."

Frequently, the assessment of impact is focused on key areas of an infrastructure, such as hardware, operating software, and middleware. Although these areas certainly deserve attention, so do the less obvious parts of your technical environment.

The XML technology platform tends to integrate differently than past platforms. It consists of a collection of processors and tools, but its close association to your corporate data allows it to infiltrate remote outer regions of your enterprise.

If you start with a high-level view of your entire infrastructure, you will be able to identify potential areas that may be directly impacted, as well as those that will be inadvertently affected (see Figure 12.2).

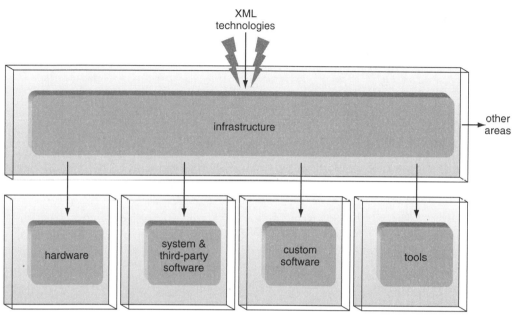

Figure 12.2
Typical areas of an enterprise infrastructure that get hit by migration shockwaves.

Common technical areas of impact to look out for include:

- Hardware requirements to facilitate additional processing overhead and increased usage volumes of legacy environments.
- Platform software and development tool upgrades that support the chosen set of XML technologies.
- Changes to custom programming logic required to interface with new processing engines, such as those used for XML documents, XSLT style sheets, and XQuery modules.
- Specialized tools that may be required to model, publish, or address specific characteristics of various XML document types.

One more thing…
Migrating to an XML platform requires not only up-front analysis time, but also a balance between thought and action. If you are working within a large enterprise,

you cannot afford to spend two years researching all these issues before you proceed with the actual migration. You need a roll-out strategy that phases in fundamental parts of the new platform, while distributing the resulting impact. XWIF provides a migration strategy that accomplishes this as part of an overall transition to a service-oriented enterprise (as explained in Chapter 14).

12.1.3 Invest in an XML impact analysis

"Perform an impact analysis to assess the cost and effort involved in large-scale migrations."

The documented results of an impact analysis will provide you with an understanding of how the XML platform will augment your established application architecture, as well as your application hosting infrastructure.

If you do not have an XML architect on staff, I highly recommend you hire someone qualified, just for this one report. There's no point in turning an impact analysis into a research project with the hopes that your project team will learn all about XML in the process.

This type of work requires the know-how of someone who's been there, and should produce the following results:

- A general risk assessment relating to the planned usage of each new XML technology. Typically, the maturity of a technology will be evaluated, along with its suitability for the intended function within the application. Often alternatives will be suggested.

- A specific risk assessment identifying security concerns relating to how the integration of each XML technology is being planned. It's always surprising how large this section of the report tends to be. If you have an authoritative security department, they may reject the use of XML altogether after reading through this part. This does not mean XML introduces unreasonable security risks. Instead, it is likely an indication that your environment may not be equipped to handle some of these concerns.

- An interoperability analysis that will highlight potential limitations resulting from the integration of an XML architecture in your application. The importance of this analysis is amplified by the quantity of legacy systems in your environment. Very often, recommendations will include an alternative design approach so that XML technology does not interfere with existing inter-application communication.

- A database integration analysis that will focus on the storage requirements of your XML data, as well as how your XML documents will relate to existing legacy repositories.

The creation of this report can be a useful exercise that tends to open people's eyes with regard to how deeply XML can penetrate an established technical environment.

One more thing…

If you don't have the budget for an Impact Analysis, then you may want to consider the following approach:

1. Classify your XML application as a prototype.
2. Build and deploy it in an isolated environment.
3. Write your own impact assessment, documenting what you learned.

The consideration here is that creating a prototype that may need to be discarded or overhauled will likely cost a great deal more than a formal Impact Analysis would have.

12.1.4 Assess the organizational impact

"All the technical changes introduced by XML technologies will need to be supported by individuals and the processes within which they operate. Therefore, the organization needs to plan for a series of adaptive changes."

Migrating to the XML technology platform will affect the organization (see Figure 12.3). Without a good impact assessment, though, you won't know how. Areas of potential impact within your organization will get overlooked, which translates into hidden costs that creep up after a migration is in its final stages. It's much better to have accounted for these expenses ahead of time.

Here are some of the more common areas you should take a close look at:

- XML will require a revision to many existing standards, and will also be responsible for introducing new ones.
- Established processes relating to document publishing, version control, maintenance, and design likely will be affected. Additionally, new processes may emerge.
- Various IT professionals will be drawn into working with and maintaining XML technologies and documents, creating a need for the definition of new roles and responsibilities. Foremost on this list is the management of XML schemas.
- With new technologies come new skill set requirements. A proper training and mentoring strategy will allow for a targeted approach to developing in-house expertise.

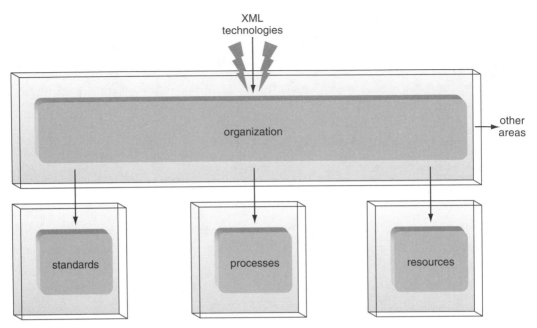

Figure 12.3
Typical areas within an organization affected by the introduction of XML technologies and products.

Each of the these organizational issues are addressed further individually, in other best practices and process descriptions.

12.1.5 Targeting legacy data

Imagine if you had the luxury of building your corporate data repositories from the ground up. For a moment, forget about redundant and fragmented data stores, poorly designed data models, and disparate database platforms. Looking at just the business data itself, you are now given the opportunity to logically group and organize this information in whatever manner you choose.

With this amount of freedom you could:

- create logical data domains that mirror or complement the organization's business model
- create granular sub-domains to whatever extent you need
- group business rules in alignment with your data bodies
- assign policies to logical data domains or to a separate layer of independent domains (as you might do with security policies)
- avoid redundancy by creating sub-domains for data shared across primary domains

You may need a background in data analysis to really get a buzz out of this particular fantasy, but most IT professionals will at least have an appreciation for the many benefits such a controllable data environment offers.

We are now in a transition to an XML-centric data representation standard. We actually have been for a number of years, but the level of acceptance within different organizations varies a great deal. Many IT environments may already be using XML technologies, but an inadvertent use of XML formatted documents does not constitute a serious effort in migrating your corporate data to a new set of data representation standards.

If, however, you take advantage of the many features provided by the XML family of specifications, you will be able to take a big step toward reclaiming control of your corporate intelligence. You first need to set your sights on what parts of your enterprise information actually would benefit from XML data representation. It is rare that an organization's entire body of corporate data needs to be fully XML-enabled. Though there are certainly benefits to achieving a universal data format within an organization, it can be difficult to justify.

Some legacy environments have always been relatively autonomous, and function just fine that way. Gateways or adapters will probably be available for integration purposes, but there may be no compelling reason to spend time and money uprooting a body of data when your return on investment will be questionable at best.

So how do you actually know what parts of your enterprise should become XML-enabled?

First of all, let's define "XML-enabled." To some this means a complete XML-compliant application hosting environment in which data freely flows as XML documents. To others, it might just be a case of plugging an adapter into a legacy application, and extracting XML formatted data from the legacy repository.

For the purpose of this discussion, let's assume the term XML-enabled refers to the adapter solution, and we'll use "XML-compliant" for applications that reside within fully XML-driven architectures.

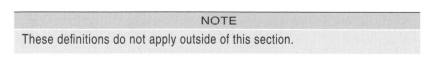

> **NOTE**
> These definitions do not apply outside of this section.

Back to our (now revised) question: How do you know what parts of your enterprise should become XML-enabled *or* XML-compliant?

The answer can be separated into two best practices, as follows.

XML-enabling a legacy application
"Enabling a legacy application to output XML formatted data should be considered only if the impact does not jeopardize the stability of the environment."

Many integration architectures and EAI solutions bridge platform gaps using adapters and other types of extensions. These technologies can disrupt the comfort zone within which legacy environments are accustomed to running. Increased usage volumes, new error conditions, and changes required to environmental configuration settings can destabilize a previously reliable system.

If addressing the problems imposed by this approach requires significant infrastructure and programming changes, then you should do some math. Carefully weigh the costs of an upgrade project to that of a complete architectural overhaul. Take into account the long-term benefits you will gain by investing in contemporary versus outdated technology.

However, if these concerns are not valid for your environment, then XML-enabling a legacy application or repository is a viable first step toward bringing legacy data into an XML-centric environment. You may not need to change this arrangement until the popularity of this integration channel increases to the point that it results in new functional and performance requirements. That's when you may have no choice but to make your legacy application XML-compliant.

Making legacy applications XML-compliant
"XML-compliance should be sought only when XML-enabling a solution is insufficient (or not possible), and if the expense justifies the value."

This option will almost always be expensive. Every situation, though, is unique. Vendors of some legacy environments may still be progressively supplementing traditional application platforms with sophisticated extensions that allow for a near-compliance to XML architecture standards. If you are fortunate enough to work with such a system, your project costs will likely be reasonable.

If, however, you are forced to rip-and-replace legacy logic in order to achieve the required level of XML compliance, then you're in for a long night writing up that ROI. Before you do, though, be certain that you've researched available alternatives.

One more thing…
XML technologies should not be integrated into legacy environments before a standardized framework is in place. This is addressed by other best practices in this chapter.

12.2 Best practices for knowledge management within XML projects

12.2.1 Always relate XML to data

XML can mean different things to different people. Given the number of uses for XML, and the many creative ways its technologies have been applied, it's easy to lose sight of for what it actually was intended. Regardless of its application or the environment in which it is utilized, there is always one constant: In some shape, way, or form, XML represents data.

Clarity of concepts
"Foster a clear understanding of XML concepts within your organization or project team."

XML, in itself, is not a programming language. It's also not a design paradigm, nor is it an implementation of technology. It's a specification that establishes a universally accepted data representation format. It can be incorporated within programming logic. Designs can be based on or around it, and technology products can process it.

The reason this distinction is relevant is because there is importance in the level of clarity with which XML concepts are communicated. You should be weary of statements like "we'll program it with XML." It's about as clear as saying "we'll program it with a database."

Statements like this may be an indication of knowledge gaps within your organization. Misperceptions can get around, and can eventually make their way to project decision makers. Poor decisions predictably lead to poor quality.

Whether it's in a board room meeting, a discussion among project team members, or a report you're writing to document the results of a research project, keep XML associated with data representation. And, explicitly quality technology-specific utilizations of XML standards.

Create a custom glossary
"Establishing a common vocabulary within your organization is a key to fostering a unified view of the XML technology platform."

I'm certainly not suggesting you go around correcting people when they use an XML term the wrong way. That would be about as annoying and embarrassing as if you corrected their grammar (especially in front of others).

A good way to establish a standard vocabulary within your organization is to put together a glossary. You can start with one of the many industry-standard glossaries available, but I highly recommend you customize it to relate key terms to existing systems within your organization's environment.

One more thing…

A common vocabulary, through whatever means implemented, is no substitute for actual training. Because of the extent to which XML technologies establish themselves within a technical environment, proper training initiatives are an important part of an organizational migration strategy, and are covered in the next set of best practices.

12.2.2   Determine the extent of education required by your organization

"Identify and recognize knowledge gaps."

A lack of education is the number one cause of failed XML application designs. The fact that XML has received so much hype has led to numerous misperceptions, fuelled primarily by vendors with a vested interest in marketing their now XML-compliant products as "open," "easily integrated," or "easy-to-use."

The truth is, you could fill a year-long university curriculum solely with courses centered around the technology of XML. And that would only give you a theoretical understanding. Once you begin using XML in the "integrated real world," you will realize that applying it correctly involves a combination of technical knowledge and thorough analysis.

Fortunately, no one person on your team will need to know it all. Additionally, the strategic use of high-level tools will alleviate the need for much of the low-level syntactical knowledge of some XML technologies.

Organize a plan to fill your team's knowledge gaps, by following these steps:

1. Define new roles within your project team, as required. (See the next section for a list of suggested roles.)

2. Select a suitable set of tools and focus the initial training effort on their usage. (See Chapter 5 for a guide to assessing XML tools.)

3. Create a training plan that incorporates instructor-led and self-study sessions. (The next best practice section provides a number of guidelines for this.)

4. Fill knowledge gaps with outside expertise and budget for mentoring. (The best practice on mentoring provides a recommended approach.)

12.2.3   Customize a training plan

The XML learning curve is as a key issue that needs to be addressed when developing an enterprise integration strategy. To build the skill set required for XML technologies to be properly applied and designed into applications, you will need to make an investment.

Creating a budget for training, however, is only the first step. Here are some guidelines for developing a productive and cost-effective training program.

Take a course to learn XML fundamentals

"Learning XML fundamentals furthers the cause of establishing a common vocabulary, and a common understanding of the XML platform."

Many corporations have a standard approach to IT training, where employees are sent on courses at external institutions. Topics covered are typically generic in nature, and courses can be up to one week long. This isn't always the best approach for XML training.

The only generic course that will be useful to a cross-section of your IT staff will be one that covers XML fundamentals. Beyond that, courses should be carefully evaluated to ensure that they address issues relevant to how those being trained will be affected by XML technologies. This leads us to defining roles.

Define roles before assigning further training

"Targeted training fosters the development of in-house experts."

Because of the pervasive nature of the XML platform, the requirement for a number of specialized skill sets will emerge. Especially when dealing with the many supplementary XML technologies, it is necessary to assign ownership to specific individuals or groups.

For instance, if your project team includes individual experts for XSLT, XSD schemas, and XQuery, you will be in good shape. On the other hand, a project made up of developers with a fragmented skill set consisting of some XML knowledge, a vague idea of what "transformation" means, and a pile of unread white papers, is heading toward "XML hell."

If you are at a point where you have a preliminary understanding of the extent to which you will be integrating XML technologies, you may be able to identify roles. Roles relate to how members of your organization or project team will be involved with XML technologies.

Here are some examples of typical roles:

- XML developer
- XML architect
- XML schema designer (or custodian)
- XSLT template designer
- XML document publisher

Make resources available to your technical staff
"Supplement platform-specific resources with vendor-neutral resources, as they can provide a clear picture of the common ground between disparate platforms."

The XML technology platform introduces a plethora of new terms, concepts, and architectural components. Most books and Internet resources are vendor-oriented, and therefore not always suitable for general-purpose reference.

If one of your goals is to build an interoperable enterprise, driven by XML technologies, then your developers will likely need vendor-neutral reference materials. They provide a clear perspective of XML concepts and functionality. This "pure" view of the platform is useful when working with disparate environments.

Also, your developers will notice that much of what they learn from vendor-neutral resources will be applicable to their respective vendor-specific environments, as most major software manufacturers strive (or at least claim) to support W3C specifications.

Spend your training budget wisely
"Books and allocated study time can be a more efficient and more cost-effective means of training than many courses."

Let's imagine it costs $1,500 for one employee to attend a week-long XML training course. For the same amount of money you could purchase a set of five $50 XML books for six employees. Of course they would need extra time to study and work with these guides, but if you believe that the self-study notion would be accepted in your organization, you should consider this approach.

The success of this strategy depends a great deal on your corporate culture. If your IT staff has traditionally received instructor-led training, they may be reluctant to buy into the do-it-yourself way. Attending courses and seminars, especially when travel is involved, can sometimes be a healthy change of scenery and a great deal more attractive than being asked to spend time reading a book in a room.

From a strictly financial perspective, though, the return on investment tends to be much higher with a self- or group-study approach. The best overall system probably lies somewhere in-between. Supplementing specific courses with books and extra study time can lead to a cost- and knowledge-effective training program.

Bring outside experts in for specialized knowledge transfer
"XML technology experts can provide unique insights and address issues specific to your technical environment."

Notice I used the word "experts" instead of "trainers." I do believe that you need a (communicative) technology expert to bring the level of insight required for many of the issues facing XML integration. If the expert is also an accomplished instructor, then that's a bonus.

Having an expert visit your organization for a few days to spend some time with key members of your IT department can result in immediate benefits. Those attending the sessions can raise issues relating to their respective projects, and discuss areas of the XML platform beyond the scope of regular text books or courses.

12.2.4 Incorporate mentoring into development projects

It's always surprising to me how often mentoring is overlooked in development projects. Even when enlisting consultants to participate in project teams, their tasks are often limited to the development work at hand. With a bit of planning, you can get a great deal more value from your consultants.

Arrange a consult-and-mentor program
"Use consultants to further in-house knowledge transfer."

Outside consultants may seem expensive, but they are a steal when compared to some training programs. If you are hiring a consultant for analysis or development work, always end that person's tenure with a knowledge transfer session. A day or two is usually sufficient for most major projects. Get a large room and pack in your team.

Unlike XML training courses that charge you per attendee, consultants are typically paid on an hourly basis. Having a consultant spend a day developing part of your application or spending that day transferring knowledge to twenty of your employees should cost you the same.

Additionally, the knowledge being transferred is specific and relevant to your organization. As long as the consultant is a competent communicator, this can be a very productive arrangement.

Get suitable mentors
"Hire consultants capable of effective knowledge transfer."

Many consultants do not share knowledge very well. They may be unable to communicate or teach effectively, or they may be protective of their knowledge in order to retain their value.

It's best to make mentoring a requirement from the beginning. Even then, give it a short trial run first. Have the consultant start with a one-day session attended by your staff. Ask many questions, and see how effectively knowledge is shared.

12.3 Best practices for standardizing XML applications

12.3.1 Incorporate standards

"Always standardize the integration of XML technologies."

A simple analogy for working with standards is to relate them to traffic lights. I don't enjoy sitting at an intersection, staring up at a red bulb, waiting for the green one to give me permission to drive, but... I know it's a necessary part of commuting. Without traffic lights and signs, there would be chaos in the streets. And though I might get to where I'm going a lot faster, it would be a much more hazardous trip.

XML technologies rely on (and sometimes demand) the inclusion of standards in order to ensure consistency and maintainability of the many inter-dependent parts of an XML architecture.

Standards exist within and apply to different domains of an enterprise. Table 12.1 provides some of the more common categories used to classify standards documents.

Table 12.1   Common standards

Development standards	Naming conventions, exception handling, grammatical language standards, and design standards limited to document structures and functional partitioning (such as modularization).
Application design standards	Standards, guidelines, and patterns that define how and when each XML technology should be used (including acceptable alternatives).
Architecture standards	A standard application architecture that acts as a blueprint for future developments projects. Standards position XML technologies conceptually and physically, and define their relationship to integration and interoperability problems.
Infrastructure standards	The application hosting environment, including server configuration, Internet access policies, security, configuration, promotion, and scalability. May also include the development environment and related tools and products.
Maintenance standards	Administration procedures, user account management, scalability, availability, and routine maintenance tasks.
Project standards	Required skill sets, processes, and an identification of any of the previously mentioned standards relevant to the immediate project (including deviations from existing application design and development conventions).

Table 12.1 Common standards *(Continued)*

Organizational standards	New organizational entities (roles or even departments) responsible for various aspects of the utilization and maintenance of XML technologies. Organization standards also establish the development tools and editors allowed by project teams. Additionally, organization standards assign ownership of the previously mentioned standards.
Enterprise standards	Typically high-level requirements that result from long-term strategic initiatives. For instance, an enterprise strategy that determines that XML is to become a key technology over the next nine months may result in an enterprise standard requiring XML to be utilized within a limited scope over the next three months.

The integration of XML technologies can affect and add to all of these standards. It would be difficult (and perhaps pointless) to build an XML-centric enterprise architecture without first revising and expanding current standards to incorporate the many new aspects introduced by this technology platform. The LSM model explained in Chapter 14 provides a migration strategy that integrates new standards incrementally, in a controlled and phased manner.

12.3.2 Standardize, but don't over-standardize

"Don't let standards over-burden projects. Achieve a balance by first integrating key standards, and then building on them."

Looking at the list of standards in the previous section, it might seem overwhelming. It might be enough to put you off wanting to bother with standards at all. It's true, XML standardization can go too far. Too many standards can hinder the progress of a project, and constrict the creativity of the project team. It is therefore important to strike a balance between the incorporation of key standards within a project, and perhaps a series of detailed standards that are provided as guidelines or patterns. This gives project teams the flexibility to use what they need.

If you are just easing into the XML technology platform, and your primary concern is getting your project completed without having to worry about complying with any grandiose enterprise standardization strategy, then at the very least:

- Assign ownership of each standard (or set of standards) to suitable project team members.
- Develop a modest maintenance process for XML documents, schemas, and style sheets.

- Add one or more standards-compliance checking stages to your project plan. Standards are useless if they aren't enforced.

12.3.3 Define a schema management strategy

Introducing XML into the enterprise will result in the creation of new data models. Two common reasons for this are:

- Existing databases and associated applications may provide little or no XML support. This often results in the need for a separate processing layer to perform data transformation into XML. The hierarchical XML data structure is different from, and often incompatible with relational data models. To represent legacy data within XML documents requires the creation of new XML data models.
- XML introduces the ability to represent a unique view, which can consist of data taken from multiple data sources. This introduces the need for new, business-centric data models.

In terms of standardization, data modeling with XML is comparable to modeling data for relational databases. Standards used to ensure consistency within the initial data model are just as important to its future state, where it may need to accommodate integration and interoperability requirements. Therefore, a strategy is required to manage, maintain, and evolve these XML data models.

Understand the importance of XML schemas
"Give XML schemas the same importance as database schemas."

XML schemas don't often get the respect they deserve. This always mystified me, but I've concluded that it is related mainly to the fact that they are generally perceived as "supplementary XML information provided in plain text files." The perhaps unconscious assumption is that unlike relational database schemas, XML schemas are not representative of and surrounded by a complete data management environment. They are, therefore, not a key part of application architecture.

Let's challenge that perception by first taking a look at the type of information XML schema definitions contain.

XML schemas:

- establish a vocabulary
- create validation boundaries
- encapsulate business rules
- associate data to logical domains (through namespaces)

Essentially, they establish a sort of data infrastructure within which all of your XML-compliant applications and repositories reside and interact. As with any technical infrastructure, standards and consistency are required to preserve its integrity.

An uncontrolled evolution of such an infrastructure will lead to:

- disparate data domains
- data redundancy
- misaligned vocabularies
- misaligned business rules

...in other words, problems.

The relationship between XML schemas and databases will also vary. Some XML schemas may be completely isolated from traditional repositories, whereas others may be partially aligned or integrated. Some databases may even be storing or outputting XML schema markup. All of these scenarios further complicate an architecture, and place even more emphasis on the need for XML schemas to be treated as carefully as any other part of your data environment.

NOTE
Chapter 5 provides a step-by-step XWIF process for managing XML schemas.

Assign an XML data custodian
"Centralize the modeling and maintenance of enterprise XML schemas."

Because XML schemas can exist as plain text files, they can be created by anyone. Developers don't even have to be proficient in an XML schema language. They can simply use a development product to auto-generate XML schema markup.

This introduces the very real likelihood that disparate data models will emerge throughout your organization. If left uncontrolled, you will not be able to take advantage of one of the fundamental benefits an XML platform has to offer: data unity. By allowing various projects to create XML schemas independently, a new layer of disparity will simply be added to your existing ones.

To prevent the proliferation of non-standard XML schema models, you will need to assign ownership. XWIF proposes that the responsibility of owning and maintaining the format, structure, standards, business rules, and validation rules associated with your XML documents be assigned to one role: the *XML Data Custodian*.

This individual would be responsible for the following.

Ownership of vocabularies   The XML Data Custodian will need to create new vocabularies on-demand for XML developers who need to work with corporate data in an XML format, and will also have to maintain and coordinate these vocabularies. This involves ensuring that XML element-types produced for vocabularies correspond correctly to definitions of the same data already residing in databases. Also, it requires that the custodian strive for normalization by trying to prevent the creation of redundant or duplicate element-types for the same corporate data sets (even if the same corporate data exists in different repositories).

Ownership of data models   Depending on which type of data validation method your organization standardizes, one person should be in control of how this validation and document structure technology is designed. XML schemas contain DDL-like[1] information that defines the structure of an XML document, the data types allowed, validation rules, and other business rule-like functionality.

So, in addition to providing an overall vocabulary, the XML Data Custodian will need to assist in defining the hierarchical structure of XML documents, as well as the contents of data integrity rules. Again, the additional challenge here is to keep this information synchronized with the data integrity and referential integrity rules already in existence.

Additional complexities can emerge when XML is used to represent data from multiple data sources. Here the XML schema may also need to represent data integrity rules for each repository.

Namespace domain administration   Finally, the responsibility of namespace partitioning will be also likely assigned to this role. Namespaces allow for the definition of a domain in which vocabularies are valid. Theoretically, an organization could be partitioned into several namespaces in which independent vocabularies exist.

12.3.4   Use XML to standardize data access logic

"Maximizing XML utilization in the data access layer increases your control over data management, and standardizes the application architecture."

XML has established itself as a key data representation technology that can bridge disparate platforms through the support of numerous supplementary technologies. When designing an XML architecture, much emphasis is therefore placed on unifying heterogeneous data sources into common data formats.

---

1.   DDL refers to the Document Definition Language used with relational databases.

This centralizes data representation, taking full advantage of one of the core features of the XML platform. There are reasons, though, to go beyond this level of standard-ization. Unifying the programming logic behind data access can introduce a number of benefits.

No longer would your application need to contend with database commands *and* XML parsing, it needs to focus only on the latter. Additionally, if all of your data access logic is driven by XML, then that narrows the skill set you need for that part of the application.

It also allows you to strategically position supplementary data access technologies. XQuery, for example, can establish centralized data access logic by creating a single entry point for a range of disparate data sources. (XQuery is further explained in Chap-ters 2 and 5.)

12.3.5 Evaluate tools prior to integration

"Carefully assess the underlying mechanics of XML products. Avoid those with proprietary hooks."

Third-party tools that allow you to edit, manage, and generate XML markup can be very handy during a development project. Making sure you choose the right tools, though, is important. Many introduce proprietary extensions and file formats that lock you into the vendor platform.

Before standardizing on any tool set, spend some time to assess the inner workings of the product properly, as well as its compatibility with your current development plat-form. (Chapter 5 provides a series of guidelines for evaluating XML tools.)

12.4 Best practices for designing XML applications

12.4.1 Develop a system for knowledge distribution

When proceeding with an enterprise-wide move to an XML-compliant architecture (or if just standardizing on a specific set of XML technologies), a number of projects will be affected.

"Implement a responsive knowledge distribution system to improve communication and to keep standards current."

In larger organizations, individual project teams will tend to deal with the challenges imposed by these initiatives individually. When working through integration or migra-tion-related issues with the XML technology platform, many will be tied directly to the environment's compatibility with whatever part of the technology is being used. In other words, a lot of problems and obstacles will be unique to that organization.

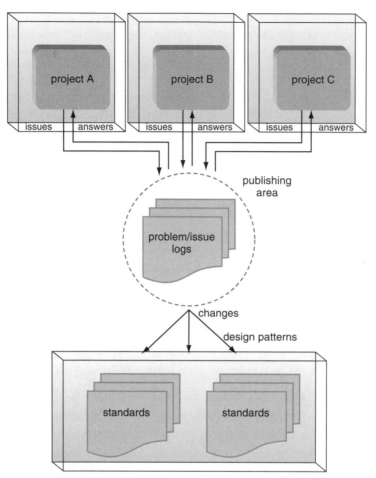

Figure 12.4
A proposed knowledge distribution system for issues relating to XML
technology.

Establishing a mechanism for logging and sharing this information (such as the model
suggested in Figure 12.4) can be extremely productive.

Two immediate benefits such a system will provide are:

- the expedited adoption of XML technologies, as project teams receive access to
  documented research and lessons learned from other projects
- the infusion of highly relevant input into project, design, and development
  standards, allowing these standards to be kept current in response to ongoing
  environmental issues

This often requires the allocation of a resource to publish and maintain these documents. Planning for this ahead of time, as part of the overall initiative, can lead to cost and effort savings for many projects to come.

12.4.2 Remember what the "X" stands for

When building any type of custom application, it's easy to get caught up with matching application features to immediate business requirements. With XML-centric environments, though, this causes some to overlook one of XML's most fundamental features: unlimited extensibility.

"Application designs with built-in extensibility allow for cost-efficient extensions to be added with a minimal impact."

This motto will likely make it into the design documents, but you need to push it further. As developers get into the details of programming routines, they are bound to encounter new opportunities for adding extensibility. Therefore, you should strive to make extensibility part of the overall development philosophy within your project team or organization.

Many in IT still assume that merely using XML automatically makes application logic extensible. The first step to fostering this culture, therefore, is to dispel this and other myths that might make extensibility less of a priority.

Building extensible XML applications includes paying special attention to the following areas:

- XML document modeling through the use of adaptive XML schema models
- modular XSD schema design (specifically using the any keyword to allow XSD schemas to be dynamically extended)
- flexible XSLT templates (such as those that incorporate variables set at runtime)
- reusable XQuery functions and XPath expressions

There are often performance trade-offs to take into consideration when developing applications with built-in extensibility. It is therefore advisable to supplement standards with metrics that can be used to assess the value of an extensible piece of application logic, when compared to the extra processing required to support it.

12.4.3 Design with service-oriented principles (even if not using Web services)

The service-oriented design model is an important (perhaps even critical) part of contemporary XML architectures, even for those not incorporating Web services. Building your applications in such a way that they support service-oriented concepts will spare you a huge amount of effort when you decide to actually make the transition to a Web services-based architecture.

"Build application logic using service-oriented principles. Otherwise, you will continue to build legacy applications with nothing more than service facades."

Even if your plans to incorporate Web services technologies are non-existent at this point, this strategy gives you the best of both worlds. Steps that you can take to begin incorporating service-oriented design characteristics into a regular XML architecture include:

- Adjust business process models to incorporate service-oriented principles, and reflect these changes in your component designs.
- Logically partition application functionality into relatively autonomous services.
- Model application components to best facilitate Web service representation. (Chapter 6 provides an entire process for modeling service-oriented components.)
- Incorporate SOAP servers and SOAP messaging. These are key parts of a service-oriented communications framework that can assist your XML architecture in standardizing message formats.

Note that I placed this best practice here, with the assumption that those of you not yet ready or interested in getting into the Web services realm will likely not read through the chapter dedicated to Web services best practices. A key requirement to carrying out this design approach, however, is a base knowledge of service-oriented design principles, as well as the technologies used by Web services. Chapter 14 provides a good introduction for both the business and technology aspects of service-oriented design.

12.4.4   Strive for a balanced integration strategy

Integration efforts often are focused on addressing immediate business problems. The resources from two or more applications need to be combined in order to meet the requirements of a new or revised business process. With each integration project, though, new communication channels get established, existing ones refined, and others mapped out. You can take advantage of projects that create or extend integration architectures by taking future interoperability requirements into consideration. This speculative approach to integration, though, can be taken too far.

Tightening the screw
"Take advantage of the integration channel creation process to build in functionality for future interoperability requirements."

Because integration projects tend to be risk-ridden, expensive, and time-consuming, the last thing you might be interested in is how the architecture you are building can be extended further to facilitate future interoperability.

The best way to avoid imposing new requirements on projects already underway, is to add a speculative analysis phase to the project, prior to finalizing requirements.

Stripping the screw

"If future requirements are vague, don't invest in speculative integration extensions. Instead, accommodate potential requirements by building an extensible integration architecture.

Understanding your requirements is the key to knowing how far you really do need to take an integration project. However, a lack of clarity around the nature of, or need for, future requirements introduces a risk for potential "over-integrate-ability."

Burdening an integration project and an integration architecture with new channels and features that may never get used is a waste of resources. It is therefore important to build integration environments carefully, and with the confidence of knowing that you will be using what you are building for tomorrow.

If some of the requirements you came up with are not yet set in stone, there is an intermediate step you can take. Limit the incorporation of these requirements to the design of the architecture only. Make any changes necessary that will allow the solution to be easily extended, should these new requirements go into effect. This dramatically lessens the effort and risk associated with "building for tomorrow."

12.4.5 Understand the roles of supplementary XML technologies

Backing up XML is an army of specifications, each of which proposes a supplementary technology that can extend the functionality and utilization of an XML-compliant application. It is important that you choose which of these technologies are part of your current and future application platforms.

Define a core technology set

"Define your core XML technology set, and treat each core technology with the same importance as XML itself."

Some specifications have had limited acceptance, some apply to very unique requirements, and others are still evolving. A chosen few specifications, however, have gained wide industry support, and have become so commonplace that they can be considered part of the core XML technology set.

For the purpose of this book, the core set of supplementary XML technologies consists of:

- DOM and SAX for programmatic data manipulation
- XSD schemas for data validation
- XSLT (and XPath) for transformation

A typical XML application architecture will rely on each of these technologies to per-form the primary tasks related to the processing of XML data. This does not mean, however, that they will necessarily become part of *your* application's core technology set. Even these established technologies have limitations and alternatives (as explored throughout Chapter 5).

Identify second-tier technologies
"Decide which emerging specifications are likely to become part of your future architecture."

Also worth mentioning are the second-tier specifications.[2] Some of these, such as XQuery and XSL:FO, are rapidly gaining support and will no doubt soon be part of the core family.

As a rule of thumb, there are two fundamental reasons for incorporating second-tier XML technologies:

- They solve immediate business problems without compromising the application architecture.
- You are confident they will eventually become a standard part of your technology platform, and you want to incorporate them now to avoid retro-fitting your application in the future.

With an understanding of the purpose and primary function of each relevant supple-mentary technology, you will gain a much better appreciation of what constitutes a complete XML architecture.

12.4.6   Adapt to new technology developments

The world of XML technology is in a constant state of evolution. New supplementary technologies, new versions of specifications, and new ways of doing old tasks are con-tinually emerging. Some leave their mark, others surface and then fade away. Those

---

2.   These are intentionally referred to as "second-tier" so that they won't be confused with the "second-generation" specifications that are part of the Web services framework.

that do catch on, though, can lead to important changes in industry standards and in the XML architecture itself.

"Abstraction is the key to an adaptive architecture."

You can't predict where this platform is going. Within a year from any given date it can change dramatically. The best way to minimize the potential impact from these technology shifts is to build in flexibility through abstraction.

By abstracting specific functional units of application logic into separate layers, you can upgrade or replace these units simply by replacing the layers themselves. The service integration layer introduced by Web services can be extremely useful in facilitating functional abstraction.

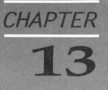

Thirty best practices for integrating Web services

W eb services introduce technology layers that reside over those already established by the XML platform. Therefore, the best practices for XML provided in the previous chapter also apply to service-oriented environments. Additionally, the contents of this chapter can be further supplemented by extracting best practices from the design and modeling strategies in Chapter 6.

NOTE
All best practices in this chapter are italicized and enclosed in quotation marks.

13.1 Best practices for planning service-oriented projects

13.1.1 Know when to use Web services

"First define the extent to which you want to use Web services before developing them. Services can be phased in at different levels, allowing you to customize an adoption strategy."

If you know that Web services will be a strategic part of your enterprise, then you need to start somewhere. A single application project, for instance, provides a low-risk opportunity for taking that first step. You will be able to integrate Web services to a limited extent and in a controlled manner. The key word here is "limited," because you do not want to go too far with a non-standardized integration effort.

Additional reasons to consider Web services include:

- The global IT industry is embracing and supporting Web services. By incorporating them sooner, your team will gain an understanding of an important platform shift that affects application architecture and technology.
- Use of Web services does not require an entirely new application architecture. Their loosely coupled design allows you to add a modest amount of simple services, without much impact on the rest of the application.
- If you are considering or already using a service-oriented design or business model, you definitely will need to take a serious look at Web services. The benefits of incorporating service-oriented paradigms within your enterprise can motivate the technical migration to a Web services framework.
- Many current development tools already support the creation of Web services, and several shield the developer from the low-level implementation details. This eases

the learning curve and allows for a faster adoption of Web service-related technologies.

13.1.2 Know how to use Web services

"Limit the scope of Web services in your production environment to the scope of your knowledge. If you know nothing, don't service-orient anything that matters."

Although the concept behind Web services has a great deal in common with traditional component-based design, it is still significantly different. Adding improperly designed Web services to your application may result in you having to redevelop them sooner than you might expect.

If you are delivering serious business functionality, you should hold off until you are confident in how Web services need to be integrated. Limit initial projects to low-risk prototypes and pilot applications, until you (and your project team) attain an adequate understanding of how Web services are best utilized within your technical environment.

13.1.3 Know when to avoid Web services

"Even though Web services are becoming an important part of the IT mainstream, you should begin incorporating them only where you know they will add value."

If you don't think that Web services will become a part of your enterprise environment anytime in the near future, then it may be premature to add them now. Technologies driving the Web services platform will continue to evolve, as will the front- and back-end products that support them.

Additional reasons to consider avoiding Web services in the short-term, include:

- The base Web service technologies (SOAP, WSDL, UDDI) are fairly established and robust, but vendor support can vary significantly for second-generation specifications. You may be better off waiting for certain standards to receive industry-wide support.

- Though development tools that support Web services will auto-generate a great deal of the markup, they will not assist in optimizing your application design. Having your developers simply attach one or two Web services to an existing application, without a real understanding of the technology behind them, could lead to a convoluted and weakened architecture.

- Some tools add proprietary extensions that will create dependencies on a vendor-specific platform. The long-term implications of these extensions need to be understood fully before too much of your application relies on them. Otherwise, opportunities for future interoperability may be compromised.

• Incorporating Web services may simply not be a requirement for autonomous application environments. Web services become a much more important consideration when taking interoperability requirements into account.

13.1.4 Moving forward with a transition architecture

"Consider a transition architecture that only introduces service-oriented concepts, without the technology."

A low-risk solution is an option if your focus is to gain experience with service-oriented technologies and concepts, and you don't have any pressing business requirements that rely on the proper delivery of Web services. You can start your transition by first delivering your application the way you normally would have, and then simply adding application proxies, or a custom designed facade (wrapper) to the functionality you'd like to expose via a service interface.

A benefit to this approach is that you can generally revert back to the traditional component-based model without too much impact to your overall application design. If your project requires a risk assessment wherein the usage of Web services is classified as a significant risk, this can become the basis for a contingency plan.

If you're just toying with the idea of introducing Web services into your application design, but aren't really sure to what extent it makes sense to do so, then you can also consider starting with a feasibility analysis. This will allow you to measure the pros and cons of the Web services platform, as they relate to your development project and your technical application environment.

Alternatively, you could avoid Web services altogether, and still build your application with a future SOA migration in mind. The XWIF modeling process in Chapter 6 provides a strategy for designing traditional component classes into service-oriented classes suitable for Web service encapsulation. These same remodeled classes can still be implemented within a non-service environment. The day you are ready to make the transition, you will already be halfway there.

13.1.5 Leverage the legacy

There are often very good reasons to replace or renew legacy environments in order to bring them into a contemporary framework. A service-oriented integration architecture, however, almost always provides an important alternative.

Build on what you have
"Always consider reusing legacy logic before replacing it."

Through the use of adapters and a service interface layer properly designed for functional abstraction, Web services can let you take advantage of what you already have. This can be a good first step to bringing application logic embedded in legacy systems into your integrated enterprise.

Compared to replacing a legacy environment altogether, leveraging existing systems is extremely cost-effective, and the process of integration can be relatively expedient. (This option also acts as a good reference point for judging the ROI of a proposed replacement project.)

Understand the limitations of a legacy foundation
"Define functional capacity boundaries around legacy applications, and do not integrate beyond."

There are challenges with bringing previously isolated applications into the interoperability loop. Although doing so can immediately broaden the resources shared by your enterprise, it can also severely tax a legacy environment not designed for external integration.

As long as you understand the boundaries within which you can incorporate legacy application logic, leveraging what you have makes a great deal of sense. Incidentally, typical EAI solutions (service-oriented or not) are based on the same principle of utilizing adapter architectures to include various legacy environments. Many mitigate the impact on legacy platforms through the use of intelligent adapters.

13.1.6 Sorry, no refunds (Web services and your bottom line)

"Budget for the range of expenses that follow Web services into an enterprise."

Web services are expensive. That is, *good* Web services require a great deal of work to ensure they truly are "good." Each service you develop can potentially become an important part of your overall IT infrastructure. Not only can services expose legacy applications and various types of business (and reusable) functionality, they can represent and even enable entire business processes.

How a service is designed requires a solid knowledge of the business model within which it will operate, as well as the technologies upon which it will be built. Services that will form (or intend to participate in) a future SOA will also need to be in alignment with the design strategy and accompanying standards that are part of the overall SOA implementation plan.

If you custom-develop services to add on to existing legacy environments, costs will typically be lower than if you start your integration by investing in enterprise service-oriented middleware products. Development costs can be especially moderate when using existing development tools that support the creation of Web services.

Also, because Web services open the door to new integration opportunities, the quality of the interface they expose is very important. Despite being classified as a loosely coupled technology, once heavily integrated into an enterprise, many dependencies upon service interfaces can still be created. Changing an interface after it has been established can be a costly (and not to mention, messy) task, especially in environments that utilize service assemblies.

Doing it right, however, will reap tangible benefits. Integration effort within a relatively standardized SOA will drop significantly. Hooking new and legacy systems into an established Web services-enabled architecture will generally require a fraction of the effort and cost than traditional point-to-point integration projects. There are definite and measurable returns to be had on your investment. It therefore pays to get it right the first time. To get it right the first time, though, you certainly will have to pay.

13.1.7   Align ROIs with migration strategies

Though many organizations have already invested in XML architectures, a move to a service-oriented design paradigm or a full-scale SOA often needs further justification. This is especially true when large investments have already been made in (non-service-oriented) EAI projects with which an organization is already quite content.

ROIs open eyes
"ROIs for service-oriented architectures can provide valuable information, beyond that required to justify the project."

Regardless of whether you are asked to justify the use of Web services or have already decided to implement them in your environment, putting together a realistic ROI can be an enlightening experience.

In addition to providing "evidence" that predicted cost savings resulting from the use of Web services will be realized, properly researched ROIs can give you a clear idea as to how long it will take for these benefits to be attained.

Iterating through ROI and migration strategy documents
"Keep revising the ROI as new information becomes available."

It is common for the results of an ROI to shape an enterprise migration strategy. Flip that thought around for a second, and consider using a migration strategy as input for the ROI.

The nature of the research that tends to be performed for migration strategies is more focused on technology and implementation, rather than high-level organizational benefits. An intelligent strategy for integrating a service-oriented architecture can lead to much greater cost benefits than an ROI originally predicted. So, even if you used an ROI to justify your migration project, you can typically refine that ROI (and often improve the justifications) using the contents of your migration strategy.

Confused yet? Have a look at the diagram in Figure 13.1.

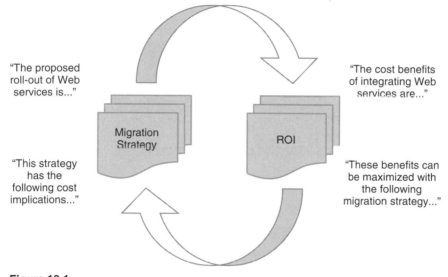

Figure 13.1
An iterative cycle between a migration plan and an ROI.

The initial SOA migration may be the most expensive part of an enterprise-wide initiative however, the scope of your ROI will likely go beyond the migration phase. Further revisions to an ROI will improve the accuracy of its predictions as they relate to subsequent phases in a long-term program.

ROIs for Web services can also be easier to justify than for other XML-based technologies. The benefits tend to be more tangible, because the interoperability enabled by the service integration layer results in immediately recognizable savings.

13.1.8 Build toward a future state

"Design a service-oriented solution to accommodate its probable migration path."

The built-in features of a Web services framework are there, whether you choose to use them or not. The foremost benefit of any service-oriented environment is the intrinsic potential for immediate and future interoperability. You can take advantage of this potential by designing application architectures for integration, even when not immediately requiring integration.

Fostering integration requires a change in design standards, application architecture development, and the overall mindset of the project team. For example, you can facilitate local requestors as well as future remote requestors by providing both coarse- and fine-grained interfaces based on standard naming and service description conventions.

To an extent, you can consider this new approach as building integration architectures, regardless of whether they will be integrating anything immediately. Perhaps a better suited term would be "integrate-able architectures."

Chapter 14 fully explains this design approach by providing future state environments for service-oriented integrated architectures and EAI solutions.

13.2 Best practices for standardizing Web services

13.2.1   Incorporate standards

"Consider standards for Web services as standards for your infrastructure."

In the corresponding section of the previous chapter,[1] I used an analogy about obeying traffic laws in order to highlight the importance of standards when integrating XML within a development project. Let's alter that analogy to define an approach for standardizing the integration of Web services.

A city's commuting infrastructure is almost always standardized. A traffic sign on the East side generally communicates a message (stop, yield, merge) the same way on the West side. You, the driver, can go from any point A to any point B with the confidence of knowing that the rules of navigation are being expressed consistently. Take your car outside of the city boundary, though, and that might change.

As with any enterprise application development project where you have different units of developers building different parts of the system, standardizing how each part is designed is important for all the traditional reasons (robustness, maintenance, etc.). In the service-oriented world, though, the real benefit is in establishing a standardized application interface. In an enterprise, this can potentially translate into a standardized system for navigating:

---

1.   The "Incorporate standards" best practice in Chapter 12.

- application logic
- integration architectures
- corporate data stores
- parts of the enterprise infrastructure

Back to our analogy: A different city, let's say in another country, will have a compatible driving platform (paved streets, intersections, traffic lights), but there will be new signs with new symbols, and often a different approach to driving altogether.

Navigating through non-standard environments will always slow your progress and introduce new risks. When developing services within your enterprise, you are establishing infrastructure through which developers, integrators, and perhaps even business partners may need to navigate in the years to come.

Simply adding a common platform for data exchange is not enough to ensure a quality service-oriented environment. You need more than streets and intersections to guarantee a safe and consistent driving experience.

13.2.2 Label the infrastructure

"Consider naming conventions as a means of labeling your infrastructure."

When assembling the pieces of an integration architecture you can end up with a multitude of interdependent components, each a necessary link in your solution. Since your environment will consist of a mixture of legacy and contemporary application components, you will already be faced with inconsistencies.

Contemporary integration solutions, however, are based on the concept of legacy abstraction. Introducing new architectural layers, such as those provided by Web services and adapters, allows you to hide the inconsistent characteristics of legacy environments. You, in fact, are given the opportunity to customize these new application endpoints. If you take a step back and look at the collection of potential endpoints that exist in your enterprise, you essentially are viewing infrastructure.

When working on a project, it's easy to label the components of an application arbitrarily. A name is something quickly added, so that you can move on to more important functional tasks. The benefits of naming standards are often not evident until later in the project cycle, when you actually have to start plugging things together. That's when introducing a naming convention can become especially inconvenient.

For instance, imagine yourself as an application architect in the midst of a development project. Surveying the environment in which developers are deploying Web services, you recognize that it is riddled with inconsistent endpoint names. You convince your Project Manager that the solution should adopt a naming convention in order to increase consistency. The project team revisits the relevant component and service interfaces they created, and your PM watches in horror as this wonderful solution begins to crumble to the ground.

The names used to identify public component and service interfaces act as reference points for other components and services. When you change a name, you therefore need to change all references to it. As a result, renaming all your solution's components and services turns into a major project in itself, during which all further development is halted.

Finally, a week later, all references seem to have been updated and the solution is online again. But… it isn't working quite as well as before. The odd error, the odd communications problem — there are still some references hidden somewhere that need to be changed. So, the solution undergoes another round of testing, the remaining references are updated, and things finally return to normal.

You call up your PM (who's been away on stress leave) and let him know everything is up and running again and your components and services have new names! After a long silence, he calmly says that he will be returning soon. He hangs up, turns back to his therapist, and finishes discussing the fantasy where *you* are the PM who has to explain the cost and time overruns to the project stakeholders, and he is the annoying architect whose only concern is that things have pretty names.

Using a naming convention will not only improve the efficiency of administering your solution, it will make the migration and deployment of new integration projects much easier. Naming conventions reduce the risk of human error and the chance that a simple adjustment will lead to your solution mysteriously breaking down. As powerful and sophisticated as enterprise solutions are these days, it can still take only one broken link to bring them to a grinding halt.

One more thing
Don't bury naming conventions amidst other standards documents. I highly recommend you place them in a separate document that gets distributed to every member of your project team. This document will act as a both a navigation and development aid that can assist developers, administrators, and many others involved with a project.

13.2.3 Design against an interface (not vice versa)

In the previous section we introduced a best practice that promoted the use of a naming convention for labeling enterprise endpoints. When modeling a service-oriented framework, we actually get to provide a complete description of these endpoints. The standardization of these descriptions, therefore, becomes very significant (see Figure 13.2).

"Consistently describing service interfaces establishes a standard endpoint model. This results in a standardized service-oriented integration architecture that can be positioned as part of enterprise infrastructure."

To ensure consistency in endpoint design, the common development process for a Web service needs to be reversed. Instead of building our application logic and then expressing this functionality through an appropriate service interface, we need to make the design of that interface our first task.

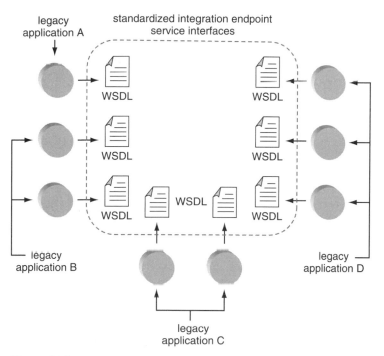

Figure 13.2
Standardized integration endpoint services establishing a service-oriented integration architecture.

This is where the fore mentioned naming conventions are incorporated with your enterprise-wide interface design standards. With a fundamental knowledge of what Web services will be encapsulating, you can create a generic, consistent interface with operation characteristics that comply to a standard model. With that in place, you can then build the back-end logic. (For a step-by-step process on how to analyze and design service interfaces using this approach, visit Chapter 6.)

The best way to ensure consistency across the interfaces within your Web services framework is to make a resource responsible for the interface design. The role of the service interface designer is explained next. Essentially this person is responsible for both the modeling of Web services as well as the design of SOAP messages.

13.2.4   Service interface designer

Designing a Web service is a separate task from its actual development. A service interface designer is responsible for ensuring that the external interface of all Web services is consistent and clearly representative of the service's intended business function. The service interface designer typically will own the WSDL document, to which developers will need to supply the implementation code. The service interface designer can also be in charge of all SOAP documents to ensure a consistent message format as well.

Typical responsibilities:

- WSDL documents
- SOAP message documents
- interface clarity
- interface extensibility
- interface standards and naming conventions

Typical prerequisites:

- a background in component design
- high proficiency in WSDL and SOAP
- a proficiency in business analysis
- a good understanding of the organization's business scope and direction

13.2.5   Categorize your services

"Use XWIF service models to classify and standardize service types."

Every Web service is unique, but many end up performing similar functions and exhibiting common characteristics, allowing them to be categorized.

This guide refers to service categories as service models. A number of service models are described throughout this book, each with a specific purpose and a list of typical characteristics. Use these as a starting point, and customize them to whatever extent necessary.

Here are some examples of how using service models can be beneficial:

- you can apply specific design standards to different service models
- the model type instantly communicates a service's overall role and position within an architecture
- models can be aligned with enterprise policies and security standards
- service models can be used to gauge the performance requirements of service-oriented applications

13.3 Best practices for designing service-oriented environments

13.3.1 Use SOAs to streamline business models

"Service-oriented designs open up new opportunities for business automation. Rethink business models to take advantage of these opportunities."

If you find yourself amidst the technology surrounding Web services, don't lose sight of one of the most significant benefits this new design platform can provide. By offering a more flexible, interoperable, and standardized model for hosting application functionality, SOAs provide an opportunity for you to rethink and improve your business processes.

For instance:

- A service-oriented architecture within your organization will increase the interoperability potential between legacy systems. This will allow you to reevaluate various business processes that rely on multiple applications or data sources.
- An array of generic business and utility services will provide a number of ways to automate new parts of your business centers
- Services can integrate with EAI solutions to deliver new business processes that, in turn, integrate existing business processes.

To learn more about service-oriented business modeling, see Chapter 14.

13.3.2 Research the state of second-generation specifications

As more and more legacy application logic is expressed and represented within service-oriented environments, the demand increases for Web services to support a wider range of traditional business automation features.

The IT community responds to these demands by improving and sometimes replacing technical specifications. The feature set of the Web services framework continues to grow, driven both by standards organizations and major corporations, many of which collaboratively produce specifications that address new functional areas for Web services to utilize.

"Approach the choice of each second-generation specification as a strategic decision-point."

If you are building serious service-oriented solutions, you will be working with second-generation specifications. Before you begin creating dependencies on the features offered by one of these standards, you need to ensure that:

- it is sufficiently stable
- it is supported by your current platform vendors
- there is no emerging specification poised to take its place
- support for the standard is (or will be) provided by middleware or development products you are considering

Don't make the mistake of classifying the selection of these specifications as a purely technical decision. It is a strategic design decision that will have implications on your architecture, technology platform, and design standards. (To stay current with Web services standards, visit www.specifications.ws.)

13.3.3 Strategically position second-generation specifications

"Design your SOA with a foreknowledge of emerging specifications."

Regardless of whether you are planning to incorporate the features offered by some of the newer second-generation Web services specifications, you should make it a point to research the feature set provided by these standards. This will allow you to identify those that may be potentially useful.

Whichever ones you classify as being significant or relevant can be positioned within your future-state enterprise architecture. This is a key step in evolving a service-oriented environment.

It is also important that you make this information publicly available to your project teams. Architects will approach the design of application logic differently with a foreknowledge of how the role a future technology may affect their application designs.

13.3.4 Understand the limitations of your platform

While traveling the roads that lead to an SOA, you are bound to run into the odd pothole or roadblock. As key industry standards continue to mature, so does the feature set required for Web services to become fully capable of representing and expressing sophisticated business logic in enterprise environments.

Until the second generation of Web services specifications is fully evolved, however, there remains a rather volatile transition period, as many middleware and development platforms compensate for the absence or immaturity of these standards by supplying solutions of their own.

Proprietary extensions (the potholes)
"Define and work within the boundaries of your development platform."

Several platforms supplement core Web services standards with proprietary extensions. Often these new features will be based on draft versions of specifications expected to become industry standards. The extent to which standards are supported, however, can vary.

When considering the use of vendor-specific extensions, make sure you understand how they are being implemented, and what dependencies they impose. Keep in mind that if you commit to using them, you may need to migrate your services away from these extensions at some point in the future.

In the meantime, however, they may very well address your immediate requirements, while allowing you to proceed with a service-oriented application design.

Exclusive proprietary extensions (the roadblocks)
"If development platform boundaries are too restrictive, reconsider the platform."

Some development platforms provide extensions to Web services at the cost of requiring that all requestors of the service be built using the same technologies. This not only defeats the purpose of designing service-oriented applications, it ties you to a platform that offers little more than traditional component-based environments.

Within a controlled environment, these features may be attractive. If open interoperability is one of your future goals, though, it's time to make a U-turn.

13.3.5 Use abstraction to protect legacy endpoints from change

The service interface layer can give you a great deal of flexibility in how you continue evolving integrated legacy applications. Since the integration layer acts as an intermediary between previously tightly bound legacy applications, a level of decoupling is achieved. This makes the Web service the only contact point for either legacy environment.

Use abstraction to improve configuration management
"Alter configuration management procedures around the abstraction benefit introduced by the service interface layer."

A side benefit to the loose coupling introduced by the service integration layer is improved configuration management of integrated legacy applications.

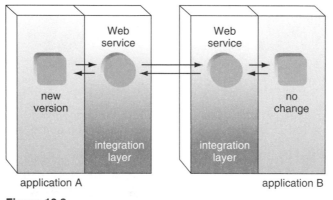

Figure 13.3
Application A is upgraded without affecting application B.

As shown in Figure 13.3, you can upgrade application A without requiring changes to application B. However, depending on the nature of the upgrade, application A's Web service may be affected. Modifying the integration layer, though, tends to be much easier than making changes to legacy logic.

Although this aspect of an SOA isn't the first benefit that comes to mind, it can have major implications on how you administer and maintain applications in your enterprise.

Use abstraction to support wholesale application changes
"Take advantage of the service integration layer by more aggressively evolving integrated legacy environments."

The level of abstraction that can be provided by service-oriented integration architectures can significantly reduce the impact of platform migrations.

Since the two applications displayed in Figure 13.4 only know of service endpoints, you can replace application A entirely without any changes required to application B. Any required modifications to application A's Web service almost always will be less disruptive than changes to application B's integration channel.

13.3.6 Build around a security model
Especially when developing second-generation Web services, incorporating a sound security model is a key part of your design process.

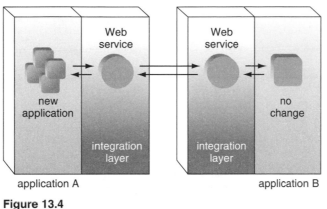

Figure 13.4
Application A is replaced without affecting application B.

Security requirements define boundaries, real boundaries
"The functional application design needs to be built upon the security model, (not the other way around)."

Putting together a design, and perhaps even building a preliminary version of your application without serious consideration for the underlying security model is a common mistake. It's like going out on stage for your performance, and then, before you can finish, getting pulled back with one of those long hooks. (It's the security requirements pulling that hook, in case you didn't get that.)

Web services security models are unique, complex, and multi-dimensional. There are many factors to consider that will result in firm boundaries that will shape and scope the remaining parts of your application design.

Define the scope of the security model
"A key part of a standardized service-oriented enterprise is a service-oriented security (SOS) model."

When we talk about a Web services security model, it can mean a number of different things. A model can represent the security rules and technologies that apply to an application. It also, however, can be standardized within the enterprise.

The enterprise SOS model displayed in Figure 13.5 establishes a standard security platform that includes policies and the technologies that enforce them. As shown in Figure 13.6, this model can be implemented within a dedicated security services layer that also becomes an application architecture standard. (For more information, see Chapter 11.)

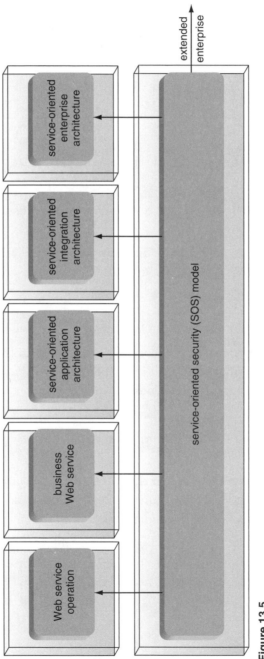

Figure 13.5
The service-oriented security (SOS) model.

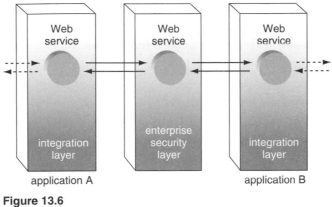

Figure 13.6
A separate security layer can implement the SOS model.

The required use of a SOS model can impose significant restrictions upon application designs. This is offset, however, by the fact that its use also alleviates application development projects from having to deal with many of the issues relating to security. Most of the decisions will have already been made; all the project team has to deliver is an application that conforms to SOS standards.

13.4 Best practices for managing service-oriented development projects

13.4.1 Organizing development resources

"Group development teams around logical business tasks."

A common mistake in development projects that incorporate a limited SOA is to have one team deliver the Web services, and the remaining team(s) develop the balance of the application. From a resourcing perspective this approach makes sense, because you have each team working with technologies that match their respective skill set. It can, however, create a disconnect between developers responsible for building parts of an application that deliver a logical unit of business functionality.

When you break an application down into its primary (or even secondary) business functions, you end up with the equivalent of a series of subprojects that collectively make up the application's feature set. Each of these subprojects will typically require the creation of a number of application components, some of which may be encapsulated within Web services. Development teams need to be grouped in accordance with these subprojects, so that the performance and functionality of individual business tasks can be streamlined.

If you have only one or two developers qualified to build Web services, then you should consider sharing them across more than one development team. As long as they are actively participating with their respective teams, they will be able to optimize the Web services to best accommodate each business task.

13.4.2 Don't underestimate training for developers

"Ensure that your developers and designers are capable of applying the right blend of business and technical intelligence to every Web service."

How much do you tip a developer? Well, that depends on how good the *service* is … OK, let's officially end my sad career in IT comedy by moving on to the importance of ensuring that your development (and design) staff has the proper skills to build and integrate Web services. If they are new to this platform, you may not want to just hand them a book and ask them to "go figure it out."

Here's why:

- In many cases, Web services affect the application's business model. The execution of an automated business task will differ within an application, depending on how Web services are utilized. Developers may not be aware of the relationship between the service they are developing and its associated business task(s). This becomes an especially critical issue when building controller and process services.

- Recurring requirements for Web services are that they be generic, openly accessible, and relatively independent. To achieve these characteristics, the functionality within a service needs to be carefully defined. This requires knowledge of the business functions an application needs to deliver now, as well as the level of interoperability it will have to provide in the future. Generally, developers are only focused on immediate project requirements.

- When teams of developers are involved with an application development project, a set of new standards will likely be required to ensure that Web services are implemented consistently. Developers can participate in the creation of these standards; typically, though, standards need to be established by those already proficient with the technologies.

- It is easy to create Web services with contemporary development tools. This can give a developer a false sense of confidence. It is, in fact, easy to create Web services, but only bad ones.

13.5 Best practices for implementing Web services

13.5.1 Use a private service registry

Once Web services establish themselves as a common part of your enterprise, they will begin to evolve, requiring interface upgrades and spawning new generations of services. Pretty soon, it will be difficult to keep track of the many service interfaces, especially since some will always be in a state of transition. (To learn more about private registries and UDDI, read through the tutorial in Chapter 4.)

Centralize service descriptions in a service repository
"Incorporate a private service registry to centralize published service descriptions into one accessible resource."

A private service registry can house the collective descriptions of all your Web services. It acts as the central repository for current service interface information to which anyone interested will go to discover and learn about an enterprise's service framework.

Its use has immediate benefits, including:

- efficient access to service interfaces (no time wasted searching)
- preserving the integrity of published service interfaces ("published" is a state represented by the repository)
- encouraging the discovery of generic and reusable services

Make the use of a service registry mandatory
"Require the use of a private service registry and keep it current. Otherwise it won't be useful."

If people lose confidence in a service registry, it can quickly become the least popular part of your IT environment. If you locate a service interface in a local UDDI registry, and you're not sure it is the latest version, you won't be inclined to use it. Instead, you'll probably phone around until you find the original service developer, from whom you'll get the most recent WSDL file.

If, however, the use of this registry is a requirement that is strictly adhered to, it will become a core part of your administrative infrastructure, supporting development projects as a resource centre for published Web service endpoints.

Assign a resource to maintain the registry
"To make enterprise service registries a functional part of an organization, assign a Service Library Manager."

Private service registries need to provide a high level of availability and dependability. Not only will the registry serve individuals who manually search it for various service details, it may also need to facilitate dynamic discovery. At that point, it could become a critical resource.

The best way to ensure that a registry is kept current and available is to assign ownership of these responsibilities. Maintaining a service registry is a unique job, in that it involves an uncommon combination of skills. XWIF provides a description of this role, and calls it the *Service Library Manager*.

Such a resource becomes especially important if your organization opens its registry to external business partners. In that case, the Service Library Manager also needs to manage the authentication and authorization of users from outside of the organization.

Responsible for maintaining the service library and the local UDDI registry, this individual may need to be included in official application design reviews so that proposed service designs can be evaluated and compared against existing and other planned services.

The Service Library Manager will also own the organization's utility services. Any changes required to these services will need to be approved by the library manager, and implemented in such a way that they are sufficiently generic for future use, and do not break existing interfaces already in use by service requestors.

Responsible for:

- service library
- publishing of service descriptions
- maintenance and design of utility services
- review of application designs incorporating services

Typical prerequisites:

- UDDI or a services broker product
- a background in component design
- a good understanding of the organization's business scope and direction

---

NOTE

In smaller IT environments, you can consider combining the roles of Service Library Manager and XML Data Custodian.

13.5.2 Prepare for administration

An often overlooked aspect of projects implementing service-oriented applications are the subsequent maintenance tasks required to keep these environments going.

"Be prepared for the costs and complexities in administering a service-oriented enterprise."

Increased interoperability results in a higher amount of dependencies between application environments, namely their Web service endpoints. With a high level of integration comes the responsibility of keeping your Web services running smoothly, regardless of what's thrown at them. High usage volumes, error conditions, and other environmental variables need to be anticipated.

Entire product suites are available to maintain Web services, although many are platform specific. If you are deploying Web services without such an environment, administration can eventually become an overly burdensome task. You may want to prevent this from happening by investigating some of the application hosting environments offered by service-oriented EAI solutions.

Either way, administration costs need to be properly represented in project budgets. Otherwise, the support infrastructure required by service-oriented architectures will not be sufficient. This, in turn, can jeopardize the success of the application and those that integrate with it.

XWIF introduces the *Service Administrator* role, a resource responsible for the maintenance and monitoring of these hosting environments.

In an environment where many Web services are deployed and utilized, an administration system needs to be in place in order to ensure a reliable runtime hosting environment.

Service administrators need to be proficient in the use of maintenance and monitoring tools. They will be the ones who need to respond to production issues relating to the availability and performance of Web services. This role is similar to that of a webmaster for a Web site. The administrator is required to keep track of usage statistics and look out for (and preemptively avoid) performance bottlenecks.

This position is especially relevant in organizations offering Web services that can be accessed externally. In order to effectively handle unpredictable usage volumes, the administrator must be able to respond quickly when performance trends start heading south.

In EAI environments, this role is often assumed by the same person managing the integration brokers. Typical responsibilities include:

- assessing the need for specific administration tools and servers
- evaluating and perhaps integrating these products
- monitoring the use of individual Web services
- analyzing usage statistics and identifying trends and patterns
- assessing the impact of the Web service use on underlying legacy applications or components
- identifying and tracking dependencies (service requestors) of deployed Web services
- managing version control over Web services
- being involved with version control of legacy applications represented by Web services

Typical prerequisites:

- proficiency in Web services administration products
- fair knowledge of WSDL and SOAP
- good understanding of service deployment techniques and related security settings

13.5.3 Monitor and respond to changes in the service hosting environments

"Be responsive to increased infrastructure requirements."

When Web services represent the endpoints to existing or new integration channels, they can easily become the busiest parts of an integrated environment. This can tax the underlying areas of the infrastructure supporting those services. To avoid performance bottlenecks, it's a good idea to survey your existing infrastructure and identify any part that may need to be upgraded.

In preparing for any new application, there will be obvious areas where upgrades will be required. New servers, more memory, and strategically located routers are all typical requirements needed to support incoming application hosting environments.

To achieve an optimized environment designed to host Web services, though, you frequently need to see them in action first. The communications framework introduced by Web services brings with it new protocols, different types of runtime processing, and an overall shift in where this processing can physically occur.

It is difficult to predict exactly where and to what extent processing requirements will change. Therefore, it is often best not to *fully* upgrade your infrastructure until you have a good idea of what the actual performance requirements will be. One way of determining this prior to making your Web services available for production use is to perform a series of stress and volume tests.

Another approach is to measure and respond to performance requirements by carefully monitoring production usage. For instance:

1. Phase in the production release of your application.
2. Closely monitor performance and study usage patterns.
3. Respond quickly with hardware upgrades where required.

13.5.4 Test for the unknown

"…but they said that if we build a service-oriented architecture, we'd be freed from the problems involved with connecting disparate technology platforms…" Sure, but you still need to build your Web services framework using a vendor-specific development platform, along with a vendor-manufactured SOAP server.

Products used to establish an environment for service-oriented data exchange may provide various levels of support for various (mostly second-generation) Web services specifications. This can lead to some discrepancies in areas such as WSDL document interpretation and SOAP message header processing.

"To guarantee the level of interoperability promised by Web services, incorporate a multi-client test phase. This precaution is especially important when working with second-generation specifications."

The simplest way to address this issue is to increase the amount of testing each newly created Web service will be subjected to. Your test strategy should require that services be tested with a range of clients representative of potential service requestors.

For instance, you may have one project team creating an application using J2EE, while the other is basing theirs on .NET. Even though neither team needs their application to integrate with the other's, their respective testing phases should still include client requestors based on both J2EE and .NET.

This issue is comparable to the age-old presentation-related problems Web page designers faced when having to accommodate Netscape and Microsoft browsers. There were a number of discrepancies in how HTML was rendered and in how client-side script was processed. Conditional logic often had to be used in order to output different page content.

When first developing a Web service, the effort to fix processing discrepancies is generally negligible. However, if these problems remain undetected until after services have been deployed, then you've got yourself a redevelopment project on hand.

Building the service-
oriented enterprise (SOE)

A service-oriented architecture is many things. It is a technical architecture, a business modeling concept, a piece of infrastructure, an integration source, and a new way of viewing units of automation within the enterprise. Building and integrating SOAs leads to the evolution of a service-oriented enterprise (SOE). For the purposes of integration, an SOE defines the ultimate future state that service-oriented integration projects strive to achieve.

From a technical perspective, a service-oriented enterprise can be viewed as standardized infrastructure, supplemented with strategically positioned XML and Web services technologies. Service-oriented architectures are a part of this standardization, designed to facilitate future inter-SOA integration within the SOE. Collectively these SOAs represent a service-oriented enterprise integration architecture.

Abstract from that the business model it is implementing, and you can view the enterprise as a collection of services and processes. Together, these two driving forces comprise an extremely powerful and flexible business automation model (see Figure 14.1).

The service-oriented enterprise is therefore more than an implementation of a new technology platform. It establishes an environment that can respond to business requirements with unprecedented agility. This, in turn, allows the business model itself to evolve in new (more service-centric) directions. Since an SOE provides a carefully designed, service-oriented view of the enterprise, it continues to evolve and adapt with an organization.

14.1 SOA modeling basics

A fundamental aspect of service-oriented business modeling is that units of business logic can be labeled in different ways, depending on the context in which they are viewed. The building blocks provided later in this chapter establish baselines units, each of which represents a common scope of business logic. Each of these blocks, however, can be classified in numerous ways.

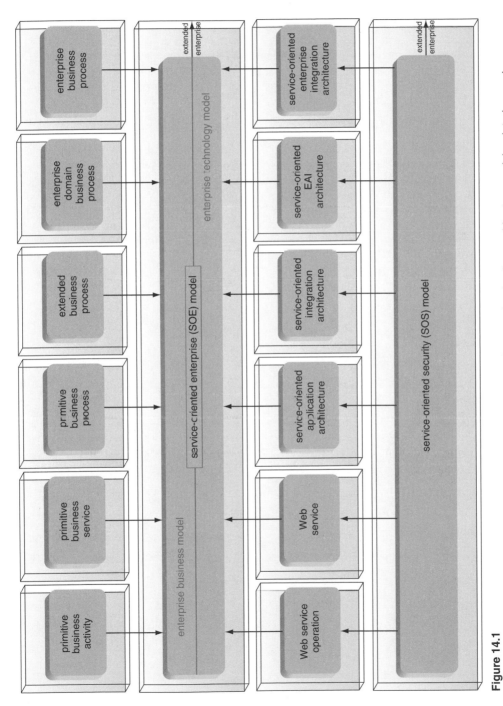

Figure 14.1

This master view of the XWIF SOE model illustrates how closely business and technology architecture models relate (one no longer exclusively drives the other).

> **NOTE**
>
> The term "service" is used in both technical and business modeling environments. The use of this term is appropriate in these contexts, as we are modeling business services that are eventually implemented through the use of Web services. For clarification purposes, within this chapter only, I refer to services within a technology architecture context as "Web services," whereas business modeling services are just "services."

> **ALSO NOTE**
>
> This entire chapter is derived from terms, concepts, processes, and ideas that form the basis of the XML & Web Services Integration Framework (XWIF). Though only the SOE model for the enterprise is covered, the full XWIF SOE encompasses the extended enterprise, which facilitates integration with external partner services. For more information, visit www.xwif.com.

There are three terms that you will see used repeatedly. Each can imply a different perspective of the same unit of business logic.

14.1.1 Activities

An activity refers to a piece of business logic that works in cooperation with others to perform some sort of business function. The scope of an activity and the function it is carrying out can vary. Therefore, three types of activities are commonly used to represent a range of scenarios.

Primitive business activity

This is the most basic business modeling building block of an SOA. It consists of a granular piece of business logic that is typically grouped with other primitive business activities that collectively represent the business logic of a complete primitive business service. Within a technical environment, a primitive business activity is most comparable to a granular Web service operation.

The primitive business activity type is further described in the "SOE business modeling building blocks" section.

Process activity

An activity within the context of a process represents an executable step within the workflow logic. Processes can consist of a series of services that are coordinated by the logic within the process workflow. Therefore, a process activity commonly corresponds to a service.

Business activity
This is a generic term typically used to represent a coarse piece of business logic. A business activity can span services and processes, and in its implemented form, roughly corresponds to a Web services activity (as defined in Chapter 3).

14.1.2 Services

Services are cohesive and autonomous units of business logic. A service can be used independently to perform a specific business task, or it may be part of an aggregation (assembly) of services that collectively complete a larger business task. When modeling services, the context in which a service is viewed can determine how it is referred to.

Primitive business service
This SOA building block defines a granular service that consists of business logic representative of a specific business function. A primitive business service typically does not encompass other services; however, it often will participate as a part of a set of composed services. Within a service-oriented architecture, a primitive business service is most comparable to a granular Web service.

The primitive business service type is described further in the "SOE business modeling building blocks" section.

Process service
Contrary to popular belief, this is not a service that participates in a process. A process service actually encapsulates the workflow logic of the process itself. A process service is different from a business service in that it is always limited to the logic of a single business process. Process Web services mirror this functional scope within a service-oriented architecture (as explained in the XWIF process service model description in Chapter 10).

Business service
This is a generic term used to identify services that can expose any level of functional granularity. A business service is self-sufficient and can represent a distinct piece of business logic, a process, or a collection of processes. In its implemented form, a business service is most comparable to the Web service building block.

14.1.3 Processes

Service-oriented processes consist of a collection of composed activities and services (Figure 14.2). The process itself is represented by a series of process activities that are coordinated through a body of workflow logic that is expressed within a process service. Each process activity can be made up of any type of service, including another process service.

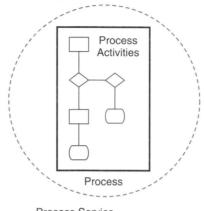

Process Service

Figure 14.2
A service-oriented process.

Service-oriented processes can inter-relate through their respective process services, as shown in Figure 14.3. Figure 14.4 illustrates how multiple processes can be represented by a single business service.

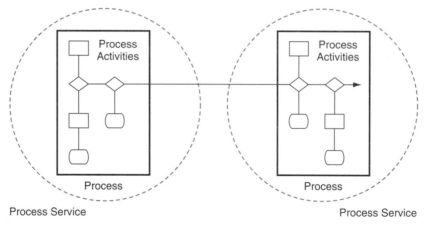

Process Service   Process Service

Figure 14.3
A relationship between two processes.

Being able to assemble activities, services, and processes in this way creates an extremely flexible enterprise model comprised entirely of business logic units with varying degrees of scope, and exposing a range of functional granularity.

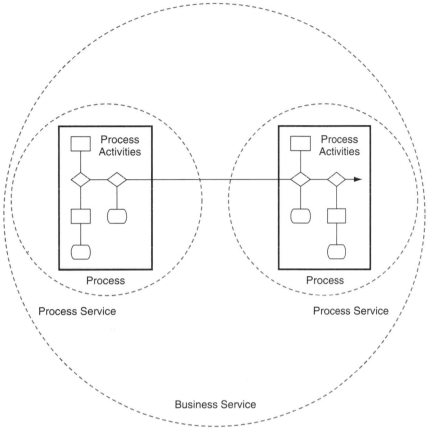

Figure 14.4
Two processes represented by a single business service.

14.2 SOE building blocks

Let's take the SOE model apart and look at each piece individually. The following descriptions separate the business modeling blocks from those associated with technology architecture. Although they are aligned in the diagram, the relationship between business and technology blocks can vary.

Throughout this section we provide examples that relate to a fictional consulting company. We use service-oriented principles to solve a series of problems, since the company is faced with a number of changes to its business model.

14.2.1   SOE business modeling building blocks

When designing (or redesigning) a business model for a service-oriented enterprise, you need to break down and partition aspects of the model into a number of primary levels. Each level represents a consistent degree of functional granularity.

The SOE building blocks (shown in Figure 14.5) provide six such levels, each of which represents business logic in increasing scope and complexity.

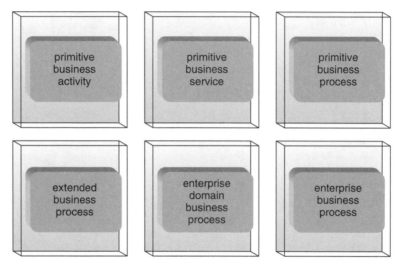

Figure 14.5
Business modeling building blocks for the SOE.

Each subsequent block encompasses the scope of its predecessor. This allows you to compose these blocks in different ways, providing a flexible model that can evolve with your business.

Throughout the following descriptions we'll provide examples relating to our fictional consulting company. We'll demonstrate how service-oriented business modeling can be used to solve the following problems.

- Consulting time billed to clients is the basis for invoices generated by the company. Hours recorded by consultants are logged on separate timesheets. Due to a recurring discrepancy between billed and logged hours, a new business rule has come into effect, requiring that before they are sent out, invoices need to be reconciled against corresponding timesheets.

- Our consulting company is merged with another. As a result, month-end sales reporting processes from each company need to be combined.

- The merger also creates a new business requirement for the invoice and timesheet reporting processes to be consolidated. Unlike the month-end sales report processes, though, the invoice and timesheet processes exist in different business domains.

The examples provided here are continued in the "SOE technology architecture building blocks" section, where we discuss how Web services can be used to implement various service-oriented business models.

Primitive business activity

A *primitive business activity* (Figure 14.6) typically represents a step executed in order to perform a business task. Groups of related activities therefore can be tightly coupled to form cohesive services. This building block represents the most fine-grained unit of business logic.

Figure 14.6
The primitive business activity.

Within our accounting system, the Retrieve Invoice Data task (service) could consist of a series of activities, such as:

- enter invoice date range
- execute search for invoice data
- return results

NOTE
Although a primitive business activity is similar in concept, it is different from a process activity or a business activity.

NOTE
The business logic represented within a primitive business activity does not constitute a service (if it did, it would be referred to as such). Typically, a primitive business activity acts as a building block for a service.

Primitive business service

A *primitive business service* (Figure 14.7) is the fundamental building block of a service-oriented business model. It represents any self-contained business task or function that can be classified as a primitive (simple) service.

Figure 14.7
The primitive business service.

Typical characteristics:

- Business logic within a *primitive business service* is autonomous in nature.
- A primitive business service consists of a collection of related primitive business activities.
- Within the service, activities can form a logical algorithm (a mini-process).

Within our accounting system, the task of Retrieve Invoice Data can be considered a primitive business service.

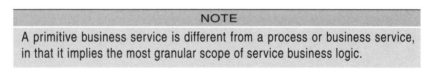

NOTE
A primitive business service is different from a process or business service, in that it implies the most granular scope of service business logic.

The primitive business process

A *primitive business process* (Figure 14.8) consists of a collection of logically related primitive business services that are composed and coordinated using workflow logic.

Typical characteristics:

- Primitive business services are composed into a sequence that forms a unit of automation (a process).
- Within a primitive business process, each service remains autonomous.
- The primitive business process in its entirety can be viewed as a process service or a coarse-grained business service.

Figure 14.8
The primitive business process.

Within our accounting system, the Process Invoice process consists of a series of primitive business services, including the Retrieve Invoice Data service (see Figure 14.9).

> **NOTE**
>
> Services and other processing steps within a business process can also be referred to as *process activities*.

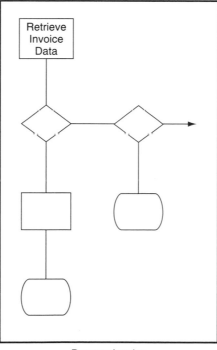

Process Invoice

Figure 14.9
A Retrieve Invoice Data service (acting as a process activity) executes a step within the Process Invoice process.

The extended business process

An *extended business process* (Figure 14.10) provides functionality beyond a single process boundary.

Figure 14.10
The extended business process.

Typical characteristics:

- An extended business process can consist of two merged primitive business processes or a single process that "borrows" a service from another.
- An extended business process can be encapsulated in a process service or a coarse-grained business service that exposes its logic to other processes and services.

Separately classifying a process as "extended" may not always be necessary. Often primitive business processes evolve with new requirements, but are still considered "primitive" in that they continue to remain focused on a specific business function. The use of this building block is therefore optional in many cases.

Figure 14.11 shows how the Process Invoice process from the accounting system is extended with the Retrieve Timesheet Data service from the Timesheet Reporting process. The new enhanced Process Invoice process may then need to introduce new business logic to manage discrepancies between the native invoice and imported timesheet data formats.

The enterprise domain business process

A domain-specific process that introduces new business logic, but is also composed of several existing processes, is referred to as the *enterprise domain business process* (Figure 14.12). The domain does not necessarily need to be organizational in nature, in that it doesn't have to represent a department or division; it can simply be a logical area of business.

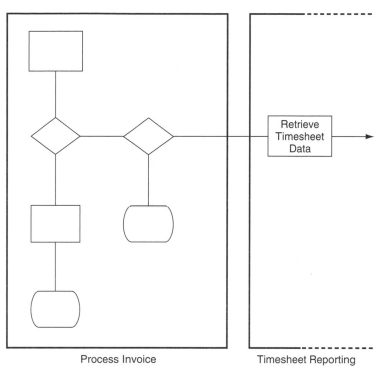

Process Invoice   Timesheet Reporting

Figure 14.11
An extended process utilizing a new service.

Figure 14.12
The enterprise domain business process.

Typical characteristics:

- An enterprise domain business process provides large-scale workflow logic that orchestrates primitive and extended business processes, as well as individual primitive services.
- An enterprise domain business process can be viewed as a process service or a coarse-grained business service.

For example, as a result of a corporate merger, our company's accounting business domain is now expanded to incorporate models from both organizations. An immediate requirement is that consolidated, domain-wide reporting be enabled. This introduces the need for an enterprise domain business process that unifies related, yet disparate business models.

Our domain process in Figure 14.13 provides new logic that coordinates the existing Month-End Sales Report processes from both companies in order to produce a combined sales total. The result is a single master report.

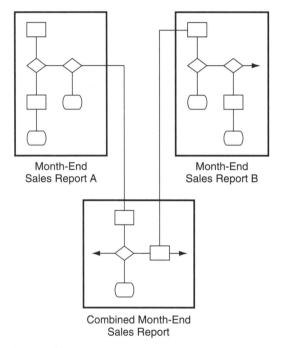

Month-End
Sales Report A

Month-End
Sales Report B

Combined Month-End
Sales Report

Figure 14.13
An enterprise domain process uniting two related
business processes.

The enterprise business process

As an enterprise-wide process that consists of business logic that spans business domains, the *enterprise business process* (Figure 14.14) represents the largest building block within the enterprise SOE.

Typical characteristics:

• This type of process can incorporate any of the previous building blocks.
• It is generally used to unite processes from separate enterprise domains.

Figure 14.14
The enterprise business process.

- The enterprise business process can be viewed as a process service or a coarse-grained business service that exposes select business functions to external partners (which takes us into the realm of the extended enterprise — see the last part of section 14.3 for more information).

In our example, another result of the corporate merger is that business logic from different domains need to be combined. Our timesheet entry process has always existed within the billing (accounting) domain. The new company, however, has their timesheet entry process within the HR domain.

Though similar in function, these processes are different in terms of the workflow logic they consist of, as well as other processes they incorporate and depend upon. Daily hours logged, for instance, is only a part of our company's timesheet process. Since we utilize a large number of subcontractors, our timesheets also consist of rate and payment term information. The new company's timesheets are designed for employees only, and are therefore considered part of Human Resources.

An enterprise business process is required to cross business domain boundaries and unite these two processes in order to provide consolidated timesheet reporting. A diagram depicting this building block would be very similar to the figure used in the enterprise domain business process description. The significance of combining processes from different domains is the scale, complexity, and level of model disparity that can be encountered.

14.2.2   SOE technology architecture building blocks

To implement a service-oriented business model, you need to assemble Web service technologies into suitably scoped service-oriented architectures. Note that the building blocks described here (and shown in Figure 14.15) do not necessarily have a one-to-one relationship with their business model counterparts. A service-oriented environment is malleable and highly adaptive, allowing for a variety of combinations and abstractions within both business and technology models.

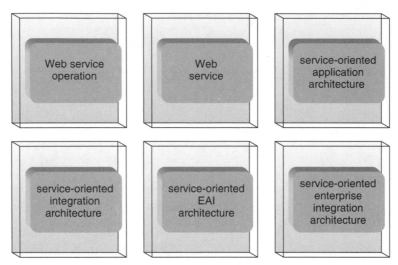

Figure 14.15
Technology architecture building blocks for a SOE.

Back to our consulting company. Let's first recap the examples and the solutions that we came up with as we stepped through the business modeling building blocks:

- We created three activities that represented the business logic within the Retrieve Invoice Data primitive business service.
- Our Retrieve Invoice Data service was part of the Process Invoice primitive business service.
- We enhanced the original Process Invoice process by incorporating the Retrieve Timesheet Data service from a separate process. This resulted in an extended business process.
- We created an enterprise domain business process to unite Month-End Sales Report processes from different parts of a business domain.
- We bridged domain gaps through the use of an enterprise business process, which merged timesheet reporting processes from Accounting and HR domains.

While describing the technology architecture building blocks, we'll demonstrate how we can realize these solutions through the implementation of Web services and service-oriented architecture environments.

Web service operation

A *Web service operation* (Figure 14.16) is an action performed by a Web service, executable via its public interface. At the lowest level within the hierarchy of a service assembly, the

Web service operation can represent the most granular piece of exposed application logic within a service-oriented architecture. At higher levels, however, the scope of an operation can vary.

For instance, an operation belonging to a controller service may contain logic that ends up executing a series of large business processes. In this case, the operation can be considered a coarse-grained part of the service interface.

Figure 14.16
The Web service operation.

If we go back to our accounting system, a Web service operation can expose functionality that relates to any of the business model building blocks.

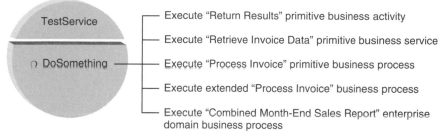

Figure 14.17
A Web service operation exposing various levels of functional granularity.

Each subsequent block increases the scope of the application logic executed by the operation, and therefore also increases the coarseness of the operation's interface.

Web service

A *Web service* (Figure 14.18) is the basic unit of application logic within an SOA. It encapsulates the logic required to execute one or more logically related self-contained functions. The scope of this function can be fine- or coarse-grained.

Typical characteristics:

- A Web service is based on one or more service models.
- A Web service can represent a single piece of business logic.
- A Web service can act as a controller, composing multiple business Web services, each representing individual business services or processes.
- A utility Web service can encapsulate a reusable piece of business or application logic.
- A single Web service can encapsulate one or more business services.
- A business process can be managed and represented by a single process Web service that coordinates the execution of process activities using multiple business Web services.

Figure 14.18
The Web service.

For example, Figure 14.19 shows how, within our accounting system, a business Web service can implement the Retrieve Invoice Data service.

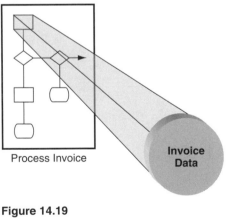

Figure 14.19
The Retrieve Invoice Data service encapsulated
in the InvoiceData business Web service.

The process Web service in Figure 14.20 can expose the functionality of an entire process, such as the Month-End Sales Report process.

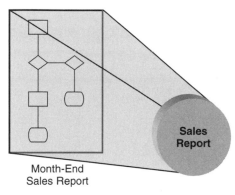

Month-End
Sales Report

Figure 14.20
The Month-End Sales Report process encapsulated
in the SalesReport process Web service.

Service-oriented application architecture

A *Service-oriented application architecture* (Figure 14.21) is an application-scoped architecture consisting of a set of Web services that implement a cohesive unit of business automation.

Typical characteristics:

- A service-oriented application architecture is typically comprised of a series of Web services that interact with legacy application logic within a physically distributed environment.

- The application logic implemented by a service-oriented application architecture typically corresponds to the business logic within a primitive business process.

- Functionality within a service-oriented application architecture can be represented and exposed by one or more coarse-grained Web services.

Figure 14.21
The service-oriented application architecture.

Our consulting company's accounting system can consist of a series of applications, each responsible for a distinct accounting function. Figure 14.22 shows how we can build a service-oriented Invoice Processing application that implements the primitive Process Invoice business process through a series of Web services deployed within a service-oriented application architecture.

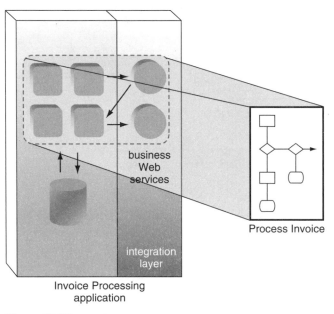

Figure 14.22
A simple SOA involving business Web services that, along with the legacy logic they represent, provide an implementation of the Process Invoice primitive business process.

Service-oriented integration architecture

When two or more service-oriented applications have been integrated it results in a *service-oriented integration architecture* (Figure 14.23) — an architecture that encompasses the application logic of each integrated application and supplements this with any new required logic to enable the integration.

Figure 14.23
The service-oriented integration architecture.

Typical characteristics:

- Each application participating in this environment is a service-oriented application by design.

- Service-oriented integration often introduces separate hub layers consisting of application-neutral Web services that facilitate the integration, and establish future interoperability opportunities.

In our example, the extended business process that was modeled to unite the Process Invoice process with the Retrieve Timesheet Data service requires that the Invoice Management and Time Tracking applications be integrated. The result is the service-oriented integration architecture displayed in Figure 14.24 that establishes an integration

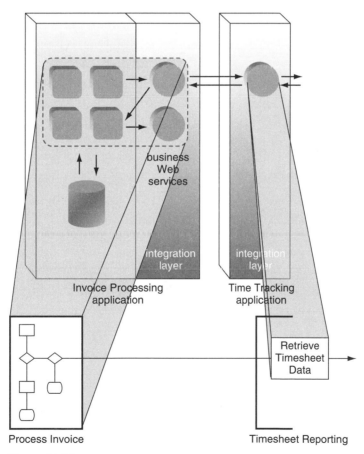

Figure 14.24
An integrated SOA, where the Invoice Processing application implementing the Process Invoice process integrates with the Time Tracking application to access the Retrieve Timesheet Data business service from the Timesheet Reporting process.

channel from the Invoice Management process to the Web service representing the Time Tracking application's Retrieve Timesheet Data service.

Service-oriented EAI architecture

Service-oriented EAI architectures (Figure 14.25) integrate two or more existing application SOAs through the use of a separate business process.

Figure 14.25
The service-oriented EAI architecture.

Typical characteristics:

- The new business process introduced by this architecture is often represented by a Web service based on the process service model.
- The functional scope of a service-oriented EAI frequently corresponds to a logical business domain within an enterprise.
- Solutions based on service-oriented EAI technology are sometimes referred to as *Service Bus* or *Service Enterprise Integration* solutions, in order to distinguish them from traditional EAI systems.

Within our example, we combine the Month-End Sales Report processes (as defined in the enterprise domain business process) through the use of a service-oriented EAI architecture (shown in Figure 14.26). The functionality of each process is exposed through a Web service.

The new domain process logic is implemented within a separate process Web service that is managed by the EAI environment's orchestration engine. Additionally, any variance in the data format received by the two Month-End Sales Report processes is resolved using an EAI broker component.

Service-oriented enterprise integration architecture

A *service-oriented enterprise integration architecture* (Figure 14.27) can span an enterprise. It is typically is required when two or more service-oriented EAI environments need to

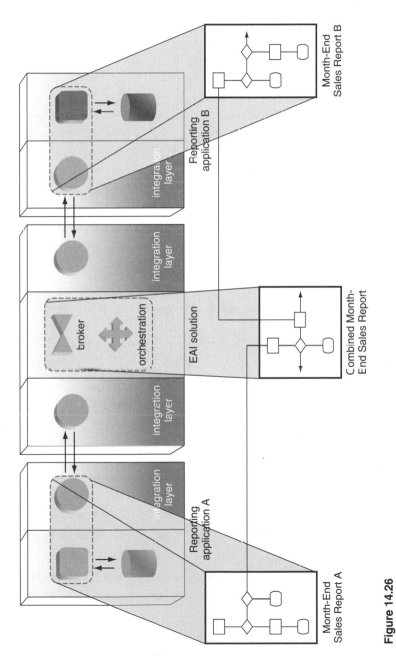

Figure 14.26

A service-oriented EAI architecture implementing the combined Month-End Sales Report enterprise domain business process.

be integrated. Regardless of whether each EAI architecture actually represents a logical business domain, this physical architecture is most concerned with bridging gaps between disparate integration environments.

Figure 14.27
The service-oriented enterprise
integration architecture.

Typical characteristics:

- The functional scope of a service-oriented enterprise integration architecture can vary significantly, but is often comparable to the business logic scope within an enterprise business process.
- This type of architecture is typically composed of existing integration architectures that expose select functionality through coarse-grained Web services.

To implement the integration required between the Accounting and HR timesheet solutions, we introduce the service-oriented enterprise integration architecture displayed in Figure 14.28. Each of the respective EAI environments exposes a service-oriented interface through which we can retrieve the required data. A master process combines this data and produces the consolidated timesheet report.

14.2.3 Service-oriented security model

Although we have been focusing on the functional implementation of business requirements so far, these implementations would not be possible without an underlying security model. Accounting and Human Resources data will likely have authentication and authorization requirements, so that only those (individuals or applications) with the proper credentials can gain access.

The *service-oriented security model* (Figure 14.29) is a single building block that persists through all possible architectures, so that the technologies and policies we use to enforce security measures remain standardized and consistent throughout the enterprise. Read through the best practices provided in the section, "Build around a security model," in Chapter 13 for more information.

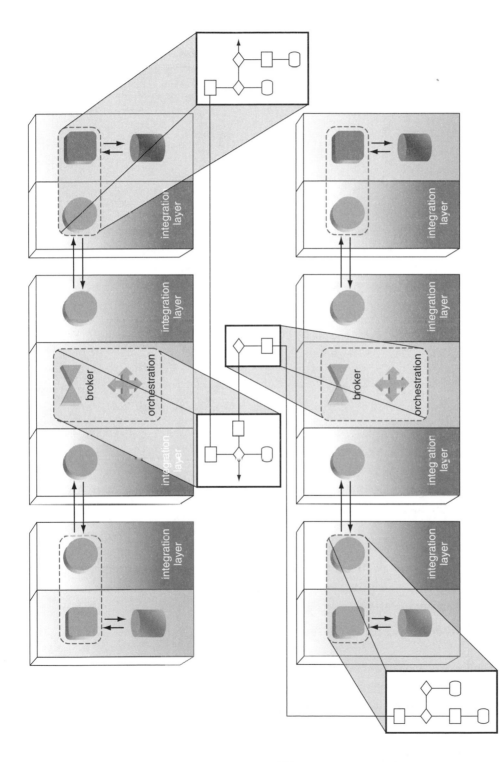

Figure 14.28
A service-oriented enterprise architecture in which two EAI solutions are integrated.

499

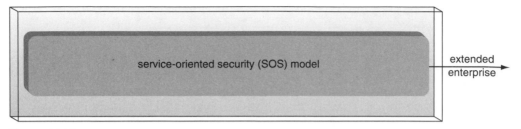

service-oriented security (SOS) model

extended
enterprise

Figure 14.29
The service-oriented security model.

14.3 SOE migration strategy

Planning and executing an enterprise-wide migration to a service-oriented enterprise can be complex and overwhelming. Since Web services and other XML technologies can be utilized and applied in numerous application architecture and information management scenarios, the scope of their potential use is extremely broad. The resulting impact — both organizational and technical — can be significant.

Tackling these challenges, however, is worth the effort. It is a golden opportunity to establish an enterprise architecture that will cut through the disparity that may have plagued your attempts at achieving true interoperability in the past. And, it's better than the alternative: allowing XML and Web Services to be used arbitrarily. As explained at the very beginning of this guide, this simply ends up replacing an existing heterogeneous environment with another.

Provided here is an XWIF migration strategy for phasing XML and Web services technologies into an enterprise in a controlled and relatively non-intrusive manner. The strategy is based on a model that is structured around a series of architectural layers that map to implementation project phases.

14.3.1 Overview of the Layered Scope Model (LSM)

The XWIF Layered Scope Model explains how the enterprise-wide standardization of XML and Web services can be controlled through a series of phases that relate to measured levels of an organization's overall architectural scope.

Following this migration path enables an organization to:

- create an environment in which the use of XML and Web services technologies is highly standardized
- mitigate the organizational and technical impact of the XML and Web services platforms

- allow the skill sets of technical resources to evolve at the same pace as their surrounding environment

- build a series of standard service-oriented architectures

- evolve a sophisticated service-oriented security model

- gradually establish a service-oriented enterprise through the incremental infusion of SOE building blocks

The LSM maps the evolution of service-oriented architecture and an enterprise-wide security model to the progression of these project phases, represented as layers within the model.

The goal of each phase is two-fold:

1. Deliver a set of standards that relates to the architectural scope defined in the LSM layer.

2. Deploy and use XML and Web services technologies, limiting the scope to the architectural boundary (zone) and the standards established in the previous step.

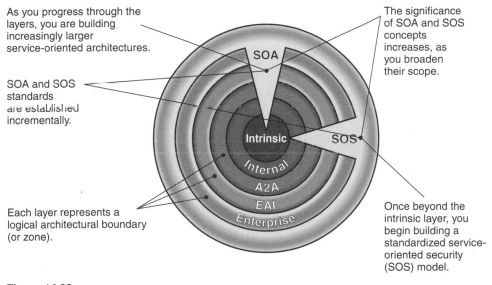

Figure 14.30
The XWIF Layered Scope Model.

As illustrated in Figure 14.30, each LSM layer identifies a specific architectural zone representing a category of applications or application functionality. The innermost (intrinsic) layer identifies the smallest anticipated scope. Each subsequent layer represents a broader classification of applications, as they relate to an organization's technical environment.

Each outer layer builds upon the standards and standardized application components established by the inner layers. Not only are standards kept in alignment, there is also an architectural relationship that evolves, where new layers incorporate the technical framework established by existing ones.

It is worth noting that the LSM applies only to the areas of an organization's technical environment that actually require XML and/or Web services. The LSM is not a rigid model — you can standardize architectural zones within your organization to whatever extent it makes sense to do so.

The SOA and SOS wedges illustrate how progression through the project phases builds standard service-oriented architectures in ever-increasing scope, while evolving the enterprise security model. Therefore, the significance of SOA and SOS design principles become increasingly important with each subsequent project phase.

Obstacles to using the LSM

This model contrasts the approach most organizations are using, in that the decision to utilize XML and Web services is often arbitrary, and not part of any long-term migration initiative. Some of the more common reasons these technologies are introduced into an enterprise this way include:

- individual development projects that identify XML or Web services as a means for addressing immediate project business requirements
- IT staff eager to work with new technologies
- vendors promoting new products, or upgrades with XML and Web services support
- new development and publishing tools that automatically generate markup and code

Using XML or Web services in a development project without coordinated migration and standardization will likely lead to subsequent projects using them in different ways. And so, a new generation of disparity begins.

Applying the LSM

To best manage the incorporation of Web services and other XML technologies into your organization, it is recommended that you structure a migration project around the LSM, matching sequential project phases to model layers. In other words, fully implement the scope of an inner layer before moving to the next. Any standardization that is established within the architectural zone represented by one layer is carried forward into subsequent zones.

Every phase within an LSM-based migration project will consist of a cycle, similar to the following:

1. Analyze applicability of XML and Web services technologies within the given architectural boundary.

2. Determine which SOE building blocks will be established within a given phase. This will also determine the extent to which process functionality can be modeled.

3. Perform an impact analysis to assess the cost, effort, and potential disruption to the existing technical environment.

4. Create standards and guidelines, incorporating any existing standards established by previous project phases (also, develop any reusable application logic, including utility services).

5. Develop and deploy an application based on these standards.

6. Repeat steps 1–4 as required, and broaden the scope of step 5 to new applications, until you are ready to move on to the next LSM layer.

Each of the strategies, best practices, and processes provided in this book come into play at some point during your progression through the LSM phases. Within each of the following LSM layer descriptions, I list the parts of this book (as well as service models and technologies) most relevant to the project phase you are working in.

Before you begin

If you haven't already, read through the following two sets of best practices for planning XML and Web services projects:

- Best practices for planning XML migration projects (Chapter 12)
- Best practices for planning service-oriented projects (Chapter 13)

The recommendations provided in these two sections will give you a better understanding of how to manage and structure LSM project phases, as they relate to your migration goals.

14.3.2 Intrinsic Layer

An application often needs to manage a set of information related only to the application itself. This is referred to as *intrinsic data* and is represented by the intrinsic LSM layer (Figure 14.31).

There are three common types of intrinsic application data:

- configuration information relating to application parameters
- state information that is stored upon application shut-down, and retrieved upon the subsequent start-up
- state information that is retrieved or dynamically generated during runtime, with a lifespan that often relates to the duration of a user session

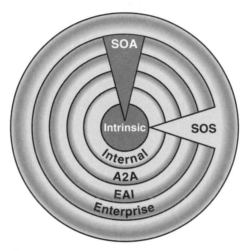

Figure 14.31
The intrinsic layer and project phase.

The scope of this data is considered intrinsic when it is certain that it will never need to be shared outside of the application boundary.

The service-oriented architecture (SOA) wedge

Though the SOA wedge is started at the intrinsic layer, there is often little in the way of standardization for service-oriented technologies in this LSM phase. The most common types of services identified here are utility services that can be reused by other applications. An example of a utility service that facilitates intrinsic application functionality is a state management service (that perhaps represents a shared IMDB).

So, why bother?

Many intrinsic standards are classified as being optional, as it may be unrealistic to enforce strict standardization at this level. Intrinsic standards can be too granular, resulting in an unacceptable bottleneck in the development process. So, why even bother at all with this LSM phase? You may not need to. In fact, it can easily be combined with the Internal phase, which broadens the scope dramatically.

The main reason to consider dedicating a project phase to the creation of intrinsic ˙dards is related to your organization's skill set and comfort level with XML.

Standardization of the intrinsic layer can mark the beginning of a modest migration to XML data representation. Standards around the use of XML within an application boundary tend not to be critical, as data sharing requirements are generally not a factor. This layer therefore provides an opportunity for a low-impact introduction of XML design standards and concepts.

Examples of intrinsic standards include XML schemas that represent intrinsic data. If XML schemas are new to you, this project phase provides an opportunity for a small-scale deployment within a production application. If you decide not to continue with XML data representation, the impact is minimal.

Processes, best practices, and strategies
The following sections of this book are relevant to this LSM layer:

- Strategies for integrating XML data representation (Chapter 5)
- Strategies for integrating XML data validation (Chapter 5)

Service models
The only Web service model commonly associated with this layer is the utility service model described in Chapter 6, although opportunities to introduce business services may also exist.

Technologies
Typical technologies utilized within this layer can include:

- XML for data representation
- XSD for XML schema definitions
- WSDL and SOAP for utility services

SOE building blocks
Building blocks likely to be introduced by this project phase include:

- primitive business activity
- primitive business service
- Web service operation
- Web service

14.3.3 Internal layer

The internal LSM layer (Figure 14.32) can represent two distinct parts of an enterprise architecture:

- the boundary of an application designed and deployed for a controlled internal environment
- the information architecture that houses corporate intelligence

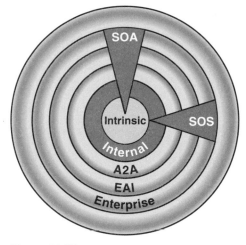

Figure 14.32
The internal layer and project phase.

The latter area refers primarily to content that can be converted or represented as XML documents. This allows corporate documents to become part of a standardized data sharing and searching platform, where data in both databases and documents can be queried, indexed, and managed together. The creation of XML documents is an optional part of this phase. Organizations that prefer to focus purely on application standardization can do so; however, the opportunity of unifying data within documents and databases is well worth considering.

Internal application standards revolve around the standardization of application tiers. This involves consistency in data representation as well as how application logic is partitioned and expressed in public interfaces. Since this phase produces a number of significant design and development standards, it will be much larger in scope than the intrinsic phase. As previously mentioned, the internal and intrinsic phases can be combined.

Building for a future state

Web services become a serious consideration, even when interoperability require-ments are not immediately evident. Without the need to actually deploy Web services technologies, there are a number of measures that can be taken to prepare an applica-tion for future participation within an SOA. Designing an application architecture for integration (even when not immediately requiring integration) is a key part of this phase (see Figure 14.33).

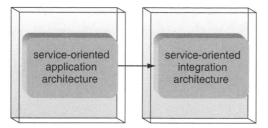

Figure 14.33
An application architecture designed to transition to
an integration architecture.

Fostering integration at this level requires a change in design standards, application architecture development, and the overall mindset of the project team. For example, you can facilitate local Web service requestors as well as future remote requestors by providing both coarse- and fine-grained interfaces based on standard naming and service description conventions.

To an extent, you can consider this new approach as building "integrate-able architectures," regardless of whether they will be immediately integrating anything.

The service-oriented security (SOS) model wedge
SOS concepts can also be introduced at this stage. Since internal applications tend to have less security requirements than for those in subsequent layers, this is a suitable starting point to begin phasing in a standard security model.

Processes, best practices, and strategies
The following sections of this book are relevant to this LSM layer:

- Strategies for integrating XML data representation (Chapter 5)
- Strategies for integrating XML data validation (Chapter 5)
- Strategies for integrating schema administration (Chapter 5)
- Strategies for integrating XML data querying (Chapter 5)
- Designing service-oriented component classes (process, Chapter 6)
- Designing Web service interfaces (process, Chapter 6)
- Strategies for integrating service-oriented encapsulation (Chapter 6)
- Strategies for enhancing service functionality (Chapter 6)
- Strategies for integrating XML with relational databases (Chapter 7)

- Techniques for mapping XML to relational data (Chapter 7)
- Best practices for knowledge management within XML projects (Chapter 12)
- Best practices for standardizing XML applications (Chapter 12)
- Best practices for designing XML applications (Chapter 12)
- Best practices for standardizing Web services (Chapter 13)

Service models
XWIF Web service models most associated with this layer are:

- utility service (Chapter 6)
- business service (Chapter 6)
- controller service (Chapter 6)

Technologies
Typical technologies utilized within this layer can include:

- XML for data representation
- XSD for XML schema definitions
- XHTML for standardization of XML document presentation syntax
- XQuery and XPath for data querying
- XSLT for different presentation renditions
- WSDL for Web service interface definition
- SOAP for inter-Web service communication
- WS-Security as the base framework for the SOS
- WS-Attachments to transport legacy files

SOE building blocks
Building blocks likely to be introduced by this project phase include:

- primitive business process
- service-oriented application architecture

14.3.4 A2A layer

The implementation of the A2A layer (Figure 14.34) can result in a very large project phase. So much so, that it may warrant a number of sub-phases. The place to start, as much of this book has been preaching, is in a standardized data exchange framework.

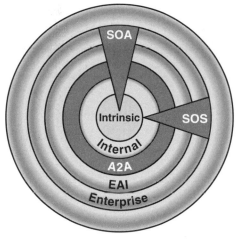

Figure 14.34
The A2A layer and project phase.

Here we take advantage of the service-oriented standards applied to single applications in the previous phase. Incorporating these applications into a service-oriented integration architecture is relatively painless, because they already provide us with standardized integration endpoint services.

Additionally, using the consistent data format established during the internal LSM phase, application interoperability is enabled more easily, allowing for the introduction of a revised standard data format to which disparate repositories can conform.

When adding service integration layers to legacy environments, whether to replace or establish integration channels between different applications, you will have a number of design options. This very likely will result in increased security requirements, broadening the technology set and standards of the service-oriented security model.

Building for a future state
Designing service-oriented integration architectures so that they can be easily incorporated within enterprise architecture environments (Figure 14.35) is a key part of the design standards established in this phase.

Often the eventual migration of an integration architecture into an EAI environment is inevitable. It makes sense for the EAI solution to want as many resources as possible in order to support the process automation within its business domain. The effort and cost associated with this migration is often related to the design characteristics of the integration architecture.

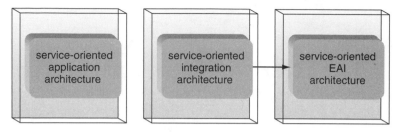

Figure 14.35
An integration architecture designed to transition to an EAI environment.

If EAI solutions are a part of your current or planned enterprise, then you should incorporate EAI characteristics in your integration architecture. In other words, prepare now for an easier transition later. For example, you can create hub services as external endpoints into integrated legacy environments and supplement business services with generic features, such as the ability to output different data formats

Processes, best practices and strategies
The following sections of this book are relevant to this LSM layer:

- Strategies for integrating XML transformation (Chapter 5)
- Strategies for integrating XML data querying (Chapter 5)
- Strategies for integrating service assemblies (Chapter 6)
- Strategies for enhancing service functionality (Chapter 6)
- Strategies for integrating SOAP messaging (Chapter 6)
- Service-oriented analysis for legacy architectures (process, Chapter 9)
- Strategies for streamlining integration endpoint interfaces (Chapter 11)
- Strategies for optimizing integration endpoint services (Chapter 11)
- Strategies for integrating legacy architectures (Chapter 11)
- Strategies for integrating Web services security (Chapter 11)
- Best practices for standardizing XML applications (Chapter 12)
- Best practices for designing XML applications (Chapter 12)
- Best practices for standardizing Web services (Chapter 13)
- Best practices for designing service-oriented environments (Chapter 13)
- Best practices for managing service-oriented development projects (Chapter 13)
- Best practices for implementing Web services (Chapter 13)

Service models

Web service models most associated with this layer are:

- utility service (Chapter 6)
- business service (Chapter 6)
- controller service (Chapter 6)
- proxy service (Chapter 9)
- wrapper service (Chapter 9)
- coordination service for atomic transactions (Chapter 9)

Technologies

Typical technologies utilized within this layer can include:

- XML for data representation
- XSD for XML schema definitions
- XQuery and XPath for data querying
- XSLT for aesthetic structural transformation
- WSDL for Web service interface definitions
- SOAP for inter-Web service communication
- WS-Security as the base framework for the SOS
- WS-Coordination to manage context
- WS-Transaction to enable distributed transactions
- WS-Attachments to transport legacy files

SOE building blocks

Building blocks likely to be introduced by this project phase include:

- extended business process
- service-oriented integration architecture

14.3.5 EAI layer

The architectural zone related to the EAI layer (Figure 14.36) can include any two applications integrated through a separate business process. The standards established in the A2A phase are fully applied here, in that the various point-to-point integration channels between the central business process and the various legacy spokes (or applications subscribed to a bus) are based on these standards.

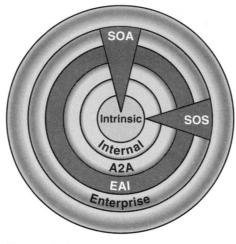

Figure 14.36
EAI layer and project phase.

SOAs evolve into full service-oriented integration architectures, further broadening the scope and complexity of the enterprise security model. Common standards created in this phase include those relating to adapters, business process modeling, and data transformation.

Building for a future state

Depending on the size of your organization, it may be important to consider cross-EAI integration as a realistic requirement when building an EAI solution (see Figure 14.37).

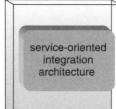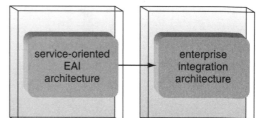

Figure 14.37
An EAI solution designed to transition to an enterprise integration architecture.

In larger organizations, multiple EAI solutions may exist, operating in relative isolation to accommodate their respective business areas. Business models, though, can change as strategic initiatives take organizations into new markets and new ways of doing business.

These changes can result in previously autonomous EAI solutions now having to integrate. The highly proprietary nature of traditional EAI platforms can make this integration effort very difficult. Fortunately, Web services have changed EAI by opening up integration opportunities both within and between EAI products.

Processes, best practices and strategies
The following sections of this book are relevant to this LSM layer:

- Strategies for integrating XML transformation (Chapter 5)
- Service-oriented analysis for legacy architectures process (Chapter 9)
- Strategies for streamlining integration endpoint interfaces (Chapter 11)
- Strategies for optimizing integration endpoint services (Chapter 11)
- Strategies for integrating legacy architectures (Chapter 11)
- Strategies for enterprise solution integration (Chapter 11)
- Strategies for integrating Web services security (Chapter 11)
- Best practices for standardizing Web services (Chapter 13)
- Best practices for designing service-oriented environments (Chapter 13)
- Best practices for implementing Web services (Chapter 13)

Service models
Web service models most associated with this layer are:

- utility service (Chapter 6)
- business service (Chapter 6)
- controller service (Chapter 6)
- proxy service (Chapter 9)
- wrapper service (Chapter 9)
- coordination service for atomic transactions (Chapter 9)
- process service (Chapter 10)
- coordination service for business activities (Chapter 10)

Technologies
Typical technologies utilized within this layer can include:

- XML for data representation
- XSD for XML schema definitions
- XQuery and XPath for data querying
- XSLT for aesthetic structural transformation

- WSDL for Web service interface definitions
- SOAP for inter-Web service communication
- WS-Security as the base framework for the SOS
- BPEL for the integration of business processes
- WS-Policy for business and security policies
- WS-ReliableMessaging for guaranteed delivery of SOAP messages
- WS-Coordination to manage context
- WS-Transaction to enable distributed transactions
- WS-Attachments to transport legacy files

SOE building blocks
Building blocks likely to be introduced by this project phase include:

- enterprise domain process
- service-oriented EAI architecture

14.3.6 Enterprise layer

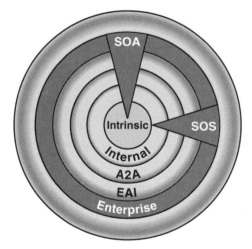

Figure 14.38
Enterprise layer and project phase.

The enterprise layer (Figure 14.38) introduces a project phase that governs inter-EAI architectures, and therefore is applicable only to large technical environments that already use process-driven, EAI-type solutions. Its architectural zone completes the internal boundary of an enterprise, and therefore may even establish interface security standards designed to facilitate interoperability with future external partners.

This layer encompasses pretty much all the strategies, best practices, processes, building blocks, technologies, and service models provided by this book.

14.3.7   The extended enterprise

The Layered Scope Model, in its entirety, spans beyond the enterprise environment. Project phases that introduce architecture and standards for external data exchange are provided, though even these build upon the internal layers that are completed first.

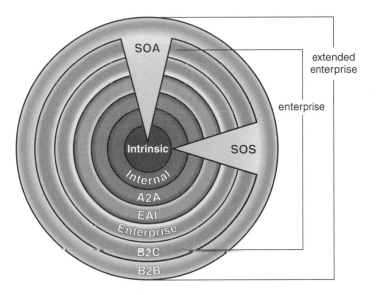

Figure 14.39
The LSM for the extended enterprise.

The complete (or extended) enterprise LSM (Figures 14.39 and 14.40) introduces new architectural zones that relate differently to internal zones. B2B and B2C architectures are allowed to evolve independently to prevent external requirements from negatively affecting internal standards.

The complete LSM is beyond the scope of this book. For more information, visit www.xwif.com.

14.3.8   Customizing the LSM

The base LSM provided in this chapter is generic in nature and slanted toward large enterprise environments. How you actually decide to apply this model, however, can

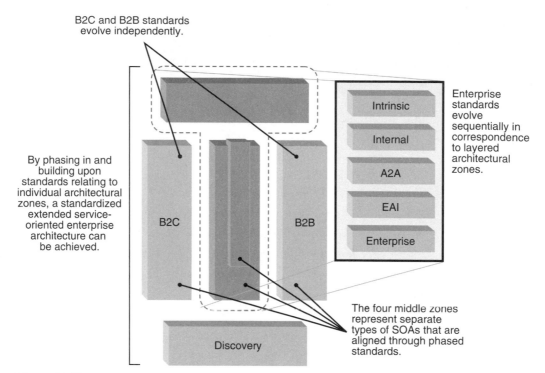

Figure 14.40
Standards are grouped into architectural zones.

vary significantly. Smaller organizations or companies with limited technical environments can create a custom migration strategy by designing unique variations of the base LSM.

Regardless of how it changes, the fundamental principles behind the LSM remain as follows:

- determine where a new technology adds value (prior to deployment)

- assess and compensate for the impact to existing environments caused by a new technology (prior to deployment)

- define standards and skill set requirements for a new technology (prior to deployment)

- establish a scalable and extensible security model based on, or incorporating, a new technology (prior to deployment)

- plan for the realistic future-state of an environment dependent on a new technology (prior to deployment)

- control the organization-wide deployment and use of a new technology
- enforce these principles by managing a phased roll-out of a new technology, where each subsequent phase represents an increasing functional or organization boundary or zone
- allow subsequent project phases to build upon and reuse standards put in place by previous phases, wherever possible

Using these principles, you can create your own custom LSM. You can design project phases and architectural zones that better suit your environment and perhaps even better fit your organization's traditional migration approaches.

For instance, you can:

- split the Internal layer into multiple layers that represent classifications of applications within your organization
- split the A2A layer into multiple layers that represent specific types of integration architectures
- add wedges to the LSM that represent ongoing standards-related initiatives
- dedicate an LSM layer to parts of an integration architecture, such as the communications framework or data transport formats
- limit the use of the LSM to the Internal layer, and use a different migration approach for integrated environments

The key is to apply patience and discipline when phasing in a new technology platform, especially one as imposing as XML and Web services. Getting the right standards and appropriate skill set levels in place before the use of a technology is out of your control is extremely important.

The consequence of not implementing this level of control is almost always an eventual level of platform disparity that compromises the quality of standard application designs.

14.3.9 Alternatives to the LSM

The Layered Scope Model may not be everyone's cup of tea. Even though it is a flexible approach that promotes standardization and controlled use of new technologies, it can introduce a migration attitude that is contrary to some organizations' cultures.

RAD and agile methodologies, for example, encourage a development philosophy that is highly responsive to changes in an organization's business model. A company may not have the luxury of waiting six months for Web services standards to become available for their integration environment, when high priority requirements demand that they begin building that environment right now. Sticking with the base LSM described in this chapter would require that they build this integration environment using legacy technologies that would then be upgraded once corresponding standards are in place.

In today's progressive business climate, though, this may not always be a suitable strategy. It may very well be that the value in using contemporary technologies to deliver some important and immediate business requirements outweighs the long-term benefits of controlled standardization. In these situations the LSM still can be considered. It can be customized further to provide "express tracks" that narrow the delivery scope of certain layers to standards relevant to critical business requirements. This benefits the project by accommodating rigid timelines, and it benefits the organization by having the project still produce reusable standards.

If, however, you are forced to build entire solutions before any foundation standards can be put in place, you can still use the LSM at a later point. It can be made part of a long-term strategic initiative, where project phases are added specifically to revisit existing code or applications of a technology, so that those implementations can be standardized as well.

Finally, using a migration strategy such as the LSM does not preclude the use of common development methodologies. It is simply a means of transitioning the state of an organization's technical environment in a planned and deliberate manner. Within the confines of the various stages of this transition, and especially once the transition itself is complete, traditional methodologies still can be utilized effectively.

About the Author

Thomas Erl is an independent consultant and Chief Architect at XMLTC Consulting Inc., in Vancouver, BC, Canada. He is widely known for inventing the Layered Scope Model for XML and Web services, and is the founder of the XML & Web Services Integration Framework (XWIF). Thomas is also responsible for eXtensinet.com, one of the world's largest XML and Web services resource portals.

Thomas is an avid photographer and artist. He provided all of the photographs used in this book, as well as the cover photo.

For more information, visit **www.thomaserl.com**.

About the Photographs

When I took these photographs in France several years ago, I never imagined they'd end up in a technical book. But, when I was asked to contribute to the aesthetic design of this guide, my collection of photographs was the first place I looked.

The theme I came up with was to represent XML with natural imagery, Web services with metalwork, and various levels of service-oriented architecture with photos of old building architecture from increasingly modern eras. The last chapter divider page intentionally departs from this theme — it introduces the service-oriented enterprise with a photograph of a contemporary piece of architectural art consisting of spheres encapsulating spheres. Appropriately, this panel of spheres was one of many with which a large building was assembled.

Finally, the photo of a large clock was chosen for the cover to tie together all of the other photographs, by representing the evolution of technology platforms through time.

For a descriptive legend of the photos used in this book, visit www.serviceoriented.ws. If you're interested in seeing some more of my work, feel free to visit www.thomaserl.com/photography/.

Index

http://www.phptr.com/

Prentice Hall PTR   InformIT   InformIT Online Books   Financial Times Prentice Hall   ft.com   PTG Interactive   Reuters

TOMORROW'S SOLUTIONS FOR TODAY'S PROFESSIONALS

Prentice Hall **Professional Technical Reference**

| Browse | Book Series | What's New | User Groups | Alliances | Special Sales | Contact Us |

Search | Help | Home

Quick Search

PTR Favorites

Find a Bookstore

Book Series

Special Interests

Newsletters

Press Room

International

Best Sellers

Solutions Beyond the Book

 Shopping Bag

Keep Up to Date with
PH PTR Online

We strive to stay on the cutting edge of what's happening in professional computer science and engineering. Here's a bit of what you'll find when you stop by **www.phptr.com**:

What's new at PHPTR? We don't just publish books for the professional community, we're a part of it. Check out our convention schedule, keep up with your favorite authors, and get the latest reviews and press releases on topics of interest to you.

Special interest areas offering our latest books, book series, features of the month, related links, and other useful information to help you get the job done.

User Groups Prentice Hall Professional Technical Reference's User Group Program helps volunteer, not-for-profit user groups provide their members with training and information about cutting-edge technology.

Companion Websites Our Companion Websites provide valuable solutions beyond the book. Here you can download the source code, get updates and corrections, chat with other users and the author about the book, or discover links to other websites on this topic.

Need to find a bookstore? Chances are, there's a bookseller near you that carries a broad selection of PTR titles. Locate a Magnet bookstore near you at www.phptr.com.

Subscribe today! **Join PHPTR's monthly email newsletter!** Want to be kept up-to-date on your area of interest? Choose a targeted category on our website, and we'll keep you informed of the latest PHPTR products, author events, reviews and conferences in your interest area.

Visit our mailroom to subscribe today! **http://www.phptr.com/mail_lists**